Classroom Assessment

A Practical Guide for Educators

Craig A. Mertler

Bowling Green State University

Pyrczak Publishing
P.O. Box 39731 • Los Angeles, CA 90039

Although the author and publisher have made every effort to ensure the accuracy and completeness of information contained in this book, we assume no responsibility for errors, inaccuracies, omissions, or any inconsistency herein. Any slights of people, places, or organizations are unintentional.

Project Director: Monica Lopez.

Cover design by Robert Kibler and Larry Nichols.

Editorial assistance provided by Sharon Young, Brenda Koplin, Cheryl Alcorn, Erica Simmons, and Randall R. Bruce.

Printed in the United States of America.

ISBN 1-884585-49-3

CONTENTS

Detailed Chapter Contents .... *iv*

Preface.. *xi*

Acknowledgments.. *xiv*

Dedication... *xiv*

Part I: INTRODUCTION TO CLASSROOM ASSESSMENT 1
   Chapter 1   Assessment in Elementary and Secondary Classrooms 3
   Chapter 2   Teaching and Assessment: The Instructional Process........................... 21
   Chapter 3   Characteristics of Assessments.. 49
   Chapter 4   Overview of Assessment Techniques 69

Part II: ALTERNATIVE ASSESSMENT TECHNIQUES 85
   Chapter 5   Informal Assessments 87
   Chapter 6   Performance-Based Assessments.. 109
   Chapter 7   Portfolio Assessments 143

Part III: TRADITIONAL ASSESSMENT TECHNIQUES 161
   Chapter 8   Objective Test Items 163
   Chapter 9   Subjective Test Items 197

Part IV: ADDITIONAL ASSESSMENT ISSUES 213
   Chapter 10   Grading Systems.. 215
   Chapter 11   Interpreting Standardized Tests.. 237
   Chapter 12   Assessing Group Work 263
   Chapter 13   Assessing Affective Characteristics... 277

Appendix A: The Standards for Teacher Competence in the Educational
              Assessment of Students.. 295

Appendix B: The Code of Fair Testing Practices in Education....................................... 303

Appendix C: A Guide to Descriptive Statistics.. 309

Classroom Assessment Glossary 319

References 327

DETAILED CHAPTER CONTENTS

PART I: INTRODUCTION TO CLASSROOM ASSESSMENT 1

   Chapter 1   Assessment in Elementary and Secondary Classrooms 3
      Overview 3
      Introduction 4
      Some Basic Definitions 4
         Assessment System, Evaluation, Measurement, Assessment, and Test 4
         Formal versus Informal Assessment 6
         Quantitative versus Qualitative Assessment 8
         Formative versus Summative Evaluation 8
         Standardized versus Nonstandardized Assessment 9
         Norm-Referenced versus Criterion-Referenced Assessment 10
         Traditional versus Alternative Assessment 10
         Objective versus Subjective Assessment 11
      Purposes of Assessment 11
         Planning, Conducting, and Evaluating Instruction 11
         Diagnosing Student Difficulties 12
         Placing Students 12
         Providing Feedback to Students (Formative) 13
         Grading and Evaluating Academic Learning (Summative) 13
      Ethical Issues Related to Assessment 13
         Teacher Responsibilities in the Classroom 13
         Motivating Students 13
         Test Administration 15
         Interpretation of Test Results 15
      Ethical Standards 16
         AFT, NCME, & NEA Standards (NCME, 1990) 16
         Code of Fair Testing Practices in Education (APA, 1988) 16
         The Family and Education Rights and Privacy Act of 1974 17
      Summary 17
      Related Web Sites 18
      Questions for Review 19
      Enrichment Activities 19

   Chapter 2   Teaching and Assessment: The Instructional Process 21
      Overview 21
      Introduction 22
      Models Connecting Assessment with Teaching 22
         The "Time-Restricted Model" 22
         The "Continuous-Feedback Model" 24
         The "Integrated Assessment Model" 26
      The Instructional Process 29
         Planning Instruction 30
            Purposes 30
            Lesson Plans 31
            Instructional Objectives 36
            Three Domains of Objectives 37
            Writing Instructional Objectives 39
            Teacher-Made versus Publisher-Developed Materials 40
         Delivering Instruction 42

Assessment During Instruction..42
 Assessing Instruction..42
  Formative Evaluation..42
  Summative Evaluation...43
Summary..44
Related Web Sites...45
Questions for Review..45
Enrichment Activities...46

Chapter 3 Characteristics of Assessments 49
Overview...49
Introduction..50
What Is Validity?..50
 Sources of Validity Evidence..52
  Content Evidence..52
  Criterion Evidence..54
  Construct Evidence...55
  Face Evidence..56
 Establishing Validity of Quantitative Assessments..56
 Establishing Validity of Qualitative Assessments 59
What Is Reliability?..60
 Establishing Reliability of Quantitative Assessments..61
 Establishing Reliability of Qualitative Assessments..63
The Relationship Between Validity and Reliability...63
Teacher Responsibilities Related to Validity and Reliability...64
Summary..66
Related Web Site..67
Questions for Review..67
Enrichment Activities...68

Chapter 4 Overview of Assessment Techniques 69
Overview...69
Introduction..70
Alternative Assessment Techniques...70
 Informal Assessments...70
  Characteristics and Examples...70
  Strengths and Limitations...72
 Performance-Based Assessments...72
  Characteristics and Examples...72
  Strengths and Limitations...74
 Portfolio Assessments..74
  Characteristics and Examples...75
  Strengths and Limitations...75
Traditional Assessment Techniques...76
 Objective Test Items...76
  Characteristics and Examples...76
  Strengths and Limitations...77
 Subjective Test Items..77
  Characteristics and Examples...78
  Strengths and Limitations...79
Summary..79
Related Web Sites...81
Questions for Review..82

Enrichment Activities...82

PART II: ALTERNATIVE ASSESSMENT TECHNIQUES...85
    Chapter 5   Informal Assessments...87
      Overview 87
      Introduction 88
      Teacher Observations...88
        Characteristics...89
        Guidelines for Use 91
        Record Keeping 93
      Teacher Questions 97
        Characteristics...98
        Guidelines for Use 98
        Record Keeping 100
      Student Reflections...101
      Validity and Reliability of Informal Assessments...102
      Advantages and Limitations of Informal Assessments 104
      Summary..104
      Related Web Sites...105
      Questions for Review 106
      Enrichment Activities...106

    Chapter 6   Performance-Based Assessments...109
      Overview 109
      Introduction 110
      Characteristics of Performance-Based Assessments...110
        Basic Requirements...113
        Process versus Product Assessment...115
      Developing Performance-Based Assessment Tasks...116
        Identifying the Purpose of the Performance-Based Assessment......................117
        Specifying Observable Performance Criteria 118
        Steps in the Development of Performance Tasks 119
        Two Examples..121
      Methods of Scoring Performance-Based Assessments..126
        Checklists and Rating Scales..126
        Rubrics...127
        Steps in the Design of Scoring Rubrics 132
        Two Examples..134
      Validity and Reliability of Performance-Based Assessments 136
      Advantages and Limitations of Performance-Based Assessments.....................137
      Summary..138
      Related Web Sites...140
      Questions for Review 141
      Enrichment Activities...141

    Chapter 7   Portfolio Assessments...143
      Overview 143
      Introduction 144
      Characteristics of Portfolio Assessments 144
      Uses of Portfolios...148
        Documentation Portfolios...149
        Showcase Portfolios..149
        Other Variations..150

Creating Portfolios 150
    Decisions on Content 155
Validity and Reliability of Portfolio Assessments 156
Advantages and Limitations of Portfolio Assessments 156
Summary 158
Related Web Sites 159
Questions for Review 160
Enrichment Activities 160

PART III: TRADITIONAL ASSESSMENT TECHNIQUES 161
  Chapter 8   Objective Test Items 163
Overview 163
Introduction 164
General Characteristics of Objective Test Items 164
    Multiple-Choice Items 169
        Guidelines for Developing Multiple-Choice Items 170
        Advantages and Limitations of Multiple-Choice Items 173
        Variations of the Basic Multiple-Choice Item 175
    Matching Items 176
        Guidelines for Developing Matching Items 177
        Advantages and Limitations of Matching Items 179
    Alternate-Choice Items 180
        Guidelines for Developing Alternate-Choice Items 180
        Advantages and Limitations of Alternate-Choice Items 182
        Variations of the Basic Alternate-Choice Item 183
Item Analysis 184
Validity and Reliability of Objective Test Items 191
Summary 191
Related Web Sites 193
Questions for Review 194
Enrichment Activities 195

  Chapter 9   Subjective Test Items 197
Overview 197
Introduction 198
General Characteristics of Subjective Test Items 198
    Short-Answer Items 200
        Guidelines for Developing Short-Answer Items 201
        Advantages and Limitations of Short-Answer Items 203
    Essay Items 204
        Guidelines for Developing Essay Items 206
        Advantages and Limitations of Essay Items 207
Validity and Reliability of Subjective Test Items 208
Summary 209
Related Web Sites 210
Questions for Review 210
Enrichment Activities 211

PART IV: ADDITIONAL ASSESSMENT ISSUES 213
  Chapter 10   Grading Systems 215
Overview 215
Introduction 216
Rationale and Purposes of Grading Systems 216

Categories of Reporting Progress and Achievement..220
   Norm-Referenced Comparisons 220
   Criterion-Referenced Comparisons..222
Specific Types of Grading Systems 223
   Letter Grades..223
   Numerical or Percentage Grades 224
   Pass/Fail..225
   Checklists...225
   Portfolios...226
   Narrative Reports..226
Calculation of Grades..226
   Record Keeping 228
Reporting Progress to Parents..228
Summary 232
Related Web Sites..233
Questions for Review 234
Enrichment Activities...234

Chapter 11 Interpreting Standardized Tests..237
Overview 237
Introduction 238
Methods of Reporting Scores on Standardized Tests..239
   Criterion-Referenced Test Scores...240
   Norm-Referenced Test Scores...240
      Raw Scores..242
      Percentile Ranks..243
      Grade-Equivalent Scores..245
      Standardized Scores..245
Interpreting Student Performance..249
   Standard Error of Measurement and Confidence Intervals 249
Uses of Test Results for Teachers...252
   Analyzing Student Performance: An Example 255
   Communicating Test Performance to Parents...257
Summary 258
Related Web Sites..259
Questions for Review 260
Enrichment Activities...261

Chapter 12 Assessing Group Work...263
Overview 263
Introduction 264
The Importance of Group Process..264
Designing Assessments of Group Process..266
   Group Papers...267
   Group Projects 267
   Group Presentations...267
   Group Skills..268
Methods for Assessing Group Process..270
   Self-Assessment..270
   Peer Assessment...271
   Teacher Assessment...272
Summary 273
Related Web Sites..274

Questions for Review...275
Enrichment Activities..275

Chapter 13   Assessing Affective Characteristics 277
Overview..277
Introduction...278
The Affective Domain and Categories of Affective Behaviors...278
   Social Adjustment..281
   Attitudes...281
   Interests..282
   Values..282
   Self-Attitudes..282
Guidelines for Developing Measures of Affective Behaviors...283
   Teacher Observations...284
   Student Self-Reports...285
Validity and Reliability of Affective Measures...289
Advantages and Limitations of Affective Measures..289
Summary..290
Related Web Sites...292
Questions for Review...293
Enrichment Activities..293

Appendix A: The Standards for Teacher Competence in the Educational Assessment of Students...........................295

Appendix B: The Code of Fair Testing Practices in Education 303

Appendix C: A Guide to Descriptive Statistics...309

Classroom Assessment Glossary 319

References..327

Subject Index 333

Notes

PREFACE

This book is designed for use in introductory-level courses on classroom assessment. It provides detailed information on (1) the functions of assessment in the classroom; (2) how to develop, administer, and interpret the results of teacher-developed assessment techniques; and (3) how to interpret the results of externally developed instruments such as published tests. Both traditional and newer, alternative assessment techniques are covered in detail with special attention to the advantages and limitations of specific techniques. A companion Web site helps both instructors and students obtain additional information on topics of special interest to them.

The *practical* nature of the book stems from the fact that it focuses almost exclusively on techniques, methods, and materials that teachers will be using in conjunction with their other everyday activities in classrooms. Teachers are shown how to "do" assessment in order to make their teaching more effective. The numerous examples of the principles and procedures discussed in the narrative make it easy for students to understand the material in this book. Measurement theory and computational procedures that are unlikely to be used by classroom teachers are de-emphasized—producing a textbook that provides comprehensive coverage for classroom teachers without being unnecessarily technical; that is, it is a *practical* book for teachers.

Audience

While this book was written primarily for undergraduates who are preparing to become teachers, it will also be useful for practicing teachers who may never have taken a course in assessment or those who learned about assessment at a time when alternative techniques were not emphasized. Thus, this textbook may be used in both undergraduate-level (i.e., preservice) and graduate-level (i.e., inservice) courses being taught to these audiences.

Note that because of the practical nature of this textbook, with its de-emphasis on mathematics and classical test theory, it is *not* designed for advanced graduate-level courses for students who are preparing for careers as leaders in assessment, such as test development specialists for test publishers or as assessment specialists who will work in advanced positions overseeing district-wide or state-wide assessments of students. These audiences will certainly need to know and understand what is in this book, but they will also need to have in-depth knowledge of test theory and statistical methods, which can be found in many other textbooks.

Organization of the Text

This textbook is organized into four parts. Part I provides an overview and introduction to classroom assessment. Chapter 1 topics include an in-depth discussion of various terminology related to assessment and the role of ethics as they pertain to assessment in elementary and secondary classrooms. Chapter 2 presents an overview of the integration of assessment and instruction. The two main characteristics of assessments—validity and reliability—are presented in Chapter 3. Finally, an overview of the various assessment techniques (to be presented in the remainder of the text) is provided in Chapter 4.

Part II focuses on alternative assessment techniques. Informal assessment techniques, such as observations and questioning, are presented in Chapter 5. Chapter 6 provides discussion of performance-based assessments, including examples and guidelines for developing scoring rubrics. Chapter 7 presents the topic of portfolio assessments.

Traditional assessment techniques are presented in Part III. Specifically, Chapter 8 focuses on objective test items (i.e., multiple-choice, matching, and alternate-choice items), while Chapter 9 concentrates on subjective test items (i.e., short-answer and essay items).

Finally, Part IV presents numerous issues related to assessment. In Chapter 10, various systems of grading student performance are discussed. Chapter 11 provides information related to the interpretation of standardized tests. Chapters 12 and 13 focus on the assessment of group work and affective characteristics, respectively.

Pedagogical Features

The following are the main pedagogical features of this text, common to each chapter:
- a chapter overview (in the form of a visual, graphic organizer);
- a comprehensive chapter summary;
- *Related Web Sites;*
- *Questions for Review;* and
- *Enrichment Activities.*

The *Questions for Review* are designed to be factual questions with answers that are either right or wrong. However, they are structured so that students cannot simply turn to earlier pages in the chapter and copy the answer. These *Questions* require a more applied type of response. The *Enrichment Activities* provide students with assignments that are broader in scope. These projects are performance-based in that they require students to develop or plan activities and then reflect on their products, responses, etc., typically in small groups. The *Related Web Sites* highlight Internet resources that supplement the content presented in each chapter. These sites may be beneficial for both instructors and students. Both URLs and brief site descriptions are provided.

In addition, there are several pedagogical elements for the book as a whole. These include the following:

- a complete glossary of assessment terms;
- three appendices (containing *The Standards for Teacher Competence in the Educational Assessment of Students*, *The Code of Fair Testing Practices in Education*, and an introductory guide to descriptive statistics); and
- a list of references.

Finally, the chapters that deal with specific assessment techniques (i.e., Chapters 4 through 13) contain one or more of the following: practical examples, step-by-step procedures for development, and specific guidelines for use.

Supplemental Materials

Accompanying this text is a Web supplement, which can be found at *http://www.pyrczak.com/assessment/mertler.htm*. The Web site is organized by chapter and, for each chapter, contains:

- a PowerPoint lecture that instructors can download and use in their courses; and
- a Web page listing the *Related Web Sites*—including their hyperlinks—as they appear in the textbook (allowing instructors to simply click on the link to view and discuss the site with students).

ACKNOWLEDGMENTS

I would like to sincerely thank Fred Pyrczak, Monica Lopez, and all the staff at Pyrczak Publishing for their professionalism, promptness, and assistance in the preparation of this textbook; they are truly incredible people to work with. I am deeply indebted to Monika Schäffner (Bowling Green State University) for her review and substantive comments related to the content of the text. Appreciation is also extended to Judy Maxey and Sherry Haskins (Word Processing Center, College of Education and Human Development, BGSU) for their assistance in formatting the text (and putting up with all my questions!). I would also like to thank students in my *Assessment and Evaluation in Education* courses over the past couple of years for providing constructive feedback on many of the activities and examples that appear in the book. Last, completion of this project would not have been possible without the support of my wife, Kate.

Craig A. Mertler

DEDICATION

For Addison...
And all his future teachers!

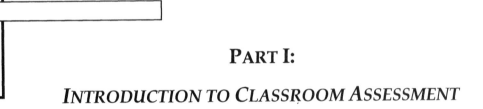

PART I:

INTRODUCTION TO CLASSROOM ASSESSMENT

Chapter 1
Assessment in Elementary and Secondary Classrooms

Chapter 2
Teaching and Assessment: The Instructional Process

Chapter 3
Characteristics of Assessments

Chapter 4
Overview of Assessment Techniques

Notes

Chapter 1

Assessment in Elementary and Secondary Classrooms

Overview of Chapter 1

WHAT IS "ASSESSMENT?"

Some Basic Definitions:
- Assessment System, Evaluation, Measurement, Assessment, and Test
- Formal versus Informal Assessment
- Quantitative versus Qualitative Assessment
- Formative versus Summative Evaluation
- Standardized versus Nonstandardized Assessment
- Norm-referenced versus Criterion-referenced Assessment
- Traditional versus Alternative Assessment
- Objective versus Subjective Assessment

Purposes of Assessment:
- Planning, conducting, and evaluating instruction
- Diagnosing student difficulties
- Placing students
- Providing feedback (formative)
- Grading and evaluating academic learning (summative)

Ethical Issues Related to Assessment:
- Teacher responsibilities in the classroom
  » Motivating students
  » Test administration
  » Interpretation of test results
- Ethical standards

INTRODUCTION

The day-to-day work undertaken by classroom teachers is multifaceted. From "minor" aspects of the job (such as taking morning attendance, supervising a kickball game on the playground, or chaperoning a dance) to much more "important" components (such as planning the instructional activities for a month-long unit, determining which students will move on to the next grade level, or developing a new curriculum), teachers are inundated with a wide variety of professional responsibilities.

None of these responsibilities is more important—or more central—to the work of teachers than that of assessing student performance. You can be one of the most energetic, interesting, and knowledgeable teachers in the world, but if you are unable to *accurately* and *consistently* assess and evaluate the performance of your students, you are not doing justice to your students.

One of the major responsibilities placed on teachers is the communication of academic and social performance and progress to a variety of audiences. These audiences include parents, administrators, the general public, and other teachers in the district, as well as individual students. If the results of assessment and evaluative judgments made about students' performances are not accurate, you will be providing *mis*information to the various recipients of your communications. In doing so, you may be harming your students instead of helping them. For exam-

ple, imagine the possible ramifications if you were to inform parents that their child was better in academic performance than was actually the case.

The purpose of this book is to assist future teachers—and perhaps, inservice teachers as well—in developing and refining their skills in student assessment. I have tried to take a very practical approach to my discussions of topics, issues, and techniques related to classroom assessment. I hope that you find the discussions, examples, and activities beneficial to your future careers as classroom teachers.

In this chapter, several important terms related to classroom assessment are defined. Next, the various purposes of assessment are described. Finally, ethical issues and standards related to classroom assessment are explained.

SOME BASIC DEFINITIONS

Assessment System, Evaluation, Measurement, Assessment, and Test

Five terms very important in classroom assessment are *assessment system, evaluation, measurement, assessment,* and *test*. There are some similarities, but also very distinct differences, among them. Airasian (2000) defines an *assessment system* as the process of collecting, synthesizing, and interpreting information to aid in educational decision making. It is important to note that this system of assessment is a process; it is not a single entity. Many people mistakenly envision a standardized test when someone refers to "assessment." Standardized tests certainly *contribute* to a system of assessment, but an assessment system is a much broader concept. It refers to a related series of measures used to determine attributes of individuals or groups of individuals (Oosterhof, 1999). The results of these related measurements—perhaps consisting of tests, homework assignments, group projects, and/or informal observations—might be used to determine a student's status on some complex cognitive characteristic. For our purposes, an **assessment system** will be defined as "all the systematic methods and procedures that are used to obtain information about behaviors and upon which educational decisions are based."

Evaluation is often described as the process of making a value judgment about student skills or capabilities. Evaluation goes beyond measurement *not only* to quantify performance, but *also* to judge the merits of that performance. Evaluation typically follows measurement and other assessment-related activities conducted by teachers. Additionally, evaluation often requires a substantial degree of professional decision making by classroom teachers. Since this type of decision making has the potential for very important repercussions, it should occur only after adequate samples of assessment information have been collected, analyzed, and synthesized. Only then can teachers make truly informed decisions and judgments. Examples of evaluative judgments made about students can range from determin-

ing if a third-grade student is prepared to advance to the next independent reading unit to whether a student has qualified for graduation from high school. It should be noted that evaluations are not limited to judgments about students; teachers, curriculum, administrators, and others are also subject to evaluative decisions. Thus, **evaluation** will be defined as "the use of assessment information to make judgments about students, teachers, or educational programs."

Since the term "measurement" was used earlier, let us now define it, as well as a couple of closely related terms. Generally speaking, *measurement* is the process of quantifying, or assigning a numerical value, to some performance. *Measurement* is a term synonymous with *assessment* (not to be confused with *assessment system*). Probably the most common example of a measurement is the development (or selection) and administration of a written test or quiz. Scoring a test usually results in a numerical description of student performance. For example, Kathleen correctly answered 45 out of 50 items on the math test; Charles correctly answered 42 out of 50. Kathleen's score is equivalent to 90% of the items answered correctly and Charles's score is equivalent to 84% correct. The math test itself is referred to as a *measure* or *assessment method*; the scores of 90% and 84% are *measurements*.

Some educators do not believe that a definition of measurement should be limited only to quantitative (numerical) descriptions (Oosterhof, 1999). They believe that measurement should also include qualitative (verbal or narrative) forms of descriptions. For example, student responses to an extended essay question might be scored as "excellent," "average," or "poor." This is an example of an alternative method of assigning a score or value to student work. For our purposes in this book, **measure** (and therefore, **assessment method**) will be defined as "a process involving a structured situation that includes samples of particular characteristics or behaviors that results in a numerical or narrative score."

Finally, a *test* is a question or task, or perhaps a series of either, designed to elicit some predetermined behavior (Gallagher, 1998). Tests are very systematic, formal procedures for gathering information about students' performance. They are one specific type of assessment method. Although not limited to this format, tests usually take the form of a pencil-and-paper activity. In sum, a **test** is "a formal set of questions or tasks, often administered to a group of students, that address particular cognitive capabilities learned in a specific course or subject area."

As you know, tests are widely used in educational settings. However, in almost all assessment systems, teachers should supplement test scores with other types of information such as samples of student work (e.g., drawings in an art class), the quality of projects developed over a span of time (such as a science project), term

papers, book reports, and so on. Thus, while this book covers tests in detail, considerable attention is also given to a wide variety of other ways to gather important information to include in a comprehensive assessment system.

Figure 1.1 summarizes the definitions of these important assessment-related terms, and Figure 1.2 shows the relationships among them.

Formal versus Informal Assessment

Classroom assessment methods can vary from extremely formal to extremely informal. This distinction is based on the level of spontaneity for each type (Oosterhof, 1999). **Formal assessment methods** are planned in advance of their administration; in other words, they lack spontaneity. These include chapter tests, unit examinations, final course examinations, graded homework, term papers, etc. Not only are the students aware of how each formal assessment method will be implemented prior to its use, but also how the teacher will utilize the results. In contrast, **informal assessment methods** are much more spontaneous and, often, less obvious. Classroom teachers conduct informal assessments when they observe a student misbehaving in class, when they pause after working a math problem on the board in order to watch the facial expressions of their students as a means of checking for the level of comprehension, or when they watch a new student to see who he or she befriends.

Figure 1.1 Summary
of definitions of
assessment system,
evaluation, measurement,
assessment, and *test*

<u>*Assessment System*</u> — all the systematic methods and procedures that are
    used to obtain information about behaviors and upon which edu-
    cational decisions are based
<u>*Evaluation*</u> — the use of assessment information to make judgments about
    students, teachers, or educational programs
<u>*Measurement*</u> (also known as <u>*Assessment*</u>) — a process involving a struc-
    tured situation that includes samples of particular characteristics
    or behaviors that results in a numerical or narrative score
<u>*Test*</u> — a formal set of questions or tasks, often administered to a group of
    students, that address particular cognitive capabilities learned in a
    specific course or subject area

Figure 1.2 Relationships
among *assessment system,*
evaluation, measurement,
assessment, and *test*

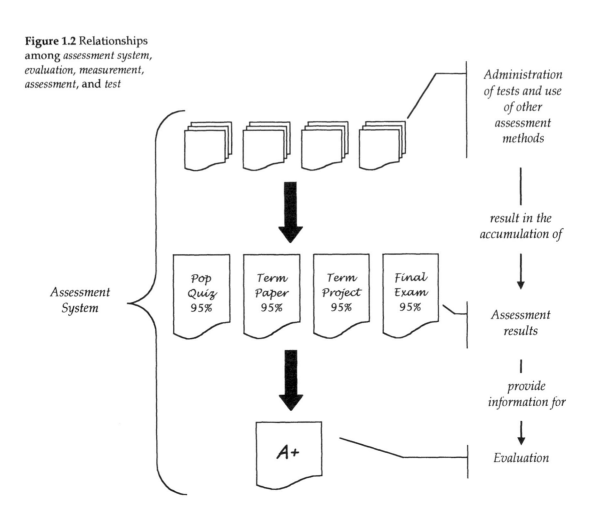

Formal assessment methods require a "break" in the instructional process (you are unable to continue teaching while your students are taking a test!); whereas, informal assessment methods often are used during instruction. Additionally, formal assessment methods are used when fewer, but more controlled, measures are required; informal assessment methods are used when you need to collect information more frequently. As with other ways of classifying assessment methods, it is typically best to utilize a balanced approach when deciding on formal or informal assessment approaches.

Quantitative versus Qualitative Assessment
There is a basic, important distinction between quantitative and qualitative assessment methods. **Quantitative assessment methods** yield numerical scores that serve as estimates of a student characteristic or behavior (e.g., 93% correct on a written test), whereas **qualitative assessment methods** result in verbal descriptions of the characteristic (Gredler, 1999). The major types of quantitative methods include teacher-constructed tests, standardized tests, checklists, and rating scales. The main types of qualitative assessments include teacher observations, anecdotal records, and informal questioning. You will learn more about both of these types in Chapter 4.

Formative versus Summative Evaluation
Often, units of instruction may span several weeks, or even months. Typically, classroom teachers will not want to wait until the unit has been completed before attempting to gauge their students' levels of comprehension and understanding. At that point, it may be too difficult—or simply too late—to go back and reteach important concepts that may have been misunderstood by many students. Perhaps more important, students may find themselves even farther behind because they failed to understand basic concepts that were taught early in the unit and upon which later conceptual information was based.

For example, in a lengthy unit on mathematical operations, students who fail to understand the basic rules for addition (e.g., the idea of "carrying" values to the next column when adding two-digit numbers) will experience even greater difficulty with more advanced mathematical operations. Teachers of this unit would probably pause after the first couple of days of instruction in order to assess where their students are with respect to their conceptual understanding for the purposes of making possible revisions to that instruction. Decision making of this type is called **formative evaluation**. Formative evaluation occurs during instruction, for the purpose of determining what adjustments to instruction should be made (Nitko, 2001; Oosterhof, 2001; Scriven, 1967). This type of evaluation is largely one of your own teaching that can provide assistance in developing and revising instruction (Trice, 2000). Feedback is provided to teachers and students about misunderstandings and other types of immediate problems (Gredler, 1999; Weber, 1999). This feedback typically is based on informal assessment methods (e.g., observations, oral questioning, etc.) but may also be based on methods that are more formal in nature (e.g., quizzes, seatwork, and homework).

In contrast to formative evaluations, **summative evaluations** occur at the end of instruction, such as at the end of a unit, semester, or school year (Nitko, 2001; Oosterhof, 2001; Scriven, 1967). It is typically at this point that we would want to assess our students in terms of our instructional objectives for purposes of assigning grades or some other "final" decisions. Summative evaluation is essentially used for administrative decision making. That is, it serves as the basis for promoting or retaining students. The purpose of summative evaluation is *not* to measure student proficiency with *each* skill in a unit (as is the purpose of formative evaluation); rather, its purpose is to provide an overview of student achievement that spans numerous skills (Oosterhof, 2001). Summative evaluation is usually based solely on formal assessment methods.

Standardized versus Nonstandardized Assessment

Standardized assessment methods (usually tests) are those that are administered,

scored, and interpreted in identical fashion for all examinees, regardless of when or where they are assessed (Airasian, 2000). In other words, these involve very specific, standard procedures. The main purpose of standardized tests is to allow educators to compare students from different schools and different states from across the country without variations in conditions (e.g., administration and scoring of the test) affecting those comparisons. Examples of standardized tests include the Scholastic Assessment Test (SAT), the Graduate Record Examination (GRE), the PRAXIS Series for the assessment of beginning teachers, the Iowa Tests of Basic Skills (ITBS), and California Achievement Tests (CAT).

Nonstandardized assessment methods are typically made by teachers for use within a single classroom and with a single set of students. These are not designed to compare students with one another. Rather, their purpose is to focus on particular areas of instruction and determine the extent to which that subject matter is being taught effectively and subsequently learned by the students. Airasian (2000) points out that it is important to note that standardized assessment methods are not necessarily better than nonstandardized ones. They simply serve different purposes. Standardization of results is important when students from different locations and different classrooms need to be compared. If comparison beyond the classroom is not desired, standardization is not necessary and would likely be less appropriate than nonstandardized assessment methods.

Norm-Referenced versus Criterion-Referenced Assessment

Norm-referenced assessments show where an individual student's performance lies in relation to other students. In most cases, standardized tests are norm-referenced. You will remember from the previous section that a major purpose of standardization is to permit comparisons of students from across different settings. Typically, student performance on tests such as the ITBS, the SAT, and the PRAXIS Series report student performance by showing how each student performed when compared to a *norm group.*

However, most classroom teachers use **criterion-referenced assessment methods**. Their purpose is to compare a student's performance to some preestablished criteria or objectives. These are sometimes referred to as *mastery, objectives-referenced,* or *competency* tests. Criterion-referenced assessment methods help determine the degree of accuracy with which a student has mastered specific content. In this case, the evaluation of an individual student's performance is not dependent on the performance of others. Most of the time, the results of norm-referenced assessment methods are quantitative; criterion-referenced assessment methods may yield quantitative or qualitative information, or a combination of both (Trice, 2000).

Traditional versus Alternative Assessment

For many years, teachers routinely assessed the performance of their students using teacher-developed multiple-choice and short-answer tests and quizzes. This system of assessment became known as **traditional assessment**. Traditional assessment typically consists of procedures such as pencil-and-paper tests and quizzes, where there is only one correct response to each test item. This type of assessment fits well into classrooms because teachers can easily and relatively quickly assess many students simultaneously. Scoring is fairly easy since all student responses can be scored as either right or wrong. However, traditional assessment very frequently encourages the memorization of lower-level facts.

Education changed substantially in the 1960s and 1970s when the movement toward more hands-on, experiential learning began to flourish. A need arose for more appropriate types of assessment methods to be developed and refined for classroom use. These newer types of assessment became known as **alternative assessment**. Alternative assessment—so named since it is seen as an *alternative* to traditional assessment—consists of several different types of assessment methods. One important type of alternative is **authentic assessment**. This involves the real application of a skill beyond its instructional context (Oosterhof, 1999). The idea behind authentic assessment is that facts and concepts are *applied* in an attempt to solve real-world problems, as compared with simply being recalled on a written test. Since these assessments require students to apply what they have learned, they necessitate the use of higher-order thinking skills by students. Learning and its assessment become more meaningful since they are related to life beyond the classroom. Nevertheless, authentic assessment methods are often more difficult and time-consuming to score. You will learn more about traditional assessment methods in Chapters 4, 8, and 9, and more about alternative assessment in Chapters 4, 5, and 7, and authentic assessment in Chapter 6.

Objective versus Subjective Assessment
One final way to classify assessment types is based on the way in which they are scored. In **objective assessment methods**, there is only one right answer per item. The term "objective" is used because the judgment of the scorer in no way influences a student's score. Examples include multiple-choice, true-false, and matching items. These are sometimes collectively referred to as *structured-response, selected-response*, or *teacher-supplied* items. This is because objective items are usually developed by the teacher—or taken from some other source, such as the teacher's edition of a textbook—and presented to the student. The student is simply required to select the correct response from a set supplied by the teacher.

In **subjective assessment**, there are several possible correct responses, or there may be only a single correct re-

sponse but several possible ways to arrive at that answer. Examples include short-answer and essay questions. They are so named because the scoring procedures involve some subjectivity on the part of the scorer, at least to some degree. It is possible that two teachers could read the same response to an essay question and award the student different numbers of points based on their individual interpretation of the response (i.e., a *subjective* scoring procedure). Subjective assessment methods are sometimes referred to as *open-ended, constructed-response*, or *supply* items.

PURPOSES OF ASSESSMENT

Planning, Conducting, and Evaluating Instruction
Classroom teachers engage in the process of assessment in order to help themselves make decisions at a variety of levels. One of the most basic and important purposes of assessment is to assist in making decisions about instruction. These can be divided into three different types of instructional decisions: those that occur prior to instruction, those that occur during instruction, and those that follow instruction.

Teachers spend countless hours planning their instructional activities. Planning for instruction might involve drafting a content outline for material to be covered next month, developing daily lesson plans for the upcoming week, previewing and selecting supplemental materials, determining the nature and length of homework assignments and student projects, and deciding on formats for assessments that will be used for formative and summative decision making. All these decisions are based on information collected from a variety of sources, including the subject matter knowledge of the teacher, the district's curriculum, students' likes and dislikes, students' capabilities, amount of classroom contact with students, scheduled school-wide activities for the students (such as an assembly), just to name a few.

The second type of instructional decisions is made during instruction. We have already briefly discussed this type of instructional decision in an earlier section. You will recall that many decisions must be made while instruction is occurring. Teachers must constantly assess and make decisions regarding the effectiveness of their teaching. Whether students are experiencing difficulty grasping a new concept, or a group of students is misbehaving and disrupting instruction in the classroom, teachers are required to "think on their feet" and make several spontaneous decisions during the course of a school day.

Finally, assessing for instruction is not complete at the end of the day when a lesson is done. Instead, effective teachers consistently assess and evaluate their instruction after its completion for the purposes of making alterations for next year, next week, or perhaps even the next class period. Reflecting on *what* you did and *how well* you did it are extremely important aspects of being a good teacher.

Diagnosing Student Difficulties
Tests and other types of assessment methods are often used prior to instruction in order to determine what students already know and can do. This sort of pretesting, or **diagnostic assessment**, is an important activity in helping teachers plan for instruction. If students already know some of the ideas and concepts basic to a unit of instruction, the teacher may decide not to cover that material or perhaps to offer only a quick review to students before moving on to new concepts.

Teachers may also notice that particular students are experiencing general types of difficulties, whether they be academic, emotional, or social. Diagnostic assessment in the form of specific tests will often enable educators to pinpoint the distinct type of difficulty a student may be experiencing. This, then, further enables teachers to be able to remedy the specific problem.

Placing Students
Classroom teachers often make decisions about placing students (Airasian, 2000). For example, teachers may use the results of assessment to divide their classrooms into reading groups based on similar levels of ability, organize students for a group project, and recommend to students appropriate sequences of courses to be taken prior to graduation. Placement decisions may be made for reasons both

academic and social in nature (Airasian, 2000).

Providing Feedback to Students (Formative)
Another very important purpose of assessment is to provide feedback to students regarding their academic progress. In our discussion earlier in this chapter, formative evaluation was defined as decision making that occurs during instruction to determine what adjustments to instruction should be made. It is a means of assessing your own instruction while that instruction is still occurring. Similarly, formative evaluation can be used to provide feedback to students during the time that they are still receiving instruction from their teacher. One of the reasons why teachers assign homework and similar academic activities is not only to monitor and assess the effectiveness of their instruction, but also to enable students to assess, as an ongoing process, their own performance and continued progress. A student who fails to perform well on a quiz three days into a month-long unit will realize that she has not understood some of the early conceptual material very well and may need to study a little harder or perhaps ask different questions in class. It is important to remember that formative evaluation of instruction goes hand-in-hand with formative evaluation as feedback to students.

Grading and Evaluating Academic Learning (Summative)
The final purpose of assessment is to grade and evaluate academic learning.

Earlier, we referred to this activity as summative evaluation. Recall that summative evaluation involves the formal assessment of academic learning following the completion of instruction. In other words, teachers grade and evaluate student learning at the end of a unit, a grading period, or a school year. This assignment of grades is typically how teachers communicate to others (i.e., parents, administrators, and other teachers, as well as the students themselves) how well students have performed under their tutelage.

ETHICAL ISSUES RELATED TO ASSESSMENT

Teacher Responsibilities in the Classroom
All students have the right to be assessed in fair and impartial ways, regardless of individual situations. Classroom teachers have various responsibilities in support of fair assessment. These responsibilities include ensuring that students are properly motivated to do their best on any type of assessment method, that all types of assessments are administered in a fair manner, and that the results of assessment are interpreted appropriately (Gredler, 1999).

Motivating Students
Teachers have the responsibility to motivate students to perform at their best in any assessment situation (Gredler, 1999). For classroom situations, teachers should make sure tests or other assessment methods have not been designed to trick students; rather, they should serve as a means for students to demonstrate what

they have learned and are able to do following instruction.

Teachers should also make sure that students do not become discouraged during the administration of a formal test or other type of assessment method. They should familiarize students with the formats of both their self-developed measures (e.g., classroom tests), and also with standardized measures. For example, students should be exposed to—and provided with opportunities to practice—multiple-choice, matching, and true-false test items, especially if those item formats are not what the students are accustomed to seeing on classroom tests. The purpose of exposing and familiarizing students with different types of assessment methods is to prevent factors external to the students' performance from confusing and adversely affecting their performance (Gredler, 1999).

Often, the real challenge for classroom teachers is to familiarize students with the *procedures* utilized in standardized testing. For example, in classroom testing situations, students are seldom, if ever, exposed to the use of computer scannable answer sheets and strictly-adhered-to time limits. Students should be provided with opportunities to practice transferring answers from a test booklet to a separate answer sheet and to practice the proper way to mark responses on the answer sheet. Additionally, they should be provided with instruction on how to manage their time effectively during a standardized testing situation. These forms of

preparation should reduce students' test anxiety, which will ultimately result in higher, and, most likely, more accurate, test scores.

It is important to note that developing students' **testwiseness skills**—the ability to use assessment-taking strategies, clues from poorly written items, and experience with particular assessment methods to improve one's score beyond that which would be attained from mastery of the content (Nitko, 2001)—is intended to enable students to demonstrate their best academic performance. However, some test preparation activities inappropriately and unethically inflate students' scores (Gredler, 1999). For example, developing a curriculum and instructional objectives that relate directly to the test, and then teaching those objectives (known as "teaching to the test") will increase test scores without improving students' overall achievement levels. That is, their achievement on the particular sample of material on the test will improve, but it will be limited to what that particular test covers. Similarly, preparing students by providing them with test questions nearly identical in content to those that will appear on the actual test is a highly unethical practice. In the end, these practices result in misleading test scores.

Oosterhof (1999) lists numerous testwiseness skills that teachers can use ethically to help prepare their students to take standardized tests. The list includes preparation activities that can help students

- follow directions carefully,
- proof their work,
- mark their answers carefully,
- work quickly and pace themselves,
- answer time-consuming items last,
- answer high-point items first,
- address specific material posed by short-answer and essay questions,
- mark items for later review and potential changing of answers, and
- eliminate incorrect alternatives.

Test Administration

Teachers also have the responsibility of maintaining a positive environment within which a test or other assessment method can be administered. Creating a positive environment assists the teacher in helping students perform to the best of their ability. A positive environment *encourages*, rather than *discourages*, higher levels of student performance. Assessment should not be used as punishment or as a means of maintaining order in a classroom. When passing out a test and explaining the directions, teachers should offer words of encouragement, such as, "I know you'll do well on this test; you've studied hard!" or "Take your time and you'll do great!" Teachers should not preface a test by making statements like, "This is a difficult test; just do the best you can" or "I've put some tricky questions on this one, so be prepared."

Teachers should discourage cheating by having students remove unnecessary materials from desktops. Also, teachers should closely monitor the class during a test to ensure that all students have an equal opportunity to perform well. Finally, in support of the idea of providing equal opportunity to everyone, clues or hints should not be given to individual students; if a problem exists with a teacher-developed test item, the entire class should receive the same clarification (Gredler, 1999).

Interpretation of Test Results

Test scores are often misinterpreted and, therefore, misused. Gredler (1999) clearly points out that a test is not a measure of the entire person. Rather, it is simply a "snapshot" or an indicator of how that person may perform. A low test score certainly does not indicate that the student is less of a person, worthless, or stupid. Teachers, as well as students, should understand that assessment methods tend to measure very specific skills and attributes. The interpretation of test scores should be limited only to those skills and attributes measured by the particular test. Inferences that extend beyond the basic purpose of the test should not be made. For example, if John does not perform well on a fourth-grade spelling test that covers words with the letters *i* and *e* in combination (e.g., ach*ie*ve, p*ie*, c*ei*ling, etc.), one should certainly not infer that he does not understand any spelling rules, will probably never learn to read, and is just not very bright. Similarly, if Sallie does not do well on a biology test because she could not correctly recall the equations for the reactions in photosynthesis, we should not infer that she does not have a "knack" for science and should therefore be counseled out of a career in that field. Although these examples are a bit extreme, classroom teachers often make similar kinds of errors (often subconsciously) in interpretation of assessment results. Overgeneralizations such as these create serious and unnecessary problems for students, such as anxiety and decreased self-esteem, and should be avoided at all costs.

ETHICAL STANDARDS

Several professional organizations have developed standards to guide teachers when they assess students. In addition, federal legislation that limits the actions of teachers and other school district employees regarding student assessment has also been enacted. All classroom teachers should familiarize themselves with these standards and laws since they have a direct impact on teachers' daily work with students.

AFT, NCME, & NEA Standards (NCME, 1990)

In 1990, a joint committee consisting of members from three national professional organizations—the American Federation of Teachers (AFT), the National Council on Measurement in Education (NCME), and the National Education Association (NEA)—published a document that delineates the responsibilities of classroom teachers with respect to student assessment (Gallagher, 1998). The document,

titled *The Standards for Teacher Competence in the Educational Assessment of Students,* contains seven major standards and includes knowledge and skills requisite for meeting those standards. The seven standards are presented in Figure 1.3. The complete version of the standards is easily accessible on the Internet at *www.unl.edu/buros/article3.html* and is also provided in Appendix A.

I strongly urge you to take some time familiarizing yourself with the standards. It is important for current and future teachers to see how those standards are interwoven into the daily practices and procedures of assessing students.

Code of Fair Testing Practices in Education (APA, 1988)

In 1988, the American Psychological Association (APA) also published a set of standards to guide the practice of classroom teachers. The *Code of Fair Testing Practices in Education* is aimed primarily at professionally developed tests such as those sold by commercial test publishers or used in formally administered testing programs, as compared with classroom (i.e., teacher-developed) tests. The four areas addressed by the code include:

- Developing and Selecting Appropriate Tests
- Interpreting Scores
- Striving for Fairness
- Informing Test Takers

The entire code is available online at *www.apa.org/science/fairtestcode.html* and is also provided in Appendix B.

Figure 1.3 Summary
of *The Standards for
Teacher Competence in
the Educational Assess-
ment of Students*

**The Standards for Teacher Competence in the Educational
Assessment of Students**

1. Teachers should be skilled in choosing assessment methods appropriate for instructional decisions.
2. Teachers should be skilled in developing assessment methods appropriate for instructional decisions.
3. Teachers should be skilled in administering, scoring, and interpreting the results of both externally produced and teacher-produced assessment methods.
4. Teachers should be skilled in using assessment results when making decisions about individual students, planning teaching, developing curriculum, and school improvement.
5. Teachers should be skilled in developing valid pupil grading procedures that use pupil assessments.
6. Teachers should be skilled in communicating assessment results to students, parents, other lay audiences, and other educators.
7. Teachers should be skilled in recognizing unethical, illegal, and otherwise inappropriate assessment methods and uses of assessment information.

*The Family and Education Rights and Privacy
Act of 1974*

Classroom teachers should also be familiar with *The Family and Education Rights
and Privacy Act (FERPA) of 1974.* This major piece of federal legislation, also known
as the Buckley Amendment, essentially
protects students and their parents from
having their personal and academic records made public without their consent
(Gallagher, 1998). Specifically, FERPA requires the following:

- Student records be kept confidential
  among the student, teacher, and parents or guardians.
- Written consent must be obtained
  from the parents prior to disclosing
  the student's record to a third party.
- Parents be allowed to challenge the
  accuracy of information kept in the
  student's records.

- Once students reach the age of 18,
  they are afforded the same rights
  formerly granted to their parents.

The confidentiality and permission requirements of FERPA apply to classroom
teachers' grade books, posting of student
grades or progress reports in public, and
discussion of students' personal and/or
academic information with a third party
(Gallagher, 1998).

SUMMARY

In this chapter, you were first introduced
to important assessment-related terms,
namely assessment, measurement, test,
and evaluation. You then became acquainted with many terms used to describe and classify various types of assessment methods. These terms included
formal and informal, qualitative and
quantitative, formative and summative,

standardized and nonstandardized, traditional and alternative, and norm-referenced and criterion-referenced assessment methods.

Important purposes of assessment—including planning, conducting, and evaluating instruction; diagnosing student difficulties; placing students; providing feedback to students; and grading and evaluating their performance—were covered. Finally, several sources of standards and guiding principles regarding ethical and legal issues in the assessment of students, with which all teachers should be well acquainted, were discussed.

🖱 Chapter 1 *Related Web Sites* 💻

Note: *Hyperlinks to all "Related Web Sites" that appear at the end of each chapter are also listed on the Web supplement that accompanies this textbook (www.pyrczak.com/assessment/mertler.htm).*

❖ **The Standards for Teacher Competence in the Educational Assessment of Students** (*www.unl.edu/buros/article3.html*)
The complete *Standards*, which describe the responsibilities of classroom teachers with respect to student assessment, can be obtained from this Web site.

❖ **Code of Fair Testing Practices in Education** (*www.apa.org/science/fairtestcode.html*)
The *Code* explains the testing practices recommended to commercial test developers.

❖ **ERIC Clearinghouse for Assessment, Evaluation, & Research** (*www.ericae.net/*)
The Educational Resources Information Center (ERIC) maintains a clearinghouse of information concerning educational assessment and evaluation. Included on the site are searchable databases containing full-text books and journal articles.

❖ **Kathy Schrock's Guide for Educators**
(*www.school.discovery.com/schrockguide/assess.html*)
Ms. Schrock, a technology specialist from Massachusetts, has assembled an impressive list of resources related to assessment for classroom teachers, including useful articles and other interactive assessment-based Web sites. *You must check this one out!*

❖ **National Center for Research on Evaluation, Standards, and Student Testing**
(*www.cresst96.cse.ucla.edu/*)
This center, funded by the U.S. Department of Education, is a great resource for teachers, administrators, and parents.

❖ **NWREL's Assessment Resource Library** (*www.nwrel.org/assessment*)
The NorthWest Regional Educational Lab's online library of assessment resources contains many downloadable resources, including several annotated bibliographies detailing assessment alternatives for specific content areas.

QUESTIONS FOR REVIEW

1. Can a multiple-choice test appropriately be called an "assessment system"? Explain.

2. A teacher noticed one child push another on the playground and made a note of it on a slip of paper. Should this be classified as formal or informal? Explain.

3. A college instructor gives a final examination at the end of a course. Should this be classified as formal or informal? Explain.

4. A superintendent has decided that she wants to test all students in the district and compare their performance to that of other students. Should she use a standardized or nonstandardized test? Explain.

5. Would it be a good idea to use a norm-referenced test to compare a student's performance with preestablished criteria? Explain.

6. In assessing a student's ability to drive a car, would a traditional or authentic assessment be more valuable? Why?

7. In the next few weeks, a science teacher will teach a unit on photosynthesis. What three types of instructional decisions will this teacher need to make? Explain why each type is needed.

8. In preparing to administer a test, a teacher announces, "This is probably the most difficult test you will take this year, so the scores may not be very good." Why should this type of announcement not be made to students?

9. Why it is important for all teachers to be familiar with *The Standards for Teacher Competence in the Educational Assessment of Students*?

10. A university researcher is conducting a study on the academic performance of students with different types of learning disabilities. The researcher approaches several classroom teachers and asks to see the academic records of their students. The teachers are told that the students will remain anonymous. Should the teachers provide the information to the researcher? Why or why not?

ENRICHMENT ACTIVITIES

1. Think back to your time in school and specifically to your experiences with testing and other assessment methods. List and discuss some of your memories regarding your experiences with various forms of assessment. For the most part, are those memories positive or negative? What caused them to be either positive or negative? Discuss your responses in small groups.

2. Collect three to five syllabi from college courses that either your friends are taking or that can be found on the Web (it is better if they are *not* from a course you have already taken). From the syllabi, identify the activities that the instructor uses to assess student learning or other performances. Try to classify the activities using the terminology presented in this chapter. Classify them in as many ways as possible. Compare your results with those of other students in your class.

3. Spend some time with a classroom teacher talking about assessment. Try to discover information concerning his or her ideas about, opinions of, and attitudes toward classroom assessment. Use the following questions to guide your interview:

   - How would you define the following terms?
     » *assessment*
     » *evaluation*
     » *measurement*
     » *test*
   - How important do you believe assessment is to the job of teaching?
   - What do you enjoy most about assessing your students?
   - What do you enjoy least about assessing your students?
   - What do you believe is the most effective method for reporting student performance and/or progress?
   - What do you find most difficult about assessing your students?

Chapter 2

Teaching and Assessment: The Instructional Process

Overview of Chapter 2

TEACHING AND ASSESSMENT

Models Connecting Assessment with Teaching:
- The "Time-Restricted Model"
- The "Continuous-Feedback Model"
- The "Integrated Assessment Model"

The Instructional Process

Planning Instruction
- Purposes
- Lesson Plans
- Teacher-Made vs. Publisher-Developed Assessments
- Educational Objectives
- Domains of Objectives
- Writing Objectives

Delivering Instruction
- Assessment During Instruction

Assessing Instruction
- Formative Assessment
- Summative Assessment

INTRODUCTION

As you know from the previous chapter, assessment is an integral part of teaching. Classroom teachers are required to make a wide variety of decisions on a continuing basis, throughout the day, the week, and the school year. Information resulting from various assessments is necessary in order for teachers to carry out this decision-making process. It is crucial for *all* teachers to be cognizant of the interrelationships among assessment and the various aspects of teaching. In this chapter, three models explaining the integration of assessment and teaching are presented. The discussions include the relative strengths and limitations of each model. The entire instructional process is then closely examined, with the discussion focusing on the three main aspects of the instructional process, namely planning for instruction, delivering instruction, and assessing instruction.

MODELS CONNECTING ASSESSMENT WITH TEACHING

There are three explicit models of the relationship between teaching and assessment (Gredler, 1999). These models are very important because they not only describe the nature of this relationship from varying perspectives but also ultimately direct teachers in how to approach the task of teaching within their individual classrooms. These three models are the *time-restricted model*, the *continuous-feedback model*, and the *integrated assessment model*.

The "Time-Restricted Model"

The time-restricted model of teaching and assessment is prevalent at the high school and, in particular, the college levels (Gredler, 1999). The key characteristic of this model is that assessment occurs only following the completion of instruction. The time-restricted model is depicted in Figure 2.1.

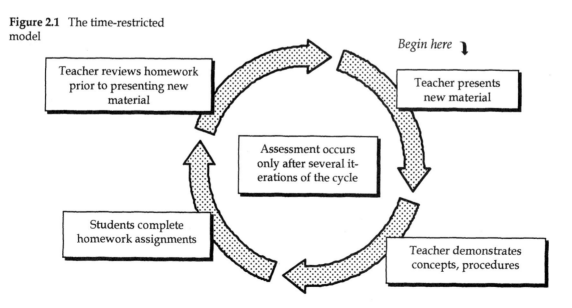

Figure 2.1 The time-restricted model

Teacher reviews homework prior to presenting new material

Begin here

Teacher presents new material

Assessment occurs only after several iterations of the cycle

Students complete homework assignments

Teacher demonstrates concepts, procedures

The instructional process begins with the classroom teacher introducing new material and then demonstrating examples of the concepts or procedures involved. At the end of that class period or lesson, the students are required to complete worksheets or other homework activities, stressing repetition of the concepts and procedures illustrated earlier by the teacher. At the beginning of the next class period or lesson, the teacher reviews the answers to the homework activities and then moves on to present new material. The cycle continues to repeat itself numerous times during the course of a unit of instruction. In the time-restricted model, assessments are administered periodically to determine the extent to which students are understanding the concepts and are able to apply them appropriately; however, they are only administered following relatively large amounts of subject matter instruction. Furthermore, the time-restricted model is routinely implemented at levels where a certain amount of material or specific content must be covered by the end of a school year or of a course (as in secondary schools and colleges). In these situations, time typically dictates the pace of instruction.

For example, Mrs. Garcia is beginning a new unit teaching her eighth-grade students all about the scientific method. On the first day, she introduces the new material by discussing what is meant by science and research and the process by which new inventions are created. She assigns her students a worksheet that re-

quires them to write definitions to the terms "science," "research," and "scientific method." At the beginning of science class the next day, Mrs. Garcia reviews the definitions of the three terms. She then proceeds to outline the basic steps in the scientific method, discussing each one and providing a single example. That evening's homework requires the students to identify a simple example of a scientific study and list the steps in the scientific method as they pertain to that topic. At the beginning of class the next day, the students share their responses and the class informally evaluates each one. This process continues for the next two weeks until Mrs. Garcia administers a formal written test to her students.

There is an assumption in the time-restricted model that classroom instruction is unidirectional. That is, teachers possess all the information and their role is to transmit that course content to the students. The students, therefore, assume an extremely passive role. Their job is to try to absorb as much of the factual information as possible.

The main advantage of this model is that it is cost-effective in terms of the time set aside for assessments. Not much time is spent on assessment; one simply administers a test at the end of the unit. However, there are several limitations to the time-restricted model. First, the assessments often prove to be difficult for students since they cover an extremely wide range of material, including both major and minor concepts, facts, and details (Gredler, 1999). Second, it often encourages memorization on the part of students in preparation for the formal assessments. Finally, since the focus of the model is a steady and continued progression through the content, it does not provide opportunities for the teacher to reteach material with which students may be experiencing difficulty.

Through high school and college, many of us were taught in this manner, so we tend to believe that this is the only way in which to assess instruction. In contrast to the time-restricted model, the remaining two models offer chances for periodic assessment as well as opportunities to revisit material that may be hampering student academic progress.

The "Continuous-Feedback Model"

The continuous-feedback model is based on the principle that the vast majority of students could master the content presented to them if provided with additional time to learn (Gredler, 1999). The key characteristic of the continuous-feedback model is that it incorporates *both* formative decision making (used only for feedback) *and* summative decision making (used for determining student grades). The continuous-feedback model is depicted in Figure 2.2.

Figure 2.2 The continuous-feedback model

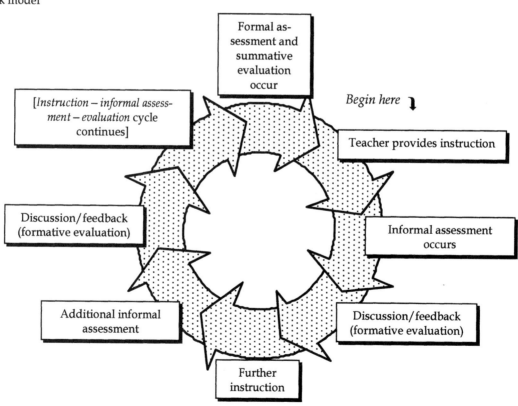

The instructional process within the continuous-feedback model builds on the time-restricted model. The main addition is the incorporation of additional informal assessment and formative evaluation into the process. Recall that the main purpose of formative evaluation is to provide feedback on student progress to teachers and students. Assessments used for these purposes are not included in the students' grades. Rather, they are designed to identify students' errors and misunderstandings during the instructional process (Gredler, 1999).

Since the focal point of the continuous-feedback model is to provide all students with the opportunity to achieve mastery of the subject matter, several assessments of various types are required throughout the process. As shown in Figure 2.2, the process begins with the introduction of new material by the teacher. This is followed by some sort of informal assessment. It is important to note that these informal assessments may be more formal in nature than their simplistic homework counterparts in the time-restricted model. They require much planning and forethought on the part of the teacher; they are not simply "activity sheets." The initial informal assessment is followed by informal individual and/or class discussion and formative evaluation of the outcome of the assessment. If the teacher determines that an individual student failed to achieve mastery of that content, he or she must receive additional instruction focusing on the missed con-

cepts or information (Gredler, 1999). This additional instruction—whether the content is repetitious or new—is then followed by additional informal assessment and discussion/formative evaluation. The key is to administer the informal assessments frequently in order to address student errors sufficiently prior to the use of graded, more formal assessments. The cycle of

informal
instruction → assessment → evaluation

continues until the end of a unit or grading period is reached. At that time, more formal assessments are administered and the results are used for establishing student grades (i.e., summative evaluation).

Gredler (1999) has identified four steps necessary to the implementation of the continuous-feedback model. These steps are:

(1) Initially, a level of mastery must be set for each unit of instruction in order to determine when students have achieved mastery and are permitted to move ahead; typically, this level of academic performance is equivalent to a grade of B.

(2) Each informal (or formal) assessment (e.g., quiz or chapter test) should be used only for purposes of providing feedback.

(3) Focused instruction must be provided to those students who do not achieve mastery on the less formal assessments, and they must

be retested following that additional instruction.

(4) A much smaller number of graded (i.e., formal) tests should be used in the course; an appropriate number may be two or three.

The advantages of this model include the potential for noticeable gains in student achievement. Students are permitted the opportunity to continually improve their understanding of course content. The frequent use of both informal and formal assessments also tends to reduce the instance of test (or other assessment) anxiety associated with the big unit test, especially when students are not sure of how they have been progressing, as with the time-restricted model. Additionally, this model, simply put, helps students learn more and better; it discourages memorization and encourages real learning.

Limitations of the continuous-feedback model include the fact that teachers must be willing to invest a great deal of time in both the development of assessments and intervention strategies for those students who experience trouble achieving mastery. In addition, there is the never-ending dilemma of how best to address the delay of instruction on new material for those students who are ready to move on while nonmastery students are receiving reinstruction on previously covered concepts.

The "Integrated Assessment Model"

The integrated assessment model is based on the notion that instruction should focus on meaningful learning and thinking (Gredler, 1999). A key characteristic of the integrated assessment model is that students are taught how to think and to apply what they have learned to new situations. The integrated assessment model is presented in Figure 2.3.

Figure 2.3 The integrated assessment model

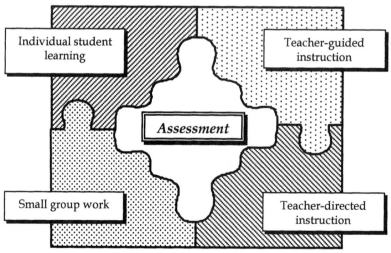

The 1980s saw a great deal of curriculum reform based on research suggesting that students were proficient at repeating facts and concepts but were unable to apply those facts and concepts in order to solve problems (Shepard, 2000; Gredler, 1999). The reform resulted in major revamping of both curriculum and instruction in order to focus on more meaningful learning and thinking.

As depicted in Figure 2.3, the integrated assessment model defines a different role for the classroom teacher. In the previous two models, especially in the time-restricted model, the teacher's role was essentially to serve as the "dispenser" of information to the students (i.e., the lower-right piece of the integrated assessment "puzzle"). In the continuous-feedback model, we saw teachers take on the additional role of helping students achieve mastery of the subject matter. However, in the integrated model, the teacher has become a guide for students and a facilitator of student learning. The amount of large group instruction is substantially reduced, and the vast majority of class time is spent with students working in pairs or small groups. Students also assume a different role in the integrated assessment model. They now possess a much higher level of responsibility for their own learning and must be able to apply it to different situations.

The process of instruction in the integrated model typically begins with the teacher introducing some new topic or material. Following this brief introduc-

tion, the teacher or the students may pose a question or problem—or, perhaps, even a series of problems or questions—related to the topic. The students then work in small groups, attempting to solve the problem(s) or answer the question(s). Finally, upon completion of the activity, the various groups of students share their respective approaches with the rest of the class.

As the name implies, assessment plays an integral part in this instructional model. However, the assessments must change (from the homework assignments and tests that we have seen in the other models) in order to meet the demands of the variety of instructional processes being used in the classroom. The assessments must now begin to focus on students' abilities to apply their knowledge and skills, in a problem-solving manner, to real-world tasks. For example, in the real world we are seldom given a task to solve along with four possible solutions where we simply have to select the best solution. As the saying goes, life is not a multiple-choice test! On the contrary, problem solving requires the application of deduction, induction, and a variety of other cognitive processes.

Assessment must be an ongoing entity throughout the *entire* process in this model. It requires the use of a variety of assessment formats in order for teachers to be well informed about students' strengths and weaknesses. For example, these formats might include informal observations and questioning, checklists, interviews, and rating scales of student products and processes. All these types of assessments will be discussed in much greater detail in later chapters.

The advantages of the integrated assessment model include the increased potential for gains in student achievement. Students begin to gain an understanding of how they think and process information. They learn how to apply what they have learned to new and different situations, settings, and scenarios. This, in turn, helps to solidify their understanding of the facts, concepts, and principles for which they are also responsible.

Student learning truly becomes more meaningful.

However, the integrated model also has its limitations. Its use requires the development of new skills on the part of classroom teachers. Inservice training, followed by continued support, is a necessity if teachers are to successfully implement an integrated assessment model of instruction in their classrooms.

The main features of the three models of the relationship between teaching and assessment have been summarized in Table 2.1.

Table 2.1 Summary of main features of the three teaching-assessment models

	Teaching-Assessment Model		
Characteristic	*Time-Restricted*	*Continuous-Feedback*	*Integrated*
Purpose of assessment	Assignment of grades	Provision of feedback and assign grades	Facilitation of meaningful learning and thinking
Nature of instruction	Unidirectional	Mastery of subject matter content	Small groups focusing on application of learning
Time of assessment	End of instructional cycle	Periodically throughout instructional cycle	Ongoing throughout instruction
Role of teacher	Dispenser of information	Dispenser of information to help students learn and achieve more	Guide and facilitator of student learning
Role of student	Passive learner	More active role taken by student	Responsible for their own learning

THE INSTRUCTIONAL PROCESS

The process of instruction is composed of three basic components: planning instruction, delivering instruction, and assessing instruction (Airasian, 2000). The step of *planning instruction* includes the specification of learning objectives, the identification of appropriate instructional materials, and the development of a coherent sequence of subject matter and learning activities. The next step, *delivering instruction*, involves the teaching of desired content and/or skills to students. Finally, *assessing instruction* includes the determination of the extent to which the learning objectives were achieved. It might appear as if this process is somewhat circular in nature—*plan* → *deliver* → *assess*, then begin again—but, in actuality, the various steps of the process are integrated throughout. The relationships among the three components of the instructional process are portrayed in Figure 2.4.

This visual representation of the process and the relationships among the three components imply that each of the three steps is dependent on the other two. For example, when planning a unit on photosynthesis (step 1), science teachers might want to consider different approaches to teaching the content (step 2). In other words, the teachers would need to make decisions regarding the types of resources, materials, and visual aids to incorporate into the unit. In addition, they would need to consider how best to determine the level of student learning and the extent to which their students understood the photosynthetic process (step 3). When developing particular assessments for the unit (step 3), they must consider not only the specific content that was taught (step 1), but also how it was presented to students (step 2). Assessment and decision making by teachers is required at each step of the instructional process (Airasian, 2000).

Figure 2.4 Relationships among steps in the instructional process

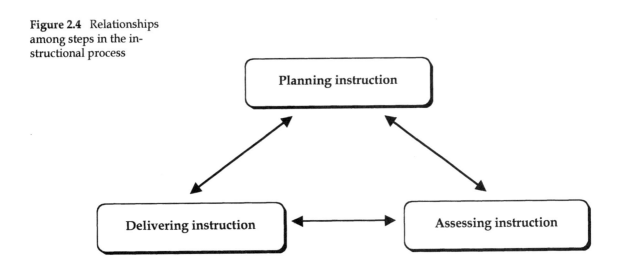

As suggested in this example, all three components must be aligned with one another in order for appropriate instruction and subsequent learning to occur. In other words, the instruction that is planned by a teacher should directly relate to the actual instruction, and the assessments should closely reflect both the planned and delivered instruction (Airasian, 2000). One of the most important things to remember about the instructional process is the following: *All three components in the instructional process must be parallel with one another.*

Let us proceed in our discussion of the instructional process, beginning with a closer examination of the first step, that of planning instruction.

Planning Instruction
Planning is an important activity in which teachers engage. They must make numerous decisions throughout the instructional process regarding things such as what they want their students to learn, whether to cover in class all topics presented in the textbook or to omit certain ones, whether the textbook material needs to be supplemented with other sources of information, how to address specific learning styles of their students, the pace of instruction, what types of homework and other formal and informal assessments should be used, and how to formally and summatively evaluate student learning. Instruction is most certainly not something you want to try to do while "thinking on your feet"!

<u>Purposes</u>
Good preparation helps teachers feel comfortable with the various tasks of teaching and also gives them a sense of ownership over the entire teaching act (Airasian, 2000). Planning for instruction occurs on a variety of levels. The most essential type of planning done by teachers is the **unit plan**. This type of plan is followed in importance by the teacher's weekly and daily lesson plans. A unit plan consists of an outline or overview of a rather large section of content material. A unit might be composed of several textbook chapters or a common theme and last several weeks to several months. The purpose of developing this overview of a unit of instruction is to allow for more specific planning in the form of weekly and daily lesson plans. Failure to begin instructional planning with a unit plan does not enable teachers to see the continuity of the "big picture" with respect to the large portion of material. Once teachers can envision the broad overview and the continuity among subsections of the material, they can better plan the specifics for the instruction of more manageable "chunks" of content material. Planning for instruction also tends to provide structure and a sense of order to the complex environments that make up classrooms.

Airasian (2000) has identified three ways in which pre-instructional planning helps teachers. First, it reduces the uncertainly and anxiety about instruction by providing a sense of purpose and focus. Second, planning furnishes teachers with opportunities to review and familiarize themselves with the material and activities prior to implementing them. Finally, it provides a framework to follow during the actual act of instruction.

Lesson Plans

Unit plans are followed by the development of more specific weekly and daily lesson plans. A **weekly plan** typically provides a brief overview of what will be covered each day of a given week for each subject, course, or class period. Within weekly plans, teachers include the instructional objectives (which will be discussed in detail below) and a concise summary of the activities for each day's lesson. An example of a weekly plan is shown in Figure 2.5.

Once the weekly plans have been specified, teachers then develop the detailed plans that will actually guide their instruction. During the development of these **daily lesson plans**, teachers should try to visualize themselves teaching while following the plans they are attempting to delineate. This allows them the opportunity to anticipate any problems or difficulties and, perhaps, address them prior to actually teaching the material or activity. This planning constitutes somewhat of a dress rehearsal for actual classroom instruction.

Much research has been conducted on various approaches to instruction and the formats of lesson plans that accompany those approaches. There is neither time nor space to address all the approaches in detail in this book. However, I will offer several suggestions or guidelines for developing lesson plans to direct your instruction. These guidelines have been adapted from Quina (1989).

Guideline #1: *There is no single way (i.e., one "correct" format) to write a lesson plan.* A common misconception, especially on the part of preservice teachers, is that there is only one way to develop a daily lesson plan. The format of a lesson plan is largely determined by the purpose of the lesson. In some instances, it may be more appropriate to focus on your behavior as well as that of the students; other times, you may decide that the focus of the lesson should be entirely on what it is the students will be doing. The detailed format of a lesson plan is not something that can be determined by someone who is not familiar with your classroom and teaching style. You must find a format that works for you and your style of planning and teaching.

Guideline #2: *Even though they are detailed, lesson plans are not written in stone and do allow for flexibility.* Lesson plans can appear rigid, if they are developed, and ultimately followed, as if they were scripts. Remember that lesson plans are guides; their purpose is to *direct* your instruction, not *dictate* your instruction. They are meant to provide direction, while at the same time allowing you to act as a professional, making appropriate decisions and adjustments as you proceed through a lesson.

Figure 2.5 Sample page
from a weekly plan book

Teacher: *Mr. Roberts*		Week: *Jan. 22 – 26, 2001*	
Grade: *4*			
Subject	**Monday**	**Tuesday**	**Wednesday**
Math (9:15 – 9:45)	*OBJ: Students will add 2-digit numbers.* (1) *Teacher works at least 5 sample problems, demonstrating rules of carrying.* (2) *Students work problems and orally share how they arrived at their answers.*	*OBJ: Students will estimate sum of 2-digit numbers.* (1) *Teacher introduces concept of "estimation."* (2) *Teacher works at least 5 sample problems, demonstrating estimation.* (3) *Students work problems and orally share how they arrived at their answers.*	*OBJ: Students will estimate sum of and add 2-digit numbers.* (1) *Teacher conducts further checks for understanding of addition and estimation.* (2) *Students will complete in-class worksheet on addition and estimation.*
Science (10:00 – 10:30)	*OBJ: Students will define "scientific method."* (1) *Teacher introduces concept of research.* (2) *Teacher introduces steps in scientific method.*	*OBJ: Students will list and describe steps in the scientific method.* (1) *Teacher reviews steps in scientific method.* (2) *Students complete worksheet describing, in their own words, the various steps.*	*OBJ: Students will apply steps in the scientific method.* (1) *Teacher reviews steps in scientific method.* (2) *Teacher provides a topic; working in groups, students apply sci. method to topic.*
Reading (10:30 – 11:00)	*OBJ: Students will define "characterization."*	*OBJ: Students will identify main character of story.*	*OBJ: Students will describe setting of a story.*

<u>*Guideline #3*</u>*: Even if you believe that you can remember what you are going to teach, lesson plans should be an integral part of the teaching process for every teacher.* Failure on the part of teachers to at least think through the planning process, if not formalize it in writing, can potentially be the greatest downfall to a particular lesson. Novice as

well as experienced teachers will always benefit from writing out a plan in advance of the implementation of a lesson. The actual process of formally writing out a plan will often enlighten teachers as to possible gaps or discontinuities in the procedures, methods, and activities of a given lesson.

Guideline #4: *Formal lesson planning does not stifle the creative process.* Another misconception often held by preservice teachers is that impromptu lessons are the most creative. On the contrary, developing lesson plans often creates opportunities for teachers to engage in professional reflection in order to anticipate potential limitations or weaknesses in a lesson, or to look back on a lesson already taught in order to identify possible ways in which a lesson can be revised and improved. Not only does this process promote creativity, it also results in the refinement of lesson content.

Regardless of its format, any lesson plan should contain, at a minimum, the following components:

- a description of the lesson topic
- the instructional objectives (these will be discussed below)
- time allotment
- required materials and supplemental resources needed
- a brief outline of the content

- an outline of the procedures for the lesson (these include expected teacher behaviors and student behaviors—for example, "...the teacher will..." and "...the students will...")
- a plan for assessing the extent to which the objectives were met.

A generic lesson plan form appears in Figure 2.6. Notice that all the required components listed above appear in the form. However, the layout and format of the lesson plan form can—and most likely *should*—be adapted to meet your specific classroom needs. It is, however, a starting point for you to begin developing a planning form that will work for you.

When using a form similar to the one depicted in Figure 2.6, most lessons can be planned and summarized in one to two pages. Often, the section for "Procedures" is rather lengthy, much more so than represented in the sample provided in the figure. In an attempt to make this process of developing lesson plans a bit more concrete, I have included in Figure 2.7 two sample lesson plans, one at the elementary level (Figure 2.7a) and one at the secondary level (Figure 2.7b). Both are actual lesson plans used by classroom teachers. For both examples, pay close attention to the different ways in which the components are incorporated into the plan.

Figure 2.6 A
sample lesson
plan form

Daily Lesson Plan

Teacher: _____   Date: _____

Subject: _____

- -

Topic:
_____

Objectives:
_____
_____
_____

Time:
_____

Materials:
_____
_____

Procedures:
_____
_____
_____
_____
_____
_____
_____
_____
_____
_____

Assessment:
_____
_____
_____
_____
_____

Figure 2.7(a) Plan for 3rd grade Language Arts lesson

Title - Past Tense Verbs [a]
Teacher - Tania Yap
Primary Subject - Language Arts
Grade Level - 3-4
Time Period - 1 hour

Objectives:
Pupils should be able to
1. understand that verbs can tell about actions that happened in the past.
2. name past tense verbs when given present tense verbs.

Strategies: Direct Teaching, Individual Activity, and Group Activity
Context: In this lesson, pupils can practice sentence construction and apply their new knowledge through creative writing.

INTRODUCTION
Tuning-in:
1. Teacher gets a pupil to do a jumping action. Asks pupils to name the verb that he is acting out (jump). Writes the verb on the board.
2. Does so for four other verbs: walk, kick, shout, laugh.
3. Teacher asks pupils to construct sentences using each of the verbs.
4. Teacher gets pupils to read the sentences.

DEVELOPMENT
PART ONE
Explaining Language Feature:
5. Teacher explains that the present tense is used when the action is done today or at the present moment. If the action was done yesterday or in the past, past tense must be used.
6. Teacher tells pupils that past tense means adding "ed" at the end of the verb.
Pupil response:
7. Teacher refers to the sentence constructed on the board and adds "ed" to the verb "jump," and adds "yesterday" to the sentence.
8. Teacher gets pupils to read the sentence.
9. Teacher asks pupils to change the other four sentences into past tense by repeating the exercise.

PART TWO
Explaining Language Feature:
10. Teacher explains that there are special words that change their spelling when they become past tense. Shows a few examples: run-ran, see-saw, come-came, go-went.
11. Teacher gets pupils to construct sentences using these past tense verbs.
12. Teacher hands out a list of commonly used past tense verbs.

CONCLUSION
13. Pupils are to do varied individual work according to their abilities.
14. The high- and middle-ability pupils are to identify and edit present tense verbs into past tense verbs.
15. The low-ability pupils are to match past tense verbs to their respective present tense verbs.

FOLLOW-UP ACTIVITY
16. Teacher arranges pupils into groups based on ability levels.
17. Each group is to write a composition based on a given picture, using past tense.

---

[a] Adapted from *http://www.lessonplanspage.com/LATeachingPastTenseVerbs34.htm*

Figure 2.7(b) Plan for junior high Social Studies lesson

Title - US Constitution [b]   Unit Topic - US Constitution
Teacher - Bryan Mallette   Grade - 8th
Subject - Social Studies   Lesson Topic - The Executive Branch
Grade Level - Junior High   Primary Teaching Method Used - Discussion

Lesson Objectives: Students will be able to
1. discuss the powers assigned to the president by the Constitution.
2. describe the electoral college process and its effect on presidential elections.
3. outline the responsibilities of the president as the commander-in-chief of the armed forces.
4. identify with 100% accuracy the four major responsibilities of the president.
5. discuss with clarity the impeachment process.

Equipment and Supplies Needed: textbook, blackboard, chalk

Anticipatory Set: Begin with a discussion of what makes a good president. Take a straw poll of the students on their
    feelings about who among the present candidates would make the best president.

Sequence of Learning Activities:
1. Anticipatory set   3. Assignment of homework
2. Discussion of Article 2 of the Constitution 4. Closure

Assignments: Read Article 3 of the Constitution.

Closure: The conclusion of this lesson will be an open discussion of what powers the students feel should or should
    not be included as presidential powers.

Adaptations: Incorporate practical examples of how the presidential powers affect what has happened in the past
    four years. Include discussion about impeachment, current presidential campaign and recent military campaigns
    or exercises.

Student Assessment: The students will be assessed on their comprehension of these concepts during the discussion
    period. They will also be tested on this information at the end of the chapter.

_____

[b] Adapted from *http://www.lessonplanspage.com/SSExecutiveBranchUSConstitutionJH.htm*

Although teachers are ultimately responsible for the planning of instruction that occurs within the four walls of their own classrooms, they are not responsible for identifying the concepts, skills, and topics that are to be taught at specific grade levels or within certain subject areas. These are dictated by individual school districts in the form of **curriculum guides,** sometimes referred to as *curriculum frameworks* or *courses of study.* Curriculum guides typically provide guidance to teachers in the form of curricular "scope and sequence" (i.e., the specific topics and the order in which they should be taught), suggested classroom activities, and expected levels of student achievement (Gredler, 1999). School districts often formulate their curriculum guides to parallel those of their respective state departments of education.

Instructional Objectives
One of the most important components in a lesson plan is the instructional objective. **Instructional objectives,** also known as

educational objectives, are statements that clearly describe what students are expected to learn or to be able to do following instruction. You may see instructional objectives referred to by several other names, including *classroom objectives, learning objectives, performance objectives, behavioral objectives, curriculum objectives, learning targets, instructional outcomes*, and *student outcomes* (Airasian, 2000; Gredler, 1999; Gallagher, 1998). Regardless of the name attached to them, instructional objectives are an essential aspect of the planning process. Not only do they describe in very precise terms what students are to accomplish as a result of instruction, they also help teachers focus their instruction by guiding that instruction toward some ultimate goal (i.e., what students should achieve by the end of a unit, chapter, or lesson). Furthermore, they serve as targets for the assessment activities that follow instruction (Gronlund, 2000). The following are examples of instructional objectives:

- *The students will list three causes of the Civil War.*
- *The students will explain the process of photosynthesis in their own words.*
- *The students will solve word problems requiring the addition of two-digit numbers.*

Three Domains of Objectives

In the mid-1950s, a group of five individuals developed the first system for classifying instructional objectives. This renowned classification system took its name from the lead author of the book in which the classification system appeared and has become known as *Bloom's taxonomy of educational objectives*, or simply as **Bloom's taxonomy**. There are actually three separate categories, or *domains*, of objectives and subsequent student behaviors. These categories are the cognitive domain, the affective domain, and the psychomotor domain. The original taxonomy was created for the **cognitive domain** and includes behaviors such as memorization, problem solving, critical thinking, and other intellectual activities. The **affective domain** involves feelings, beliefs, attitudes, interests, and values. The **psychomotor domain** includes behaviors that are physical and/or manipulative in nature. For our purposes, we will focus on the cognitive domain of instructional objectives.

The cognitive domain of Bloom's taxonomy is organized into six levels. These levels constitute somewhat of a hierarchy; that is, each level represents more complex cognitive behaviors and thinking skills than the level or levels that precede it (Airasian, 2000). The six levels in the taxonomy, from simplest to most complex, are knowledge, comprehension, application, analysis, synthesis, and evaluation. It is important to note that the taxonomy represents a hierarchy of thinking skills; it is *not* a teaching hierarchy. The hierarchical arrangement of Bloom's taxonomy is depicted in Figure 2.8.

Figure 2.8 The hierarchical arrangement of levels in the cognitive domain of Bloom's taxonomy

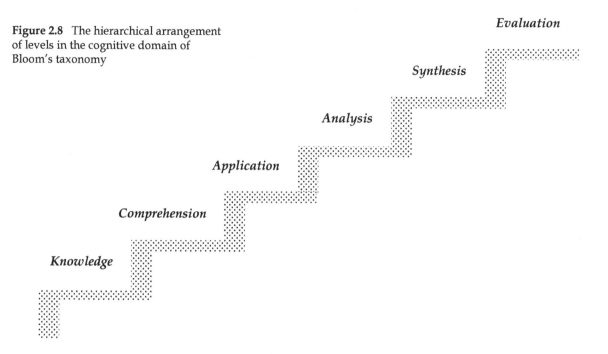

Each level is characterized by typical behaviors (i.e., those behaviors that students should be able to exhibit). The type of behavior that exemplifies each level of the cognitive domain in Bloom's taxonomy is shown below:

- *Knowledge*: memorization behaviors, in particular the recall of previously encountered information
- *Comprehension*: understanding behaviors, such as being able to explain terms and concepts in your own words
- *Application*: behaviors characterized by being able to use previously encountered information, often abstract concepts, in order to solve an unfamiliar problem
- *Analysis*: behaviors characterized by the ability to break down large pieces of information into component parts

- *Synthesis*: behaviors typified by the ability to combine several smaller bits of information into a new generalization or conclusion
- *Evaluation*: the ability to judge the value or worth of something, based on evidence

The six levels of the cognitive domain can be further simplified by placing them into a two-category system that distinguishes lower-level cognitive behaviors from higher-level cognitive behaviors. **Lower-level cognitive behaviors** tend to focus on basic thinking strategies, such as rote memorization, recall of information, and simple understanding of subject matter. In Bloom's taxonomy, the knowledge and comprehension levels represent lower-level thinking skills. **Higher-level cognitive behaviors** include thinking skills beyond simple memorization and understanding, as they are arranged in the hierarchy. These include application, analysis, synthesis, and evaluation.

It is important for teachers to be aware of the distinction between lower- and higher-order cognitive behaviors because it is easier to teach and assess lower-level thinking skills. Hence, some teachers fall into the trap of unintentionally overemphasizing lower-level skills. To avoid this potential trap, it is important to classify all instructional objectives according to Bloom's taxonomy while asking yourself whether both levels of skills are included.

Writing Instructional Objectives

Gronlund (2000) suggests that when writing instructional objectives, there are several important things that teachers should bear in mind. First, instructional objectives should be written in terms of student behaviors, not behaviors exhibited by the teacher. Remember that the purpose of instructional objectives is to focus instruction on behaviors that *students* should be able to exhibit or on skills they should be able to perform upon completion of an instructional unit. As a reminder of this fact, instructional objectives often begin with phrases such as "The student will..." or "The learner can..." In either case, objectives remind the teacher to focus instruction and assessment on desirable student outcomes.

Second, instructional objectives must focus on observable and measurable student characteristics or behaviors. Students must be provided with the opportunity to demonstrate that they have learned, and teachers must be able to observe and assess that "presentation" as evidence that the learning has occurred. Behaviors such as *think, know,* or *understand* are too vague and cannot be measured. For example, try to imagine the difficulties you might encounter if you attempted to determine the extent to which your students *understood* some key concept. It is virtually impossible to directly "see" or "touch" an individual's level of understanding. As teachers, we must provide opportunities for students to *demonstrate* that they understand the concept. In other words, teachers must give students something *to do* that will serve as a demonstration of their understanding. This "something" typically takes the form of an assessment (e.g., a homework activity, a quiz, a test, or a project). Through completion of those types of assessment tasks, students demonstrate that they either do or do not understand the concepts being taught.

Third, the specific content, skill, or behavior to be demonstrated by students must be included within each instructional objective. The objective should be clearly specified so that both the behavior and how the student is to demonstrate the behavior are made very clear. Airasian (2000) summarizes the basic requirements of instructional objectives and states that they should include the specification of:

- the student behavior that should result from instruction in terms that can be observed;

- the content on which the behavior is to be performed.

Airasian (2000) has also provided a simple model for writing instructional objectives:

The student will [*observable behavior*] [*specific content*].

Three examples of instructional objectives follow. Notice how all three fit into this simple model.

- *The students will translate a written German passage into English.*
- *The students will compare and contrast the circulatory system of vertebrates to that of invertebrates.*
- *The students will count to 100 aloud in increments of 5.*

Notice that in all three objectives, the student behavior has actually been specified by the verb in each statement. Not only have the behaviors been specified, but behaviors are also observable. The verbs *translate, compare* and *contrast*, and *count* are all actions that teachers are able to observe and assess. These verbs are known as **action verbs** and serve as the basis for specifying the observable behaviors in instructional objectives. Each level of Bloom's taxonomy has several distinctive action verbs that act as specific observable behaviors for objectives written at the various levels of the taxonomy. Sample action verbs for each level are provided in Table 2.2.

Since the specification of instructional objectives is part of the lesson planning process, it obviously occurs prior to instruction. It is difficult to anticipate the flow that the delivery of instruction will take or the possible obstacles to learning that students might experience during the course of a lesson. Similarly to the development of lesson plans, teachers must be flexible in their approach to using instructional objectives. When a given situation warrants, teachers must be willing to adapt to these unforeseen hindrances. Teachers must rely on their professional discretion to determine how precisely they follow the instructional objectives that were developed prior to beginning actual instruction (Airasian, 2000).

Teacher-Made versus Publisher-Developed Materials

Textbooks, as well as other resources such as the Internet, can provide teachers with a wealth of resources for use during all three phases of instruction (Airasian, 2000). Textbook publishers often develop teacher's editions, teacher's guides, or other types of supplemental materials. During the planning stage, one can find resources such as unit and lesson objectives, unit and lesson plans, and ideas for introductory activities. (Some similar types of Internet resources are highlighted later in this chapter.) Resources such as lesson overviews, guiding questions, content outlines, visual aids, transparency masters, and homework assignments or worksheets can provide assistance during the delivery of instruction. Finally, unit or chapter tests, as well as end-of-book "final exams" have also been developed for teacher use.

Table 2.2 Sample action verbs for levels of the cognitive domain of Bloom's taxonomy

Level	Sample Action Verbs
Knowledge	*list, define, tell, describe, identify, show, label, collect*
Comprehension	*summarize, describe, interpret, predict, associate, distinguish, estimate, discuss*
Application	*apply, demonstrate, calculate, complete, illustrate, show, solve, examine, modify*
Analysis	*analyze, separate, order, explain, connect, classify, arrange, divide, compare*
Synthesis	*combine, integrate, modify, rearrange, substitute, plan, create, design, compose*
Evaluation	*assess, decide, rank, recommend, convince, select, judge, discriminate, support*

These prepackaged lesson objectives and plans, visual aids, activities, assessment items, and other teacher resources can prove very valuable to the classroom teacher. However, there is sometimes a tendency for teachers to rely solely on these types of materials and resources. Teachers who rely exclusively on these types of materials are in potential violation of a basic tenet of classroom teaching that was stressed earlier in this chapter: *All three components in the instructional process — planning, delivering, and assessing instruction — must be in alignment with one another.* Textbook publishers have no way of knowing what a given teacher's instructional goals and objectives are, or the types of methods that a teacher uses in his or her classroom. Additionally, they cannot know the individual instructional needs of each student in that teacher's classroom. Rather, these materials are designed with the typical teacher in mind (i.e., these resources are developed such that *most* teachers and students would benefit from them). If a teacher chooses to utilize these types of materials, it is the responsibility of that teacher to ensure that they are adapted appropriately for use (1) by that teacher, (2) with those students, (3) with the particular instructional objectives and content, and (4) with the appropriate assessments. Adoption of these resources requires a thorough examination of their strengths and limitations. Making the decision to use these materials should most certainly not occur before school on the day in which the lesson will be taught or the assessment administered. Although readily available and a time-saver, prepackaged instructional materials and resources tend to focus on lower-level thinking skills and, when used in the absence of critical review, can lead to inappropriate instruction for some students (Airasian, 2000).

Delivering Instruction

The second phase of the instructional process is the actual delivery of instruction to students. Although this is not a teaching methods textbook, there are some important things to remember about the delivery of instruction and the impact that assessment has on that instruction.

Assessment During Instruction

According to Airasian (2000), teachers should engage in two tasks once instruction has begun: (1) deliver the instruction that they have planned, and (2) constantly assess and evaluate the effectiveness of their instruction in order to alter it when the situation warrants. Often, things do not go according to a teacher's well-developed plans. Teachers must attend to student questions, off-task behaviors, and various levels of interest in the subject matter. In addition, there exist a variety of school-based events that can interrupt teachers' delivery of instruction, such as assemblies, fire drills, and the unexpected classroom visit from the principal. All these things can force teachers to alter their instruction.

Teachers must assess the progress that their particular instruction is making on the ultimate goal of student learning, and then subsequently make decisions about that progress (e.g., "Are the students getting this?"; "Is my teaching enabling the students to show that they have met my objectives?"; "Should I proceed, or do I need to review that last concept and provide more examples?"). This assessment-evaluation process is carried out in an on-going, never-ending manner. Teachers do it constantly every day and throughout every lesson. Teachers continuously gather assessment information—usually in the form of informal assessments (i.e., by making observations, asking questions, etc.). They are careful to notice things such as unusual student reactions or behaviors, nonverbal cues (i.e., a "wrinkled brow," perhaps indicating a lack of understanding), or unanticipated student questions that may lead a teacher to conclude that the instruction and subsequent learning are not progressing well. A teacher's knowledge of his or her own class and subject matter, coupled with the information provided by these ongoing assessments of progress, allow the teacher to adapt the instruction to truly meet the instructional needs of the students. It is important to remember that seldom, if ever, do instructional lessons go exactly as you planned them. You must be prepared to assess and adapt them.

Assessing Instruction

The third and final phase of the instructional process is the formal assessment of the instruction delivered to students. In Chapter 1, you read about the differences between formative and summative evaluations. Those concepts are now applied to the instructional process.

Formative Evaluation

Formative evaluations have been described as those evaluations that occur during instruction, for the purpose of determining what adjustments need to be made. The primary application of formative evaluations to the instructional process was actually discussed in the preceding section. Most formative decision making occurs during instruction and typically results from informal assessments. Recall that these types of assessments are spontaneous and include unplanned assessments such as visual observations and oral questioning.

However, some formative evaluations may be based on assessments that are more formal. Assessments such as take-home worksheets, individual seatwork activities, and brief written quizzes certainly differ from informal assessments since they must be planned in advance of their administration. These more formal assessments occur at specific planned breaks or pauses in instruction (e.g., at the end of a section that constitutes part of a large book chapter). Although these are planned assessments, their purpose is still to help in making decisions about adjustments to instruction. For example, if students do not perform well on an oral quiz or homework sheet, a teacher may decide to revisit previously covered material since the students apparently failed to understand the material or concepts. More important, this information is gathered and the decision made prior to the administration of much more formal assessments that will ultimately be used as the basis for assigning grades (i.e., summative evaluations).

Summative Evaluation

Much more formal assessments are administered following the completion of a unit or some other major cycle of instruction. Summative decision making typically follows written tests or other large-scale projects and performances. Results are typically used for the purposes of assigning grades to students as measures of their achievement levels, but can also be used as final measures of the overall effectiveness of instruction (Gallagher, 1998). They provide information to teachers regarding the extent to which the instructional objectives were met as a result of instruction, as well as information regarding the implications for future cycles of instruction on the same topic or of the same unit. In this latter application, summative decisions are actually being used in a formative manner. In other words, they are being used as feedback to guide future instruction.

Gallagher (1998) has identified three major uses of the results of summative evaluations. First and foremost, they provide feedback, information, and direction to the teachers and students who were directly involved in the instruction. Second, these assessments provide feedback and information to stakeholders who do not have direct involvement in the process, such as parents and school administrators. Finally, depending on the nature of the instruction and assessment, the results may be used by other groups of individuals, such as guidance counselors or school psychologists.

It is critical to remember that not all students in your classroom will achieve the instructional objectives you establish, unless they are very low-level objectives. For a variety of reasons, some students will have a more difficult time experiencing success. When trying to determine the *overall* effectiveness of your instruction, there will most certainly be some outcomes of your instruction that should be achieved by nearly all students; however, for some outcomes, this expectation may be less reasonable (Gallagher, 1998).

SUMMARY

The instructional process consists of three phases: planning instruction, delivering instruction, and assessing instruction. Assessment is an integral part of all three phases. Information must be gathered and informed decisions made prior to, during, and following instruction.

Three models depicting the relationship between teaching and assessment were discussed. The time-restricted model involves assessment only at the end of instruction. The continuous-feedback model incorporates assessment for both feedback and the assignment of grades. Finally, the integrated assessment model blends assessment and instruction so that instruction focuses on more meaningful thinking and learning.

In order for classroom instruction to be effective, the three components of the instructional process must be aligned with one another. In other words, decisions made during the planning phase should also take into consideration both the delivery and assessment of instruction. Similarly, decisions made about the delivery and assessment of instruction should consider the remaining two phases. All three components should be parallel.

Many important decisions must be made during the planning of instruction. Unit plans, weekly plans, and daily lesson plans provide the structure for the scope and sequence of instruction. The starting point for any lesson plan is the specification of instructional objectives. These objectives should be developed on the basis of the six levels of the cognitive domain of Bloom's taxonomy. Instructional objectives consist of two basic components: an action verb (which specifies the observable student behavior) and the specific content being addressed. Prepackaged instructional objectives, lesson plans, and other resources are available; however, teachers should utilize them only after they have been carefully evaluated for appropriateness.

🖰 **Chapter 2** *Related Web Sites* 💻

❖ **Bloom, et al.'s Taxonomy of the Cognitive Domain**
(*chiron.valdosta.edu/whuitt/col/cogsys/bloom.html*)
Dr. Bill Whuitt of Valdosta State University maintains this site where he provides a definition, a list of several action verbs, and a sample behavioral objective for each of the six levels of Bloom's cognitive domain.

❖ **The Lesson Plans Page** (*http://www.lessonplanspage.com*)
This site provides more than 1,000 lesson plans developed by classroom teachers. You begin by selecting a subject area (math, science, language arts, computers, social studies, art, physical education and health, or multidisciplinary), followed by a specific level (grades PreK–1, 2–3, 4–5, 6–7, junior/high school, or multiple). The site is free of charge and is also searchable by topic. However, I reiterate one major caution: These lesson plans were developed by teachers for use in *their* classrooms, not yours. *Please* make sure you take the time to scrutinize the objectives, content, materials, and activities, and adapt them to meet your individual needs.

❖ **AskERIC Lesson Plans** (*www.askeric.org/Virtual/Lessons*)
ERIC, the Educational Resources Information Center, also maintains a database of lesson plans developed by classroom teachers. Once again, please make sure that you take the time to closely examine all aspects of the lesson plan and adapt them to meet your individual needs. The database is searchable by topic and grade level. Also included is a link (*www.askeric.org/Virtual/Lessons/Guide.shtml*) to AskERIC's "Write-a-Lesson Plan Guide," which provides some very useful planning advice, as well as more links to lesson plan Web sites.

QUESTIONS FOR REVIEW

1. A teacher is overheard saying, "I make sure my students master the content of my lessons by incorporating all the work they complete into their final course grades." What, if any, problems are there with this statement? Explain.

2. Why might you expect that several teachers within the same school and teaching the same grades and subject matter would have lesson plan formats that differ from one another?

3. How would you respond to a teacher who says, "I don't believe in formal planning. I don't do weekly or daily lesson plans because I never end up following them anyway"?

4. How do curriculum guides relate to unit and lesson plans?

5. Consider the following instructional objective: *The students will list the three primary colors.* Would you classify this objective as addressing lower- or higher-order thinking skills? Explain.

6. In which specific level of Bloom's taxonomy would the objective listed in Question 5 above be classified? Explain.

7. Consider the following objective: *The students will classify the leaf samples into like categories based on similar characteristics.* Which higher-order skill of Bloom's taxonomy is being addressed? Explain.

8. A fifth-grade teacher is searching the Internet for resources related to a unit on the Civil War to be taught next month and stumbles on an entire unit plan. Excitedly, the teacher prints out the unit plan and all the related student activities. You enter the room just in time to hear the teacher say, "Wow! That was easy. Now I can relax until it's time to begin the unit." Having just taken an assessment course, what advice would you offer this teacher?

9. Why is it important to constantly assess your instruction *during* the time the instruction is occurring?

10. Since summative assessments typically occur at the end of an instructional cycle, is there any way that they might be used in a formative manner (i.e., to provide feedback)? Explain.

ENRICHMENT ACTIVITIES

1. (a). Select a topic in a subject matter area with which you are familiar and a unit in that area. Ideally, it should be in an area you would like to teach someday. Using the suggestions and guidelines presented in the chapter, write five to seven instructional objectives. Remember that your objectives should be written for key or major skills that students should be able to perform upon completion of the unit, not for each isolated piece of content in the unit.

   (b). After you have written your instructional objectives, classify each according to the level of skill it represents in Bloom's taxonomy. If you determine that all of your objectives are assessing lower-level thinking skills, select two or three and rewrite them so that they assess higher-order thinking skills. Be prepared to share your objectives with the class.

2. Select one or two of the instructional objectives that you developed in Activity number 1 above. For these objectives, and using the lesson plan format as shown in Figure 2.6, develop a lesson plan for teaching that content. In addition to your instructional objectives, be sure to include the following in your lesson plan:
   - the approximate timeframe
   - materials and other resources necessary for the lesson

- clearly outlined procedures (specify what you will be doing and what you will expect your students to be doing)
- the plan for assessing the extent to which your objectives have been met.

3. Working in small groups (preferably organized by common subject areas), select one chapter from a textbook. If grouping into common subject areas is not feasible, you might use this textbook. Based on the content of the chapter, write one instructional objective for each level of Bloom's taxonomy. Be prepared to share your objectives.

Notes

Chapter 3

Characteristics of Assessments

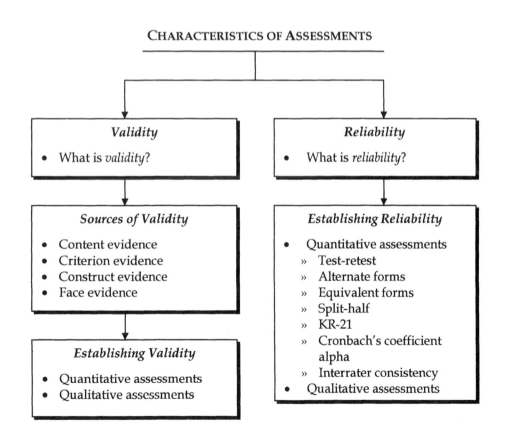

CHARACTERISTICS OF ASSESSMENTS

Validity

- What is *validity*?

Reliability

- What is *reliability*?

Sources of Validity

- Content evidence
- Criterion evidence
- Construct evidence
- Face evidence

Establishing Reliability

- Quantitative assessments
  - » Test-retest
  - » Alternate forms
  - » Equivalent forms
  - » Split-half
  - » KR-21
  - » Cronbach's coefficient alpha
  - » Interrater consistency
- Qualitative assessments

Establishing Validity

- Quantitative assessments
- Qualitative assessments

INTRODUCTION

As you have seen, assessment is the process of gathering information and using it to make educational decisions. We hope that educational decisions made by classroom teachers are the best and most appropriate for a given situation. However, the quality of those decisions is *only* as good as the information that leads to them. If the information gathered is inappropriate for a specific individual or situation or if it is collected in a less-than-precise manner, the decisions that follow will logically be inaccurate.

This chapter focuses on the two most important characteristics of any assessment: *validity* and *reliability*. Ensuring that assessments are both reasonably valid and reliable is key to developing educational assessments and making subsequent educational decisions that are accurate and appropriate.

WHAT IS VALIDITY?

The concept of **validity** is formally defined as "the degree to which evidence and theory support the interpretations of test scores entailed by proposed uses of tests" (American Educational Research Association, American Psychological Association, & National Council on Measurement in Education, 1999, p. 9). Validity emphasizes not the results themselves but, rather, how you use the results. In other words, validity is less about the quality of the assessment and its actual results (e.g., students' scores) but is more about the *decisions* that follow the inter-

pretation of those results. Therefore, it is not appropriate to talk about the validity of assessment results, the validity of measurement instruments (such as tests), or the validity of the assessment procedures. Validity is the most fundamental consideration when developing and evaluating tests and other assessments (AERA, APA, & NCME, 1999).

Let us consider a concrete example. Assume that you teach in a school district that recently decided to administer the SMART (Science, Mathematics, and Reading Test—a fictitious test to be used in our discussion) to students in grades 3, 6, 8, and 10. The teachers in the district decided that they would like to use the results of the SMART in several ways. Mrs. Johnson suggested that the results of the reading portion be used to group her new students next year into above average, average, and below average reading groups. Mr. Chan, a seventh-grade science teacher, would like to be able to use the results to describe each student's comprehension of science vocabulary and concepts. Mrs. Goldman, the calculus teacher, suggested that the math results could be used as prerequisite scores for admission into upper-level, advanced mathematics courses. Finally, Mr. Riley, an American history teacher, would like to use the results of the reading portion of the SMART as a means of identifying students who would be successful in an advanced placement history course.

Granted, this is an oversimplified example, but we can use it to illustrate two points. First, it appears that the first three uses of the SMART scores as identified above potentially could be legitimate, valid ways to interpret and use the results. (Of course, since we do not know what types of items are asked on the test, or what types of student skills are required, we cannot be sure of our determination.) Mrs. Johnson could very likely use the reading scores as an indicator of reading ability for each student and subsequently place her students into three appropriate groups based on those scores. Similarly, Mr. Chan could conceivably conclude, and ultimately describe, each student's level of comprehension of science terms and concepts. Finally, Mrs. Goldman could feasibly make reasonable decisions about which students should be permitted to enroll in advanced mathematics courses based on their SMART mathematics scores.

The second point is more critical. The reading portion of the SMART measures student skills such as reading comprehension, vocabulary, and the ability to identify the main idea in a story. It should be fairly obvious that using the reading results in order to determine whether a student would be successful in advanced history is an *in*appropriate use of those particular scores. In this situation, the results are being used inappropriately, which would likely lead to inaccurate decisions (i.e., a lack of validity).

The key in our working example is whether there is alignment among four critical factors: (1) the objectives for in- struction, (2) the actual instruction that preceded the administration of the SMART, (3) the assessment items that appeared on the test, and (4) the decisions or conclusions based on the interpretation of the resulting scores. These conclusions will be valid if they follow logically from the preceding three factors (i.e., the objectives, instruction, and assessment).

Notice that I did not discuss the SMART being a "valid assessment," in and of itself. I referred only to the idea of "valid results" or "valid conclusions." Quite often, an assessment may have a high degree of validity for one use but may not have a high degree for some others. Nitko (2001) identifies three important points to keep in mind when discussing the validity of assessment results. Two of them help summarize our discussion to this point:

- The concept of validity applies to the various ways that teachers interpret and use assessment results and not to the assessment itself.
- Assessment results have different degrees of validity based on different purposes and/or situations.

Nitko's third point is also worthy of mention. He states that:

- Judgments about the validity of specific uses of assessment results should only be made after examination of several types of validity evidence.

For example, if we really want to know if Mrs. Johnson's intended use of the reading scores from the SMART would be valid, we should look closely at the items presented to students on the test. Do the items appropriately address the skills and content that they claim to? Do those items accurately represent the objectives that served as the foundation for the actual reading instruction presented to the students?

Whenever teachers want to determine if their assessments are valid (or if they want to determine their relative degrees of validity), they must gather evidence that demonstrates that validity. There are several sources of evidence that support an assessment's validity, which are presented in the next section.

Sources of Validity Evidence

Validity is an abstract concept; we cannot directly observe it. At best, we only hope to be able to gather evidence in support of it. There are several different sources of evidence that can support validity. In the past, these different sources of evidence were actually considered to be different types of validity. However, the current representation of validity is that it is a unitary concept (AERA, APA, & NCME, 1999), not an entity consisting of several distinct forms of validity (Nitko, 2001; Gredler, 1999). The various sources of evidence that support validity include content, criterion, and construct.

Content Evidence

With respect to teacher-developed assessments, the most important source of evidence used in the determination of validity is content-related evidence. **Content evidence of validity** focuses on the extent to which the *content* addressed by the assessment items, tasks, or activities adequately samples (i.e., is representative of) the larger domain of performance (Nitko, 2001; Oosterhof, 1999). In other words, content evidence determines the degree to which an assessment measures the intended content area (Gallagher, 1998). The determination of validity based on content evidence is based almost solely on professional judgment.

When attempting to determine the extent to which the results of an assessment are valid, the primary source of evidence for classroom teachers is content-related. There are two sources of content-related evidence with which teachers should be familiar. The first, referred to as *relevance* (Nitko, 2001; AERA, APA, & NCME, 1999), is concerned with the degree to which the test items or other assessment tasks emphasize what has been taught. Assume that a classroom teacher wants to test students on their knowledge of World War II. If students are given a test that consists of 100 items, all of which specifically required the students to recall and apply their knowledge of World War II, we could conclude that the test exhibited content-related evidence of validity. On the other hand, if the test consisted of 100 items, some of which asked questions related to the Vietnam War, it would not have a very high degree of validity based on content evidence. The students' knowledge of Vietnam does not inform the teacher in any way about their knowledge of World War II. Imagine the consequences of drawing conclusions about student performance relative to World War II based on questions about a different war.

The second source of content-related evidence is called *representativeness* (Nitko, 2001; AERA, APA, & NCME, 1999). Representativeness is concerned with how well the assessment items or tasks represent the total content area. To continue our previous example, suppose the teacher developed her test of World War II by focusing *only* on the causes of the war. There are certainly many more World War II topics for which items could have been written and included on the test. This situation is especially problem-

atic if the objectives and instruction covered all these other topics (e.g., specific battles, key leaders of the opposing sides, etc.). In this case, the items appearing on the test were not representative of the entire content that was taught (i.e., it lacks content-related evidence of validity).

It is important to note that assessments require both sources of evidence in order to establish their validity based on content evidence. They need to (1) cover the intended objectives and (2) adequately sample those objectives. One method that teachers can use to assist them in the preparation and assessment of validity involves the development of a two-way table, such as the one shown in Table 3.1.

Table 3.1 Test item numbers for test on World War II

	Areas of Content				
Bloom's Levels	*Causes*	*Geography*	*U.S. Involvement*	*Key Leaders*	*Major Battles*
Knowledge	1, 5, 7	6, 8	9, 10		
Comprehension	11, 12	2, 3, 4			
Application					
Analysis	15, 16, 17				18, 19
Synthesis			13, 14	20	
Evaluation	21			22	

This two-way table specifies the major content covered during instruction in the columns and the six levels of Bloom's taxonomy in the rows. The cells are filled in with the various test item numbers based on the intersection of content and the appropriate taxonomic level that is being tested. In Table 3.1, for example, test items 9 and 10 cover content related to the involvement of the U.S. in World War II by requiring students to use simple recall skills. In contrast, test items 13 and 14 cover the same content but require students to synthesize several different pieces of information related to U.S. involvement in the war. Of course, not every cell in the table needs to be filled in. It is likely that other types of student work (e.g., a term paper or project) will cover some of the higher-level skills. Coverage within the table depends on the types of content and the nature of the instructional objectives. By using this type of table to assess content-related evidence of validity, teachers think not only about content coverage but also skill levels being assessed.

As previously stated, content evidence of validity is the most important source of evidence with which classroom teachers need to be concerned. This is because content-related evidence allows teachers to determine the extent to which there exists alignment between the instructional objectives, the content of instruction, and the subsequent assessment. This fact reiterates—and continues to stress—the importance of the relationships among the three key components of the instructional process.

Criterion Evidence

A second source of evidence that can help establish the validity of assessment results is criterion-related evidence. **Criterion evidence of validity** is a measure of the extent to which the scores resulting from an assessment are related to the scores on another, well-established assessment (AERA, APA, & NCME, 1999; Gallagher, 1998). This previously established assessment is called the *criterion*. Criterion-related evidence is typically not of concern to classroom teachers but is of greater consequence in standardized testing programs.

There are two types of criterion-related evidence that can be obtained, depending on the nature of the criterion. **Predictive evidence of validity** is a form of criterion-related evidence in which the criterion is measured sometime in the future. Predictive evidence is of particular importance for aptitude tests. These types of tests measure an individual's potential to perform certain skills or tasks in the future. For example, suppose we administer an algebra aptitude test to middle school students and later (perhaps, two to three years) record their grades in a high school algebra course. If those students who scored well on the aptitude test also performed well in the course (and if those who did poorly on the aptitude test also did poorly in the course), the aptitude test is said to have predictive evidence of validity. In contrast, if students performed well on the test but poorly in the course, the aptitude test would lack validity based on predictive evidence.

The concept of predictive evidence of validity is very important to tests such as the Scholastic Assessment Test (SAT) and the Graduate Records Examination (GRE). Both tests are used for selection and admission to college and graduate school, respectively, because there is some evidence that they are modest predictors of academic performance. In other words, there is a modest tendency for high school students who score high on the SAT to earn high GPAs as undergraduates in college.

The second type of criterion-related evidence is called **concurrent evidence of validity** because the criterion is measured at the same time or consists of some measure that is available at the same time. Suppose that a newly developed test purports to measure the same content and skills as the SMART. In order to determine if the new test is valid, we might administer the SMART on one day and the new test a few days later. Once again, if those students who scored well on the SMART also perform well on the new test, the new test is said to have validity based on concurrent evidence.

Construct Evidence

The third and final source of evidence used to establish assessment validity is construct evidence. **Construct evidence of validity** is the degree to which there is a fit between the hypothetical construct being measured and the nature of the responses actually engaged in by the students (AERA, APA, & NCME, 1999). A *construct* is a human characteristic or trait that cannot be *directly* observed. For example, "depression" is a construct. We cannot reach out and touch someone's depression nor can we measure it with a ruler. In fact, it exists only as a construct, which we *infer* from observing some of its parts. Crying, downcast eyes, and a listless tone of voice are some behaviors that might lead to a diagnosis of depression, even though we cannot directly see the depression itself.

Determining the extent to which an assessment task is valid based on construct evidence involves the careful identification of performances that are direct indicators of a student's skills or abilities in that particular area. Those skills and abilities are typically identified through the complex theories that define that particular construct (Chase, 1999). Similar to criterion evidence, construct-related evidence is not a major concern to classroom teachers but is of much greater consequence in standardized testing programs, especially those dealing with psychological traits (e.g., intelligence, anxiety, self-esteem, personality, etc.).

Construct evidence of validity is often seen as an "umbrella" for all sources of validity evidence (Chase, 1999). If one can gather construct-related evidence in support of validity, there exists a logical assumption that the particular test items or assessment activities are accurately representing the content area in question (content evidence). Also, if those items or activities are closely related to skills that students are currently able to perform (concurrent evidence), or should be able to perform at some later time (predictive evidence), the more likely the activities are to appropriately assess what the theory says it should assess. Therefore, construct-related evidence embodies both content and criterion evidence of validity (Chase, 1999).

Face Evidence

Although typically not considered a formal source of evidence used to establish validity, there is a fourth type that deserves consideration. **Face evidence of validity** is an informal measure of the extent to which the users or takers of tests believe that the tests are valid. If examinees do not believe that a given test *appears*, taken at "face value" (henceforth, the name "face evidence"), to be valid, they may believe there is no point in trying to perform well on it. Since face evidence essentially relies on mere superficial perceptions of individuals, it is not considered to be a formal means of establishing an assessment's degree of validity.

I do, however, believe that face evidence of validity plays an important role in education and, in particular, for the classroom teacher. If teachers develop and administer written tests to their students, they would certainly hope that the students recognize that the material covered by the test items corresponds to their instruction. If the students believed that the test covered information that they had not been taught, they might assume (and logically so) that they would not perform well on the test. When this type of assumption is made, it often becomes a self-fulfilling prophecy for students. If they believe that they will not perform well on a test, and therefore do not try very hard, in all likelihood, they will not do well.

Since the content coverage of the assessment is an important feature of face evidence, if is often said that face evidence stems from content-related evidence (Chase, 1999). It does not involve the level of scrutinization that is required in the examination of formal content evidence. However, as you saw in the preceding paragraph, and perhaps more important, face evidence of validity is relevant from a student motivational perspective (Chase, 1999).

Establishing Validity of Quantitative Assessments

As previously discussed, the main source of evidence with which classroom teachers should be concerned is content-related evidence of validity. There is no formula or specific set of guidelines to follow in order to establish the validity of quantitative assessments. However, Nitko (2001) offers a set of criteria that can be used for purposes of improving the validity of classroom assessments. The set of criteria involves an extremely comprehensive list of nineteen criteria to be attained in order to ensure the validity of your self-developed assessments. The set of criteria that I offer is presented in Table 3.2. These criteria appear in the form of guiding questions and have been adapted from Nitko's original set of criteria (pp. 39–43).

Notice that Guiding Questions 1 through 3 all address the similarities between instructional goals and/or objectives and the specific content that was taught in class. If, after *careful* examination of your assessments, you are able to answer all three questions in the affirmative, then you have content-related evidence that your assessments are valid. You should also be aware of the fact that, since face evidence stems from content evidence, affirmative answers to these three questions will also provide face evidence of validity, especially with respect to question 1. If there is a close parallel between what was taught and the assessments with which you provide your students, the assessments will appear to them as valid.

Table 3.2 Guiding questions for enhancing the validity of quantitative assessments

Category	Type of Evidence[a]	Guiding Questions
Content relevance and representativeness	Content	1. *Does my assessment procedure emphasize what I have taught?* 2. *Do my assessment tasks accurately represent outcomes specified in my school's, district's, or state's curriculum guide?* 3. *Is the content in my assessment procedure important and worth learning?*
Consistency with other assessments	Criterion	4. *Is the pattern of results for my students consistent with what I expected based on my other assessments of them?* 5. *Did I make the assessment tasks too difficult or too easy for them?*
Student perceptions	Face	6. *Do students perceive that the problems or tasks on my assessment emphasize the concepts and other material that I have taught?* 7. *Do students generally believe that the assessment measures the appropriate behaviors, skills, or characteristics as they were taught?*

[a] Note that construct evidence does not appear in this column. It is assumed that if content and criterion evidence exist, construct evidence logically follows.

Guiding Questions 4 and 5 specifically address the degree to which similarities exist between the assessment in question and other assessments that supposedly measure the same or similar behaviors, knowledge, or skills. Once again, only after careful scrutiny of your assessments and the subsequent results, if you are able to answer the two questions favorably, you have criterion-related evidence of the consistency of your assessment results.

In addition to the first three content-related questions, answers to Guiding Questions 6 and 7 also provide specific evidence of validity related to content, but from the perspective of the students. If your assessments *appear* to measure the content, concepts, skills, and behaviors that were taught, then all students will see those assessments as being fair to them. This, in turn, results in a higher level of motivation for students to provide maximum effort. When students believe that a particular assessment item or activity addresses something that was not taught (or that was taught differently), their motivation to perform to the best of their ability can be seriously jeopardized. In this case, your assessment does not appear to be valid, at least to those students.

The above discussion pertains directly to teacher-developed assessments designed for use within their own classrooms. With respect to standardized tests and other large-scale assessments, evidence of validity, especially criterion-related evidence of validity, is often established through statistical analysis. The idea behind both predictive evidence and criterion evidence is to be able to demonstrate that a relationship exists between the two assessments. From a statistical perspective, the degree of relationship between two tests or other assessments is measured using a correlation coefficient. **A correlation coefficient** (symbolized r) is a statistical value that indicates the extent to which the scores on one measure agree with the scores on another measure. The values for correlation coefficients range from –1.00 to +1.00. Positive correlations indicate that high scores on one test correspond with high scores on the second; negative correlations indicate that high scores on one correspond with low scores on the other. A correlation coefficient specifically used as a measure of validity is known as a **validity coefficient**.

Briefly, correlation coefficients equal to –1.00 and +1.00 indicate perfect relationships between measures. In other words, the scores on the first measure correspond perfectly with the scores on the second. This phenomenon never occurs in educational testing. If we were trying to establish a test's validity using criterion-related evidence, we would hope to obtain positive validity coefficients as a result of our analyses. High scores on one test and low scores on the other would certainly not demonstrate consistency between the two measures. Furthermore, the closer the validity coefficient is to +1.00, the stronger the relationship and, therefore, the stronger the evidence supporting valid test results. Table 3.3 provides a general scheme for interpreting the values of correlation coefficients with respect to describing the extent of the relationship. Greater detail concerning correlation coefficients and the method of calculating them, including examples, can be found in Appendix C.

Table 3.3 General scheme for interpreting correlation coefficients

Value of Coefficient (r)	Extent of Relationship
$.85 \leq r \leq 1.00$	Very strong
$.70 \leq r < .85$	Moderately strong
$.50 \leq r < .70$	Moderate
$.30 \leq r < .50$	Moderately weak
$.00 \leq r < .30$	Very weak

Adapted from Chase (1999).

Establishing Validity of Qualitative Assessments

In addition to establishing the validity of formal, quantitative assessments, classroom teachers must also be concerned with the validity of their less formal, qualitative assessments. Recall from Chapter 1 that qualitative assessments include such things as informal observations, oral questioning, and anecdotal records. Since qualitative assessments are largely informal, and therefore unstructured, they typically represent only a "snapshot" of student behavior as it is occurring (Gredler, 1999). A great deal of caution must be exhibited when attempting to draw conclusions from such a limited sample of student behaviors or performances. A list of guiding questions (adapted from Gredler, 1999) that can be used with qualitative assessments is provided in Table 3.4.

Table 3.4 Guiding questions for enhancing the validity of qualitative assessments

Category	Guiding Questions
Representativeness of observations, notes, etc.	1. *Have I limited my observations to concrete behaviors, as opposed to more global impressions of students?* 2. *Have I observed/noted the specific behavior a sufficient number of times in order to draw definitive conclusions?* 3. *Have I observed/noted the behavior in different settings or situations?*
Nature of inferences drawn	4. *Have I based my conclusions only on the information that I have gathered?* 5. *Are there plausible, alternative explanations for the given behavior?*

Guiding Questions 1 through 3 provide the classroom teacher with appropriate evidence in order to determine the extent to which specific student behaviors are representative (i.e., typical). If the behaviors cannot be classified as typical, it could be that they represent isolated incidents, or that they are "global impressions" of individual students. In other words, when a teacher observes a student exhibiting off-task, the teacher needs to determine if that behavior is an isolated one or if it occurs more frequently, indicating that the student may have some sort of learning difficulty. Additionally, teachers want to be sure that they do not arrive at negative conclusions concerning a *specific* behavior simply because they dislike the student *in general.*

The second category of Guiding Questions provides teachers with evidence to help them determine the extent to which their conclusions follow logically from the information they have collected as a result of their observations, questions, etc. They also provide classroom teachers with an opportunity to reflect on their conclusions and decisions in order to determine if alternative, yet still credible, interpretations might exist. This notion of reflecting on your assessment information and resulting conclusions is an important activity for teachers. It often provides the much-needed chance to consider whether your judgments may have been influenced by factors other than your specific observations and notes about students'

behaviors and their academic performance.

WHAT IS RELIABILITY?

Validity is the most important characteristic that assessment results should possess. A second essential characteristic is reliability. **Reliability** is formally defined as the consistency of measurements when the testing procedure is repeated on a population of individuals or groups (AERA, APA, & NCME, 1999). Validity addresses accuracy; whereas, reliability addresses consistency. In other words, reliability speaks to the consistency of the assessment scores and their subsequent interpretation and use. It is not a characteristic of the assessment itself. So, to reiterate, one should not refer to a "reliable test" but to "reliable scores from a test."

The consistency of scores resulting from an assessment can be affected by many things, some of which are temporary factors and others which are permanent (Gallagher, 1998). For example, if an achievement test is administered to a large group of students, some may not perform as well as they are capable of doing. One student may have *error* introduced into his score due to the fact that he or she was ill on the day of the test (i.e., a temporary factor). Another student may not perform well because a large number of items appeared on the test that concerned content not actually taught in class (i.e., a permanent factor). These errors that occur in measuring knowledge, skills, abilities, and aptitudes may be either random or systematic. Random errors affect reliability; systematic errors affect validity (Gallagher, 1998). The illness experienced by the first student will affect the consistency of his or her scores. If the student were to take the test again when feeling healthy, he or she would likely perform better. In contrast, the second student who did not perform well owing to the poor coverage of content that appeared on the test would, in all likelihood, not perform better if he or she were to take the test again. These results would certainly be reliable (i.e., the student failed the test each and every time!), but the results would most assuredly not be valid.

Establishing Reliability of Quantitative Assessments

The reliability of quantitative assessments is typically established by correlating test results with themselves or with other forms of the test (Charles & Mertler, 2002). **Reliability coefficients**—that is, correlation coefficients representing measures of reliability—are interpreted in similar fashion to validity coefficients. When attempting to determine the reliability of an assessment, one would anticipate that high scores on one form or administration of the assessment are associated with high scores on the other form or second administration, thus resulting in a positive reliability coefficient. The same general guidelines as previously shown in Table 3.3 would also apply to the interpretation of reliability coefficients.

There are several different ways to establish reliability of quantitative assessment results. Some methods estimate reliability over time. The primary method of estimating consistency over time is the **test-retest method**. The test-retest method involves the following sequence of steps:

1. Administer the test to a group of students.
2. After a short period of time, administer the *same* test to the *same* students.
3. Correlate the scores from the two administrations.

The resulting reliability coefficient is specifically called a **coefficient of stability**. If the two sets of scores are very similar (i.e., high–high, low–low), the results can be considered stable or reliable. The main problem associated with the test-retest method for classroom teachers is that we do not typically give our students the identical test on two occasions. The test-retest method for estimating reliability is more appropriately used on standardized tests, although could you imagine taking the SAT twice?

Other methods of establishing reliability relate more to equivalence. Two such methods are the **alternate-forms method** and the **equivalent-forms method**. The alternate-forms method involves the administration of different forms of a test. Specifically, alternate forms of the same test would present students with *different* items of the same difficulty and covering the same content. In contrast, equivalent forms of the same test include the *identical* items, simply arranged in different sequence. Standardized tests often have alternate forms that can be used interchangeably. Both forms of a test are designed to measure the same skills and abilities, but use somewhat different content. For example, alternate forms of a standardized math test might test the same types of math skills but present students with different numbers with which to work. The following steps outline the procedure for establishing alternate-forms reliability:

1. Administer Form A of the test to a group of students.
2. Shortly afterward, administer Form B of the test to the same students.
3. Correlate the scores from the two administrations.

The resulting reliability coefficient is called an **alternate-forms coefficient**.

The main problem associated with the alternate-forms method of estimating reliability is that it is also not very feasible for classroom teachers. Imagine trying to give your students two tests that cover the same content.

There are, however, methods that are appropriate for use by classroom teachers. These methods are generally classified as **internal consistency** methods of estimating reliability.[1] Internal consistency methods involve only one administration of a test and are most appropriately used when a teacher is assessing essentially the same behavior or area of content knowledge (Gallagher, 1998), as is typical on chapter or unit tests. The basic idea is that, if the *individual* items or tasks appearing on the test or other assessment activity correlate well with one another, we can assume that the entire test or assessment is reliable. In essence, each item is treated as its own individual test (Chase, 1999).

There are three specific methods of establishing the internal consistency for classroom assessments. The first procedure is known as the split-half method. The **split-half method** involves dividing one test into two comparable halves and follows these steps:

1. Administer one long test to a group of students.
2. Separate the items on the test into two equal halves (this is typically done by placing all even-numbered items into one subtest and all odd-numbered items into the other).
3. Correlate the scores from the two shorter tests.
4. Correct for estimate based on two shorter tests.

Notice that a critical step has been added to these procedures in the form of step 4 above. Because shorter tests tend to be less reliable than longer tests, the obtained reliability coefficient will not be a true representation of the consistency for the original longer test. Therefore, the coefficient must be corrected to account for the fact that it was based on two shorter (ac-

---

[1] Specific formulas and sample calculations for measures of internal consistency appear in Appendix C.

tually, half-length) tests. The method for correction is known as the *Spearman-Brown prophesy formula*.

This method can be reasonably used by classroom teachers, but it tends to provide an "over-correction" or slightly higher final reliability coefficient than would be obtained using other methods (Gallagher, 1998).

A second method for establishing internal consistency is called the **Kuder-Richardson methods**, and specifically their *KR-21 formula*. The Kuder-Richardson methods essentially result in an estimate of reliability equal to the average of all possible split-half combinations. The KR-21 formula is the most accurate and widely used method of estimating reliability for a single use test (Gallagher, 1998). Calculation of a KR-21 reliability coefficient involves only the number of test items, as well as the mean and standard deviation of the test scores.[2]

A third, and final, method of estimating reliability from one administration is **Cronbach's alpha (α) method**. Cronbach's α is a special case of the KR-21 formula where individual items or tasks may be scored with different point values (KR-21 assumes that all items are scored either "correct" or "incorrect"). It is a special case of the KR-21 formula but interpreted in the same manner.

Establishing Reliability of Qualitative Assessments

The primary method of establishing the reliability of qualitative assessments is interrater consistency. **Interrater consistency** basically involves the calculation of the percent agreement between two or more raters of student performance or products that are more appropriately scored on qualitative criteria.

The use of this percent agreement technique is most appropriate for assessments such as performance assessments, works submitted as part of a portfolio, physical or musical performances, or even simple essay examinations. The calculation of the percent agreement serves as an indication of the extent to which the raters consistently scored the student performances or products.

THE RELATIONSHIP BETWEEN VALIDITY AND RELIABILITY

I alluded earlier to the relationship between validity and reliability of assessment results. A couple of observations can be made with respect to that relationship. First, validity is the more important feature, for if the results of an assessment are valid, it logically follows that they will also be reliable—reliability is a prerequisite to having validity (Oosterhof, 2001). In other words, if the items that appear on a written test *accurately* assess the specific domain of content in which we are interested, the resulting scores will also be relatively consistent.

---

2 Information concerning the calculation of a mean and standard deviation as well as KR-21 are also presented in Appendix C.

Let us return to the fictitious example we examined at the beginning of this chapter. Recall that science, math, and reading teachers wanted to utilize the results of the SMART, all of which were closely related to classroom decisions that needed to be made by those teachers. If students were to take the SMART several times (provided the validity had been established), the scores resulting from the multiple administrations would very likely be compatible as well.

Second, reliability is an important characteristic and a necessary condition for validity. However, reliability is *not* a sufficient condition for the presence of validity. In other words, simply because the results of an assessment are consistent does not guarantee that those results are also valid. The social studies teacher wanted to use the results of the SMART for the purpose of accurately being able to determine students' ability to succeed in an advanced history course. Even if students did score consistently on the SMART, evidence of validity would demonstrate that the results were being used inappropriately for their intended purpose (i.e., there were no items appearing on the test that specifically addressed critical thinking skills as they relate to historical content). This would ultimately lead to inaccurate decision making on the part of the classroom teacher.

Let us consider another example. Suppose that a student who is new to this country and does not speak English is given a math word problem test *written in English*. Although the student is quite proficient in math, she fails miserably on the test. Surprised at the low score, the naïve teacher administers the same test to the student over and over. Each time, the student fails. (The test is providing a reliable assessment—the results are *consistent* even though they are *not valid*.)

The following summarizes the relationship between validity and reliability:

Valid test results are also reliable, but reliable test results are not necessarily valid.

This relationship between validity and reliability is visually represented in Figure 3.1. Notice the differing types of results based on the various combinations of validity and reliability. The "bullseye" in each target represents the information that is desired from each student. Assessment results that are both valid and reliable would be indicated by the accumulation of scores in the bullseye.

TEACHER RESPONSIBILITIES RELATED TO VALIDITY AND RELIABILITY

Teachers have several responsibilities that are directly related to assessment validity and reliability. However, teachers sometimes do not see these types of quality assurance measures as being their responsibility. In a recent study, Mertler (2000) surveyed K–12 teachers regarding their classroom assessment practices. Among other items, teachers were asked to indicate how they determined that their assessments were both valid and reliable. In

Figure 3.1 The relationship between validity and reliability (each dot represents an individual score)

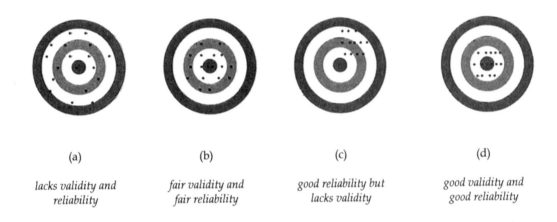

(a)	(b)	(c)	(d)
lacks validity and reliability	*fair validity and fair reliability*	*good reliability but lacks validity*	*good validity and good reliability*

Adapted from Fraenkel & Wallen (2000).

addition, they were asked to indicate how often they did so. Nearly one-tenth of the teachers who responded indicated that they never worried about determining whether or not their assessments resulted in valid or reliable results. Many cited the fact they did not know how to make these determinations, did not have the time to make them, or that it simply was not their responsibility to do so.

On the contrary, if classroom teachers do not ensure that *their own* assessments are both valid and reliable, who will? Claiming ignorance or a lack of responsibility is certainly not justification for simply assuming that your classroom assessments are valid and reliable. Teachers, and only teachers, are responsible for determining the extent to which their classroom assessments meet certain standards

of quality. Nitko (2001) states that "the fact that you cannot afford to conduct validity [and reliability] studies does not mean that you may ignore concerns about the validity [and reliability] of your assessment results" (p. 44). A lack of resources, time, or knowledge does not justify using classroom assessments that are likely to produce invalid results or cause inaccurate and inappropriate decisions to be made about students.

Teachers have a professional responsibility—to students, parents, other teachers, and to themselves—to ensure the quality of their self-developed or selected classroom assessments. If you require additional proof of this fact (other than simply my word), revisit Appendices A and B and examine how the concepts of validity and reliability run throughout both *The*

Standards for Teacher Competence in the Educational Assessment of Students and *The Code of Fair Testing Practices in Education.* Classroom teachers must take the time to gather the pertinent evidence and to ensure that their assessments result in legitimate and accurate conclusions about student behaviors and academic performances.

SUMMARY

Validity is the soundness of the interpretations of student assessment results made by teachers. The focus of validity is not on the assessment itself or on the actual results but on the decisions that are made following the interpretation of the results. Evidence must be continually gathered and examined in order to determine the degree of validity possessed by decisions. Three formal sources of evidence that support the existence of validity include content, criterion, and construct evidence. Content evidence relies on professional judgment; whereas, criterion and construct evidence rely on statistical analyses. Content evidence of validity is the most important source of evidence for classroom assessments. Validation is also important when considering less formal, qualitative assessments.

Reliability is the consistency with which intended methods are measured. As with validity, reliability addresses assessment scores and their ensuing use. Five methods of establishing the reliability—all of which incorporate the use of statistical analyses—for quantitative assessments include test-retest, alternate-forms, split-half, Kuder-Richardson, and Cronbach's alpha methods. Interrater consistency is the primary mean of establishing the consistency of qualitative assessments.

The relationship between validity and reliability is an important one. Reliability is a necessary, but not sufficient, condition for validity. Valid test results are also reliable, but the reverse is not necessarily true.

Teachers usually have the sole responsibility for establishing the validity and reliability for the results of their classroom assessments. They have a professional responsibility to continually gather evidence in support of these essential assessment characteristics. Only by doing this will they have confidence in the educational decisions they must make about their students.

⌐🐭 **Chapter 3 *Related Web Site*** 🖳

❖ **Assessment — Reliability and Validity**
(*seamonkey.ed.asu.edu/~alex/teaching/assessment/reliability.html*)
Dr. Chong Ho (Alex) Yu of Arizona State University maintains this Web site, which highlights classroom assessment validity and reliability. He describes conventional views of both reliability and validity, discusses ways of establishing both, and provides some very good examples of content evidence of validity. He provides some "alternative" views of validity and reliability offered by several leading scholars. Finally, Dr. Yu offers an extremely good piece of advice: Even if you adopt a validated instrument, remember that it was not validated on your students. Classroom teachers must still check the validity and reliability with their own students, specifically with respect to the decisions they intend to make using the scores.

QUESTIONS FOR REVIEW

1. Use Table 3.1 to answer the following questions:
   a. How many questions on the test deal with the geography of WWII?
   b. How many questions deal with key leaders involved in WWII?
   c. How many questions deal with the memorization of facts?
   d. How many questions require students to "pull together" several separate pieces of information?
   e. How many total questions appear on the test?

2. Test developers designed a science fiction trivia test. They claim that scores on this test will accurately predict performance in science classes that require the memorization of unrelated facts. What type of evidence would be appropriate to test this claim?

3. For the test described in Question 2 above—and based on your response to Question 2—how would you go about determining if the scores resulting from the test were valid?

4. Imagine a college course that emphasizes the development of Web sites. Instruction in the course focuses on how to incorporate images, links, etc., into a site. As the final project, each student in the course must develop his or her own site containing these elements. When assessing these projects, what source of evidence of validity would be most important to the instructor? Why?

5. Early in the school year, an elementary teacher observes John push Billy on the playground. The next day, the teacher observes John hit Billy on the arm. The teacher concludes that John will likely be the class bully. Based on the Guiding Questions that appear in Table 3.4, comment on the validity of the teacher's conclusion.

6. How might the teacher described in Question 5 above establish the reliability of the observations?

7. Which methods for establishing reliability for quantitative assessments (i.e., test-retest, alternate forms, equivalent forms, split-half, KR-21, and Cronbach's α) are most appropriately used by classroom teachers? Why?

8. When determining test-retest reliability, it is important that a *substantial* amount of time *not* pass between the first and second administrations of the test. Why is this a crucial component of this type of reliability?

9. In your own words, briefly explain what is meant by the following statement: *Valid test results are also reliable, but reliable test results are not necessarily valid.*

10. How might you respond to a teacher who says, "I don't have time to worry about the validity of my tests"?

ENRICHMENT ACTIVITIES

1. Think of written tests that you have taken in previous courses. Have you ever taken a test that you believe had a poor sample of content? Have you ever taken a test that was not aligned well with the objectives, instructional materials (e.g., textbook), and actual instruction? Discuss your responses in small groups.

2. For a test you identified and discussed in Activity 1 above, discuss how your instructor *should* have collected evidence of validity for the test. What sources of evidence of validity would have been appropriate? How could your instructor have collected that evidence? Use Table 3.2 as a guide, and be prepared to discuss your responses.

3. For the content covered by that same test, briefly describe how your instructor could have *informally* (i.e., using qualitative data) assessed the class during the unit of instruction. Using Table 3.4 as a guide, discuss how you would go about collecting evidence, and what that evidence would consist of, in order to establish the validity of those assessments. Share your responses in small groups.

4. For that same test, which method of determining reliability should your instructor have used? Are there alternative ways that he or she could have determined the reliability of the test? Be prepared to discuss your responses.

Chapter 4

Overview of Assessment Techniques

Overview of Chapter 4

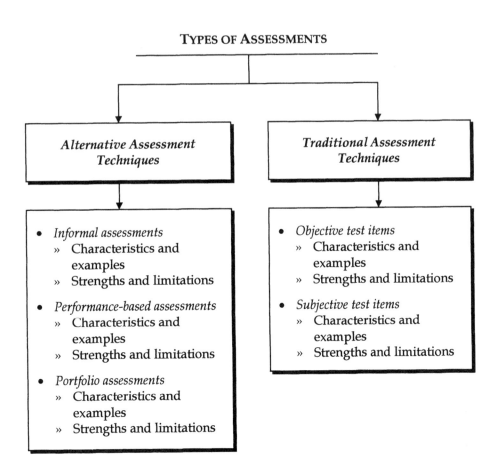

TYPES OF ASSESSMENTS

Alternative Assessment Techniques

Traditional Assessment Techniques

- *Informal assessments*
  - » Characteristics and examples
  - » Strengths and limitations
- *Performance-based assessments*
  - » Characteristics and examples
  - » Strengths and limitations
- *Portfolio assessments*
  - » Characteristics and examples
  - » Strengths and limitations

- *Objective test items*
  - » Characteristics and examples
  - » Strengths and limitations
- *Subjective test items*
  - » Characteristics and examples
  - » Strengths and limitations

INTRODUCTION

Teachers have available a wide variety of classroom assessment possibilities. However, decisions regarding the use of different types of assessments should not be taken lightly. Teachers must examine information such as the instructional objectives, the content to be taught, as well as necessary skills and behaviors, before they can adequately decide on the appropriate type of assessment.

This examination may point them in the direction of either formal (versus informal) assessments, quantitative (versus qualitative) assessments, or perhaps objective (versus subjective) assessments. In any case, as you have previously read, the assessment must appropriately match both the objectives and the instruction. In this chapter, you will be exposed to a broad overview of assessment techniques, which will be classified under two broad categories of alternative and traditional assessment techniques.

ALTERNATIVE ASSESSMENT TECHNIQUES

In the 1980s, criticism of multiple-choice tests and other types of "pencil-and-paper" testing began to increase fairly dramatically. Educators began looking for different forms of assessment that would help focus instruction on more meaningful student learning. These educators wanted to incorporate into the classroom setting assessments that would (1) allow students to demonstrate the ability to directly *apply* learned knowledge and skills and (2) reflect higher levels of *real-world* application. They wanted these assessments to reflect the actual types of cognitive challenges faced by adults in the day-to-day activities that made up their professional and personal lives (Gredler, 1999). These characteristics were missing from more traditional forms of assessment. These newer assessments were named **alternative assessments** because they overcame the limitations of traditional pencil-and-paper tests. Those alternative assessments that specifically address real-world applications of knowledge and skills have become known as **authentic assessments**.

The main types of alternative assessments include informal assessments, performance-based assessments, and portfolio assessments. Characteristics of each type will be described and examples provided below. The general strengths and limitations of each will also be explained.

Informal Assessments
As you read in Chapter 1, informal assessments are spontaneous and often occur unnoticed. This general type of assessment typically results in verbal information. Informal assessments include the specific assessment methods of *teacher observations* and *teacher questions*.

Characteristics and Examples
Teacher observations and questions are by far the most common forms of informal assessment used in classrooms. Informal observations and questions occur in an

ongoing—and never-ending—manner in classroom settings. Oosterhof (1999) has stated that in all likelihood, greater than 90% of all measures of student performance involve casual and informal observations and questions.

Teacher **observations** involve watching and/or listening to students as they carry out some activity (Airasian, 2000). Observations of students can be a valuable technique in which to engage due to the important role they play in planning, delivering, and revising instruction. For example, imagine that an elementary school teacher is teaching a lesson on exponents. Specifically, the instruction covers the steps involved in squaring and cubing whole numbers. The teacher completes a sample problem on the chalkboard and then puts the following problem on the board for the students to try:

$$2^2 + 3^2 = \quad ?$$

As the students attempt the problem, the teacher is met with perplexed stares from several children, something like...

Almost immediately, the teacher can sense that the students are confused by something in the lesson or by the sample problem on the board. At this point, the teacher realizes that it is necessary to stop, reflect, and restructure the instruction.

Similar to observations, teacher **questions** can be informal, unplanned, and spontaneous oral inquiries posed by the teacher to be answered by students. Questioning is particularly useful during instruction (Airasian, 2000), and especially with respect to assessing the extent of understanding (Gredler, 1999). There are essentially two types of questions that teachers can ask. *Lower-order questions* usually have predetermined correct answers. *Higher-order questions* require additional student thought and evaluation of information (Gredler, 1999).

Let us return to our example of the elementary mathematics lesson on exponents. After observing the confusion on the faces of the students, the teacher would likely try to determine the nature of the confusion. He or she might begin by asking a few lower-order questions, such as "What answer did you get for the sample problem?" and "Who can list the steps we use to find the square of a number?" If the answers to these questions do not provide sufficient information to guide the revision of instruction, the teacher may decide to ask a series of higher-order questions such as "Who can describe what we are actually doing when we square a number?" or "Who can describe how we might find the value of a number raised to the 4th power? What about finding the value of a number raised to the 10th power?"

Strengths and Limitations

Informal observations and questions are techniques we engage in as part of nearly everything we do. When driving a car, shopping at the mall, or talking with friends, we are constantly observing and making mental notes of what we see. In addition, we constantly ask for clarification about the things we have observed. Informal assessments allow us to observe events simultaneously or in rapid succession, without the formality of being written down. Furthermore, observations and questions are very efficient; it is not necessary to plan in advance of their use.

There are, however, several limitations to the use of informal assessments. First, observations require inference. In other words, just because you observe a confused look on the faces of several students does not necessarily mean that they do not understand what you have just taught them. That particular assumption is drawn by you based on your experiences. Therefore, a lack of experience can also become a limitation, especially with respect to the accuracy of your inferences. Second, since observations and questions result in undocumented information, they are often forgotten or distorted by the classroom teacher (Oosterhof, 1999). A final limitation to the use of teacher questions is that classroom teachers often do not provide students with adequate time to respond to informal questions. You will learn more about informal assessments in Chapter 5.

Performance-Based Assessments

A second type of alternative assessment is the category of **performance-based assessments**, also known as *performance assessments* and sometimes referred to as "PBAs." PBAs allow students to demonstrate what they *know* and can actually *do* in a real situation; they involve true application of acquired knowledge and skills (Airasian, 2000).

Characteristics and Examples

The most important characteristic of a performance-based assessment is that it provides direct observation of student performance (Oosterhof, 1999). Many performance-based assessments are also classified as **authentic assessments**, which means that the assessment involves the real application of a skill beyond its instructional context. When using traditional assessments, teachers simply ask students if they *know* something; with performance-based assessments, teachers require students to demonstrate that they know *how to use* that knowledge. Therefore, performance assessment occurs whenever a student is asked to demonstrate a skill, is involved in an activity, or produces a product, *and* when the teacher assesses the quality of that demonstration, performance, or product (Chase, 1999). In other words, performance assessments require that students must do something, and the teacher must see it being done and subsequently evaluate it.

As with any type of assessment, performance assessments must also be linked to instructional objectives and must parallel the delivered instruction. Teachers must ensure that the skills students are being required to demonstrate during the activity or performance have been taught as part of the instruction. Additionally, they are often used in conjunction with written tests, since they measure different types of student skills (Oosterhof, 1999).

Based on the nature of their design, assessing the results of performance assessments necessitates some degree of subjective, but professional, judgment on the part of the classroom teacher (Chase, 1999). The development of this professional judgment does take some time and requires practice and experience. Often, these activities, performances, or products cannot be evaluated on the basis of "right-and-wrong." There are typically multiple correct answers or products that students may develop. Or, if only one correct answer exists, there may be multiple ways in which students may arrive at the single, particular answer. Typically, the results of performance assessments are assessed using scoring guides such as *rating scales*, *checklists*, or *rubrics*.

Performance assessments can take a variety of forms; in fact, the number of possibilities is almost limitless. For example, performance assessments can include such activities as lab experiments, a sculpture, a formal speech or debate, or a letter-writing campaign. Even some assessment activities that are typically thought of as more traditional—such as an essay or a formal report—can actually

be considered forms of performance assessment, depending on their structure and specifically on what is required of the students. The following are three specific examples of performance assessments spread across the K–12 curriculum.

(1) In an attempt to determine the level of students' fine motor skills, an early childhood teacher sets up five stations in the classroom: cutting paper with a pair of scissors; drawing a circle with a crayon; picking up beans using only the thumb and forefinger; stacking small blocks; and following a line of print with a finger. The teacher assesses each student on each of the five skills using a checklist.

(2) At the end of a unit on the scientific method, a middle school science teacher requires students to conduct a formal scientific experiment utilizing all components of the scientific method. The projects last six weeks, and students must carefully document in a journal their procedures throughout the entire process. Using a rating scale, the teacher evaluates them on both the process (how well were the specific steps followed as evidenced by his or her observations and the students' journals) and the product (what were the formal results of each scientific experiment).

(3) Each grading period, a high school language arts teacher requires students to select a controversial topic, conduct research on it, and then formally debate the topic. Students are

evaluated through the use of a rubric on several criteria, including the level of research preparation, the extent to which each side's argument is compelling and convincing, and the degree of professionalism with which the oral arguments and rebuttals are delivered.

Strengths and Limitations

The main advantage of performance assessments is that they allow for the assessment of skills that could not be measured through the use of traditional methods. The preschool teacher in example (1) above could not administer a written test to the students in order to assess their fine motor skills. Furthermore, the science teacher in example (2) might also give students a written test on the steps in and application of the scientific method, but having students conduct scientific experiments enables the teacher to determine the extent to which the students can *actually do* an experiment following the correct procedures, as opposed to simply describing *how to do* an experiment.

A second important strength of performance assessments is that they can be used to evaluate both processes and products. By examining the students' journals, the science teacher will have a good idea about the students' levels of understanding of the process of conducting an experiment. That information would not be obtained by simply asking students to list the steps of the scientific method on a pencil-and-paper test. When

a math teacher requires students to show all their work, he or she does so in order to assess the process used by students to answer the problem.

A final strength is that performance assessments can also be used to make informed decisions about instruction. Determining where students are making mistakes during their attempts to work math problems provides the teacher with specific information that can be used during reinstruction.

A limitation of performance assessment is that it can be very time-consuming. As you will see in Chapter 6, developing performance assessments and their scoring guides, as well as implementing the actual assessment activity, may require a great deal of the classroom teacher's time. For this reason, performance assessments often are not used as the sole means for assessing students.

As was alluded to earlier, a second limitation of performance assessments is that they require a high degree of subjective decision making by teachers. This subjectivity can result in bias and, therefore, lower levels of validity and reliability for the assessments (i.e., processes and products may not be evaluated consistently across all students in a class).

Portfolio Assessments

Often, teachers assess their students with somewhat of a "snapshot" assessment—in other words, results of a given assessment show what the student was able to do today or in a given unit. In contrast, **portfo-**

lio assessment allows teachers and students to gather evidence of student abilities and skills over an extended period of time.

Characteristics and Examples

Portfolios contain samples of student work, typically selected by the student based on guidelines prepared by the teacher. It is a very purposeful collection of information (Chase, 1999). This system of assessment permits the individual student to take a more active role in the evaluation of his or her academic work. The process becomes a collaborative effort between student and teacher. Therefore, portfolio assessment emphasizes the performance of the *individual* student, as opposed to an entire class (Oosterhof, 1999).

Furthermore, portfolios focus on the *accomplishments* of students, with particular emphasis on their best work or growth over a period of time. The idea of a portfolio is to showcase the types of things at which the student excels, not to demonstrate the things they are unable to do. In addition, the focus is on the assessment of products, not processes (Oosterhof, 1999).

An additional feature of portfolios is that students and teachers may decide to include evaluative commentary on certain pieces of work. This allows both the teacher and student the opportunity to reflect on work over the course of instruction. Students may comment on what they liked about the piece, why they believed it to be a sample of good work, or ways in which they might improve it. Teacher

comments may indicate how the piece pertains to specific educational standards or instructional objectives. They may also make comments on the quality of the piece and how it might be improved (Chase, 1999).

There are several types of portfolios depending on their particular purposes. In Chapter 7, you will learn more about these various types or purposes of portfolios, which include *documentation*, *showcase*, *class*, and *evaluation* portfolios.

Strengths and Limitations

There are several strengths associated with the use of portfolio assessments (Chase, 1999). As previously mentioned, portfolios empower students by including them in the assessment process and also allowing them to evaluate their own work. Additionally, portfolios foster communication between students and teachers. A critical component of a portfolio assessment system is the inclusion of dialogue between teachers and their students. Two final strengths are that portfolios show growth in student skills, and they allow students opportunities for incorporating experiences from their own personal lives.

Limitations of portfolios include the fact that they usually should not be used as an exclusive means of assessment. (A major exception is in fine arts classes where evaluation of the students' portfolios of artwork may be the only assessment procedure.) Some educational decisions—such as assigning final course grades—often should not be made solely with portfolio information. Additionally, assessing the contents of large portfolios can be extremely time consuming. Finally, due to their subjective nature, results of portfolio assessments are often subject to validity and reliability problems.

TRADITIONAL ASSESSMENT TECHNIQUES

For years in American education, there existed a singular approach for assessing what students could and could not do. This primary means of assessment, which involves the use of pencil-and-paper testing, is known as **traditional assessment**. Even though the majority of assessments of student performance are informal, in practice, the majority of assessments upon which grades and other evaluative decisions are based come from these formal, written tests. Two main categories of traditional test items are objective and subjective items.

Objective Test Items

Many classroom tests (i.e., teacher-developed tests)—as well as standardized tests—are known as **objective tests** based on the way in which they are scored. These tests are scored objectively, meaning that there is a single correct answer for each question appearing on the test. There are no teacher-related judgments involved in scoring objective test items.

Characteristics and Examples

Objective test items have only one correct response, which is determined prior to the time the test is administered to students (Chase, 1999). Regardless of who—or what, in the case of computers—scores a given test consisting of objective test items, the resulting scores will be identical. There is no subjectivity involved in scoring this type of test item.

Objective test items may vary in their format, but the overriding characteristic is that they present a question or problem, along with several options. It is the task of the student to select the correct response from the set provided. For this reason, objective test items are also referred to as **selected-response items**. Objective test items include multiple-choice, alternate-choice, and matching items.

Multiple-choice items are the most popularly used type of objective test item (Chase, 1999). Most of us are very familiar with this item format. Multiple-choice items consist of a *stem* and a set of possible answers known as *options*. One of the options is the correct answer, while the others are called *distractors*, or incorrect responses. The following is an example of a multiple-choice item, with these components labeled:

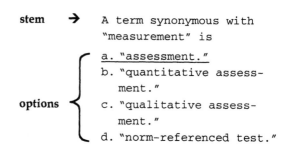

```
stem    →    A term synonymous with
             "measurement" is

             a. "assessment."
             b. "quantitative assess-
                ment."
options  {   c. "qualitative assess-
                ment."
             d. "norm-referenced test."
```

In the example, the underlined option (a) is the correct response. Options (b), (c), and (d) are distractors.

A second type of objective test item is the **alternate-choice item**. These items are similar in structure to a multiple-choice item, but they contain only two possible responses. The most popular type of alternate-choice item is a true-false item. True-false items consist of a declarative statement, where the student must decide if the statement is true or false. The following is an example of a true-false item:

```
T   F   If a test is reliable, it is,
        by definition, valid.
```

Students simply circle "T" if they believe the statement is true or "F" if they believe that it is false (hopefully, they circle "F"!). Another example of an alternate-choice item might be one that consists of a "Yes-No" response set.

The final type of objective test item is a matching item. **Matching items** typically consist of two lists of terms. The list on the left is called the *stimuli*, and the list on the right is known as the *responses*. The following is an example of a matching item:

```
Match each state with its appropriate
capital city.

    ___   1. Ohio            a. Albany
    ___   2. New York        b. Pierre
    ___   3. Florida         c. Atlanta
    ___   4. Georgia         d. Columbus
    ___   5. South Dakota    e. Tallahassee
```

You will learn much more about the construction of objectively scored test items in Chapter 8.

You will learn much more about the construction of objectively scored test items in Chapter 8.

Strengths and Limitations

Objective test items are very appropriately used in the assessment of lower-order thinking skills, such as knowledge and recall. They can also be used to assess students' knowledge of concepts. A final strength, albeit an important one, is that objective items are efficient to score.

The greatest limitation to objective test items is that they are subject to guessing. Since all the correct answers are provided to students on the test, they may be able to accurately guess the correct answer, at least part of the time. With alternate-choice items, students have a 50% chance of guessing the correct answer. Additionally, it is sometimes difficult for classroom teachers to write high-quality objective test items that are clearly understood by students. Developing good items requires a good deal of practice. Although it is possible, developing objective test items that assess higher-order thinking skills is a difficult task.

Subjective Test Items

Subjective test items are so named because, due to their construct, subjectivity enters into the scoring process. Subjective items require students to develop their response to a question. The correct answer is not provided; they must construct it themselves. For this reason, subjective test items are sometimes also referred to as **constructed-response items** or **s u p p l y items**.

Characteristics and Examples

It is possible for subjective test items to have more than one correct answer. Based on that fact, scoring of these test items is often contingent on the individual teacher. Subjectivity, and possible bias, potentially have a substantial role in the scoring procedures.

Collectively, subjective test items are open-ended. That is, they require students to analyze the prompt or question provided to them and subsequently develop their own unique response. There are two main types of subjective test items. **Essay items** consist of a problem, situation, or question known as a *prompt*. Based on their knowledge, students must construct their response to the prompt. Responses to essay items may be as short as a couple of sentences or as long as several pages. This feature distinguishes the two types of essay items, known as **restricted response** and **extended response**. Restricted response essay items limit what the student is permitted to answer (Nitko, 2001). Restricted response essay items are also sometimes referred to as **short-answer items**. The following is an example of a restricted response essay item:

1. List two similarities and two differences between the continuous-feedback and the time-restricted models of teaching and assessment. Focus your response on the roles of the teacher and the student.

Extended response essay items allow students to respond by freely expressing their own ideas and to use their own organization of their answers (Nitko, 2001). Using content similar to the previous example, the following is an example of an extended response essay item:

2. Compare and contrast the three teaching-assessment models. In what ways are they similar? In what ways are they different? Which model will you use in your classroom, and why?

Clearly, the second item could be answered in brief fashion or in several pages, depending on the level of detail provided. Also, notice how scoring responses to this prompt could be quite subjective.

Completion items, also known as *fill-in-the-blank items*, are similar to essay items in that the student must provide the response. However, responses to completion items are typically limited to one or two words. Although there is usually a single correct answer that the teacher has in mind, variations of that answer may still be scored correctly. The following are two examples of completion items:

1. The capital city of Ohio is _____.

and

2. The most advanced level of the cognitive domain of Bloom's taxonomy is _____.

You will learn much more about the construction of subjectively scored test items in Chapter 9.

Strengths and Limitations

Subjective tests are typically easy to construct. This is especially true of essay tests since these tests require fewer total items. Essay items require students to utilize more complex thinking skills, as well as stress the importance of communication skills (Chase, 1999). There is a substantially lower chance of guessing correctly on both completion and essay items than on objective test items.

Limitations of subjective items include the fact that students' abilities to write can affect their scores. If students know the material, but fail to convey it well, they typically receive fewer points. Furthermore, although students cannot guess on an essay item, some will try to "bluff" their way through it (Chase, 1999). They may write something, but it could be far from the anticipated response. Finally, responses to essay items are time consuming to score.

Completion items suffer from some similar limitations. Spelling can be an issue for completion responses. Decisions must be made about awarding partial credit for correct responses that are spelled incorrectly. Additionally, completion items are almost always restricted to the assessment of lower-order thinking skills.

SUMMARY

Two broad categories of assessment techniques are alternative and traditional assessment. Alternative assessments address several of the limitations inherent in traditional assessments. Alternative assessments permit greater levels for the application of student learning, as opposed to the simple recall of information. However, alternative assessments are typically very time consuming to develop and score.

Traditional assessments can appropriately address both lower- and higher-order thinking skills. They are limited by the effects of guessing. However, in most cases, they are efficient to develop and score, especially compared to alternative assessments.

Table 4.1 provides a summary of the various assessment techniques discussed in this chapter, including descriptions of the general technique and major strengths and limitations.

Table 4.1 Summary of general assessment methods and their respective strengths and limitations

General Method of Assessment	Specific Techniques (if appropriate)	Description	Major Strengths	Major Limitations
Informal assessments	• teacher observations • teacher questions	• watching and/or listening to students as they carry out some activity • unplanned and spontaneous oral inquiries	• very familiar • can observe many events simultaneously • efficient; do not need to be planned ahead	• require inference • require practice and experience • observations or responses may be forgotten or distorted • ample time to respond must be provided
Performance-based assessments		• provide direct observation of student performance • must be linked to objectives • require teacher's judgment	• assess skills that cannot be measured through traditional methods • can evaluate both process and product • can be used to improve instruction	• time consuming • subjective decision making • lack of consistency in scoring
Portfolio assessments	• documentation portfolio • showcase portfolio • class portfolio • evaluation portfolio	• gather evidence of student abilities and skills over extended period of time	• empower students • foster communication between teachers, students • show growth in student skills • allow opportunities for personal experiences	• cannot be used with certain types of decisions • can be time consuming • may have problems with validity and reliability

Table 4.1 Continued

General Method of Assessment	Specific Techniques (if appropriate)	Description	Major Strengths	Major Limitations
Objective test items	• multiple-choice items • alternate-choice items • matching items	• no subjectivity in scoring • correct response selected from set of options provided	• appropriate for lower-order thinking skills • can be used with conceptual information • efficient to score	• subject to guessing • writing good items takes practice • difficult to assess higher-order thinking skills
Subjective test items	• completion items • restricted- and extended-response essay items	• response must be constructed by student • subjectively scored	• relatively easy to construct • reduced chance of guessing • essays stress communication, higher-order thinking skills	• completion limited to lower-order skills • writing and spelling skills become an issue in scoring • bluffing is a possibility

---

⌐ Chapter 4 *Related Web Sites* 🖥

❖ **Consider Alternatives to Traditional Assessment**
(*www.nea.org/helpfrom/student/meas3.html*)
This brief page provides simple examples of performance and portfolio assessments, as well as some other less common alternative types of assessment.

❖ **Alternative Assessment** (*www.emtech.net/Alternative_Assessment.html*)
This Web site provides a wealth of information about alternative assessment. Following descriptions of alternative assessments, more than 100 links to sites with various kinds of information about alternative assessment are provided.

QUESTIONS FOR REVIEW

1. A teacher wants to conduct informal assessments during instruction and develops several brief written tests to be administered daily over the next two weeks. Describe what is wrong with this approach to assessment.

2. An art teacher wants to know how well students can incorporate perspective into their drawings. Should the teacher use a multiple-choice test or a performance-based assessment in this situation? Why or why not?

3. Why are authentic assessments typically not graded solely on the basis of "right-and-wrong"?

4. Is it possible for a sample of student work (in authentic assessment) to be evaluated differently by different teachers? Explain.

5. Which types of traditional test items do you think would most appropriately be used when developing a test to be taken in a restricted timeframe (e.g., 40 minutes)?

6. If a teacher wants to reduce the opportunity for students to correctly guess the answers on a test, what types of traditional test items should be avoided?

7. What characteristic of portfolios makes it more difficult to rely solely on them for evaluative decisions about students?

8. What is meant by an "objective" test item versus a "subjective" test item?

9. Distinguish between the terms "selected-response" items and "constructed-response" items.

10. Which assessment techniques discussed in the chapter can be used to make informed decisions about instruction? (Be careful...this is a bit of a trick question!)

ENRICHMENT ACTIVITIES

1. In a paragraph or two, describe content for a lesson or unit that you would like to teach someday. Discuss how you would most appropriately assess your students using *informal* methods, focusing on specific techniques and your selected content. Share your responses in small groups.

2. For the same content you selected in Activity 1 above, describe how you would most appropriately assess your students using *alternative* methods, focusing on specific techniques and your selected content. Discuss your responses in small groups.

3. For the same lesson you selected in Activity 1 above, describe how you would most appropriately assess your students using *traditional* methods, again focusing on specific techniques and your selected content. Discuss your responses in small groups.

4. Based on your responses to the activities above, do you believe that it is preferable to assess students using a variety of methods? What are the advantages and disadvantages of doing so?

Notes

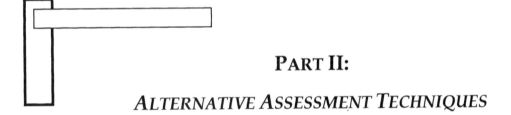

PART II:

ALTERNATIVE ASSESSMENT TECHNIQUES

Chapter 5
Informal Assessments

Chapter 6
Performance-Based Assessments

Chapter 7
Portfolio Assessments

Notes

Chapter 5

Informal Assessments

Overview of Chapter 5

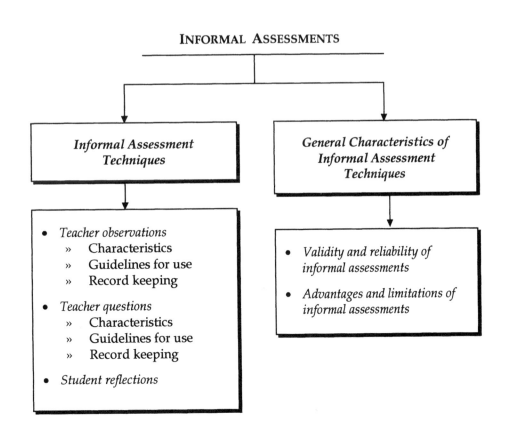

INFORMAL ASSESSMENTS

Informal Assessment Techniques

- *Teacher observations*
  - » Characteristics
  - » Guidelines for use
  - » Record keeping
- *Teacher questions*
  - » Characteristics
  - » Guidelines for use
  - » Record keeping
- *Student reflections*

General Characteristics of Informal Assessment Techniques

- *Validity and reliability of informal assessments*
- *Advantages and limitations of informal assessments*

INTRODUCTION

In Part II of this book, you will learn more about the various types of alternative assessment techniques. Specifically, in this chapter you will learn about the main types of informal assessments, namely teacher observations, teacher questions, and student reflections.

As you read in Chapter 4, informal assessments are the most commonly used assessments in classrooms; in fact, the overwhelming majority of assessments are informal. These assessments typically are ongoing and continuous. Although the benefits of informal assessments are numerous, teachers must be cautious in their strict reliance on such assessments, as you will discover in the latter sections of this chapter.

TEACHER OBSERVATIONS

One of the most important aspects of teaching is the observation of children's learning (Meisels, Harrington, McMahon, Dichtelmiller, & Jablon, 2002). **Observations** conducted by teachers involve watching and/or listening to students as they perform some activity or judging material that they have produced (Airasian, 2000). Observation is often seen as a primary, but often underutilized, tool for assessing learning and instruction (Johnson & Johnson, 2002). Its purpose is to record and describe student behavior *as it occurs in a natural setting.* Johnson & Johnson (2002) identify three major areas in which teacher observations provide data:

(1) *The quality of student performances.* Many of the types of performances or products completed by students can be assessed only through observation. Examples include performances such as giving a presentation, participating in a group activity, reciting a dramatic reading, and properly hitting a golf ball.

(2) *The processes and procedures students use to complete assignments.* In order to improve and learn, students must continually receive feedback about the ways in which they complete assignments or perform on assessments; in other words, feedback concerning *how* they learn.

(3) *The processes and procedures teachers use in providing instruction.* Similarly, in order for teachers to improve, they must continually receive feedback regarding their actions in conducting instructional lessons.

Much of what teachers learn about students is a direct result of informal observations. Through observations, teachers are made aware of student behaviors, such as interacting in group settings, feeling ill, bullying other students, losing concentration, failing to stay on-task or to sit still, listening carefully, having trouble seeing the chalkboard, or appearing confused.

Teachers also learn a great deal about themselves and their instruction as a result of observing students. During the course of a lesson, if a teacher observes students nodding their heads in approval, smiling attentively, and anxiously raising their hands to answer questions, that teacher can feel confident that, generally speaking, the students appear to be engaged in the lesson and understanding the material. It would, therefore, be appropriate to continue moving forward with new content. In contrast, if the students appear confused and none are raising their hands to offer answers to questions, the teacher might believe that some degree of reinstruction is in order and would likely pause and reexamine the pace of the lesson. All the preceding examples show how observations produce information that influence educational decisions.

Characteristics

Oosterhof (1999 & 2001) offers several characteristics of informal teacher observations. Familiarizing yourself with these characteristics will enable you to observe students engaged in classroom activities more effectively and with a higher level of accuracy. The following list, which is reiterated in Figure 5.1, briefly summarizes Oosterhof's predominant characteristics.

- *Many events in the classroom are observed either simultaneously or in very quick succession and are observed at various levels of detail.* With anywhere from 20 to 30 students in a classroom, the number of events that could possibly be observed at any given time is quite likely astronomical. It would be virtually impossible for teachers to see everything that occurs in a classroom at a given moment in time. Additionally, those events that are observed will be seen at a variety of levels of detail. For example, while walking around a classroom, a teacher might observe—in quick succession—several students working diligently in a science center conducting experiments with electricity, several others reading quietly in a corner of the room, and two students who are clearly off-task and exhibiting disruptive behavior. The teacher should focus attention and closer observation on the two disruptive students.

- *Classroom observations often become focused on one event. When this occurs, observations of other critical events must be maintained.* It would be understandable if the attention of the teacher described above was suddenly focused on the two disruptive students. However, teachers must be cautious that focusing their attention on specific events does not result in other events going completely unnoticed. For example, while attending to the disruptive students, imagine what could happen if the students working in the science center were essentially ignored by the teacher. A student could be injured while working with electricity; the injury might have been preventable had the teacher continued to watch those students while attending to the disruptive ones.

- *Teachers should depend on the observations of students.* Students can assist teachers by learning how to observe events in the classroom, how to initiate corrective actions, and what constitutes an appropriate situation warranting the teacher's attention. Teachers must assist students in this effort by modeling these observational and corrective behaviors with examples that occur within the classroom.

- *Realize that most events that go on in the classroom go unnoticed.* As was mentioned earlier, the number of events that could occur within a classroom setting during a given period of time are simply too numerous to notice. Additionally, most events—such as the acquisition of knowledge and student achievement—are not directly observable. Teachers, especially those who are in the early stages of their careers, must be aware that most events go unnoticed and should not try to observe *everything*. To do so would be an impossible task.

- *Observations are often quickly forgotten or distorted when recalled.* Continuous observation is essential when used for formative purposes. Since most assessment conducted in classrooms is informal, the sheer volume of observations dictates that much of what is observed will quickly be forgotten. If not forgotten, the event will likely be distorted if recalled at a later time. One of the best practices in which teachers can engage is to write down what is observed in order to retain a higher degree of accuracy. It is im-

portant to remember that, from a practical perspective, it is possible to make notes on a very small percentage of what is actually observed.

- *Observations often require inferences, which may be erroneous.* When teachers observe students, they cannot *directly* observe what they understand, what they are thinking, or what they feel. *Inferences*—conclusions arrived at through logic and deduction—must be made by the classroom teacher. For example, if a teacher gives an assignment requiring students to write their responses in cursive, but then observes a student printing a response, the teacher might infer that the student does not know how to form cursive letters. This inference may not be correct; perhaps the student was not aware of or forgot that particular requirement for the assignment. In contrast, the opposite situation might also occur. Perhaps the teacher inferred that the student was not paying close attention to the directions and subsequently reprimands the student. In actuality, the student may not have known how to write cursive letters and was embarrassed to admit the fact. Although logic is often beneficial, the resulting inferences may not be accurate and, in fact, may be in complete error. Furthermore, experience in conducting classroom observations will most certainly result in the improved quality of those observations (Oosterhof, 1999). Teachers with less experience tend to focus on very specific types of or simply very isolated behaviors. As they gain experience in the classroom, teachers are able to effectively observe several events concurrently.

Guidelines for Use

Beginning teachers cannot really learn *how* to observe by reading a textbook. Learning to observe continuously—and accurately—throughout the school day can only be learned through experience. The following guidelines (Oosterhof, 1999 & 2001) should help you to refine your skills in informal observation as you gain experience. They are all aspects of observational techniques of which you should not only be aware, but also try to practice whenever you are observing students. These guidelines are also summarized in Figure 5.1.

- *Know what to observe.* As discussed previously, the number of events that teachers are responsible for observing is quite large. Without a pre-established plan for observation, the teacher is left to determine what to observe during the actual course of a lesson. This is extremely difficult to do. As with any aspect of an instructional lesson, the best time to make decisions about what you specifically intend to observe during the lesson is when the lesson is being planned. For example, while developing a lesson plan, determine what you believe would constitute on-task behavior, try to antici-

pate the types of off-task behaviors you might expect from your students, and determine what types of student behaviors would serve as indicators that the students are understanding the content of the lesson. Of course, this task becomes somewhat more efficient as a school year progresses and you learn more about each of your students. Also, this is not meant to imply that you should not be open to observing events of an unplanned nature.

- *Know when to place limits on how much is being observed.* Sometimes, the severity of student behaviors—both good and bad—requires teachers to focus their attention and concentrate on a small number of events. If a lesson requires students to apply a complex set of skills during a classroom activity, the teacher may need to concentrate observations on that particular set of skills. This information may be necessary in order to determine whether or not students are prepared to move on to more difficult topics, or if some degree of reinstruction is required.

- *Be familiar with what is being observed.* Familiarity with students as well as with the content being taught will result in a teacher being a much more effective observer within a classroom setting. A teacher who is knowledgeable about the subject matter being taught can actually be more observant and subsequently respond more appropriately to students' questions or various levels of confusion. This familiarity comes from experience in the classroom.

- *Avoid extended inferences; begin with hypotheses and look for substantiating evidence.* Inferences on the part of teachers are required during observations since it is impossible to see what students know, feel, or are thinking. Extended inferences are those that are based more on assumption and less on evidence. In other words, extended inferences are the result of "inspired guesswork" as opposed to well-informed decision making. Extended inferences often result in erroneous conclusions. A prime example is a quote attributed to one of Albert Einstein's teachers, who told Einstein's father that "It doesn't matter what he does, he will never amount to anything!" (Children's Museum of Indianapolis, 1999) To avoid this potentially negative situation, begin by making a *hypothesis* (a tentative explanation) following the observation of some event. Then proceed to gather additional evidence through more observations or other methods, prior to drawing firm conclusions.

- *Recognize that observations may overestimate achievement.* The vast majority of teacher observations occur during or immediately following instruction. Since the content of a lesson is still being retained in students' short-term memories, observations made at that

time tend to reveal that most students understand what was taught to them. If observations were made after the passage of some time, the effects of short-term memory loss would be much more apparent (Oosterhof, 1999). Teachers need to be aware that as time passes, students will retain less information from a lesson. Early observations will make it appear as if more learning and retention has transpired than what actually occurred.

- *Document observations that must be recalled at a later time.* As students' short-term memories are adversely affected with the passage of time, so too are the short-term memories of teachers. As time passes, unrecorded observations tend to be forgotten or their contents substantially distorted. Most observations are not recorded simply because of the amount of time required to do so, in addition to the fact that in many instances, recording them would necessitate the interruption of instruction. However, in situations where the recollection of details may be important, it is critical for teachers to document—as precisely as possible—what they observed, or risk losing it. Documentation typically involves the development and maintenance of either written or electronic records. At the elementary level, teachers might develop and maintain an ongoing observation file (either written or on a computer) for each student in the class; at the secondary level, they often develop a file for each class period or subject taught.

Record Keeping

As mentioned earlier, most observations made by teachers are not recorded in any manner. However, when an observation is significant, it is crucial that teachers record what they have seen. Oosterhof (1999 & 2001) states that the details of most observations that are not documented are typically not remembered for more than one hour. It is, therefore, of great importance to somehow record observations. There are three basic techniques for recording the details of teacher observations. These techniques include anecdotal records, checklists, and rating scales.

Figure 5.1 Characteristics and guidelines for the use of informal teacher observations

Characteristics

1. Many events in the classroom are observed either simultaneously or in very quick succession and are observed at various levels of detail.
2. Classroom observations often become focused on one event. When this occurs, observations of other critical events must be maintained.
3. Teachers should depend on the observations of students.
4. Realize that most events that go on in the classroom go unnoticed.
5. Observations are often quickly forgotten or distorted when recalled.
6. Observations often require inferences, which may be erroneous.

Guidelines for Use

1. Know what to observe.
2. Know when to place limits on how much is being observed.
3. Be familiar with what is being observed.
4. Avoid extended inferences; begin with hypotheses and look for substantiating evidence.
5. Recognize that observations overestimate achievement.
6. Document observations that must be recalled at a later time.

Anecdotal records are used primarily to document an individual student's behaviors for later reference by teachers, parents, counselors, or administrators (Airasian, 2000; Oosterhof, 1999 & 2001). These records consist of short narratives that describe both the behavior and the specific context in which it occurred (Oosterhof, 1999). In some instances, it may be appropriate to also include some interpretation of the behavior, as well as a possible recommendation. However, care must be taken to ensure that the record documents the behavior in an objective manner, preventing the inclusion of any teacher bias. Finally, Airasian (2000) points out that only observations that have special importance and that cannot be obtained through any other more formal means of classroom assessment should be included in an anecdotal record. An example of an anecdotal record appears in Figure 5.2.

Figure 5.2 Example of an anecdotal record

Student	*Michelle Carter*	Date	*10/15/02*
Observer	*Mr. Roberts*		

Observation: *Students were asked to complete their journal assignments. Michelle refused, stating that she would do it later. She then proceeded to read a magazine and disrupt other students sitting near her. When redirection was attempted, she seemed to withdraw.*

Interpretation: *This is the third time this term that Michelle has intentionally seemed to disrupt the class. It always seems to occur during journal time, however. It could have something to do with a dislike of writing in her journal or of writing, in general. Will continue to monitor...*

Recommendation: *None (at this time)*

A **checklist** consists of a list of behaviors or student outcomes, where the teacher simply indicates whether each behavior or outcome has been observed. The use of checklists is somewhat limited to situations and settings where the presence or absence of a given condition is to be determined (Moskal, 2000; Oosterhof, 1999); in other words, an "either–or" type of situation. Those behaviors that are observed are indicated with a checkmark; those that are not observed are left blank.

Since checklists are more structured, they provide a more detailed record of student behavior or performance than do anecdotal records (Airasian, 2000). There are, however, limitations associated with checklists. The nature of checklists allows the teacher only two possible options for the observation: performed or not performed, present or not present, observed or not observed, yes or no, etc. A sample checklist for a word processing activity is shown in Figure 5.3.

Figure 5.3 Example of an observational checklist

	Student Michael Vance	Date 11/30/02

Word Processing Skills

		Yes	No
1.	Hands in proper location on keyboard	☑	☐
2.	Places fingers on "home keys" at rest	☑	☐
3.	Types with eyes on text, not keyboard	☑	☐
4.	Strikes appropriate keys with each finger	☐	☑
5.	Utilizes proper techniques for formatting of paragraphs, etc.	☑	☐
6.	Uses ENTER key only at end of paragraphs	☐	☑
7.	Able to move rather than retype relocated text	☐	☑
8.	Uses TAB key instead of space bar	☑	☐
9.	Changes margins for indented paragraphs	☑	☐
10.	Saves work at reasonable intervals	☑	☐

Rating scales are similar to checklists but permit teachers more specificity in their feedback to students (e.g., indicating the *frequency* or *degree* to which a student exhibits a characteristic, instead of simply indicating the presence or absence of it). Rating scales can be used both formatively—to provide feedback to students—and summatively—for purposes of assigning grades to specific academic work. Examples of student performances and products that can be assessed with rating scales include oral presentations, experiments, research reports, and artwork (Gredler, 1999).

Rating scales are also referred to as **scoring rubrics**. There are two basic types of scoring rubrics, namely *holistic* and *analytic* rubrics. You will learn much more about scoring rubrics, including how to develop your own, in the next chapter on performance assessment. However, a sample rubric or rating scale is presented in Figure 5.4. Notice that the same skills addressed in the checklist shown in Figure 5.3 are reiterated here, but the student is being assessed along a continuum instead of according to a dichotomy.

Figure 5.4 Example of a rating scale

| Student | Michael Vance | Date | 11/30/02 |

Word Processing Skills

Key:
- 1 = student **never or almost never** performs skill
- 2 = student **seldom** performs skill
- 3 = student **often** performs skill
- 4 = student **always or almost always** performs skill

		1	**2**	**3**	**4**
1.	Hands in proper location on keyboard	☐	☐	☐	☑
2.	Places fingers on "home keys" at rest	☐	☐	☐	☑
3.	Types with eyes on text, not keyboard	☐	☐	☑	☐
4.	Strikes appropriate keys with each finger	☐	☐	☑	☐
5.	Utilizes proper techniques for formatting of paragraphs, etc.	☐	☑	☐	☐
6.	Uses ENTER key only at end of paragraphs	☐	☑	☐	☐
7.	Able to move rather than retype relocated text	☑	☐	☐	☐
8.	Uses TAB key instead of space bar	☐	☐	☑	☐
9.	Changes margins for indented paragraphs	☐	☐	☑	☐
10.	Saves work at reasonable intervals	☐	☐	☑	☐

TEACHER QUESTIONS

A second type of informal assessment involves a seemingly commonplace classroom activity: teachers asking questions of their students. In most cases, **teacher questions** are informal, unplanned, and spontaneous oral inquiries posed by teachers to be answered by students. Questioning can be especially useful during instruction as a means of informally assessing the extent to which students understand what is being presented to them (Airasian, 2000; Gredler, 1999).

Through the use of questions, teachers can assess student understanding across the continuum of the cognitive domain of Bloom's taxonomy. *Lower-order questions* typically have a single predetermined correct answer. They are therefore appropriately used to assess lower levels of Bloom's taxonomy, such as knowledge and comprehension. Examples of lower-order questions would include the following:

- *How many sides does a parallelogram have?*
- *All living organisms have what element in common?*
- *What are the three primary colors?*

In contrast, *higher-order questions* often require students to apply or, in some other manner, critically examine information they have learned. They may be required to apply concepts in a different setting or within a different scenario; to analyze a complex situation; to take concepts or entities presumably unrelated to one another and synthesize them into a new, more complex composite; or to evaluate a series of alternatives based on given information. Higher-order questions often do not have predetermined correct responses. There may be multiple correct responses or, if there is a single correct answer, there may be multiple ways by which students could arrive at that response. Examples of higher-order questions would include the following:

- *Is it possible for the square root of a number to be negative? Why or why not?*
- *How serious is the impact of terrorism in America? Explain.*
- *Which is the more appropriate sentence for capital crimes, life imprisonment or the death penalty? Explain.*

With the implementation of more and more formal alternative assessment, higher-order questions have also taken on an additional application. As you will learn in Chapter 6, as a component of formal assessments, students are encouraged to think critically and evaluate their *own* learning processes and thinking strategies. In many cases, students are asked to explain and justify their thinking strategies (Gredler, 1999). Teachers have the responsibility of motivating students to engage in these critical-thinking activities, often through the use of questions. These questions are typically asked as follow-up questions to content-based inquiries. Examples of questions that would promote student self-reflection might include the following:

- *Which of the following would cost more: 10 apples at 5¢ each, 15 apples at 3¢ each, or 20 apples at 2¢ each? Show how you know.*

- *Is it possible for the value of a standard deviation to be negative? Explain your answer.*

Characteristics

As with informal observations, Oosterhof (1999 & 2001) also offers several characteristics of teacher questions. The following list, which is reiterated in Figure 5.5, briefly summarizes these characteristics of informal teacher questions.

- *Questions are obtrusive.* When students expect questions to be asked, as is typical during a lesson, they tend to pay greater attention to what is being taught. Knowing that questions might be asked in front of the entire class may promote *maximum* performance from students, as opposed to *typical* performance.

- *Questions must be interpreted by others; therefore, they must be stated clearly.* When teachers pose questions in class, students are forced to make inferences about what the teacher is asking since they cannot see what the teacher is thinking. Unless questions are stated clearly, students may make incorrect inferences and provide responses that are not what the teacher had intended. The quality of a student's inference—and subsequent response to the question—will be only as good as the quality of the question initially asked.

- *Questions can be directed to individuals or to groups.* Classroom questions are often posed to the entire class, instead of individual students. The advantage to this technique is that greater participation is encouraged. However, if questions continue to be asked of an entire class over an extended period of time (e.g., throughout an entire lesson or class period), control over *who* responds becomes substantially reduced. This can be a problem if only a subset of students repeatedly answers the questions, leaving other students as nonparticipants.

- *Details of questions asked and their subsequent responses are quickly forgotten.* As with informal observations, student responses to teacher questions may be quickly forgotten unless they are somehow recorded. It is for this reason that students' responses to informal teacher questions should be used primarily for purposes of formative assessment, and not for summative purposes such as grading.

Guidelines for Use

Similarly to the use of informal observations, learning how to pose good questions is best learned through experience. Several guidelines (Oosterhof, 1999 & 2001) should help you structure and refine your skills in posing questions to your students. These guidelines are also summarized in Figure 5.5.

- *Develop questions from instructional objectives.* As with any form of assessment, when trying to gauge student understanding and comprehension, teachers must be sure that they are in fact measuring the skills and concepts they intend to measure. Asking questions that parallel the information provided to students will serve two purposes. First, doing so will enable students to demonstrate their levels of understanding. Second, asking appropriate questions allows teachers to draw proper conclusions concerning what students do and do not understand.

- *Provide a clear problem for students to address.* Even though teacher questions are considered informal and spontaneous, they should not be posed without some degree of forethought. If questions are truly asked "off the top of one's head," students will likely—and repeatedly—ask for clarification. At a minimum, they may respond initially to a teacher's question with looks of confusion. Prior to asking a specific question, teachers should try to anticipate possible student responses in order to determine if any clarification is needed.

- *Allow sufficient time for students to respond to oral questions.* This guideline is essential in terms of providing students with ample time to formulate and develop appropriate responses to your questions. When teachers pose questions to an entire class, a period of silence that lasts for two to three seconds may seem like an eternity, but in many cases is barely enough time for

students to even process the question, let alone arrive at a response they might be willing to share with the class. For lower-order questions, a few seconds may be sufficient time, but for higher-order questions that require a great deal of cognitive processing, five to ten seconds might be more appropriate. It may seem like quite a long time to you, but try to provide your students with enough time to process the question and provide a good response.

- *Avoid embarrassing students.* One major drawback to teacher questions is that they are public. Most other forms of assessment permit students to respond much more privately. The potential for students to feel embarrassed or intimidated when responding to teachers' questions must always be considered. The teacher must make every effort to ensure that each student is comfortable in responding to various classroom inquiries.

- *Exhibit caution when reacting to student responses.* The major source of embarrassment and intimidation often stems from the teacher's reaction to a student's response. Teachers must be cautious in their use of both verbal and nonverbal communication when responding to students. Some facial expressions, as well as verbal comments with negative connotations, may serve only to discourage future student participation.

Figure 5.5 Characteristics and guidelines for the use of teacher questions

Characteristics

1. Questions are obtrusive.
2. Questions must be interpreted by others; therefore, they must be stated clearly.
3. Questions can be directed to individuals or to groups.
4. Details of questions asked and their subsequent responses are quickly forgotten.

Guidelines for Use

1. Develop questions from instructional objectives.
2. Provide a clear problem for students to address.
3. Allow sufficient time for students to respond to oral questions.
4. Avoid embarrassing students.
5. Exhibit caution when reacting to student responses.

Record Keeping

When documenting the use of teacher questions, there are very few structured techniques that can be used to maintain records regarding student participation or quality of responses. In most cases, teachers would likely customize some sort of variation of a checklist in order to document student participation and responses. Some form of a checklist would be most appropriate since teachers would want to avoid a substantial interruption to classroom instruction, yet still be able to quickly indicate whether or not a particular student had answered a question correctly.

An example of this type of checklist appears in Figure 5.6. In this particular variation, all students are included on a single checklist; students' names are listed vertically down the left side (each student constitutes a row) and dates are listed across the top (each constitutes a column). Notice that one copy of the checklist could be used for each class or class period. During the course of a lesson, the teacher simply indicates by checking the appropriate box each student who was asked a question or whether the student was able to answer the question correctly. Listing each student on a single page is much easier to maintain than having a separate checklist for each student.

Figure 5.6 Partial example of a checklist for teacher questions

QUESTIONING CHECKLIST								PERIOD 2
Student	Date							
	2/1	2/2	2/3	2/4	2/5	2/8	2/9	2/10
Able, Jonathon	☐	☐	☐	☐	☐	☐	☐	☐
Adams, Stephanie	☐	☐	☑	☐	☑	☑	☐	☑
Bouking, Monica	☐	☐	☑	☐	☐	☑	☑	☑
Chan, Natalie	☑	☐	☐	☐	☐	☐	☐	☐
Christopher, Raul	☑	☐	☐	☐	☑	☐	☐	☐
Cristie, Paul	☑	☐	☐	☐	☐	☐	☐	☑
Everman, Gloria	☐	☑	☐	☐	☐	☐	☐	☐
Florentine, Gino	☑	☐	☐	☐	☐	☐	☐	☐
Gray, Michelle	☑	☐	☑	☑	☑	☐	☐	☐
Hernandez, Edward	☑	☐	☑	☑	☑	☐	☐	☐
Johnson, Angela	☐	☐	☑	☐	☑	☑	☐	☐
Light, Robert	☐	☐	☐	☐	☐	☑	☑	☑

One of the advantages of this type of checklist is that teachers can maintain an ongoing record of the frequency with which certain students are asked oral questions during instruction, the frequency with which students voluntarily respond to questions, or the quality of students' responses (e.g., **+** = "very good," √ = "good," **-** = "poor"). In the example, it is clear that Jonathon Able has not been asked a question in several days; whereas, several other students are asked questions with much greater frequency. This teacher would likely notice that more questions should be asked of Jonathon, as well as Natalie, Gino, and Gloria.

STUDENT REFLECTIONS

In an attempt to provide students with opportunities to evaluate their *own* understanding of material being presented to them during a lesson, teachers often expose students to a process of reflection. **Student reflections** are brief narratives or self-reports written by students concerning the subject matter being studied

(Johnson & Johnson, 2002). These student reflections are essentially variations of journals or learning logs (Johnson & Johnson, 2002). Periodically throughout a unit of instruction, students write short narrative entries in a reflective journal on aspects related specifically to the instructional content. These entries may consist of summaries of the material, questions raised by a class discussion or activity, characteristics of their work on a project, or an apparent connection between the material being studied and a current event in the news (Johnson & Johnson, 2002; Gredler, 1999).

Student reflections provide opportunities for the teacher and student to discuss the student's comments and questions. Teachers have the chance to read what each student is thinking about as a result of the material being studied, to learn a little more about how each student is processing the material or what difficulties individual students may be having. This, in turn, enables teachers to provide feedback to each student based on the individualized need (Trice, 2000). Furthermore, from a student perspective, student reflections provide a safe environment within which to share thoughts, concerns, and questions. Many students might not be comfortable asking questions in class, especially if they feel that they are the only ones who do not understand the material, for example. No person other than the teacher and individual student has access to that particular student's reflective journal.

A widely used variation on student reflections is known as the "one-minute paper." The *one-minute paper* can be used quickly and efficiently to ascertain students' understanding of a class or specific concept (Magnan, 1991). The one-minute paper procedure is relatively straightforward. Students are given the last few minutes of class to respond—in writing and anonymously—to one or two questions specified by the teacher. The responses are collected and synthesized in any manner deemed appropriate by the teacher. The teacher then responds to them in some manner at the beginning of the next class period. One-minute papers emphasize student responsibility to listen and process during class (McGovern, 2001b). Some commonly used questions or prompts that can be used to facilitate one-minute papers include:

- *What was the most important thing you learned from today's class?*
- *What question do you still have following today's class?*
- *I would like to know more about…*
- *I am still unsure about…* (McGovern, 2001a; Magnan, 1991).

VALIDITY AND RELIABILITY OF INFORMAL ASSESSMENTS

Informal assessments typically result in reduced validity and reliability due to their subjective nature. They can, however, result in valid and reliable decisions about student behavior and performance, provided several pitfalls are avoided. Recall that validity is the degree to which the results of assessments are interpreted and used appropriately. The validity of teacher observations and questions can be adversely affected by two potential problems (Airasian, 2000). First, there exists a tendency for teachers to sometimes prejudge students or anticipate the nature of their behaviors. This often occurs as a result of rumors overheard in the teachers' lounge; comparing the previous behavior or performance of siblings; student behavior in nonclassroom settings; or a teacher's cultural, gender, racial, or disability biases or stereotypes. Teachers must make every effort to remain objective, especially with respect to the results of informal assessments.

Second, teachers sometimes select inappropriate indicators when attempting to assess specific student characteristics. When this occurs, they have essentially *in*validated any decision reached as a result of the particular observation. It is often tempting to try to "read more into" an individual observation of a student or a given student response. It would certainly be easier if we could observe a student for a brief period or ask a single question and have valid information regarding motivation, academic achievement, social skills, and self-confidence. Obviously, one observation or question could not be structured in such a way as to capture this diversity of student information.

Reliability was described earlier as the degree of consistency in decisions resulting from assessment information. The reliability of teacher observations and ques-

tions can also be affected by two potential problems (Airasian, 2000). First, reliability can be severely affected by a lack of adequate sampling of student behaviors. Too few observations prevent teachers from drawing accurate conclusions regarding specific behaviors. You can witness a specific characteristic during an isolated observation, but it would be incorrect to assume or infer that the particular characteristic represented "typical" behavior. Additional observations would be necessary in order to substantiate or refute your initial conclusion.

Second, and somewhat related to the previous point, not only is it dangerous to draw inferences about student behaviors from isolated observations, it is also a bit risky to assume that conclusions drawn about behaviors observed in one setting will carry over into other settings. Just because students are seen exhibiting disruptive behaviors in the lunchroom does not necessarily mean that the same type of behavior will be displayed in the classroom during an academic lesson.

The keys to valid and reliable results from informal assessments are first and foremost to remain objective when implementing informal assessments, but also to ensure that teachers limit the conclusions to what was specifically observed, and to collect enough information to draw accurate conclusions.

ADVANTAGES AND LIMITATIONS OF INFORMAL ASSESSMENTS

There are several advantages to the use of informal assessments in classroom settings. Observations and questions are efficient and adaptable. Numerous events can be observed or questions asked in quick succession and, if need be, with little preparation. Additionally, informal assessments can be built into the flow of a lesson. They can be used effectively as a means of monitoring events as they occur during the course of a lesson or to gauge the current level of students' understanding. Individual teacher questions can function quite well as a follow-up to teacher observations.

As with any form of assessment, informal assessments also have limitations. Observations are limited to those behaviors that occur naturally. If a student is not observed exhibiting a characteristic or performing a given skill, it might be assumed by the teacher that the student has already demonstrated the behavior or skill, is incapable of doing so, or for a variety of reasons has simply chosen not to, any of which might be erroneous conclusions. Furthermore, teachers observe only a fraction of student behaviors and characteristics and do so in spontaneous fashion, therefore resulting in less technical conclusions. The majority of student characteristics must be assessed in other ways, utilizing other techniques. Finally, as discussed earlier, many informal observations and questions go undocumented, implying that most will be forgotten or distorted by the classroom teacher.

SUMMARY

Informal assessments occur in a continuous, ongoing manner. The main types of informal assessments include teacher observations, teacher questions, and student reflections. Teacher observations involve watching or listening to students as they perform some activity or behavior that occurs naturally. Characteristics of observations include their simultaneous nature, tendency to focus on a single event, and the requirement of inference when interpreting observations. It is important for teachers to avoid extended inferences, recognize that observations may underestimate or overestimate achievement, and document observations for later reference. Observations may be documented through the use of anecdotal records, checklists, or rating scales.

Teacher questions are typically informal, unplanned oral inquiries of students. They may be used to assess both lower- and higher-order thinking skills. Oral questions are characterized by being obtrusive, requiring interpretation by someone other than the responding student, and their details and subsequent responses may be quickly forgotten. Teachers should base questions on instructional objectives, allow sufficient time for students to respond, and avoid embarrassing students through the use of questioning.

Student reflections consist of student self-reports of the subject matter being studied. They provide opportunities for students to clarify their own understanding of the material and for teachers to identify individual difficulties or misconceptions. Reflections may be as comprehensive as a journal or as brief as a one-minute paper.

Valid and reliable information can result from informal assessments, provided teachers collect enough information in order to make accurate conclusions and remain objective when implementing informal assessments.

Chapter 5 *Related Web Sites*

* **Classroom Questions** (*www.ericae.net/pare/getvn.asp?v=6&n=6*)
  This brief article appears in *Practical Assessment, Research, & Evaluation*, a peer-reviewed electronic journal, and is authored by Amy C. Buraldi. Characteristics of both good and bad questions are discussed. Additionally, suggestions are provided for research-based questioning practices that foster higher student achievement.

* **Effective Questioning Techniques** (*darkwing.uoregon.edu/~tep/lizard/questions.html*)
  This Web site has been developed by the Teaching Effectiveness Program at the University of Oregon. In the first paragraph, the authors state, "Good questioning skills are part of the artistry of teaching." To this end, they offer ten brief, but very appropriate, suggestions for developing and using oral questions.

* **Tutoring Tips: Questioning Techniques** (*www.casaa-resources.net/peer-helping/tutoring-tips/asking-questions.html*)
  This page, maintained by the Canadian Association of Student Activity Advisors, takes a slightly different approach from the Web sites above. The authors present suggestions—and examples—of techniques to *avoid* when posing oral questions to your students. Additionally, they provide a follow-up page (*www.casaa-resources.net/peer-helping/tutoring-tips/answers.html*), which provides suggestions for how to handle correct and incorrect student responses.

* **Effective Techniques of Questioning**
  (*www.campbell.k12.ky.us/programs/ktln/questions.htm*)
  This Campbell County (KY) Schools site provides a brief list of tips on asking questions for effective interaction between teacher and students.

QUESTIONS FOR REVIEW

1. A physical education teacher wants to assess students' abilities to accurately keep score for a bowling tournament. Would a series of observations or oral questions be the more appropriate method of informal assessment? Why?

2. During the course of a science lesson, an elementary school teacher wants to know if an entire class understands the definition of "hypothesis." Would a series of observations or oral questions be the more appropriate method of informal assessment? Why?

3. Describe what is meant by an *inference*. Why should teachers exhibit caution when drawing inferences about student behaviors or characteristics? What is the best way to avoid drawing incorrect inferences?

4. Distinguish between checklists and rating scales. What are the similarities and differences?

5. Explain why observations tend to overestimate academic achievement.

6. A middle school mathematics teacher is trying to assess students' knowledge of the proper order of math operations. The teacher decides to provide problems in the form of seatwork, observe the students as they complete the work, and maintain anecdotal records for each student. If the teacher asked for your reaction to this assessment plan, how would you respond?

7. How can rating scales be used effectively for purposes of *formative* evaluation?

8. What is the major advantage of using student reflections?

9. Briefly discuss any advantages and limitations to the use of a "one-minute paper."

10. With respect to the validity and reliability, what is the most important aspect of informal assessments for teachers to remember?

ENRICHMENT ACTIVITIES

1. In a paragraph or two, describe content for a lesson or unit that you would like to teach someday. Discuss how you could informally assess your students' understanding of the subject matter or skills using observational and questioning techniques. Share your responses in small groups.

2. Most oral questions are informal and spontaneous. In a lesson plan, however, teachers will sometimes note particular questions they want to remember to ask of students. For the same content you selected in Activity 1 above, list four to five *specific* oral questions

that could be used to assess student understanding during a lesson. Share your questions in small groups.

3. For the same content you selected in Activity 1 above, list three *specific* questions or incomplete statements that could be used as prompts for one-minute papers. Share your prompts in small groups.

Notes

Chapter 6

Performance-Based Assessments

Overview of Chapter 6

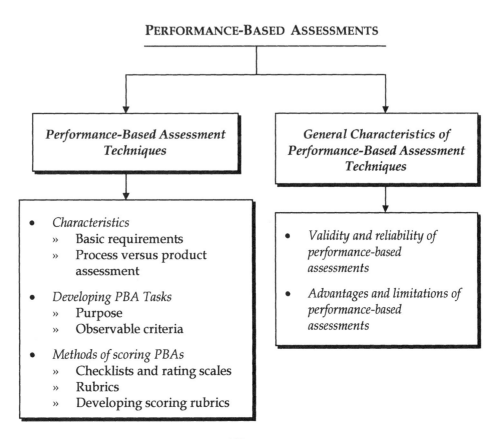

PERFORMANCE-BASED ASSESSMENTS

Performance-Based Assessment Techniques

- *Characteristics*
  - » Basic requirements
  - » Process versus product assessment

- *Developing PBA Tasks*
  - » Purpose
  - » Observable criteria

- *Methods of scoring PBAs*
  - » Checklists and rating scales
  - » Rubrics
  - » Developing scoring rubrics

General Characteristics of Performance-Based Assessment Techniques

- *Validity and reliability of performance-based assessments*

- *Advantages and limitations of performance-based assessments*

109

INTRODUCTION

This chapter introduces a second category of alternative assessment techniques. This type of assessment requires students to directly apply their knowledge and skills, often from several content areas, in order to complete a task or activity. *Performance-based assessment*, or more simply, *performance assessment*, has many purposes and can be used as the basis for both formative and summative evaluative decisions. Although more labor- and time-intensive from the perspective of the classroom teacher, there are many important advantages to the use of performance assessments.

CHARACTERISTICS OF PERFORMANCE-BASED ASSESSMENTS

Many assessments, and the information that results from them, narrowly focus on students' comprehension. In other words, these assessments help teachers answer the following question: What do my students know? Although teachers are often concerned about what students *know*, they may also be interested—and, in many instances, more interested—in what students are *capable of actually doing*. This different focus of assessment requires the use of different forms of assessment; the same techniques used to assess comprehension will not suffice when trying to assess actual student capabilities. Performance assessments permit teachers to assess these types of capabilities.

Performance assessments present to students a hands-on task or some other performance-based activity that students must complete either individually or in small groups. Furthermore, performance assessments use specifically defined and preestablished criteria for evaluating the work completed by students (Nitko, 2001). Therefore, performance assessments consist of two components: (1) the *performance task* and (2) the preestablished scoring criteria, usually in the form of a *scoring rubric* (Nitko, 2001). A **performance task** is the actual prompt or activity supplied to students as part of a performance assessment; it specifies to students exactly what they are to do. A **scoring rubric** is a scoring guide, consisting of specific preestablished performance criteria, used in evaluating student work on performance assessments. You will learn much more about the characteristics and development of scoring rubrics later in this chapter.

Performance assessment permits the direct observation of student skills and capabilities (Oosterhof, 1999 & 2001). In other words, the results of performance assessments provide teachers with information about the extent to which students are capable of actually *applying* specific knowledge or actually *executing* a specific set of skills. This is dramatically different from the information that results from the assessment of students using more traditional pencil-and-paper tests. These latter types of assessments typically assess the extent to which students understand facts and concepts and, perhaps, know *how* to execute a set of skills. However, knowing how to do something and *actually* doing it are two very different things. For example, a commonplace activity in an industrial arts class is the disassembly and subsequent reassembly of a small engine. Many students may be able to *tell* their teacher how to reassemble the engine (in other words, they know *how* to do it), but it takes a different set of skills and capabilities to be able to *actually* reassemble the engine. Additionally, if it is important that students be able to put the engine back together (i.e., it is a specific instructional objective), then the industrial arts teacher should not assess the objective by merely asking students if they can describe how to assemble an engine but, rather, have them do it (Trice, 2000).

Performance assessment, like all forms of assessment, must be linked to the instructional objectives (Chase, 1999). If the teacher is trying to guide students to the performance of a specific skill through the course of a lesson or unit, students must obviously receive instruction on the particular skill or behavior. Instruction on that skill or behavior should initially be guided by its inclusion in an instructional objective.

Another key component of performance assessment is that it tends to be less abstract than more traditional forms of assessment (Tanner, 2001). Since actual student demonstrations of learning are central to performance assessments, specific assessment activities tend to be much more practical and based on "real-world" activities. This is the focus of assessment activities that are classified as *authentic assessments*. **Authentic assessments** are those that present assessment activities that are directly meaningful to students (Nitko, 2001). In other words, authentic assessments, by themselves, are meaningful learning activities. They require students to develop a response to a task that replicates a real-life event (Chase, 1999). They are designed to provide a greater transfer of learning from the setting in which learning occurs (i.e., a classroom) to the real world outside the confines of the classroom (Tanner, 2001). For example, a teacher may ask students to complete a worksheet that contains several mathematics problems, such as the following:

$$
\begin{array}{ll}
1. \quad 150 & 2. \quad 175 \\
\ \ \times \ .06 & \ \ \times \ .05 \\
\hline
\end{array}
$$

These problems, as presented, do not represent authentic real-life applications. Few of us will go to work one day and be asked by a supervisor to complete a worksheet containing 50 multiplication problems as one of our routine, job-related activities. In contrast, the following task permits students to show that they know how to multiply by placing those skills in a more meaningful setting:

1. You approach your parents about wanting to purchase a new stereo for your bedroom. You tell them that the cost for the stereo is $150 and that you have just that amount saved. However, they remind you that you will also have to pay sales

```
tax. Your parents tell you that
if you can show them what the
total cost (including the sales
tax) would be, they will give
you the additional amount to
cover the tax. The tax rate in
your state is 6%. Prepare a
written statement itemizing the
total cost of the stereo.
```

Notice that this more meaningful version is actually the same problem (i.e., addresses the same skills and uses the same numerical values) as number 1 in the first set. Authentic assessments are just one type of alternative assessments. Furthermore, performance assessments are one form of authentic assessments. This relationship is depicted in Figure 6.1.

The concept of performance assessment is not new. For years, many exhibition- or presentation-based subjects—such as art, music, physical education, and vocational education—have a tradition of using more of an applied, authentic approach toward assessing students. Furthermore, medical schools and flight-training schools have relied on simulations as a basis for assessment for many years. Only in the past 15 years or so has performance assessment become more integral in assessing student performance in academic subject areas (Tanner, 2001).

Figure 6.1 Relationship between alternative, authentic, and performance assessments

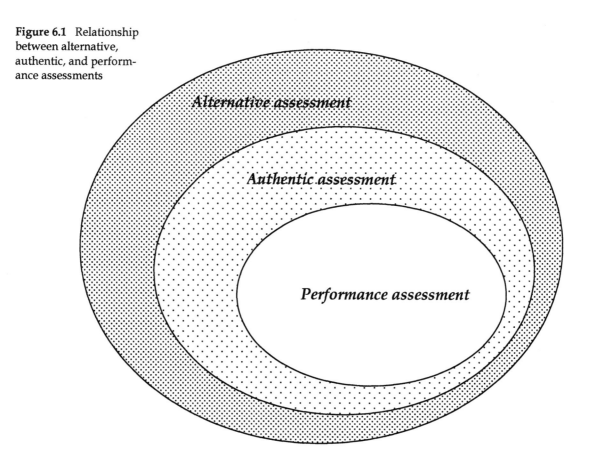

Finally, it is important to note that performance assessments can appropriately be used for both formative and summative purposes (Chase, 1999). Because of their structure, performance assessment tasks often provide important information about student strengths and weaknesses. In fact, when used correctly, they can actually provide a profile of strengths and weaknesses for individual students. This is a highly beneficial aspect of performance assessment for teachers as they progress through an instructional unit (i.e., formative assessment). Implementing performance assessments in this manner can provide very meaningful diagnostic feedback to teachers and students and, therefore, help guide or refine instruction. Additionally, at the end of a unit, teachers need to ensure that all instructional objectives have been achieved by their students (i.e., summative assessment). Since performance assessments should be linked directly to instructional objectives, they can also be used quite effectively as a culminating activity to assess the overall effectiveness of instruction at the end of a unit of instruction.

Basic Requirements

Compared to some other forms of assessment, the basic nature of performance assessment tends to be much more diverse and is, therefore, more difficult to describe concretely (Oosterhof, 1999 & 2001). Performance assessments may include observations and formal assessments of hands-on tasks or other performance-based ac-

tivities such as lab experiments, oral presentations, term papers, musical performances, dance and other physical performances, work habits, group or social interactions, and writing a persuasive letter. Performance assessments are typically framed so that multiple correct responses may be possible (Nitko, 2001). Alternatively, if there exists only a single correct response to a task, there may be multiple ways of reaching that conclusion, as well as perhaps multiple ways of expressing the answer (Nitko, 2001). Due to this open-ended and broad-based nature of performance assessment, its characteristics are much more difficult to specify than those of informal assessments or more objective forms of assessments (i.e., multiple choice, true-false, and matching items). However, Oosterhof (1999 & 2001), Nitko (2001), and Gredler (1999) have identified some necessary characteristics that have been combined below in an attempt to describe the basic requirements of performance assessment:

• *Specific behaviors or capabilities should be observed.* As with any form of assessment, teachers must be able to identify the specific behaviors or skills they wish to see exhibited by their students. Even though they tend to be relatively open-ended, performance assessment tasks should be structured to provide students with the appropriate opportunities to demonstrate that they possess the identified behaviors and capabilities.

- *Complex capabilities or skills that cannot be measured with pencil-and-paper tests should be measured with performance assessments.* Performance assessments should focus on higher-order thinking skills, specifically application, analysis, synthesis, and evaluation from Bloom's taxonomy. Lower-order skills—such as knowledge and comprehension of definitions and concepts—can be much more appropriately and *efficiently* assessed using more traditional pencil-and-paper forms of assessment.

- *Tasks must focus on teachable processes.* Although performance assessments should focus on higher-order thinking skills, those skills identified by the teacher must still be taught as an integral part of the instructional unit or lesson. One should not expect students to be able to apply knowledge and concepts to new or different situations without having been taught how to do so. The skills or capabilities must be ones that can be taught to students; the performance assessment task should not require the use of intuition or insight, but should allow students to demonstrate the use of teachable skills and behaviors.

- *Performance tasks make it possible to judge the appropriateness of student behaviors or the level of understanding or proficiency, which provides information about strengths and weaknesses.* As you will see illustrated later in this chapter, responses to performance assess-ments are typically not scored on the basis of being correct or incorrect. Rather, they are assessed using a continuum of knowledge, understanding, or proficiency. This is the essential characteristic that categorizes performance assessment as an alternative technique and distinguishes it from traditional forms of assessment. Traditional pencil-and-paper tests are ordinarily scored by indicating whether the student response to a multiple-choice or true-false item, for example, is correct or incorrect (a relatively simple dichotomous outcome). Student products resulting from a performance assessment task are often judged according to some continuum or range of "correctness." It may be possible to have four, five, or even six levels of proficiency or understanding. This characteristic, in turn, provides a potential wealth of information to both teachers and students. As opposed to the limited information provided by knowing that a student answered a question correctly or incorrectly, performance assessments may be designed to provide feedback about specific areas of strength or weakness in a student's response.

- *Performance assessments require products or behaviors that are valuable in their own right.* A simple hands-on activity, worksheet, or seatwork does not necessarily constitute a performance assessment. The key is that the actual performance task must provide for students a valuable learning experience in and of itself. In other words, through the application of higher-order thinking skills, even if their work was not being evaluated, students would still learn as a result of the experience.

- *Performance tasks should encourage student reflection.* In Chapter 5, you read about the use of student reflections, which are intended to provide opportunities for students to evaluate their *own* understanding of subject matter. A similar procedure can be incorporated into performance assessment tasks by requiring students to reflect on and discuss—either in written or oral form—the steps they followed, or the thinking processes they used, to arrive at their response. Additionally, teachers might require that students reflect on their own strengths and weaknesses. This is most simply accomplished as the final component of a performance task by asking students to explain their answers or justify their conclusions.

These six basic requirements are summarized in Figure 6.2.

Process versus Product Assessment

One important way to further categorize performance assessments is for the assessment to focus on a process, a product, or both. A **process assessment** is one that specifically targets the procedures used by students to solve a problem or complete a task (Gredler, 1999; Oosterhof, 1999 & 2001). In contrast, a **product assessment** is one that results in a tangible outcome (Oosterhof, 1999 & 2001). In an earlier example, students were required to disassemble and then reassemble a small engine. Assessing the way that students use the appropriate tools for disassembly and reassembly would be a *process* assessment; assessing the quality of the completely rebuilt engine would be a *product* assessment.

In some cases, teachers will be more interested in the final product that students submit. For example, they may be interested in the overall quality of a finished painting, the persuasiveness of a public awareness campaign, or the appropriate use of supporting facts, along with the grammar, punctuation, and spelling, of an essay. In other situations, the process or procedures used by students serve as the basis for the assessment. For instance, assessment of the execution of a dance routine, where each individual move is essential, would be appropriate for a process assessment. Depending on the learning objective, you may want to assess either the process or the product, or both (Nitko, 2001; Tombari & Borich, 1999), although most performance assessments are typically concerned with only the process or only the product, or at least emphasize one as being more important than the other (Oosterhof, 1999 & 2001).

Figure 6.2 Basic requirements for the use of performance assessments

Basic Requirements

1. Specific behaviors or capabilities should be observed.
2. Complex capabilities or skills that cannot be measured with pencil-and-paper tests should be measured with performance assessments.
3. Tasks must focus on teachable processes.
4. Performance tasks make it possible to judge the appropriateness of student behaviors or the level of understanding or proficiency, which provides information about strengths and weaknesses.
5. Performance assessments require products or behaviors that are valuable in their own right.
6. Performance tasks should encourage student reflection.

To illustrate, imagine that a teacher designs a performance task that requires students to develop a research proposal. It might be appropriate for the teacher to assess various stages of development or possibly drafts of specific sections — such as the hypotheses, literature review, or methodology — of the proposal during the process of development.

In the end, however, the teacher is ultimately interested in the overall quality of the final version of the research proposal. In this particular situation, both process and product are being assessed, but the product would be weighted more heavily than the process. Decisions about assessing processes or products are ones that must be made by classroom teachers prior to the implementation of the performance assessment task and are based largely on the nature of the specific instructional objectives being targeted by the performance assessment task.

DEVELOPING PERFORMANCE-BASED ASSESSMENT TASKS

Airasian (2000 & 2001) has identified four essential features to keep in mind when developing performance assessment tasks. He suggests that all performance assessment tasks (1) have a clear purpose that specifies the decision that will be made about the assessment, (2) identify observable aspects of the students' performance or product that will be judged, (3) provide an appropriate setting for completing the task and judging the performance, and (4) result in one or more scores that describe the students' performance. All four of these features are central to the development and implementation of performance assessments, as you will soon see outlined in the step-by-step process of task design.

Although our present focus is on the development of performance assessment tasks, it is important to note that a variety of educational resources exist where teachers can select previously developed performance assessments. Sources for performance assessment materials might include other teachers in your district, district curriculum and/or assessment specialists, professional educational publications, and materials produced by educational (textbook) publishers (Gallagher, 1998). However, it is also crucial to note an important caveat: These materials were *not* developed by you or for use with your students, in your classroom, using your instructional objectives (Mertler, 2001b). As you will recall from Chapter 2, Figure 2.4 stressed the importance of the alignment among three entities: the planning, the delivery, and the assessment of instruction. If you decide to use existing performance assessments, you must make sure that the assessments match your instructional objectives and instruction you actually deliver. Otherwise, the ultimate outcome of using these assessments may be inaccurate conclusions about student performance. Existing performance tasks must be carefully examined by teachers who wish to use them in their classrooms. The criteria and guidelines that are used to design performance tasks can also be used to judge the quality of previously developed tasks in terms of the potential application in your classroom (Gallagher, 1998).

Identifying the Purpose of the Performance-Based Assessment

In all likelihood, the most crucial step in designing a performance assessment task is to determine its purpose. The initial determination of purpose will drive a variety of decisions concerning the development of the task (Gallagher, 1998). Some of these latter decisions might include in what specific context the task will be placed, the types of skills and subsequent indicators of those skills that teachers want to observe in students, and the types of conclusions the teacher wishes to make as a result of the students' performances. Oftentimes, information that will guide decisions about the purpose of the assessment will come directly from the stated instructional objectives (Chase, 1999).

It is important for teachers to decide ahead of time whether the performance or product will be used for formative or summative purposes. Judgments made by a teacher would be quite different, depending on the nature of the conclusions to be reached. When the performance assessment is being used formatively, the purpose is to provide specific feedback to students regarding strengths and weaknesses while they are striving to acquire a set of skills. When being used in summative fashion, the purpose of performance assessment is to determine if students have achieved or mastered some set of skills, and this determination will likely become some sort of grade. Regardless of the purpose of the performance assessment, it should be thoroughly specified at the beginning of the process of assessment development so that the appropriate standards of performance and the procedures for judging students' work can be delineated (Airasian, 2000 & 2001).

Specifying Observable Performance Criteria

A second crucial component in the design of performance assessment tasks is the specification of observable performance criteria. **Performance criteria** are defined as the specific observable standards by which student performances or products are assessed (Airasian, 2000 & 2001; Weber, 1999). In other words, these criteria comprise the specific behaviors or skills that students must perform when they complete a performance or produce a product (Airasian, 2000 & 2001). It is important to stress that these criteria must be *observable*. Airasian (2000 & 2001) has stated that this is the area of performance assessment design in which the majority of problems are encountered by teachers.

Prior to deciding what criteria to observe, teachers must determine whether a process, product, or both will be observed (Airasian, 2000 & 2001). For example, a performance task might involve writing a friendly letter. The teacher must determine if the process (e.g., writing skills, penmanship, and format of the letter) or the product (e.g., the overall quality of the final handwritten letter) will be assessed. The teacher would also have the option of assessing both, but that determination

must be made at the outset, prior to implementing the task.

Once these decisions have been made, the overall performance or product must be broken down into its component parts (Airasian, 2000 & 2001). In the letter-writing task, for example, assessing "format of the letter" is much too broad—and potentially too subjective—an activity for teachers to perform accurately. Students' abilities to format a letter must be broken down into more specific and observable skills. The specific criteria corresponding to the letter-formatting skills might include:

Broad Skill	Performance Criteria
Formatting of a friendly letter	• Inclusion of date and address • Proper spacing between elements • Date is right justified; all others left justified • Each paragraph indented five spaces • Appropriate greeting and closing for friendly letter • Letter is signed appropriately

Notice that all the specific performance criteria are observable and could easily be identified in a student letter.

Further, it is important for performance criteria to be stated clearly (Airasian, 2000 & 2001). A suggested rule of thumb is that the criteria are sufficiently clear if another teacher at the same grade level or from the same subject area can use the performance criteria without additional explanation from the authoring teacher.

Finally, the number of performance criteria to be observed should be limited to a reasonable and manageable number (Airasian, 2000 & 2001). This tends to be less critical when teachers assess a product since an overall assessment of the final product will be made. Process assessments will often result in the identification of numerous criteria. A common recommendation is to limit the number of criteria to no more than ten.

Steps in the Development of Performance Tasks

A series of steps designed to facilitate the development of performance tasks is presented below. These seven steps summarize the entire process of designing a performance assessment, including both the task and scoring instrument. Our immediate concern will be with the first four steps, namely the design of the performance task. We will examine the development of the scoring instrument in detail later in this chapter. Information for this particular step-by-step procedure to be used in the design of performance assessment tasks was compiled from various sources (Airasian, 2000 & 2001; Gallagher, 1998; Mertler, 2001b; Nitko, 2001;

Tombari & Borich, 1999). They are summarized and discussed, followed by presentations and explanations of the design of two sample performance tasks, one at the elementary level and one at the secondary level.

Step 1: *Determine the purpose of the assessment.* As previously discussed, determining the purpose of the task is an essential component in the design and should be addressed first. Be sure that the purpose is aligned with the instructional objectives.

Step 2: *Specify the skills and outcomes, along with their respective taxonomic level.* (See Chapter 2, page 38, to review the taxonomic levels.) This step will help you ensure that the performance task matches appropriately both the content and skill level(s) of the original instructional objectives being assessed by the task.

Step 3: *Specify the performance criteria that will be used to judge students' work and identify observable indicators of those criteria.* In this step, the performance criteria are specified. Only indicators of key skills and outcomes should be identified. Keep the number of indicators manageable.

Step 4: *Create an authentic and meaningful context for the task.* Performance assessments must be placed in a context that is based in the real world. Furthermore, the setting for the task must, in and of itself, constitute a meaningful learning experience for students. The task should not consist of artificial or abstract situations, scenarios, or settings.

Step 5: *Develop a scoring instrument.* The scoring instrument allows teachers to consistently judge student performances or products. Its development follows many of the decisions made earlier by describing various levels or degrees of the performance criteria. We will discuss scoring instruments in much more detail below.

Step 6: *Generate or select exemplary student responses.* Prior to the first time a task is implemented, it is a good idea to generate possible student responses that exemplify various

levels of competency on the identified performance criteria. In essence, this creates a series of benchmarks that will aid in the judgment of student work. After the task has been implemented once or twice, teachers may select actual samples of student work to serve in this capacity.

Step 7: *Revise the task, as necessary.* Like many activities in education, seldom will a task work perfectly the first time. Be prepared to reflect on the quality of the task, focusing on what worked and what did not work, and revise it prior to its next implementation.

These seven steps involved in the design of performance tasks have been summarized in Figure 6.3.

Figure 6.3 Step-by-step procedure for the design of performance assessment tasks

---

Designing Performance Assessment Tasks:
Step-by-Step Procedure

Step 1: Determine the purpose of the assessment.

Step 2: Specify the skills and outcomes, along with their respective taxonomic level.

Step 3: Specify the performance criteria that will be used to judge students' work and identify observable indicators of those criteria.

Step 4: Create an authentic and meaningful context for the task.

Step 5: Develop a scoring instrument.

Step 6: Generate or select exemplary student responses.

Step 7: Revise the task, as necessary.

Two Examples

Two sample performance assessment tasks are presented next. Although these examples are relatively brief, it should be noted that some tasks may be quite lengthy and may span long periods of instructional time. However, these two examples typify the process of task development. Furthermore, for illustrative purposes, some of the steps outlined in Figure 6.3 have been combined in the respective discussions.

Example 1:
Subject – Mathematics
Grade Level(s) – Upper Elementary

Mr. Harris, a fourth-grade teacher, is planning a unit on the topic of data analysis, focusing primarily on the skills of estimation and interpretation of graphs. Specifically, at the end of this unit, he wants to be able to assess his students' mastery of the following instructional objectives:

- Students will properly interpret a bar graph.
- Students will accurately estimate values from within a bar graph.

Since the assessment will be administered at the end of the unit, the results will be incorporated into the students' grades (*Step 1*). Furthermore, he believes that a performance task is the most appropriate means of assessing these objectives and skills.

Based on the nature of the instructional objectives, Mr. Harris determines that the specific skills he wants to see his students demonstrate include reading and interpreting a bar graph and estimating different values based on the information presented in the graph. He identifies the proper interpretation of a bar graph as a comprehension skill, and the estimation as an application skill. Additionally, he wants his students to be able to explain or justify their reasoning and thinking when they are interpreting information and estimating values—an analysis skill (*Steps 2 and 3*).

Next, Mr. Harris must determine the specific observable indicators of the skills identified above; in other words, what can he observe that will draw him to conclude that individual students have either mastered the skills or need additional practice and reinforcement? After some brainstorming, he decides that by providing his students with a graph and directly asking them questions regarding the information contained in that graph, he should be able to arrive at the appropriate conclusions (*Step 3*).

Finally, Mr. Harris knows that for a performance assessment to be effective, he must "personalize" the learning experience in order to make it more meaningful for his students. He recalls that a new sandwich shop, American City Delicatessen, has recently opened in town and everyone has been praising the quality of the food. He has even heard several of his students talk about eating there with their parents. Since many students are familiar with the new restaurant, he decides to put the performance assessment task in that context (*Step 4*).

Mr. Harris' resulting performance assessment task appears in Figure 6.4. (We will examine Steps 5 and 6 associated with this task in the next section of this chapter on designing scoring instruments.)

Figure 6.4 Sample performance assessment task for upper elementary mathematics

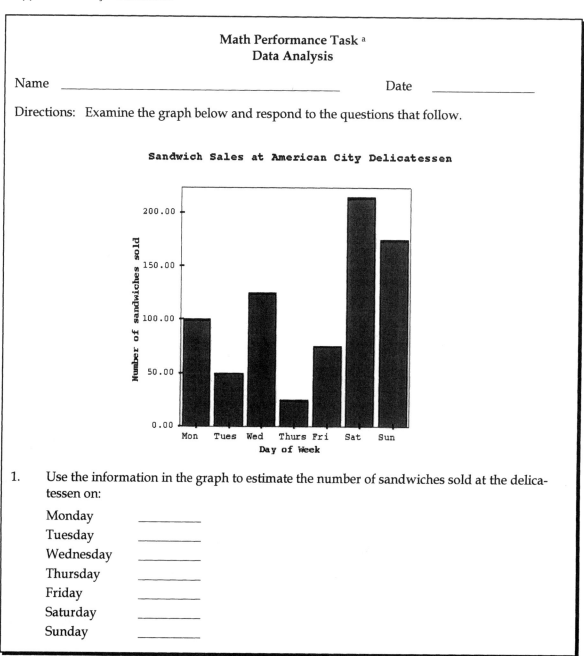

Math Performance Task [a]
Data Analysis

Name _____   Date _____

Directions: Examine the graph below and respond to the questions that follow.

Sandwich Sales at American City Delicatessen

1.   Use the information in the graph to estimate the number of sandwiches sold at the delicatessen on:

Monday   _____
Tuesday   _____
Wednesday   _____
Thursday   _____
Friday   _____
Saturday   _____
Sunday   _____

Figure 6.4 Continued

2. A waiter at the delicatessen wants to take one day off each week. Which would be the best day for the owner to choose? Which would be the worst day? Explain your answers.

    _____

    _____

    _____

    _____

3. The delicatessen needs to close for two days for repairs. Which two days would be the best? Why? Which would be the worst? Why?

    _____

    _____

    _____

    _____

    _____

    _____

4. Estimate how many more sandwiches are sold on Saturday than on Monday. Show your work.

5. Compare the number of sandwiches sold during the week to the number sold during the weekend. Were more sandwiches sold during the week or during the weekend? Show your work.

[a] Adapted from "Arlington (NY) Central School District: Performance Assessment Tasks" (http://www.arlingtonschools.org/Curriculum/Assessment/math4dat.html)

Example 2:
Subjects — Social Studies;
Probability and Statistics
Grade Level(s) — 9 - 12

Ms. Wolfe is a high school American government teacher. She is beginning a unit on the electoral process and knows from past years that her students sometimes have difficulty with the concepts of sampling and election polling. She decides to give her students a performance assessment so they can demonstrate their levels of understanding these concepts. The main idea that she wants to focus on is that samples (surveys) can accurately predict the viewpoints of an entire population. Specifically, she wants to be able to assess her students on the following instructional objectives:

- Students will collect data using appropriate methods.

- Students will accurately analyze and summarize their data.

- Students will effectively communicate their results.

Ms. Wolfe wants the assessment to focus on the provision of specific feedback to her students regarding their strengths and weaknesses (*Step 1*).

After examining the instructional objectives, Ms. Wolfe identifies several skills on which she will assess her students (*Step 2*). First, students must be able to use proper sampling techniques for surveying individuals from the population (an application skill). Second, they must be able to design a written survey or develop an interview guide in order to gather the appropriate data (a synthesis skill). Third, following some sort of compilation of their data, students should be able to interpret and summarize the results of their poll (a comprehension skill). Finally, students must demonstrate the ability to effectively communicate the results of their poll (also a comprehension skill).

The product of this performance assessment task will be a written report and oral presentation of the entire polling process and subsequent results. The specific performance criteria must be included in the written report, as well as summarized accurately in the oral presentation. The criteria include (1) appropriate descriptions of the sampling technique used and the nature of the questions asked in the survey or interview, (2) a brief summarization of the statistical analyses conducted and the results of those analyses, and (3) effective communication demonstrated by the quality of the written report and the brief oral presentation (*Step 3*).

Since there is a national presidential election in the next month, Ms. Wolfe decides to place the performance task in the context of a mock presidential election (*Step 4*). She will ask that her students sample the student population in the school in an attempt to accurately predict the next president, as determined through the mock election. Furthermore, a former student, now the owner of a local advertising agency, liked Ms. Wolfe's idea of the mock election so much that the agency decided to offer summer jobs to the students who most accurately predict the outcome of the mock election.

The resulting performance task appears in Figure 6.5. (Again, note that the scoring instrument will be examined later.)

Figure 6.5 Sample performance assessment task for secondary social studies and/or probability and statistics

Performance Task [b]
Population Sampling

Our national presidential election is approaching quickly. To better understand the polling and election process, we will hold a mock election in our school. Working in pairs, your task is to sample—using either a random or a stratified sampling technique—your high school student body in an attempt to predict the outcome of the actual mock election. As an incentive, a local advertising agency has guaranteed summer jobs to the students who most accurately predict the outcome of the actual presidential election through our mock election process.

For the final product that you will submit to me, you are required to prepare a written report documenting all procedures used to collect your data (including sampling plan and survey or interview questions), statistical calculations, and other procedures used to arrive at your conclusions. You must also include a rationale that supports your conclusions and speaks to the accuracy of your prediction. In addition, please attach your raw data as an appendix. Finally, you will give a 10-minute oral presentation summarizing the results of your poll.

You will have one week (five entire class periods) to work on the task. All written reports are due one week from today.

[b] Adapted from "Pattonville (MO) School District: Show-Me Classroom Performance Assessment Project, Performance Assessments Index (High School)"
http://www.pattonville.k12.mo.us/services/showme_assessment/pdfdocs/HScannam.pdf

METHODS OF SCORING PERFORMANCE-BASED ASSESSMENTS

One of the more difficult aspects of developing performance assessments is the design of scoring instruments. Remember that performance assessments do not typically have simple right or wrong answers; students' products or performances must be assessed along some sort of continuum based on the nature of the identified performance criteria.

It is sometimes tempting to limit your criteria to those aspects of the product or performance that are easiest to rate (Tombari & Borich, 1999). For example, teachers sometimes unknowingly identify right-and-wrong type questions as criteria, such as, "Did the student submit the project on time?" or "Was the response sheet completed?" Notice that these questions require a simple "yes" or "no" as answers and, therefore, as assessments. The performance criteria and subsequent scoring criteria should be specified such that *degrees* of quality, proficiency, or understanding can be observed in student work. It requires time to accomplish this task, but the overall result is a much more sound performance assessment.

Since performance assessments are more open-ended in nature and often result in a variety of types of student products, there exists the potential for teachers to rate student work with a good deal of subjectivity and bias. For example, when scoring student products or performances without an actual scoring instrument, teachers may be subjective. This often causes individual students to be evaluated differently, even though the students might have similar performances that are being evaluated by the same teacher. Through the process of specifying the performance criteria and developing a concrete scoring guide, this potential for subjectivity and bias is greatly reduced (Tombari & Borich, 1999).

Before examining specific forms of scoring instruments, it is important to discuss one more essential feature of performance assessment scoring instruments. Once again, due to the open-ended nature of performance tasks and the fact that there may be multiple correct responses to a given task, students should be provided with some degree of guidance prior to beginning work on their performance or product, while still allowing them to exhibit creativity. An efficient way to accomplish this is to share the scoring instrument with them from the outset (Gallagher, 1998; Mertler, 2001b; Montgomery, 2001). Doing so allows students to see the specific criteria on which their work will later be judged. Some researchers (e.g., Montgomery, 2001; Stix, 1996) have even suggested that the development of the scoring guide—including the performance criteria—be a joint task between teachers and students, thus giving students some sense of ownership in the performance assessment.

Checklists and Rating Scales

There are two basic categories of scoring instruments that can be used with performance assessment tasks: checklists and rating scales. Both of these techniques were discussed earlier in Chapter 5 and will be reviewed here. Recall that a **checklist** is composed of a list of behaviors, skills, or characteristics and is used by simply indicating whether each behavior or skill has been observed. The nature of checklists allows the teacher only two possible options for each action or skill: performed or not performed, present or not present, observed or not observed, yes or no, etc. (Moskal, 2000). With respect to performance assessments, checklists are best suited for tasks that involve complex behaviors that can efficiently be broken down into a series of very specific actions or skills (Tombari & Borich, 1999). They are probably best utilized with performance tasks where the results will be used formatively. They can provide students with a quick indication of where their specific strengths and weaknesses lie. You saw an earlier example of a checklist in Figure 5.3.

Rating scales are also used to assess complex products and processes, but are more appropriately used for those that do not lend themselves to "either–or" types of judgments (Tombari & Borich, 1999). Unlike checklists, rating scales permit teachers to indicate the frequency or degree to which a student exhibits a particular behavior, characteristic, or skill. In essence, this allows teachers to note finer distinctions of abilities and skills beyond simply noting the presence or absence of the characteristic (Gallagher, 1998). Recall that rating scales can be used both formatively — to provide feedback to students — and summatively — for purposes of assigning grades to specific academic work. Rating scales might appropriately be used with oral presentations, experiments, research reports, paintings, and writing samples (Gredler, 1999), but can also be used as a measure of student attitudes, interests, and self-evaluations. You saw an earlier example of a rating scale presented in Figure 5.4.

Rubrics are rating scales that are specifically used with performance assessments. Characteristics of two different types of scoring rubrics will be discussed in the next section. These various scoring instruments are shown in Figure 6.6.

Rubrics

Rubrics are formally defined as scoring guides, consisting of specific pre-established performance criteria, used in evaluating student work on performance assessments. Rubrics are typically the specific form of instrument used when evaluating student performances or products resulting from a performance task.

There are two types of rubrics: holistic and analytic. A **holistic rubric** requires the teacher to score the overall process or product as a whole, without judging the component parts separately (Nitko, 2001). In contrast, with an **analytic rubric**, the teacher scores separate, individual parts of the product or performance first, then sums the individual scores to obtain a total score (Nitko, 2001).

Figure 6.6 Types of scoring instruments for performance assessments

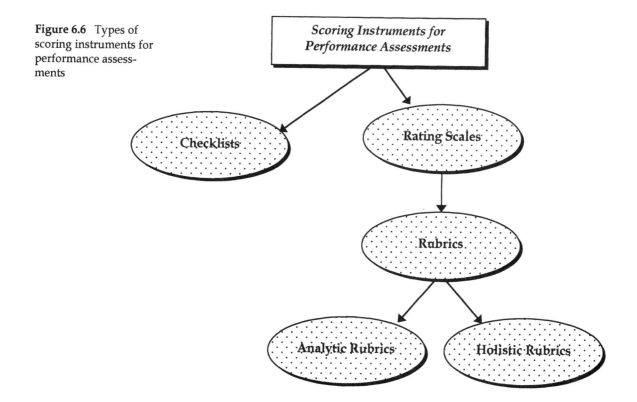

Holistic rubrics are customarily utilized when errors in some part of the process can be tolerated, provided the overall quality is high (Chase, 1999). Nitko (2001) further states that use of holistic rubrics is probably more appropriate when performance tasks require students to create responses when there is no definitive correct answer. The focus of a score reported using a holistic rubric is on the overall quality, proficiency, or understanding of the specific content and skills; it involves assessment on a unidimensional level (Mertler, 2001a). Using holistic rubrics can result in a somewhat quicker scoring process than when using an analytic rubric (Nitko, 2001). This is basically be-

cause the teacher is required to read through or otherwise examine the student product or performance only once in order to get an "overall" sense of what the student was able to accomplish (Mertler, 2001a). Since assessment of the overall performance is the key, holistic rubrics are also typically, though not exclusively, used when the purpose of the performance assessment is summative in nature. At most, only limited feedback is provided to the student as a result of scoring performance tasks in this manner. A template for holistic scoring rubrics is presented in Figure 6.7.

Analytic rubrics are usually preferred when a fairly focused type of response is required (Nitko, 2001); that is, performance tasks where there may be one or two acceptable responses, and creativity is not an essential feature of the students' responses. Furthermore, analytic rubrics result initially in several scores, followed by a summed total score: Their use represents assessment on a multidimensional level (Mertler, 2001a). As previously mentioned, the use of analytic rubrics can cause the scoring process to be substantially slower, mainly because assessing several different skills or characteristics individually requires a teacher to examine the product several times. Both their construction and use can be quite time consuming. A general rule of thumb is that a

student's work should be examined a separate time for *each* of the specific performance tasks or scoring criteria (Mertler, 2001a). However, the advantage to the use of analytic rubrics is quite substantial. The degree of feedback offered to students—and to teachers—is significant. Students receive specific feedback on their performance with respect to each of the individual scoring criteria—something that does not happen when using holistic rubrics (Nitko, 2001). It is possible to then create a "profile" of specific student strengths and weaknesses (Mertler, 2001a). A template for analytic scoring rubrics is presented in Figure 6.8.

Figure 6.7 Template for holistic scoring rubrics

Template for Holistic Scoring Rubrics

Score	Description
5	Demonstrates complete understanding of the problem. All requirements of task are included in response.
4	Demonstrates considerable understanding of the problem. All requirements of task are included.
3	Demonstrates partial understanding of the problem. Most requirements of task are included.
2	Demonstrates little understanding of the problem. Many requirements of task are missing.
1	Demonstrates no understanding of the problem.
0	No response/task not attempted.

Figure 6.8 Template for analytic scoring rubrics

	Beginning 1	Developing 2	Accomplished 3	Exemplary 4	Score
Criteria #1	Description reflecting beginning level of performance	Description reflecting movement toward mastery level of performance	Description reflecting achievement of mastery level of performance	Description reflecting highest level of performance	
Criteria #2	Description reflecting beginning level of performance	Description reflecting movement toward mastery level of performance	Description reflecting achievement of mastery level of performance	Description reflecting highest level of performance	
Criteria #3	Description reflecting beginning level of performance	Description reflecting movement toward mastery level of performance	Description reflecting achievement of mastery level of performance	Description reflecting highest level of performance	
Criteria #4	Description reflecting beginning level of performance	Description reflecting movement toward mastery level of performance	Description reflecting achievement of mastery level of performance	Description reflecting highest level of performance	

Template for Analytic Scoring Rubrics

Total Score = _____

Prior to designing a specific rubric, a teacher must decide whether the performance or product will be scored holistically or analytically (Airasian, 2000 & 2001). Regardless of which type of rubric is selected, specific performance criteria and observable indicators must be identified as an initial step to development. The decision regarding the use of a holistic or analytic approach to scoring has several possible implications. The most important of these is that teachers must first consider how they intend to use the results. If an overall, summative score is desired, a holistic scoring approach would be more desirable. In contrast, if formative feedback is the goal, an analytic scoring rubric should be used. It is important to note that one type of rubric is not inherently better than the other; you must find a format that works best for you (Montgomery, 2001). Other implications include the time requirements, the nature of the task itself, and the specific performance criteria being observed.

As you saw demonstrated in the templates (Figures 6.7 and 6.8), the various levels of student performance can be defined using either quantitative (i.e., numerical) or qualitative (i.e., descriptive) labels. In some instances, teachers might want to utilize both quantitative and qualitative labels. If a rubric contains four levels of proficiency or understanding on a continuum, quantitative labels would typically range from "1" to "4." When using qualitative labels, teachers have much more flexibility, and can be more creative. A common type of qualitative scale might include the following labels: master, expert, apprentice, and novice. Nearly any type of qualitative scale will suffice, provided it "fits" with the task. The following list offers several suggestions for qualitative descriptors (Stix, 1996).

Lowest ⟵⟶ Highest			
Novice	Apprentice	Proficient	Master
Attempted	Acceptable	Admirable	Awesome
Lead	Bronze	Silver	Gold
Amateur	Semi-Pro	Professional	Hall of Fame
Byte	Kilobyte	Megabyte	Gigabyte
Minnow	Goldfish	Tuna	Shark

One potentially frustrating aspect of scoring student work with rubrics is the issue of somehow converting them to "grades." It is not a good idea to think of rubrics in terms of percentages (Trice, 2000). For example, if a rubric has six levels (or "points"), a score of 3 should not be equated to 50% (an "F" in most letter grading systems). The process of converting rubric scores to grades or categories is more a process of logic than it is a mathematical one. Trice (2000) suggests that in a rubric scoring system, there are typically more scores at the average and above-average categories (i.e., equating to grades of "C" or better) than there are at below-average categories. For instance, if a rubric consisted of nine score categories, the equivalent grades and categories might look like this:

Rubric Score	Grade	Category
8	A+	Excellent
7	A	Excellent
6	B+	Good
5	B	Good
4	C+	Fair
3	C	Fair
2	U	Unsatisfactory
1	U	Unsatisfactory
0	U	Unsatisfactory

When converting rubric scores to grades (typical at the secondary level) or descriptive feedback (more typical at the elementary level), it is important to remember that there is not necessarily a correct way to accomplish this. The bottom line for classroom teachers is that they must find a system of conversion that works for them and fits comfortably into their individual system of reporting student performance.

Steps in the Design of Scoring Rubrics

Similarly to the steps used in the design of performance tasks, a step-by-step process for designing rubrics is presented below. Information for these procedures was also compiled from various sources (Airasian, 2000 & 2001; Mertler, 2001a; Montgomery, 2001; Nitko, 2001; Tombari & Borich, 1999). The steps will be discussed and summarized (see Figure 6.9), followed by presentations of rubrics corresponding to the two sample performance tasks developed earlier.

Step 1: *Reexamine the learning objectives to be addressed by the task. This allows you to match your scoring guide with your objectives and instruction.*

Step 2: *Identify specific observable attributes that you want to see (as well as those you don't want to see) your students demonstrate in their product, process, or performance. Specify the characteristics, skills, or behaviors you will be looking for, as well as common mistakes you do not want to see.*

Step 3: *Brainstorm characteristics that describe each attribute. Identify ways to describe above-average, average, and below-average per-*

formance for each observable attribute identified in Step 2.

Step 4a: *For holistic rubrics, write thorough narrative descriptions for excellent work and poor work incorporating each attribute into the description. Describe the highest and lowest levels of performance combining the descriptors for all attributes.*

Step 4b: *For analytic rubrics, write thorough narrative descriptions for excellent work and poor work for each individual attribute. Describe the highest and lowest levels of performance using the descriptors for each attribute separately.*

Step 5a: *For holistic rubrics, complete the rubric by describing other levels on the continuum that range from excellent to poor work for the collective attributes. Write descriptions for all intermediate levels of performance.*

Step 5b: *For analytic rubrics, complete the rubric by describing other levels on the continuum that range from excellent to poor work for each attribute. Write descriptions for all intermediate levels of performance for each attribute separately.*

Step 6: *Collect samples of student work that exemplify each level. These will help you score in the future by serving as benchmarks.*

Step 7: *Revise the rubric, as necessary. Be prepared to reflect on the effectiveness of the rubric and revise it prior to its next use.*

Figure 6.9 Step-by-step procedure for the design of performance assessment scoring rubrics

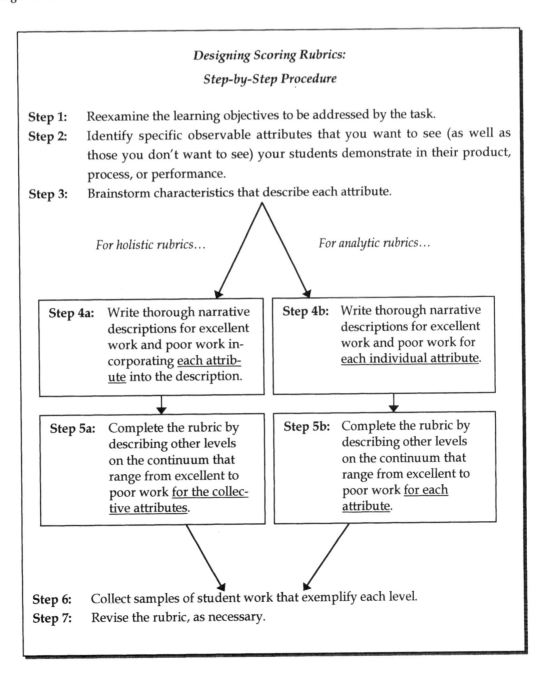

Designing Scoring Rubrics:

Step-by-Step Procedure

Step 1:   Reexamine the learning objectives to be addressed by the task.

Step 2:   Identify specific observable attributes that you want to see (as well as those you don't want to see) your students demonstrate in their product, process, or performance.

Step 3:   Brainstorm characteristics that describe each attribute.

For holistic rubrics...   *For analytic rubrics...*

Step 4a: Write thorough narrative descriptions for excellent work and poor work incorporating <u>each attribute</u> into the description.

Step 4b: Write thorough narrative descriptions for excellent work and poor work for <u>each individual attribute</u>.

Step 5a: Complete the rubric by describing other levels on the continuum that range from excellent to poor work <u>for the collective attributes</u>.

Step 5b: Complete the rubric by describing other levels on the continuum that range from excellent to poor work <u>for each attribute</u>.

Step 6:   Collect samples of student work that exemplify each level.

Step 7:   Revise the rubric, as necessary.

Two Examples

Two sample scoring rubrics for the performance assessment tasks we developed earlier are presented next. Brief discussions precede the actual rubrics. For illustrative purposes, a holistic rubric is presented for the first task and an analytic rubric for the second. It should be noted that either a holistic or analytic rubric could have been designed for either task.

Example 1:
Subject — Mathematics
Grade Level(s) — Upper Elementary

Recall that Mr. Harris is planning a unit, focusing on the skills of estimation and interpretation of graphs. He wants to assess the following instructional objectives:

- Students will properly interpret a bar graph.

- Students will accurately estimate values from within a bar graph. (*Step 1*)

Since the purpose of his performance task is summative in nature, he decides to develop a holistic rubric. He identifies the following four attributes on which to focus his rubric: estimation, mathematical computation, conclusions, and communication of explanations (*Steps 2 and 3*). Finally, he begins drafting descriptions of the various levels of performance for the observable attributes (*Steps 4 and 5*).

The final rubric for this task appears in Figure 6.10.

Figure 6.10 Sample holistic rubric for example task #1

Math Performance Task – Scoring Rubric
Data Analysis

Name _____   Date _____

Score	Description
4	Makes accurate estimations. Uses appropriate mathematical operations with no mistakes. Draws logical conclusions supported by graph. Sound explanations of thinking.
3	Makes good estimations. Uses appropriate mathematical operations with few mistakes. Draws logical conclusions supported by graph. Good explanations of thinking.
2	Attempts estimations, although many inaccurate. Uses inappropriate mathematical operations, but with no mistakes. Draws conclusions not supported by graph. Offers little explanation.
1	Makes inaccurate estimations. Uses inappropriate mathematical operations. Draws no conclusions related to graph. Offers no explanations of thinking.
0	No response/task not attempted.

Example 2:
Subjects — Social Studies;
Probability and Statistics
Grade Level(s) — 9 - 12

Recall that Ms. Wolfe is beginning a unit on the electoral process and wants to be able to assess her students on the following instructional objectives:

- Students will collect data using appropriate methods.

- Students will accurately analyze and summarize their data.

- Students will effectively communicate their results. (*Step 1*)

Since the purpose of this performance task is formative, she decides to develop an analytic rubric focusing on the following attributes: sampling technique, data collection, statistical analyses, and communication of results (*Steps 2* and *3*). She drafts descriptions of the various levels of performance for the observable attributes (*Steps 4* and *5*).

The final rubric for this task appears in Figure 6.11.

Figure 6.11 Sample analytic rubric for example task #2

Performance Task – Scoring Rubric
Population Sampling

Name _____   Date _____

	Beginning 1	Developing 2	Accomplished 3	Exemplary 4	Score
Sampling Technique	Inappropriate sampling technique used	Appropriate technique used to select sample; major errors in execution	Appropriate technique used to select sample; minor errors in execution	Appropriate technique used to select sample; no errors in procedures	
Survey/ Interview Questions	Inappropriate questions asked to gather needed information	Few pertinent questions asked; data on sample is inadequate	Most pertinent questions asked; data on sample is adequate	All pertinent questions asked; data on sample is complete	
Statistical Analyses	No attempt at summarizing collected data	Attempts analysis of data, but inappropriate procedures	Proper analytical procedures used, but analysis incomplete	All proper analytical procedures used to summarize data	
Communication of Results	Communication of results is incomplete, unorganized, and difficult to follow	Communicates some important information; not organized well enough to support decision	Communicates most of important information; shows support for decision	Communication of results is very thorough; shows insight into how data predicted outcome	

Total Score = _____

VALIDITY AND RELIABILITY OF PERFORMANCE-BASED ASSESSMENTS

If properly constructed, performance assessments can *appear* to have a great deal of comparability with instructional objectives and outcomes. However important face evidence (i.e., "on the surface" appearance) might be, it is not enough to ensure content and criterion evidence of assessment validity (Gallagher, 1998).

Since performance tasks are typically more open-ended, teachers must instruct students on the desired performances or products and share with them the criteria that will be used to judge their work (Airasian, 2000 & 2001). This is sometimes difficult to accomplish since teachers want to avoid providing too much guidance during the course of a performance assessment. However, by not providing some degree of initial guidance, students may spend a great deal of time and effort developing a product or performance that does not capture the desired behaviors, characteristics, or skills. This situation would most likely lead to invalid decisions about student performance.

Furthermore, teachers must ensure that an individual student's performance is not task specific (Gallagher, 1998). In other words, does the student perform at a high level simply as an outgrowth of the task itself (e.g., a mock job interview in a classroom)? In a different situation or setting (e.g., in a real job interview), would the same student also be able to perform at that particular level? If the answer to the second question is "no," drawing broad conclusions based on the limited demonstration of skills might lead to inaccurate decisions.

When performance tasks require students to use complex thinking skills, there is also the issue of prerequisite skills (Gredler, 1999). In order for the results of a performance assessment to be valid, students must possess the necessary prerequisite knowledge and skills. Many performance tasks, even in mathematics for example, require a great deal of reading and writing. If a particular student performs poorly on a math task, the teacher might conclude that the student is incapable of performing the specific mathematical skills. In actuality, the student may have performed poorly because of an inability to read and comprehend the directions or to effectively develop a written response.

Teachers must also be sure that performance tasks are fair for all students (Gallagher, 1998; Gredler, 1999). If a performance assessment task requires the use of specific equipment or resources, those items must be made available to all students. For example, if students are required to complete a task outside of class, and to do so using the Internet, teachers need to make sure that all students have access to the Internet via a personal computer at home.

There are also important issues related to the reliability of performance assessments. The main concern centers around the fact that even with well-constructed scoring rubrics, many subjective judgments must be made by teachers when scoring responses to performance tasks (Gallagher, 1998). The specific steps for the design of tasks and scoring rubrics presented earlier in this chapter should help ensure a reasonable degree of reliability in classroom performance assessments.

Similarly, the reliability of teacher ratings can be adversely affected by personal bias (Airasian, 2000 & 2001). For example, teachers' scores of written responses in social studies might be affected by sloppy penmanship or misspelled words. Expectations of this type will again lead to scores that are not consistent with students' actual levels of understanding or performance. It is difficult for teachers to be completely unbiased, but with experience, teachers can learn to focus their judgments on the specific outcomes of interest and not miscellaneous distracting factors.

ADVANTAGES AND LIMITATIONS OF PERFORMANCE-BASED ASSESSMENTS

Performance assessments have several distinct advantages over other types of assessments. First and foremost, performance tasks assess students' abilities "to do" as opposed to "knowing how to do" (Nitko, 2001). In performance assessments, knowledge must be applied and skills demonstrated by students. Typically, performance tasks—especially those that are more complex and span a longer period of time—go a step further by requiring students to integrate knowledge,

behaviors, and skills (Nitko, 2001). These types of assessment tasks create much more meaningful learning experiences for students. Additionally, since they require application of knowledge and skills, they more appropriately mirror real-life situations.

In many cases, performance tasks can assess skills that cannot be assessed through the use of more traditional written tests, specifically higher-order thinking skills, such as analysis, synthesis, and evaluation (Gallagher, 1998; Oosterhof, 1999 & 2001). Performance tasks offer students and teachers a variety of ways to express learning, as opposed to the simple correct or incorrect response to a written question (Nitko, 2001).

Another advantage of performance assessments over written tests is that they allow teachers to assess thinking processes as well as final student products (Nitko, 2001; Oosterhof, 1999 & 2001). If students answer a written test item incorrectly, teachers often are unsure of the steps used to arrive at an incorrect answer since, typically, only the final answer is provided by the student and scored by the teacher.

Finally, performance assessments can be used to improve instructional practice (Gallagher, 1998; Oosterhof, 1999 & 2001). Since performance assessments are usually scored according to gradations of quality, proficiency, or understanding, results from these assessments can provide substantial feedback regarding weaknesses in student comprehension that may require revisions to the instruction delivered. This is an extremely beneficial way in which the results of performance assessments can be utilized in an informal manner.

There are, of course, limitations to the use of performance assessments in K–12 classrooms. The main limitation to their use is arguably the time requirements (Gallagher, 1998; Nitko, 2001; Oosterhof, 1999 & 2001). Creating high-quality tasks and rubrics is extremely time consuming, not to mention difficult. Furthermore, completing performance tasks takes students a good deal of time. Many performance tasks span several weeks; even shorter tasks may take students 30–60 minutes to complete. Additionally, as you saw in the discussion of rubrics earlier, scoring products and performances, especially those resulting from complex tasks, is very time intensive. Using holistic instead of analytic scoring is a means by which the time factor may be reduced.

A related limitation is that performance assessment tasks are extremely inefficient when used to assess lower-level thinking skills, such as knowledge and comprehension (Gallagher, 1998). Student outcomes at these levels are much more appropriately assessed through the use of written tests.

Due to the subjectivity involved in scoring performance tasks, the reliability of these scores tends to be lower than scores resulting from more traditional forms of assessment (Gallagher, 1998; Nitko, 2001). Also, these scores are subject to greater degrees of teacher bias and expectations than assessments scored more objectively (Oosterhof, 1999 & 2001).

Finally, due to the open-ended nature of performance tasks and the fact that they are designed to encourage creativity, students of lower ability levels may experience higher levels of frustration and discouragement than others (Nitko, 2001). This may be due in part to less ability to apply higher-order thinking skills and the necessary requirement that students must sustain their interest levels over long periods of time, especially with more complex tasks. Permitting students to work in groups may reduce the effects of or alleviate this obstacle.

SUMMARY

Performance assessments present students with some performance-based activity or task that students must complete. Performance assessments consist of two components: a performance task and a rubric scoring, or other type of scoring guide. These assessments permit the direct observation of students engaged in the application of actual skills and behaviors. Performance assessments are also a type of authentic assessment, in that they should be designed to mirror real-life events and situations. They can be used for both formative and summative decisions.

The basic requirements for performance assessments include the matching of the assessment task to appropriate instructional objectives and the identification of specific behaviors or skills to be observed. The task should be designed to permit student work to be assessed along a continuum of understanding and may include assessment of products, processes, or both. Finally, performance assessments should encourage student reflection on their own thinking skills and processes.

When developing performance tasks, it is important that the task has a clear purpose, identifies observable aspects of the product or performance (i.e., the performance criteria), provides a meaningful setting for its completion, and results in one or more scores that describe a student's performance. If selecting a performance task from an existing resource, care must be taken to ensure that the task is aligned with your objectives, instruction, and plan for assessment. The step-by-step process for designing performance tasks was presented in Figure 6.3.

Student products or performances can be scored with checklists or, more commonly, with rating scales, typically referred to as rubrics. Holistic rubrics result in a single overall score and are effectively used for summative decisions. Analytic rubrics result in several scores, as well as a total summed score. They are most appropriately used to provide formative feedback to students.

Invalid decisions about student performance can result from the use of per-formance tasks when a lack of guidance is provided by teachers and if students need but are not provided with any necessary prerequisite skills. Reliability in the resulting scores can be adversely affected by personal bias and expectations on the part of teachers.

Advantages of performance assessments include the ability to assess students' abilities to *actually* perform a task or produce something tangible, as opposed to simply knowing *how* to accomplish it. Higher-order thinking skills can efficiently be assessed through the use of performance tasks. Finally, performance assessments can provide teachers and students with substantial formative feedback.

Limitations of performance assessments include the significant amount of time required to develop, administer, and score the results of performance tasks. This time factor also limits the use of performance assessment in efficiently assessing lower-level thinking skills, which may be more appropriately assessed using other forms of assessment. The subjectivity involved in the scoring process can result in lower reliability. Finally, care must be taken when using performance assessments with lower ability level students, in order to ensure that they do not experience an inordinate amount of frustration and discouragement.

✍ **Chapter 6 *Related Web Sites* 💻**

❖ **Implementing Performance Assessment in the Classroom**
(*www.ericae.net/pare/getvn.asp?v=6&n=2*)
This brief article appears in *Practical Assessment, Research, & Evaluation,* a peer-reviewed electronic journal, and is authored by Amy C. Buraldi. She provides information on defining the purpose of the assessment, choosing an appropriate activity, defining performance criteria, and developing scoring rubrics.

❖ **Scoring Rubrics: What, When, & How?** (*www.ericae.net/pare/getvn.asp?v=7&n=3*)
This article also appears in *Practical Assessment, Research, & Evaluation* and is authored by Barbara M. Moskal. The article discusses what rubrics are, and distinguishes between holistic and analytic types. Examples and additional resources are provided.

❖ **A Process for Designing Performance Assessment Tasks**
(*www.pgcps.pg.k12.md.us/~elc/designsteps.html*)
Staff in the Prince George's County (MD) Public Schools have developed this page that provides a very informative description of the steps involved in the design of performance tasks. This page provides an overview of the steps and includes links provided to more detailed information and discussions, including a page
(*www.pgcps.pg.k12.md.us/~elc/scoringtasks.html*) that provides rubric samples.

❖ **Performance Assessments Index**
(*www.pattonville.k12.mo.us/services/showme_assessment/gradelevel.html*)
Faculty and staff in the Pattonville (MO) School District have collected samples of performance tasks, including rubrics, and categorized them by grade level.

❖ **Performance Assessments Tasks Table of Contents**
(*www.arlingtonschools.org/Curriculum/Assessment/mathassess.html*)
The Arlington (NY) Central School District maintains this page with samples of mathematics performance tasks in grades K through 8.

❖ **Rubrics from the Staff Room for Ontario Teachers**
(*www.odyssey.on.ca/~elaine.coxon/rubrics.htm*)
This site is a collection of literally hundreds of teacher-developed rubrics for scoring performance tasks. The rubrics are categorized by subject area and type of task. This is a fantastic resource...check it out!

❖ **Rubistar Rubric Generator** (*rubistar.4teachers.org/*) and
Teacher Rubric Maker (*www.teach-nology.com/web_tools/rubrics/*)
These two sites house Web-based rubric generators for teachers. Teachers can customize their own rubrics based on templates on the site. In both cases, rubric templates are organized by subject area and/or type of performance task. These are very informative resources for teachers!

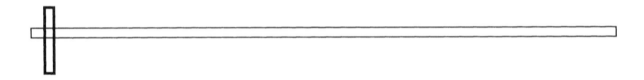

QUESTIONS FOR REVIEW

1. Following the completion of a health lesson, a middle-school teacher wants to determine the extent to which her class understands the definition of "hygiene." Would a performance assessment be appropriate in this case? Why or why not?

2. Explain what is meant by a "direct observation." How is it different from an "indirect observation"?

3. Describe the relationships between the following terms: alternative assessment, authentic assessment, and performance assessment.

4. In what ways can teachers encourage students to reflect on their performance or product resulting from a performance assessment?

5. Explain what is meant by the term "performance criteria."

6. In Example #1 presented in this chapter, Mr. Harris decides to use a holistic rubric to score his students' responses about graph interpretation and estimation. Could he have used an analytic rubric? Why or why not?

7. Compare and contrast holistic and analytic rubrics. What similarities and differences exist?

8. An elementary teacher wishes to develop "student profiles" for her students' academic performances in various subject areas. To accomplish this, she knows that she will need to design and implement several performance assessments throughout the year. What type of scoring instrument should she use and why?

9. Describe ways in which teachers might improve the reliability of their rubric scores for performance assessments.

10. What are the relative advantages of performance assessments over traditional pencil-and-paper tests?

ENRICHMENT ACTIVITIES

1. In a paragraph or two, describe content for a lesson or unit that you would like to teach someday. Identify skills or capabilities that you could appropriately assess using a performance assessment and consider how you might do so. Discuss your responses in small groups.

2. Identify two or three specific instructional objectives from content you would like to teach someday. Describe a performance assessment task that could be implemented as

a means of assessing those objectives. Using the steps outlined in the chapter, design a *holistic* rubric to be used with the task. Share your rubrics in small groups.

3. For the same content, objectives, and performance task you identified in Activity 2 above, design an *analytic* rubric to be used with the task. Would you prefer to use the holistic or analytic version of the rubric? Why? Share your responses—as well as any issues raised—in small groups.

Chapter 7

Portfolio Assessments

Overview of Chapter 7

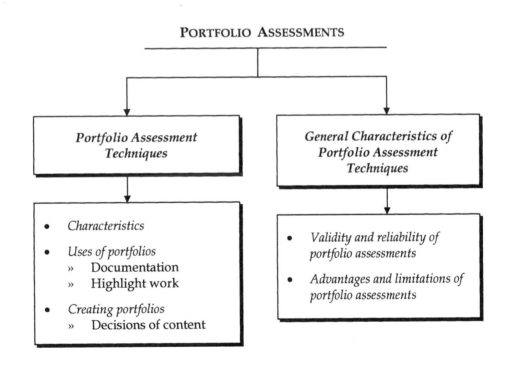

PORTFOLIO ASSESSMENTS

Portfolio Assessment Techniques

- *Characteristics*
- *Uses of portfolios*
  - » Documentation
  - » Highlight work
- *Creating portfolios*
  - » Decisions of content

General Characteristics of Portfolio Assessment Techniques

- *Validity and reliability of portfolio assessments*
- *Advantages and limitations of portfolio assessments*

INTRODUCTION

This chapter presents the third, and final, category of alternative assessment techniques. *Portfolio assessments* are substantially different from what we have examined up to this point. In contrast to the idea of observing a single event, product, or series of related skills, portfolio assessments require the accumulation of evidence over an extended period of time. There are, of course, both advantages and limitations to the use of portfolio assessments within classroom settings. However, many subject areas or specific classroom settings view assessment of students' portfolios as having a different focus compared to the previous forms of assessment we have examined. As you will soon see, portfolio assessments offer unique purpose and perspective in these situations.

CHARACTERISTICS OF PORTFOLIO ASSESSMENTS

Since the early 1990s, the use of portfolios has become increasingly popular among classroom teachers. The reason may be due in part to the fact that many teachers believe that portfolio assessment is the one strategy that "does it all"—it engages students in content learning, helps students become reflective learners, documents student learning, and facilitates communication with parents (Danielson & Abrutyn, 1997a).

Portfolio assessment can be described as a method of alternative assessment that allows teachers and students to assemble

purposeful evidence of student abilities and skills over an extended period of time. A formal definition for **portfolio assessment** is a purposeful, organized collection of student work that can be used to describe students' efforts, progress, or achievement in a subject area (Airasian, 2000 & 2001; Danielson & Abrutyn, 1997a; Johnson & Johnson, 2002). The idea of an academic portfolio is derived from an artist's or writer's portfolio, designed to showcase his or her creativity and style (Airasian, 2000 & 2001; Gallagher, 1998). Portfolios may be used to document a student's work over a brief period of time (e.g., during an instructional unit or course) or to reflect work in a specific discipline over several years (Tanner, 2001).

Portfolios provide a means for students to show what they can really do (Tombari & Borich, 1999). For this reason, portfolio assessment is considered to be based in the "real world"; that is, it mirrors real-world circumstances. Hence, it is another example of authentic assessment (Montgomery, 2001). For years, professions such as architecture, advertising, art, photography, journalism, creative writing, music, and acting have relied on the compilation of portfolios to demonstrate and showcase their work for prospective clients or employers (Montgomery, 2001; Oosterhof, 1999 & 2001). In classrooms, portfolios serve a very similar purpose. Samples of student performances or products are compiled in an effort to show a student's accomplishments or improvements over time (Airasian, 2000 &

2001). Portfolios serve as tangible evidence for showing teachers, parents, administrators—as well as the students themselves—what students know and can actually do (Tombari & Borich, 1999).

It is important to note that portfolios are not simply composed of random work samples, nor are they collections of every performance or product (Airasian, 2000 & 2001). Successful portfolio assessment begins with the *purposeful* collection of student work representing products, processes, or progress in one or more areas (Montgomery, 2001). They may include examples of a student's best work or benchmarks that demonstrate a student's progress over time. Several features of student portfolios differentiate them from simple work sample folders (Montgomery, 2001, p. 78). These include the following:

- Students must be included in the process of selecting work to be included in the portfolio.
- Specific criteria for the selection of work to be included must be identified.
- Specific criteria for judging the value of the work must be developed.
- There must be evidence of student reflection in the portfolio process.

Note that an essential characteristic of portfolio assessment is the direct involvement of individual students in the process. Student ownership is key to the success of a portfolio assessment system (Oosterhof, 1999 & 2001). Typically, teachers provide guidelines (i.e., the selection

criteria) and then work collaboratively with the individual student to identify specific goals of the portfolio and the types of work samples to be contained in the portfolio. The student is then responsible for actually selecting the materials for inclusion. By approaching the portfolio in this manner, it provides evidence that the student is able to pursue academic work over an extended period of time and can implement standards of excellence, based on the preestablished criteria (Gredler, 1999).

Since the student has ownership of the portfolio, both the teacher and student have continuous access to its contents (Oosterhof, 1999 & 2001). The portfolio typically remains in the classroom, but the student may examine it whenever time permits. The portfolio may be shared with whomever the student wishes, including other students or teachers. This concept of an "open system of assessment" is a stark contrast to the historically private grade book maintained by the classroom teacher. This is the main reason that portfolio assessments are seen as being more student centered as opposed to teacher centered (Oosterhof, 1999 & 2001).

Building on this notion of student-centered assessment, portfolios can also be easily adapted to meet individualized instructional needs (Oosterhof, 1999 & 2001). Teachers work collaboratively with individual students on *each* student's own portfolio. Theoretically, each student could select an entirely unique set of work samples for inclusion in the portfolio, depending on the instructional goals for that individual student. This is a unique feature of portfolio assessment that separates it from traditional written tests or even performance assessments. With both written tests and performance assessments, there is typically a common set of test questions or a common performance task that is administered to every student in a class. It would not be logistically feasible—or, at least, would be extremely difficult and time consuming—to customize written tests or performance tasks to meet the unique needs of every student.

One of the most important characteristics and contributions of portfolio assessment is the inclusion of a student self-evaluation component (Airasian, 2000 & 2001). These student reflections provide students with opportunities to think about how they think—to reflect on ways in which they successfully learn and increase their understanding, as well as to reflect on ways in which they fail to learn (Montgomery, 2001). As a result, students take the initiative to assess their own progress and to revise their work in order to achieve some standard. Incorporating student reflections into the portfolio assessment process engages students in the very important process of self-assessment (Montgomery, 2001).

The idea of student reflection is one to which students are not accustomed (Airasian, 2000 & 2001). Typically, after submitting one day's assignments, papers, and performances, the student is forced to move on to the next day's work. The pre-

vious day's assignments are discarded—at least figuratively, if not literally (Airasian, 2000 & 2001). Students can experience a great deal of growth by taking the time to critically think about and compare their work over time. Students are actually able to see their own improvement in order to help them determine what resulted in the most effective learning.

Portfolio assessment is seen by many as one of the best methods to show both the methods and thinking used by a student—that is, the processes—as well as the student's final level of achievement—that is, the products (Airasian, 2000 & 2001; Oosterhof, 1999 & 2001; Tombari & Borich, 1999). Portfolios can show the completed paper, final sculpture, or finished project, but can also document the steps taken by the student that led up to the final product. These steps might comprise rough drafts, early sketches, or pilot studies. By including—and, ultimately, examining and assessing—these steps in the portfolio, the audience (e.g., teachers, parents, and administrators) has a much better sense of the student's effort, reflection, growth, and final mastery of the learning criteria (Tombari & Borich, 1999).

The general focus of portfolios is another way that this form of assessment differs from more traditional forms of assessment. Written tests and other types of formal assessments tend to focus on students' mistakes, as opposed to their achievements and proficiency (Oosterhof,

1999 & 2001). Although not always the case, marks made by teachers on written tests usually identify errors made by students and scores posted at the top of the paper typically indicate the number of questions missed. Discussions following the test often focus on questions that students answered incorrectly, instead of reviewing information and concepts of which students demonstrated understanding. Even standardized achievement tests—as you will later see in Chapter 11—tend to emphasize the negatives of student performance. Some standardized tests report results by identifying skill areas in which a student is deficient. Other types of tests report results by indicating the areas in which the student performed below average.

In contrast, portfolios accentuate student strengths. Students are encouraged to select for inclusion examples of their best work. Student reflections and discussions with the teacher focus on the strengths exhibited by the student, and not what the student was not able to demonstrate in the selected works. If student deficiencies are observed, they are not the focal point of discussions or reflections. They are, however, utilized in that they serve as the stimulus for new goals to be mastered and illustrated by future samples of work (Oosterhof, 1999 & 2001).

It is important to note another characteristic of portfolio assessment. Using portfolios as a basis for assessment of student performance can be a time-consuming endeavor. In contrast to what many believe, the preparation of the actual portfolio does not require much additional time, since most of the material included in a portfolio would be produced anyway as a normal component of student work in a class or subject (Oosterhof, 1999 & 2001). The review aspect of the process of portfolio assessment is time consuming. At periodic, scheduled intervals, teachers must review students' portfolios and meet individually with students to discuss the contents and their relation to the students' individual goals. Oosterhof (1999 & 2001) states that this review and discussion portion of the process can take up to one hour per student. The amount of time associated with the use of portfolios is dependent on the frequency with which the teacher reviews the portfolios with individual students. Frequent reviews—approximately four to six weeks—are preferable; however, the time requirements must be anticipated in relation to the other responsibilities held by teachers. Based on a class size of 30 students, elementary teachers might expect to spend approximately 30 hours for each session of portfolio review; whereas, secondary teachers would probably need a substantially greater period of time to complete their reviews. This fact tends to be a major reason why portfolio assessments are not widely used; many teachers believe that it is an inefficient use of time.

The characteristics of this type of alternative assessment can be summarized by highlighting the three main features of any form of portfolio assessment. As outlined by Airasian (2000 & 2001) and Gallagher (1998), in order for a collection of student work to be classified as a portfolio, these three features must be included:

- The collection of student work must have a specific purpose.
- Students must be actively involved in the process of selecting work to be included in the portfolio.
- Students must actively engage in self-reflection.

USES OF PORTFOLIOS

Since their inception and inclusion into classroom settings, portfolios have been implemented in a variety of ways. Due to the different uses of portfolios, educators have developed different types in order to meet specific needs or goals. However, all the various uses and types are based on a common, generic template. Gredler (1999) refers to this common template as the "ideal format." This "ideal" portfolio format is designed to meet two major objectives. The first of these is that the portfolio should model personal responsibility in reflecting on one's own work. The second objective is to document student growth and development over time. This format essentially results in a working document where portfolio entries are added and removed throughout the year as the student experiences growth and insight about the content, as well as his or her own learning.

The "ideal" format consists of three main components (Gredler, 1999). These are:

- *Documentation of the development of major works.* For any large-scale project, evidence of the process undertaken by the student should be included. This evidence might include notes, drafts, revisions, and diagrams, as well as the final version of the project. This type of evidence serves as an indicator of the depth of the student's work.
- *Evidence of the range of student work.* Different types of student work samples should be included in the portfolio. This informs the teacher of the student's abilities over a wide range of academic skills. This evidence serves as an indicator of the breadth of the student's work.
- *Student reflections.* Of course, no portfolio is complete without the inclusion of written self-reflections and self-analyses of the student's own work.

Note the similarities between the main features of portfolios, as discussed earlier in this chapter, and the main components of the "ideal" portfolio. This parallel can be seen in Figure 7.1.

Several variations of this "ideal" format for portfolio development have been cited in the literature. However, there are two main types—or uses—of portfolios: those used to document student work and those used to highlight student work.

Figure 7.1 Similarities between main portfolio characteristics and components of "ideal" portfolio format

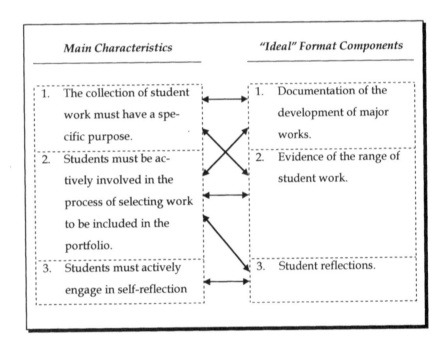

Main Characteristics	**"Ideal" Format Components**
1. The collection of student work must have a specific purpose.	1. Documentation of the development of major works.
2. Students must be actively involved in the process of selecting work to be included in the portfolio.	2. Evidence of the range of student work.
3. Students must actively engage in self-reflection	3. Student reflections.

Documentation Portfolios

Documentation portfolios, also known as "assessment portfolios" (Danielson & Abrutyn, 1997b), "growth portfolios" (Nitko, 2001; Rolheiser, Bower, & Stevahn, 2000), and "progress portfolios" (Montgomery, 2001), represent a very common use for portfolios in classroom settings. The main purpose of a **documentation portfolio** is to provide an ongoing record of student progress (Gredler, 1999). The emphasis of this type of portfolio is on the accumulation of evidence in one or all of the following areas: effort, progress, or achievement. Since effort and progress are more difficult to assess than achievement (and are often seen as nonachievement factors in grading), portfolios are a very

efficient way to assess and document those characteristics.

The documentation portfolio may also include the results of other types of assessments (Gredler, 1999). Teacher checklists, anecdotal records, results of performance assessments, and even the results of written tests may be included. This type of portfolio is not restricted specifically to student products. Its focus is on providing evidence of a *holistic* nature about the individual student's progress and achievements.

Showcase Portfolios

Showcase portfolios, also known as "best work portfolios" (Danielson & Abrutyn, 1997b; Nitko, 2001; Rolheiser, Bower, &

Stevahn, 2000), "display portfolios" (Danielson & Abrutyn, 1997b), and "product portfolios" (Montgomery, 2001), represent the second most common use for classroom portfolios. The main emphasis of a **showcase portfolio** is to highlight and display student accomplishments (Gallagher, 1998; Gredler, 1999).

A showcase portfolio is a collection of the student's best or favorite work, which should be selected primarily by the student (Gredler, 1999). Often, samples selected for inclusion in a showcase portfolio were previously included in a documentation portfolio. Evidence of both product or process may be included in a showcase portfolio (Rolheiser, Bower, & Stevahn, 2000). The real key is that the samples included should demonstrate the student's highest levels of achievement. This tends to foster in students a great sense of pride and accomplishment and provide for them the opportunity to say "Here is what I can do!" (Danielson & Abrutyn, 1997b)

The student self-reflection component is typically a key aspect of this type of portfolio. Since students are responsible for selecting samples of their best work, the reflections often provide insight into *why* an individual student believed them to be the "best" work and, therefore, selected them for inclusion in the portfolio (Rolheiser, Bower, & Stevahn, 2000).

Other Variations

Gredler (1999) describes two additional variations on the "ideal" portfolio format.

These have unique applications that do not typically lend themselves to regular, day-to-day use in the classroom. A *class portfolio* is used as a summary document to illustrate the various achievements of all students in a class, but does not need to include any student reflections. It is primarily used as a reporting mechanism to parents and administrators.

A final variation for portfolio formats is an *evaluation portfolio*. This type of portfolio is used exclusively to report to the general public or to government agencies. Often, school districts participate in state or national reform efforts, curriculum projects, or grant-funded research studies. Evaluation portfolios are used to report to the various sponsoring agencies regarding the effectiveness of the district's academic programs and instructional efforts.

CREATING PORTFOLIOS

There are several issues to be considered and addressed when creating a portfolio assessment system. First and foremost, teachers must be clear about the purpose to be accomplished by the portfolios. This is essentially the equivalent to determining how the portfolio will be used (Nitko, 2001). Since documentation and showcase portfolios have different overall purposes and goals, an initial decision about whether the portfolios will be used to document growth or to show best works is a crucial one. This decision ultimately influences later decisions regarding the selection of specific portfolio entries, the frequency with which they are added and removed, and the criteria used to judge them (Airasian, 2000 & 2001; Gallagher, 1998). Since students have some degree of ownership of the portfolio, it is paramount that they understand its purpose.

As with any type of assessment, and especially with performance-type assessments, the identification of specific criteria that will be used to assess the individual portfolio samples is a critical step in the process. Without specification of the criteria, the assessment of student work cannot be consistent either within or across portfolios (Airasian, 2000 & 2001). Additionally, teachers must ensure that the products or other types of work that make up the portfolio parallel the objectives and actual instruction provided to students. The procedure used to identify the criteria is very similar to that used in the specification of performance criteria to be assessed as a result of performance assessment tasks (see Chapter 6). As you will see below, one reason for the similarity is the fact that checklists and rubrics are also used to judge the works included in a portfolio.

Important decisions, logistical in nature, must also be made by teachers prior to implementing portfolio assessments. These decisions address the broad issue of managing the sheer volume of material that can be accumulated in student portfolios. Portfolios might contain items such as journals, projects, video- and audiotapes, and other work samples, along with scoring rubrics, checklists, and self-reflections (Montgomery, 2001). The key is

trying to find something reasonable in which to store this variety of materials. Possible containers for portfolios include folders (especially the expandable or accordion-style variety), three-ring binders, scrapbooks, shoeboxes, plastic crates, "cubbies" with pull-out bins, filing cabinets, computer disks, and compact disks (Forgette-Giroux & Simon, 2000; Gallagher, 1998; Montgomery, 2001). Ideally, the management system should be individualized; in other words, each individual student should have a separate box, binder, or cubbie. This way, portfolio containers can be personalized by their owners and are accessible only by the teacher and that particular student (Gallagher, 1998).

A further issue related to the management of portfolios centers around the timeframe for portfolio maintenance. Decisions regarding this issue are also largely dependent on the purpose of the portfolio (Rolheiser, Bower, & Stevahn, 2000). For example, if documentation or growth portfolios are being developed, one would likely maintain the same portfolio over the course of an entire year, periodically adding new entries and removing others. If the purpose of the portfolio is to showcase best work, the portfolio may need to be maintained for a grading period or semester. At the end of the respective term, all contents may be removed and the process begins again. Rolheiser, Bower, & Stevahn (2000) suggest that teachers consider their students' relative familiarity with portfolio assessment before determining a specific timeframe. It may be advisable that students with little or no portfolio experience be given a shorter timeframe; whereas, students with substantial experience may be better able to handle long-term portfolios since they are more familiar with the idea of self-directed learning and reflection.

Some students may require assistance with the notion of self-reflection. Since this is a critical part of portfolio assessment, teachers must be prepared to help them along. Questions of a general nature may be posed to students as prompts in order to stimulate them to think about their learning (Nitko, 2001). For example, the following questions might serve as self-reflective prompts:

- What is the process you went through to complete this assignment?
- Where did you get your ideas? How did you revise your thinking as you gathered more information?
- Why did you decide to include this project in your portfolio? What makes it more effective than other things you have completed?
- What are the strengths of your work? What do you think you still need to work on?

Responses to these questions might consist of entries in a journal, responses to a teacher-developed self-assessment rating scale, or in a "student reflection form," as shown in Figure 7.2.

Figure 7.2 Sample student self-reflection form

Student Portfolio Reflection Form [a]

Name: _____   Date Completed: _____

1. I think this is my best work because _____
    _____
    _____.

2. One important thing I learned from completing this project is _____
    _____
    _____.

3. I think my work has improved because _____
    _____
    _____.

4. Some things I still need to improve on are _____
    _____
    _____.

[a] Adapted from Gallagher (1998).

A final issue, albeit an extremely important one, is the scoring of portfolios. Scoring portfolios is very time consuming, as not only the individual entries must be judged, but also the summarized work and self-reflections (Airasian, 2000 & 2001). Additionally, the entries are typically complex performances or products resulting from performance assessments. Specifying performance criteria and developing a concrete scoring guide can certainly facilitate this process. Airasian (2000 & 2001) and Gallagher (1998) suggest that the criteria and scoring guides used for individual entries be different from those used to assess the overall portfolio. For example, individual entries might be judged using a guide similar to an analytic rubric, where the overall portfolio might be judged using a rubric more holistic in nature.

Since students have some ownership in the portfolio process, it is important to include them in the process of identifying performance criteria and developing the specific scoring rubrics (Airasian, 2000 & 2001). This activity reemphasizes to students the important role they play in this particular assessment system. They will also begin to think through the development of the products they will eventually select for inclusion.

A series of steps is presented next in an attempt to guide the development of student portfolios. These steps represent a planning process, as opposed to the actual implementation of a portfolio assessment system. The specific procedure outlined below was compiled from various sources (Gallagher, 1998; Nitko, 2001; Oosterhof, 1999 & 2001; Tombari & Borich, 1999).

Step 1: *Determine the purpose to be served by the portfolio.* Decide if the portfolio will be used primarily to document growth or to showcase best works. As previously mentioned, this is a crucial step, as it influences many of the decisions to follow.

Step 2: *Identify the content, concepts, and skills to be assessed by the portfolio.* As with any form of assessment, the content, concepts, and skills to be assessed should emerge directly from the instructional goals and objectives. Early specification of the subject matter and skills to be assessed helps to reinforce the purpose of the portfolio.

Step 3: *Identify the approach to organization.* At this stage, it is important to identify the particular types of student products and other activities that will permit you to assess the content, concepts, and skills you specified in Step 2. These decisions can be somewhat open-ended, to allow students the flexibility to develop and select their works that meet the criteria, but should establish basic parameters within which they should develop their products. Also important at this stage is the determination of logistical issues. Decisions about how and where the portfolio contents will be stored and maintained should be resolved during this step.

Step 4: *Plan for an efficient review process.* Develop a timeframe for portfolio review and student conferences that fits appropriately with your other responsibilities as a classroom teacher. It is crucial to plan ahead (for the entire school year, if possible) since becoming overwhelmed at any point with portfolio reviews will only make the task more daunting.

Step 5: *Specify how and when students will be involved in the process.* Determine how extensively students will participate in the selection of contents for the portfolio. Additionally, plan if you will involve them in the specification of the contents and/or scoring rubrics.

Step 6: *Develop scoring rubrics.* Analytic or holistic rubrics should be developed based on the overall purpose to be accomplished by the portfolios.

Step 7: *Arrange for multiple reviewers in order to improve reliability.* Although reliability for portfolio reviews is not formally established, having more than one reviewer examine portfolio contents will aid in the facilitation of improved consistency in scores.

Step 8: *Plan for the final conference.* An end-of-term or -year conference gives students an opportunity to examine their overall growth and final achievement. However, you should plan in advance for this time-consuming endeavor.

These steps have been summarized in Figure 7.3.

Figure 7.3 Step-by-step procedure for creating portfolio assessments

---

Creating Portfolios:
Step-by-Step Procedure

Step 1: Determine the purpose to be served by the portfolio.
Step 2: Identify the content, concepts, and skills to be assessed by the portfolio.
Step 3: Identify the approach to organization.
Step 4: Plan for an efficient review process.
Step 5: Specify how and when students will be involved in the process.
Step 6: Develop scoring rubrics.
Step 7: Arrange for multiple reviewers in order to improve reliability.
Step 8: Plan for the final conference.

Decisions on Content

When creating portfolios, one of the most important decisions facing a teacher is who determines the eventual content of the portfolio. Some educators (e.g., Tanner, 2001; Trice, 2000) believe that the primary responsibility for selecting work samples should rest with the teacher, although the student should have some input. The belief is that if portfolios are to be accurate indicators of student learning as evidenced through the specific samples, students may not be the most appropriate judges of those indicators. By handing over the selection process to the student, the teacher has essentially removed all professionalism from the process.

However, most educators (e.g., Chase, 1999; Oosterhof, 1999 & 2001) firmly believe that the more students are responsible for selecting the contents of their portfolios (whether entirely or in collaboration with the teacher), the greater the ownership and pride they experience. It truly becomes a documentation of *their* work. However, in these situations, it is vitally important that the teacher makes clear the specific criteria to be met by the selected work samples. Teaching students how to effectively make their selections is yet another way to help prepare them for life outside school.

Once it has been determined who will be responsible for selecting the samples to go into the portfolio, teachers must also decide what kinds of samples can be included. There really is no limit regarding what can be included in a portfolio; teach-

ers are bound only by the degree of creative thinking represented in their instructional planning (Montgomery, 2001). Portfolios can contain almost anything (Gallagher, 1998; Trice, 2000). However, care must be taken to ensure that there is alignment between the goals and objectives for instruction and the products that will ultimately serve as the basis for assessment. Though, after factoring in those considerations, the list of possible portfolio entries seems limitless. The following is a list of possible entries that teachers may want to consider (Airasian, 2000 & 2001; Montgomery, 2001; Tanner, 2001):

- journals
- letters
- essays and other written reports
- poetry
- maps
- group projects
- inventions
- photographs
- audiotapes and videotapes
- posters
- laboratory reports
- artwork
- written solutions to problems
- quizzes and tests

It is important to remember that processes can also be represented in a portfolio by including both rough and final drafts of written work, artwork, and problem-solving activities (Airasian, 2000 & 2001).

VALIDITY AND RELIABILITY OF PORTFOLIO ASSESSMENTS

Three important concerns exist when trying to establish the validity of portfolios. These are (1) the student capabilities represented by the work samples, (2) the representation of the subject domain by the portfolio samples, and (3) the match between the scoring rubric and the actual samples (Gredler, 1999; Tombari & Borich, 1999). First, the specific student capabilities being represented by the included samples must be determined in advance. It is not good practice to first select work samples for the portfolio and then try to match them to specific skills.

Teachers must also be sure that the work selected for inclusion in the portfolio adequately represents the entire domain of the given subject area. If the samples portray only limited topics and skills within the domain of content knowledge, inaccurate decisions regarding overall student progress and achievement will likely be made by the teacher.

It is important to realize that portfolios will most often comprise a variety of materials, including writing samples, audio recordings, sketches, written reports, and others. When using a rubric to score, or otherwise assess, a portfolio, teachers must ensure that the contents of the scoring rubric appropriately parallel the work included in the portfolio. Otherwise, what is being assessed and the criteria on which it is being assessed will be mismatched.

Reliability of portfolio assessments is typically interpreted as interrater agreement (Gredler, 1999). In other words, it is determined by the consistency with which multiple raters assign scores to the particular work samples. Having multiple raters of your students' portfolios is not always a reasonable feat to accomplish. Other teachers in your school will have responsibilities with their own students; many of those teachers will not have nor want to take the time to assess your students as well. One way that classroom teachers can facilitate this type of assistance in reviewing portfolios is to ask other teachers to review a sample of your students' portfolios. The ratings from those teachers can then be compared to your ratings in an attempt to establish their consistency.

There is actually very little published information about the consistency of portfolio ratings (Oosterhof, 1999 & 2001). Most evidence indicates that the reliability of these ratings tends to be poor. At a minimum, teachers should be exceptionally cautious when relying on portfolios as the sole means of assessing individual student performance.

ADVANTAGES AND LIMITATIONS OF PORTFOLIO ASSESSMENTS

Arguably, the most important advantage of portfolio assessment is the substantial involvement of students in the assessment process (Chase, 1999; Gallagher, 1998; Johnson & Johnson, 2002). This collaborative and participatory form of classroom assessment empowers students by giving them an active role in their own assessment. They have a substantially higher degree of responsibility in terms of directing their own assessment activities (Chase, 1999). Students are typically in control of the activities, projects, and products that are created and refined for inclusion in the portfolio. They are permitted to assess their own learning, determine which items best represent their learning, and establish future goals (Johnson & Johnson, 2002).

Portfolios also show student growth and development over time, as opposed to a single "snapshot" representing one moment in time (Chase, 1999; Gallagher, 1998; Johnson & Johnson, 2002). As products are removed and new (or revised) ones added, teachers and students are able to observe the development of knowledge and skills over time and determine the extent to which they meet the learning goals.

The use of portfolios fosters communication between teachers and students (Chase, 1999). Traditional assessment offers only a one-way flow of assessment feedback—from the teacher to the student. Through the direct involvement of students in the assessment process and the inclusion of the reflective aspect, students also have the opportunity to communicate to teachers about their learning. This continuous flow of information and feedback serves to keep both teachers and students better informed about student progress and achievement.

Additionally, the use of portfolio assessments requires substantial changes in

the assessment roles of both teachers and students (Gredler, 1999). Depending on your perspective, this may be an advantage or a limitation. Portfolios necessitate that the teacher's role change from a dispenser of information—and grades—to a facilitator and guide for student growth and reflection. The concept of collaborative assessment will likely be new to both teachers and students. Students will need guidance with respect to their roles—mainly, the selection of portfolio entries and nature of the self-reflections. Teachers should help students see what each entry says about them and what the entire portfolio indicates about their progress and achievement. Teachers will also need to restructure their classroom instruction and activities to meet this type of assessment. There will be less reliance on textbook-based instruction, worksheets, and chapter questions and greater focus on hands-on and problem-solving activities (Gredler, 1999). This shift in respective roles has the potential to produce problems, but most certainly will create opportunities for both teachers and students.

The greatest limitation associated with the use of portfolio assessment are the costs (Gredler, 1999). Managing, reviewing, and scoring portfolios is both time and labor intensive. Previously mentioned was the fact that teachers can expect to spend approximately one hour per student reviewing the portfolio contents and subsequently discussing the results with individual students.

Various logistical issues arise when implementing a portfolio assessment system (Gallagher, 1998). A sizable amount of material is produced by students and included as entries into their portfolios. Often, class storage space is minimal or limited, at best. Advanced planning with respect to the actual physical organization and maintenance of portfolios is another key role of the teacher.

Finally, as discussed in the previous section, there are some potentially severe problems associated with the validity and reliability of decisions resulting from portfolio scores (Chase, 1999). Teachers must ensure that portfolios are not used for purposes for which they were not intended, such as evaluating teachers or ranking schools (Gallagher, 1998).

SUMMARY

The use of portfolios is becoming more popular among teachers as a means of assessing their students. One of the reasons behind this increase in popularity is the authentic nature of portfolio assessment. Portfolios are used in a variety of professions as a method of demonstrating and showcasing the work of individuals. Albeit for different audiences, the use of portfolios in the classroom serves essentially the same purpose.

Portfolios do not consist of random samples of student work. Rather, they represent the purposeful collection of a student's products, processes, and evidence of progress. Basic characteristics of portfolios include student involvement in the selection of portfolio entries, the flexibility to be individualized based on particular student needs, the ability to demonstrate processes as well as products, their focus on student strengths, and student self-assessment components. Portfolios depict a student-centered, open system of classroom assessment.

The basic format for portfolios consists of three main components: documentation of the development of major works, evidence of the range of student work, and student reflections. There exist two main variations of this "ideal" format: documentation portfolios and showcase portfolios. Documentation portfolios provide an ongoing record of student progress throughout a term or school year. Showcase portfolios highlight and display students' best works. Class and evaluation portfolios are two additional variations that have unique applications, typically outside the classroom setting.

When creating portfolios for classroom use, several important issues must be considered. The specific purpose to be met by the portfolios must be identified. Specific performance criteria and subsequent scoring rubrics—which parallel instruction and planning—must be delineated. Decisions of content (i.e., *who* will select entries and *which* entries will be selected) must be made. Finally, logistical issues such as storage, maintenance, and a timeframe for reviewing portfolios must also be specified.

As a means of establishing the validity of portfolio assessments, care must be taken by the teacher to ensure that the work samples adequately represent the individual students' capabilities as well as the subject domain. Reliability, although not formally calculated, can be enhanced through the use of multiple reviewers.

There are substantial advantages to the use of portfolios, which include the involvement of students in the process of assessment, their ability to document growth and development over time, and the establishment of a reciprocal flow of information and feedback between teacher and student. The primary limitation centers around the substantial amount of time required to maintain, review, and score portfolios. Additionally, considerable planning must occur in order to facilitate the storage of all the student work samples which make up their portfolios.

⌁ Chapter 7 *Related Web Sites* ⌨

❖ **Organizational Issues Related to Portfolio Assessment Implementation in the Classroom** (*www.ericae.net/pare/getvn.asp?v=7&n=4*)
This brief article from *Practical Assessment, Research, & Evaluation* reports the results of a research study that investigated issues arising when portfolio assessment was implemented in eleven classrooms. Important issues raised include the time requirements and management issues related to storage and access to the portfolio contents.

❖ **Student Portfolios: Classroom Uses**
(*www.ed.gov/pubs/OR/ConsumerGuides/classuse.html*)
This brief "Education Research Consumer Guide" produced by the Office of Research in the U.S. Department of Education provides a good overview of portfolio assessment, highlighting its appropriate classroom uses, advantages, and limitations, as well as what research says about its use.

❖ **Portfolio Assessment** (*www.pgcps.pg.k12.md.us/~elc/portfolio.html*)
Staff in the Prince George's County (MD) Public Schools have developed this page that describes what portfolios are and why teachers may want to consider using them. Included are links to additional pages discussing characteristics of effective portfolios, different types of portfolios, and how to get started and evaluate student portfolios.

QUESTIONS FOR REVIEW

1. Explain how portfolios reflect "real-world" learning. (Hint: Consider how portfolios are used outside classrooms.)

2. What is meant by the "purposeful collection of student work" when we discuss portfolios?

3. Why is it important for students to have active involvement in the selection of items to be placed in their portfolios?

4. Explain why it is important to incorporate a student self-assessment component into portfolios.

5. Briefly explain how portfolios accentuate strengths over weaknesses.

6. Discuss the importance of the three main features of any portfolio assessment.

7. Discuss the parallels (as shown in Figure 7.1) between the main portfolio characteristics and the components of the "ideal" format.

8. When developing a scoring rubric for a documentation portfolio, should you design a holistic or an analytic rubric? Why?

9. Which specific type of portfolio allows students to declare, "Hey, everyone, look what I did!"?

10. Explain why some students experience difficulty when required to reflect on their learning. As a teacher, how might you facilitate this process?

ENRICHMENT ACTIVITIES

1. Identify a specific subject area and grade level. Think about important content in the subject, as well as student capabilities at the particular grade level, and make a list of possible materials that could be included in a student portfolio. Discuss your lists in small groups.

2. Identify a two- or three-chapter unit covering content you would like to teach someday. Using the steps outlined in the chapter, develop a template for a showcase portfolio you could use to assess your students over the unit's content and skills. Specify the types of work samples you would suggest to your students that they include in their portfolios. Share your template with others in your class.

3. For the showcase portfolio system you described above, design both a holistic and an analytic rubric that could be used to assess the portfolio contents. Would you prefer to use the holistic or analytic version of the rubric? Why? Share your responses in small groups.

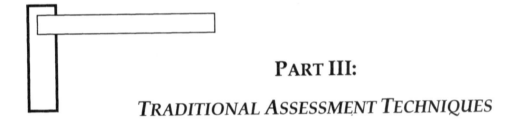

PART III:

TRADITIONAL ASSESSMENT TECHNIQUES

Chapter 8
Objective Test Items

Chapter 9
Subjective Test Items

Notes

Chapter 8

Objective Test Items

Overview of Chapter 8

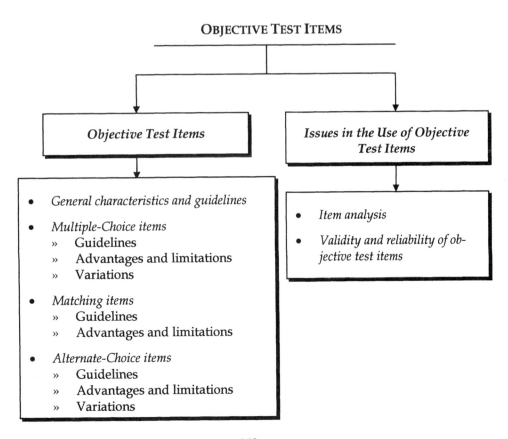

OBJECTIVE TEST ITEMS

Objective Test Items

- *General characteristics and guidelines*

- *Multiple-Choice items*
  - » Guidelines
  - » Advantages and limitations
  - » Variations

- *Matching items*
  - » Guidelines
  - » Advantages and limitations

- *Alternate-Choice items*
  - » Guidelines
  - » Advantages and limitations
  - » Variations

Issues in the Use of Objective Test Items

- *Item analysis*

- *Validity and reliability of objective test items*

INTRODUCTION

This chapter introduces traditional assessment techniques—that is, those techniques that typically result in written, pencil-and-paper classroom tests. In this chapter, our discussion focuses on *objective test items*; the topic addressed in the next chapter is *subjective test items*. In contrast to the alternative techniques previously discussed, traditional assessment techniques have been utilized in classrooms for many years. Although variations on the basic item formats continue to be developed by educators, these basic formats have not changed since their early use.

Since many of us have been exposed to pencil-and-paper tests for nearly all of our educational careers as students, there is a tendency among educators to believe that the development of these test items is relatively simple and straightforward. However, this is not typically the case. As Gallagher (1998) reasoned, "...developing *a* test is easy, but developing a *good* test requires considerable knowledge, skill, [and] time..." (p. 132). As we examine the characteristics, guidelines for development, and advantages and limitations of various item types, you will see that her appraisal is quite accurate.

GENERAL CHARACTERISTICS OF OBJECTIVE TEST ITEMS

Classroom teachers have used objective test items for quite some time. These test items are so named based on the way in which they are scored. **Objective test** items have a single correct response and regardless of who actually scores a set of student responses, an identical score will be obtained. In other words, the judgment of the scorer in no way influences an individual student's score (Chase, 1999; Gredler, 1999; Trice, 2000). These types of test items are also referred to as *selected-response* and *structured-response* items since students are simply instructed to select their response from options provided, or structured, by the teacher. Trice (2000) also refers to objective items as *recognition* items, due to the fact that students are simply required to recognize the correct answer from a list of possibilities, as opposed to recalling from memory or providing their own response. Specifically, objective test items include multiple-choice, matching, and alternate-response items.

Objective test items typically assess lower-level student skills, such as knowledge, comprehension, and application (Trice, 2000; Gredler, 1999). These item formats can be used to assess higher-order thinking skills (i.e., analysis, synthesis, and evaluation); however, these items are much more difficult to write (Airasian, 2000 & 2001; Gredler, 1999). In the case of evaluation skills, items typically involve judgments of quality or worth, which cannot necessarily be scored as correct or incorrect. Additionally, they tend to require much more time to develop. Teachers who develop classroom tests at the last minute—which is obviously not good practice, in and of itself—would find it extremely difficult to create an objective test that addressed higher-order student thinking.

Some of the advantages of objective test items include the fact that they are relatively easy to administer, score, and analyze (Johnson & Johnson, 2002). They can be administered to large numbers of students simultaneously and can be scored with relative ease, in some cases even by computers. Also, since students are simply selecting a response, as opposed to constructing one from scratch, teachers can sample more of the content in a given amount of testing time than would otherwise be possible by using other assessment techniques (Tanner, 2001). Finally, reliability of objective tests tends to be quite good (Johnson & Johnson, 2002; Tanner, 2001).

Even though time is saved in the administration and scoring of objective items, writing high-quality items requires a great deal of time (Tanner, 2001). Writing high-quality objective test items and doing so quickly is something even experienced item writers cannot achieve (Tanner, 2001). Another limitation of objective items includes the fact that, although subjectivity in scoring is all but removed, a substantial degree of subjectivity exists in the determination of the content (i.e., sampling of the content domain) to be addressed by the items on the test. Furthermore, since the correct answer to an item always appears for the student, guessing is always a distinct possibility (Tanner, 2001). A final limitation is that poor read-

ers may be unjustly penalized (Johnson & Johnson, 2002). Students may understand the content being addressed by an objective test question, but they may select an incorrect response simply because they were unable to understand the prompt provided to them.

Several authors have advanced general guidelines that can assist teachers in the development of their objective classroom tests. The following list, discussed and then summarized in Figure 8.1, represents a compilation of the most pertinent guiding principles (Airasian, 2000 & 2001; Gredler, 1999; Johnson & Johnson, 2002). These principles include:

- *Objective test items should cover important content and skills.* Classroom goals and objectives should be clearly reflected by the items that appear in the test. If this alignment does not exist, the resulting scores on the test will not be accurate indications of student learning.

- *The reading level and vocabulary of each item should be as simple as possible.* If students are to respond appropriately to a test question, they must be able to understand the question.

- *Each objective item should be stated in an unambiguous manner, and confusing sentence structure and wording should be avoided.* Similar to the previous principle, nothing is accomplished by confusing or "tricking" students on any form of assessment. To that end, objective items should also be kept short and to the point.

- *Objective items should not consist of verbatim statements or phrases lifted from the text.* An objective test should not be designed as an exercise in rote memorization of textbook passages. Questions of this type most certainly will not reflect student learning.

- *Clues to the correct answer should not be provided.* The focus here is not on avoiding problems that inhibit students from doing their best, as the previous principles demonstrated. Rather, our concern is to avoid helping students answer an item correctly when they have not actually learned the content being assessed. These clues may be grammatical (for example, the word *an* at the end of a question indicates that the correct answer begins with a vowel), may include implausible options (for example, a seemingly ridiculous option that has nothing to do with the content), or may include specific determiners (such as *always, never, all,* and *none,* which are seldom the correct response).

The next several principles address issues for formatting and assembling a test. When teachers follow these guidelines, students tend to experience less confusion and their task appears clearer.

- *Vary the types of items that appear on classroom tests.*

- *Group items similar in format together so that each type appears in a separate section (e.g., all multiple-choice items should be grouped together).*

- *Each section should be preceded by clear directions.*

- *Within each section, order the items from easiest to most difficult.*

- *Although all item types will not appear on every test, a good order of items is: true-false, matching, short answer, multiple-choice, and essay.*

- *Provide adequate space for students to respond to each item.*

- *Avoid splitting items between two pages.*

A good way to begin the development of a written objective test is to prepare a table of specifications. A **table of specifications** is a chart showing the relation between objectives, instructional content, and taxonomic levels of Bloom's cognitive domain (Trice, 2000). The rows of the table specify the content and/or instructional objectives to be covered through the instruction. The columns represent the six levels of Bloom's cognitive domain. The intersecting cells in the table are filled in with instructional objectives and the number or percentage of test items that will be developed to assess particular content at that specific cognitive level. These percentages of items may often reflect the relative amount of instructional time spent on given topics. A sample table of specifications is shown in Figure 8.2.

Notice that in the figure, not all cells in the table of specifications are filled. Rarely, if ever, will you develop a written test that will test *all* content at *each* level of Bloom's taxonomy. It is the responsibility of the teacher to match content with appropriate student skills to be assessed.

Figure 8.1 General guidelines for developing objective tests

> *Developing Objective Tests:*
>
> *General Guidelines*
>
> 1. Objective test items should cover important content and skills.
> 2. The reading level and vocabulary of each item should be as simple as possible.
> 3. Each objective item should be stated in an unambiguous manner, and confusing sentence structure and wording should be avoided.
> 4. Objective items should not consist of verbatim statements or phrases lifted from the text.
> 5. Clues to the correct answer should not be provided.
> 6. Vary the types of items that appear on classroom tests.
> 7. Group items similar in format together so that each type appears in a separate section (e.g., all multiple-choice items should be grouped together).
> 8. Each section should be preceded by clear directions.
> 9. Within each section, order the items from easiest to most difficult.
> 10. Although all item types will not appear on every test, a good order of items is: true-false, matching, short answer, multiple-choice, and essay.
> 11. Provide adequate space for students to respond to each item.
> 12. Avoid splitting items between two pages.

Further, notice that each cell in the table contains a learning objective. For example, the first cell contains the objective "The student will identify the main causes of the war." This particular objective (i.e., specific student skills coupled with content) will be assessed on the written test using five items to be written by the teacher at the knowledge level of the cognitive domain of Bloom's taxonomy. These five items will constitute 14% of the total 35 items that will eventually appear on the written test.

Tables of specifications provide teachers with assurance that their tests will assess a representative and accurate sample of the content and skills that have been covered in the learning unit (Johnson & Johnson, 2002). Since teachers do not typically have ample time to test students on *everything* that was covered in class, written tests only provide a sample of what students can do and should know how to do. In essence, a table of specifications helps teachers greatly in ensuring that their tests have content validity.

Figure 8.2 Sample table of specifications for test covering World War II

Content	Knowledge	Comprehen-sion	Application	Analysis	Synthesis	Evaluation
1. Causes	[a]...identify the main causes. {5/14%} [b]	...summarize main causes. {3/9%}		...order the causes appropriately {3/9%}		...support U.S. decision to enter war {3/9%}
2. Geography	...label geographic locations. {2/6%}	...interpret map showing key locations {3/9%}				
3. U.S. Role	...describe ways U.S. involved. {3/9%}				...combine roles from various war fronts {3/9%}	
4. Key Leaders					...compose synopsis of leaders and their roles {5/14%}	...judge the success of key leaders {3/9%}
5. Major Battles				...compare and contrast major battles {2/6%}		

[a] Each objective is preceded by "The student will..."
[b] Indicates the number and percentage of total items on the test addressing the particular content area at a specific taxonomic level.

At this point, it is important to discuss another option for objective tests. At some time in our educational careers, we have probably all taken chapter or unit tests found in the teachers' editions of textbooks. Teachers are often confronted with the question of whether to construct their own classroom tests or use those found in their textbooks. Because textbook tests already exist, many teachers find them quite appealing, especially since they accompany the text and seem to measure exactly what appears in the text (Airasian, 2000 & 2001). Teachers should consider several issues before making the decision to use an existing test or develop one of their own. First and foremost, teachers must consider the basic question of validity: Do the items on the test match the instruction provided to students? (Airasian,

2000 & 2001). Textbook tests must be critically and professionally examined in order to determine the extent to which the items are aligned with actual instruction. There often exists a misalignment between textbook tests and the actual content that appears in the chapter (Gredler, 1999). This misalignment potentially invalidates any inferences made about student performance as evidenced by the resulting tests scores. Additionally, research has shown that the focus of textbook tests is primarily on the recall of information; in other words, only the lowest levels of Bloom's taxonomy are being addressed by the actual test items (Gredler, 1999). There is nothing inherently wrong with using textbook tests, provided teachers thoroughly and critically evaluate them item by item in order to ensure their appropriateness.

Objective test items are the easiest type of written test item to score. Students are usually instructed to indicate their responses to items by writing, circling, or somehow marking their choice. The responses are then scored by comparing students' responses to those that appear on the teacher's answer key. An **answer key** simply consists of a copy of the test with all correct answers listed (Airasian, 2000 & 2001). Scoring objective items takes very little time and can be done by someone with little content expertise (Gallagher, 1998). The final test score is typically equal to the number of items the student answered correctly.

In the following sections, the three main types of objective items—namely, multiple-choice, matching, and alternate-choice—will be discussed. Guidelines for the specific development of each will be summarized, as will the advantages and limitations of each. You should notice that the advantages clearly explain their popularity, while the limitations shed light on why they are so often criticized (Tanner, 2001).

Multiple-Choice Items

The multiple-choice item is probably the most popular format of objective test item used in classroom testing, especially in secondary schools (Chase, 1999; Oosterhof, 1999 & 2001). As you read in Chapter 4, the basic format of a multiple-choice item consists of two essential components: a **stem** and a set of **response options**. Of the response options, one is the correct answer, while the others are referred to as **distractors**. The stem defines the problem or provides the prompt to which students must select the correct response (Chase, 1999; Oosterhof, 1999 & 2001). The stem may be written as either an incomplete statement or as a question (Gredler, 1999). Typically, there are three to five options that make up the response set. An example of a multiple-choice item with these components appropriately labeled appears in Figure 8.3.

Figure 8.3 Sample multiple-choice item from science

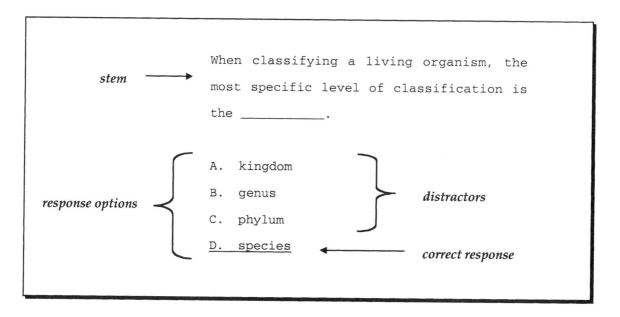

Multiple-choice items are used for assessing the recall and application of knowledge (Gredler, 1999). These skills most accurately address the lower levels of Bloom's taxonomy (i.e., knowledge and comprehension). Additionally, these items can also be used to assess higher-order thinking skills, such as application, analysis, synthesis, and evaluation (Airasian, 2000 & 2001; Gredler, 1999), although these items tend to be much more difficult to write.

Guidelines for Developing Multiple-Choice Items

This section provides several guidelines and suggestions for crafting well-written multiple-choice test items (Chase, 1999; Frary, 1995; Gallagher, 1998; Gredler,

1999; Kehoe, 1995; Nitko, 2001; Oosterhof, 1999 & 2001; Trice, 2000). They are as follows:

- *The stem should clearly present the problem to be addressed by the student.* If the stem is vague or misleading, students read the options and try to determine their response without really knowing what problem they are to solve. Sometimes presenting the stem as a question, as opposed to an incomplete sentence, will improve the item's clarity. Consider the following pair of stems, in which the second version poses a clearer problem to students:

1) "Objective" refers to _____.

2) To what does the term "objective" refer when describing a test item?

- *All response options should be parallel, or homogeneous, in type of content.* When response options vary in their form or content, students are required to compare them, but must do so based on different characteristics. Often, the result is more than one conceivably correct answer. Consider the following multiple-choice item:

```
Which of the following repre-
sents the longest distance?

A) 10 centimeters
B) 3 inches
C) 30 millimeters
D) the length of your thumb
```

The first three options are specific, well-defined, and familiar scales of measurement. The fourth option would likely vary from person to person. The correct answer could be A) or D).

- *Options should avoid the use of repetitive words.* If a word or phrase is repeated at the beginning of each option, it should be removed and placed as part of the stem. This tends to make the options easier to read and the stem clearer. Consider the following item:

```
1) When classifying living or-
   ganisms,

  A) the most specific level is
     the kingdom.
  B) the most specific level is
     the genus.
  C) the most specific level is
     the phylum.
  D) the most specific level is
     the species.
```

```
2) When classifying a living
   organism, the most specific
   level of classification is
   the _____.

  A) kingdom
  B) genus
  C) phylum
  D) species
```

Notice how the second version presents a clearer task, and the options become much easier for the student to read and evaluate.

- *Adjectives or adverbs that substantially alter the meaning of a stem or option should be emphasized.* If the inclusion of a single word changes the problem posed or the nature of a response in an important way, it should be underlined, capitalized, italicized, or otherwise emphasized to draw students' attention to it so they can respond appropriately. For example, here are two stems with such words highlighted:

```
Which of the following is a
necessary component of an in-
structional objective?

Which of the following is NOT
an advantage of portfolios?
```

- *All distractors in the response set should be plausible.* From an assessment perspective, placing a seemingly ridiculous distractor among the options of a multiple-choice item accomplishes nothing. It might be a nice "tension reliever" for students, but it does not permit teachers to distinguish between those students who know the material and those who do not. For example,

Which of the following best describes an octagon?

A) it has five sides
B) it has eight sides
C) it has ten sides
D) it lives in the sea

Option D) would not logically be selected by any student, even one who does not know what an octagon is. If you are struggling to come up with a fourth option that sounds plausible, simply make the decision not to include one.

- *The grammar in each option should be consistent with the stem.* Students should not be able to detect any grammatical clues from the stem itself. If these are present, students can quickly rule out options that clearly do not flow with the stem, in terms of completing the sentence. Consider the following item:

A large body of water is called an

A) ocean.
B) pond.
C) creek.
D) stream.

Clearly, option A) is the correct answer. Even if the definition was not known, a student could easily determine that "ocean" is correct since it is the only option that fits grammatically into the stem. Here is a possible remedy for this problem:

A large body of water is called a/an

A) ocean.
B) pond.
C) creek.
D) stream.

Sometimes, the *a(n)* or *a/an* notations confuse students. Another possible solution would be:

A large body of water is called

A) an ocean.
B) a pond.
C) a creek.
D) a stream.

- *Items should not have "all of the above," "none of the above," or any equivalents as response options.* These options are typically intended to increase the number of options, but actually function in the opposite manner. When "all of the above" is used, it is possible for students to quickly narrow their possible choices. If they can determine that one of the other options is incorrect, they have in essence also eliminated "all of the above," since that one could no longer be correct either. Similarly, if students can determine that two options are correct, they do not need to know anything about the remaining options, so "all of the above" must be the correct response. Similar fallacies also exist when "none of the above" is used. It is best to avoid the use of these options altogether.

- *The use of absolute terms should be avoided.* Absolute terms such as "always," "never," "all," and "none" typically provide clues to students that these options are incorrect. In our world, seldom—if ever—can we guarantee that a particular phenomenon will always occur, or never occur.

- *Items should remain independent of one another*. Information—specifically the correct response—from one item should not be necessary in order to answer a subsequent item correctly. Consider the following pair of items:

```
1) A man stands at the center
   of a circle. He measures the
   distance to the edge of the
   circle as 3 feet. What is
   the diameter of the circle?

   A) 3 feet
   B) 6 feet
   C) 9 feet

2) What is the circumference of
   the circle in question 1
   above?

   A) 6 feet
   B) slightly more than
      18 feet
   C) 30 feet
```

A student who incorrectly answers the first question does not stand a chance of answering the second one correctly, since the correct answer for question 1) is a necessary component for the calculation needed to answer question 2). Even if the student knows the formula for the circumference of a circle—*pi* (or 3.14) times the diameter—but answered question 1) incorrectly, the student will be penalized since the wrong value for the diameter would be substituted into the formula.

- *Avoid nongrammatical clues, such as a key term appearing in both the stem and correct response*. In situations when students honestly do not know the correct answer, these types of clues will often direct students to the correct response. For example,

```
1) What  is  the  name  of  the
   large ocean located to the
   west  of  the  continental
   United States?

   A) the Great Salt Lake
   B) the Pacific Ocean
   C) the Mississippi River
```

This could be easily corrected by inserting the phrase "large body of water" in place of "large ocean."

These guidelines have been summarized in Figure 8.4.

Advantages and Limitations of Multiple-Choice Items

Multiple-choice test items have several advantages over other types of written test items. They allow a test to comprehensively sample the content domain (Chase, 1999; Oosterhof, 1999 & 2001). Multiple-choice items provide an efficient means of assessing a variety of content, especially compared to subjective (i.e., completion and essay) items. This is mostly because students can answer them quicker since they are required only to select the correct response, instead of construct their own. Finally, multiple-choice items can be used effectively for assessing learning outcomes in virtually all subject areas taught in schools (Chase, 1999).

Figure 8.4 General guidelines for developing multiple-choice items

Developing Multiple-Choice Items:
General Guidelines

1. The stem should clearly present the problem to be addressed by the student.

2. All response options should be parallel, or homogeneous, in type of content.

3. Options should avoid the use of repetitive words.

4. Adjectives or adverbs that substantially alter the meaning of a stem or option should be emphasized.

5. All distractors in the response set should be plausible.

6. The grammar in each option should be consistent with the stem.

7. Items should not have "all of the above," "none of the above," or any equivalents as response options.

8. The use of absolute terms should be avoided.

9. Items should remain independent of one another.

10. Avoid nongrammatical clues, such as a key term appearing in both the stem and correct response.

A second advantage of multiple-choice items is that they can be scored relatively quickly (Chase, 1999; Gallagher, 1998; Oosterhof, 1999 & 2001). Students respond to each item with a single mark (e.g., a circle, a letter, etc.) that can be assessed very quickly by comparing it to the answer key. If students use answer sheets separate from their test papers, which are scannable, all scoring and analysis of the test data may be accomplished by the computer. Special equipment is required, but in recent years, this type of equipment has become economical and accessible, even for individual schools.

Third, responses to multiple-choice items are scored objectively (Gallagher, 1998; Oosterhof, 1999 & 2001). The subjective judgments of the scorers (i.e., teachers) do not enter into the scoring process. Not only does this increase the reliability of the test scores, but it also facilitates the logistics of scoring. Students, teachers' aides, and scoring machines can efficiently score the responses to multiple-choice items since there is a single correct answer to each item, as identified on the scoring key.

A final advantage to multiple-choice items is that they can provide diagnostic information about difficulties that a particular student may be experiencing (Nitko, 2001). This can be done by examining the distractors that students choose. However, in order for these items to function effectively as diagnostic tools, the distractors must be extremely well written. Obviously, this places an even greater burden on the classroom teacher.

In contrast, there are limitations to using multiple-choice items on classroom tests. First, multiple-choice items are susceptible to guessing (Oosterhof, 1999 & 2001). This is a basic limitation of any form of selected-response type of item. Since the correct responses to items are provided to students directly on the test—and they simply have to identify them—guessing becomes a possible method of response for students who do not truly know the material being tested. The positive aspect of this particular limitation is that relatively few multiple-choice items are answered correctly by students as a result of "blind guessing" (i.e., selecting a response without knowing anything about the material being tested).

Multiple-choice items can reduce the potential of guessing correctly, especially when compared to other types of items such as alternate-response (e.g., true-false) items (Chase, 1999; Gallagher, 1998; Nitko, 2001). If a multiple-choice item contains four options, students would have a 25% chance of blindly guessing the correct answer. Alternate-choice items, since they contain only two possible responses (as you will soon see), increase to 50% a student's chances of blindly guessing the correct answer.

Second, multiple-choice items are time consuming to construct. In fact, more time is required to construct a test consisting of multiple-choice items than any other kind of written format (Gallagher, 1998; Oosterhof, 1999 & 2001). The main reason for this is that for each item, a clearly posed stem must be provided to students along with a correct answer and two to four effective distractors. As you saw in the guidelines presented in Figure 8.4, a good deal of care must go into the development of well-written response options. Furthermore, multiple-choice items that assess higher-order thinking skills are even more difficult—and time consuming—to create (Chase, 1999). Writing legitimate options for lower-level thinking skills is difficult enough; developing effective options at a higher level substantially increases that level of difficulty.

Variations of the Basic Multiple-Choice Item

In addition to the basic format of a multiple-choice item, there are several variations that have been used quite extensively. Two common variations are the *correct-answer* multiple-choice item and the *best-answer* multiple-choice item (Gallagher, 1998; Nitko, 2001). Items involving mathematical computations and the identification of elements based on atomic weights are examples of correct-answer items. In these situations, students are presented with stems that clearly have only one correct answer. The examples that we have examined thus far in this chapter have been correct-answer multiple-choice items.

In contrast, best-answer items focus on students' problem-solving abilities. Students are provided with several options and, although all may be legitimate choices, one of the options is clearly better than the others. In other words, all options may be correct to some degree. The following is an example of a best-answer item:

> Imagine that you are the owner of a restaurant. A customer approaches you to complain about the quality of your food. Which would be the best way to solve this problem?
>
> A) Tell the customer that there is nothing you can do.
> B) Offer the customer a complimentary meal.
> C) Inform the customer that he can order more food, but will have to pay for it.

Another variation of the basic format is a combination of a multiple-choice item along with a short-answer essay (C. S. Mertler, personal communication, September 10, 1991). Students are provided with correct-answer multiple-choice items and are instructed to respond to them accordingly. However, the students must then construct brief explanations justifying why the distractors are not correct.

Care must be taken to ensure that students do not simply insert words that indicate an opposite meaning (such as, "not") into the otherwise verbatim distractor statements.

A final variation, similar to the previous one, is a metacognitive multiple-choice item. "Metacognition" literally means knowledge about one's own knowledge. Metacognitive test items offer students the opportunity to reflect on and explain their thinking. The following is an example of a metacognitive multiple-choice item:

> 1) A man stands at the center of a circle. He measures the distance to the edge of the circle as 3 feet. What is the diameter of the circle?
>
> A) 3 feet
> B) 6 feet
> C) 9 feet
>
> 2) Explain your response to question 1 above.

Notice that this type of item furnishes information similar to that provided by student reflections in portfolios (see Chapter 7). It allows the teacher to better understand how a student mentally decided on a particular response from the options provided. These types of items are often appropriate to include as components in performance assessment tasks.

Matching Items

A matching item consists of two lists. The list on the left typically consists of concepts or names that are called the **stimuli**, and the list on the right contains possible

responses. There is a one-to-one correspondence between members of each list, which students need to categorize and associate (Johnson & Johnson, 2002; Tanner, 2001). Matching items are considered to be a special case of multiple-choice items in which each item shares the same set of options—both correct and distractors (Airasian, 2000 & 2001; Oosterhof, 1999 & 2001). An example of a matching item, with appropriate components labeled, appears in Figure 8.5.

When presented with lists of related data such as appears in matching items, students' knowledge of facts as well as comprehension skills can be efficiently assessed (Gredler, 1999; Tanner, 2001). They are especially useful in measuring students' understanding of concepts or terms that are interrelated (Trice, 2000).

Guidelines for Developing Matching Items

This section describes guidelines for developing quality matching items for classroom tests (Chase, 1999; Gallagher, 1998; Gredler, 1999; Johnson & Johnson, 2002; Nitko, 2001; Oosterhof, 1999 & 2001; Trice, 2000). They are:

Figure 8.5 Sample matching item from chemistry

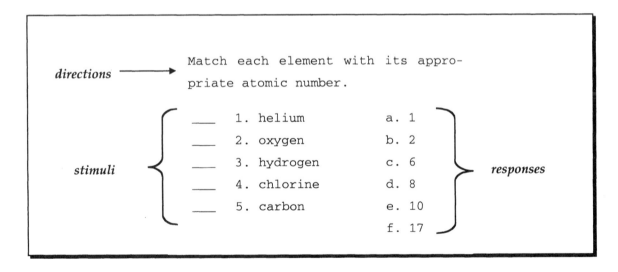

- *The lists should be homogeneous.* All responses should appear as plausible options for each stimulus. The more homogeneous, or similar, the lists are, the finer the level of discrimination required. This permits the teacher to more precisely determine what the student knows. If sets are not homogeneous, students can easily eliminate improbable options and improve their chances of guessing correctly. Consider the following item, which consists of heterogeneous lists of stimuli and responses:

```
__ causes some islands   A. hot, humid
   to be formed          B. Shanghai
__ climate of SE Asia    C. volcanoes
__ ledge on a hillside   D. 35%
__ largest city in       E. terrace
   China
__ percentage of
   population living
   in Asia
```

These stimuli and responses are not similar (i.e., not homogeneous), and students could eliminate options and blindly guess with relative efficiency. For organizational purposes, it is sometimes helpful to provide a title for each of the lists. If you cannot come up with a clear, specific title for each list, the lists are probably too heterogeneous.

- *The directions (i.e., the basis for matching) must be made clear.* For the most part, these directions add clarity to the similar characteristics contained in each list. In the item that appears in Figure 8.5, the simple directions make it clear that the list on the left contains the names of elements and the list on the right contains the atomic weights of those elements.

- *Avoid "perfect matching" by placing more items in the response list than in the stimulus list.* Perfect matching (i.e., having the same number of stimuli as responses) can give away at least one answer to students through a process of elimination. By including one or more responses that do not match any of the stimuli, this problem can be avoided. Another technique is to provide fewer items in the response list than in the stimulus list and inform students in the directions that the responses may be used more than once.

- *Use relatively short lists of stimuli and responses.* For a single matching exercise, 10 to 15 elements in a stimulus list is appropriate. If more elements are included, it becomes increasingly difficult to keep the items homogeneous. Additionally, students spend too much time "searching" the response list for the correct answer. When necessary to incorporate more items in the list, try to find a way to develop two separate matching exercises.

- *Place longer phrases in the stimulus list and shorter ones in the response list.* This simply makes the process of examining and matching options more efficient for students since they will be scanning the list of responses once for each item on the stimulus list.

- *Arrange the lists in some logical order.* This also facilitates the searching process and saves time for the student. Dates should be arranged chronologically, numbers in order of magnitude, and names or vocabulary terms in alphabetical order.

These guidelines have been summarized in Figure 8.6.

Advantages and Limitations of Matching Items

Arguably, the main advantage of matching items is that they permit efficient assessment of related sets of ideas, facts, or concepts (Chase, 1999; Johnson & Johnson, 2002; Nitko, 2001; Oosterhof, 1999 & 2001). Assessing a large set of related concepts could be accomplished with multiple-choice items, but numerous multiple-choice items would have to be developed, as opposed to one matching exercise.

Along those lines, matching items are relatively easy to construct (Chase, 1999; Oosterhof, 1999 & 2001). This is mainly because the same set of options is being used for each stimulus. Much less time is required to write matching items than to write multiple-choice items, where separate sets of options must be developed for each item. Additionally, since the same set of options is being used throughout the matching exercise, a minimal amount of reading is required of the student (Chase, 1999).

Figure 8.6 General guidelines for developing matching items

Developing Matching Items:
General Guidelines

1. The lists should be homogeneous.

2. The directions (i.e., the basis for matching) must be made clear.

3. Avoid "perfect matching" by placing more items in the response list than in the stimulus list.

4. Use relatively short lists of stimuli and responses.

5. Place longer phrases in the stimulus list and shorter ones in the response list.

6. Arrange the lists in some logical order.

Since matching items are a type of objective test item, a final advantage—albeit a repetitive one—is that responses to matching exercises can be scored easily and without subjective bias (Chase, 1999; Johnson & Johnson, 2002). An answer key, similar to one developed for multiple-choice items, is prepared and serves as the basis for comparison.

The most substantial limitation is that in order for a matching item to be developed, a relatively large number of related (i.e., homogeneous) concepts or ideas must be available within a given unit of study (Chase, 1999; Gredler, 1999; Nitko, 2001). This is not always feasible. However, a well-developed table of specifications can sometimes help teachers see the extent to which there exists closely related concepts or facts (Chase, 1999).

Finally, matching items are best for measuring factual knowledge. They are difficult, if not impossible, to design in order to measure higher-level cognitive skills.

Alternate-Choice Items

You have seen that matching items are often considered to be special cases of multiple-choice items. Similarly, alternate-choice items are also essentially a special case of multiple-choice items where the options are limited to only two choices. The most popular type of alternate-choice item is the true-false test item. Other possible choices for the responses include yes or no, correct or incorrect, fact or opinion (Airasian, 2000 & 2001). You will see

shortly that there are several variations of this item type.

True-false items typically get quite a bit of negative press (Tanner, 2001), but if they are written carefully, they can be highly effective. Specifically, they provide an efficient means of assessing lower levels of Bloom's taxonomy. However, it is also believed that true-false items tend to overestimate student learning, since students have a 50% chance of correctly guessing the answer to an individual item they do not know (Trice, 2000). Unfortunately, this increases the potential of lower reliability for the overall test.

The format of a traditional true-false item consists of a statement, followed by the two options—true and false. Typically, students are instructed to circle, or otherwise indicate, their response. For example,

```
1. The body of water that
   borders Ohio to the
   north is Lake Erie.    T   F
```

Guidelines for Developing Alternate-Choice Items

This section comprises guidelines and suggestions for developing quality true-false items (Chase, 1999; Gallagher, 1998; Johnson & Johnson, 2002; Tanner, 2001; Trice, 2000). Although these guidelines are discussed from the perspective of true-false items, they also apply to other types of alternate-choice items. These guidelines include:

- *Avoid the use of absolute terms and other specific determiners.* This suggestion was previously discussed in relation to multiple-choice items. Words like "all," "none," and "never" provide clues to students. Since few things are complete absolutes (i.e., there is no guarantee that they will "always" or "never" occur), statements containing these words are almost always false or incorrect. Similar to these terms are "vague" terms, such as "usually," "sometimes," and "frequently." These words typically indicate a correct statement or a true response. What makes these words even more frustrating for students is that they cannot be sure of their definitions. For example, a student's definition of "sometimes" or "usually" may be quite different from that of a teacher. For example, consider the next item, which contains the vague term "long time," followed by an improved version:

```
1. The American Revolution
   took place a long time
   before the Civil War.     T   F

2. The American Revolution
   took place less than 100
   years before the Civil
   War.                      T   F
```

Here is another example in which the meaning of the first item is vague:

```
1. Sometimes multiple-choice
   items are superior to
   true-false items.         T   F
```

```
2. When trying to reduce the
   amount of guessing,
   multiple-choice items
   are superior to
   true-false items.         T   F
```

- *Avoid testing trivial knowledge.* There is a tendency for these items to be written such that overly simplistic information is requested from students. True-false items are no different from any other type of assessment in that they should follow a teacher's instructional objectives. Furthermore, they should stress the main content, concepts, and skills taught to students.

- *Items should be stated positively.* Some teachers tend to use negative terms in true-false statements. This often confuses students. Consider the next item and its revised version:

```
1. It is not important for
   a test to be valid.      T   F
```

```
2. It is important for a
   test to be valid.        T   F
```

Sometimes, it is necessary to include negative terms; if so, teachers should format the term (i.e., underline, bold, or italicize the word) so as to draw students' attention to it.

- *Roughly half of the test items should be keyed true and half false.* This simply reduces the chances of students guessing if they have figured out that a teacher always puts more false than true statements on a test.

- *True statements and false statements should be of equal length.* In order to be sure that true statements are totally true, teachers sometimes describe the true statements in greater detail than the false ones, making them too lengthy. Students will quickly notice this pattern. The length of an item should have nothing to do with its truth or falsity.

- *True-false items should be entirely true or entirely false.* One must consider all possibilities when drafting true-false items. If a statement might not be true, then it will always be false. Consider the following:

```
1. Apples are red.          T   F
```

For a preschool student learning primary colors, this statement would likely be true, since we tend to associate the color red with apples. How-ever, we all know that other varieties of apples exist that are yellow and green, for example. True, apples are red; however, not *all* apples are red.

These guidelines have been summarized in Figure 8.7.

Advantages and Limitations of Alternate-Choice Items

Relatively speaking, alternate-choice items are quick to construct, answer, and score (Chase, 1999; Gallagher, 1998; John-son & Johnson, 2002; Oosterhof, 1999 & 2001). This makes them highly efficient since large amounts of material can be sampled in relatively short time. It is es-timated that students may be able to an-swer twice as many alternate-choice items versus multiple-choice items in a given period of time (Oosterhof, 1999 & 2001).

Figure 8.7 General guidelines for develop-ing alternate-choice items

Developing Alternate-Choice Items:
General Guidelines

1. Avoid the use of absolute terms and other specific determiners.
2. Avoid testing trivial knowledge.
3. Items should be stated positively.
4. Roughly half of the test items should be keyed true and half false.
5. True statements and false statements should be of equal length.
6. True-false items should be entirely true or entirely false.

As with the other item types examined thus far, alternate-choice items can be scored efficiently and objectively (Chase, 1999; Gallagher, 1998; Oosterhof, 1999 & 2001). Like multiple-choice, they can be scored by hand or by computer, and without subjective bias.

In contrast, alternate-choice items are highly susceptible to guessing (Gallagher, 1998; Johnson & Johnson, 2002; Oosterhof, 1999 & 2001; Tanner, 2001). Even if students know nothing about the content, they are most likely to answer half the questions correctly as a result of blind guessing. As you will see in the next section, some of the variations address this issue of guessing.

Furthermore, predominantly lower-level skills are appropriately assessed with alternate-choice items (Johnson & Johnson, 2002). If carefully written, however, they may be used to assess all levels of the cognitive taxonomy (Chase, 1999).

Variations of the Basic Alternate-Choice Item

Several variations of the basic, traditional true-false item have been developed. A simple variation, called a **yes-no item**, simply changes the stem from a statement to a question and the response options to "yes-no" (Nitko, 2001). For example,

```
1. Is it possible for a
   test to be reliable
   but not valid?        Yes No
```

This type of item can be highly effective for students in early elementary grades who may not yet have an understanding of true and false.

Another commonly used variety of alternate-choice item resembles one of the variations of multiple-choice items we looked at earlier. This item type is known as the **correction true-false item** (Nitko, 2001; Oosterhof, 1999 & 2001). This item requires students to rewrite statements that they indicate as being false. An example of a correction true-false item follows:

```
Indicate whether the following is
true or false. If it is false, re-
write the statement to make it
true.

1. A reliable test is
   also a valid test.        T   F
```

A third variation of a basic true-false item is called an **embedded alternate-choice item** (Oosterhof, 1999 & 2001). This type of item consists of a series of alternate-choice items embedded in a paragraph. This is often effectively used when testing students on spelling or grammar. An example is provided below:

```
Indicate whether each numbered and
underlined word is spelled cor-
rectly, by marking (A) or (B) on
your answer sheet.

    (A) spelled correctly
    (B) spelled incorrectly

Frogs and toads have [1]sharred the
world with humans as far back as
our species' memory extends. With
their huge eyes, their quadrupedal
[2]bodies, their love of and need
for water, and their [3]eerie
```

voices, frogs and toads are both distinctly alien to humans and uncannily like us. [4]<u>Cultures</u> the world over and throughout history have [5]<u>soght</u> stories to explain these creatures who share our world.

A final type of alternate-choice item is a **multiple true-false item** (Nitko, 2001; Oosterhof, 1999 & 2001). This is sort of a hybrid between a multiple-choice item and a true-false item. A multiple true-false item consists of several statements, each utilizing the same stem, and requiring a determination of truth or falsity. An example of this variation follows:

```
Read each option and indicate
which are true and which are
false.

A CD-ROM disk

1. can have information
   stored on it by you.        T   F

2. can store more
   information than a
   standard floppy disk.       T   F

3. requires a special type
   of disk drive.              T   F
```

Although they resemble multiple-choice items, this type of item is more similar to true-false items. Each individual numbered statement presents its own problem to be solved or addressed, even though they share a common stem.

ITEM ANALYSIS

As with any form of assessment, objective items should be evaluated in order to de-

termine their quality. There are two optimal opportunities to evaluate assessment items (Tanner, 2001). The *first* occurs when the items are actually being drafted. Utilization of a table of specifications, as previously discussed in this chapter, will greatly assist the classroom teacher in ensuring that the assessment is aligned with the instructional objectives and actual instruction delivered, as well as appropriately measure desired students' skill levels. In terms of item format, quality can also be enhanced by following the guidelines presented earlier in Figures 8.1, 8.4, 8.6, and 8.7. By using these guidelines alongside a well-developed table of specifications, teachers can have greater assurance that the content and format of their items are appropriate for assessing what they intend to assess (i.e., they have content evidence of validity).

The second opportunity occurs *following* the administration of a test and involves the analysis of students' response patterns (Tanner, 2001). You might be asking yourself what benefit could be realized from this, since your students have already taken the test. The benefit may not be experienced by your current students, but the ultimate outcome will consist of the refinement of your individual test items. More important, this refinement is based on actual student data, not on subjective judgments made about the content of individual items. It is important to remember that even though a large number of students might perform poorly on a test, it may not be necessary to "throw out" the entire test and start from scratch. Based on the evidence, you may determine that several items functioned quite well, but the low scores really resulted from poor performance on a specific subset of the items. Furthermore, this low performance may be due to characteristics of the items, such as being confusing or being too difficult or too easy.

In situations such as these, it may be necessary to analyze the statistical characteristics of each item for purposes of making decisions about the items through a process known as **item analysis**. There are four basic statistics reported in the analysis of item characteristics: item difficulty, item discrimination, distractor analysis, and reliability. **Item difficulty** is defined as the proportion of students who answer the item correctly. **Item discrimination** is the difference between the proportion of correct answers for the highest-scoring students and the proportion of correct answers for the lowest-scoring students. **Distractor analysis** provides information about the pattern of responses for incorrect options.

Before discussing these statistical analyses, it is critical that we examine a basic belief about classroom tests. Many teachers design their pencil-and-paper classroom tests to be *criterion-referenced* tests. Recall from Chapter 1 that criterion-referenced tests compare students' performances to some preestablished criteria or objectives. The basic belief is that if teachers have provided adequate instruction on a topic and students are aware

that they will be tested on it, there is the expectation that most (if not all) students will answer a given item correctly. In other words, if students have mastered the material, they are *expected* to answer the item correctly. If the results of an item analysis show that many students answered a question incorrectly (potentially indicating a poorly written item), but the item covers basic and critical material, a teacher should not simply remove the item, especially if it clearly addresses the instructional objectives and mirrors what was taught. This basic belief is important in the interpretation of item analyses.

Let us then continue with our examination of the three new indices resulting from a formal item analysis before discussing reliability. *Item difficulty*, or the item difficulty index, is symbolized by a lowercase, italicized letter *p* (for "proportion"). It involves the relatively simple mathematical calculation of dividing the number of students who answered the item correctly by the total number of students who attempted to answer the item, or

$$p = \frac{[\text{number of students who answered item correctly}]}{[\text{total number of students attempting item}]}$$

Since it is a proportion, the possible values can range from .00 to 1.00. If the item was extremely easy (i.e., nearly everyone answered it correctly), we would expect to see a relatively high value for *p*; if it was a difficult item (i.e., nearly everyone missed the item), we would expect to see a low value for p. For example, if 45 students took a test and 36 answered item 1 correctly, the item difficulty would be equal to .80, indicating that 80% of the students answered the item correctly.

There is some disagreement on the ideal value for item difficulty for a classroom test item. One legitimate recommendation, which is supported here, is that teachers should examine closely and consider revising any item whose difficulty index is extremely easy (e.g., .85 or above) or extremely difficult (e.g., .20 or below) (Chase, 1999).

Of course, teachers should use good judgment as well as statistics when evaluating the difficulty of test items. For example, suppose an important instructional objective in a current events class is that all students know the name of the chairman of the Federal Reserve and his or her job functions. If a teacher stressed this information, presented it in various ways, and made it clear to students that they would be tested on it, it might not be surprising if all students answered a basic question on this topic correctly. Under these circumstances, the resulting difficulty index of 1.00 indicates that all is well. It confirms what the teacher wanted to know: Students mastered the concept.

The second index is known as *item discrimination*, and is symbolized by an uppercase, italicized letter D (for "discrimination"). The purpose of item discrimination is to examine how well each item discriminates among different levels of learning. If an item is functioning well, it should be answered correctly by most of the students who perform well on the entire test (i.e., those students who have likely mastered the content) and incorrectly by those students who performed poorly on the test (i.e., those students who have not mastered the content). In contrast, if an item does not discriminate well, it is likely that more poorly performing students will answer the item correctly than those who performed well on the test. In situations like this, there is probably something wrong with the item itself. For example, ambiguity in an item might mislead high-achieving students, causing them to mark a distractor. At the same time, low-achieving students might not recognize the ambiguity and mark the choice keyed as correct. Such items should be revised, or possibly discarded altogether, by the teacher.

In computing an item's discrimination index, one must first separate the class into upper- and lower-level groups. This is typically accomplished by rank ordering all students in the class based on total test score, and placing the top 1/4 and bottom 1/4 into the high and low groups. Nitko (2001) advises that any percentage of students ranging from 1/4 (the top and bottom 25%) to 1/3 (the top and bottom 33%) is appropriate. The remainder of the calculation involves the comparison of the proportion of students in the upper group who answered the item correctly to the proportion in the lower group. The comparison is then accomplished through simple subtraction, as follows:

$$D = \begin{bmatrix} \text{proportion} \\ \text{of students} \\ \text{answering} \\ \text{correctly} \\ \text{in upper} \\ \text{group} \end{bmatrix} - \begin{bmatrix} \text{proportion} \\ \text{of students} \\ \text{answering} \\ \text{correctly} \\ \text{in lower} \\ \text{group} \end{bmatrix}$$

or, since these proportions are equivalent to the item difficulty for each group:

$$D = p_{Upper} - p_{Lower}$$

The discrimination index can range from –1.00 to +1.00 (Nitko, 2001; Oosterhof, 1999 & 2001; Tanner, 2001). Items with positive values are known as *positively discriminating items*, and those with negative values are called *negatively discriminating items* (Nitko, 2001). An index of "+1.00" indicates perfect discrimination between the two groups. In other words, every student in the upper group answered correctly, and every student in the lower group answered incorrectly. An index of "–1.00" indicates that all low scorers answered correctly and all high scorers answered incorrectly—obviously representing a substantial problem with the item. Item discrimination values typically range between +.10 and +.60; any negatively discriminating item should either be discarded or substantially revised (Chase, 1999).

Again, there is some disagreement concerning the optimal values for item discrimination. Values greater than or equal to +.30 indicate fairly good quality.

The following represents a commonly used guideline (Chase, 1999):

.50 and up	very good item; definitely retain
.40 to .49	good item; very usable
.30 to .39	fair quality; usable item
.20 to .29	potentially poor item; consider revising
below .20	potentially very poor; possibly revise substantially or discard

Teachers should not rely too heavily on the value of a discrimination index in judging the quality of an item. A discrimination index can only provide information if there is variability in the performances of the students; for example, you cannot form "high scoring" and "low scoring" groups if all students perform well on a test. If these groups cannot be formed, the discrimination index cannot be calculated. Even if *almost all* students answered all items correctly, the proportions of students in both the high- and low-scoring groups who answered an item correctly will be very high. Thus, the difference in the proportion of each group who answered it correctly (i.e., the discrimination index) will naturally be small. For example, suppose a multiple-choice item asked second-graders what number to dial in an emergency (i.e., 9-1-1) and almost all students answered correctly. Such an item would have a low discrimination index but should probably be retained in future tests because it taps an extremely important piece of information, and the teacher will undoubtedly want to check that all students in future years have also mastered it. Thus, while a low discrimination index suggests that an item might need additional inspection, it does not necessarily mean that it should be rejected or even revised.

The third component of an item analysis is the *distractor analysis*. This informal type of analysis allows the teacher to examine how each distractor for an individual item is functioning. It basically consists of the number of students who selected each possible option, including the correct response. If an item's discrimination index is good, there is typically little reason to examine the distractors, since there is probably not a specific distractor that served to confuse any of the students (Oosterhof, 1999 & 2001). For instructional purposes, however, a distractor analysis will help teachers identify misconceptions students may have, which can then be remedied.

The final component included in an item analysis is the calculated reliability. Recall from Chapter 3 that the reliability of quantitative assessment data can be estimated through the use of *reliability coefficients*. For classroom test data, the method used to estimate reliability is one of internal consistency involving the application of the KR-21 formula. The resulting reliability coefficient ranges from .00 to +1.00. Desirable reliability values for classroom tests should range from .70 to 1.00 (Nitko, 2001). Some teachers may want to examine the internal consistency reliability of their classroom tests. The method of calculating KR-21 reliability is provided in Appendix C.

A portion of sample item analysis resulting from a test that I recently gave to my students is shown in Figure 8.8. The test was composed of fifty items; however, only the results for the first ten are shown here. A brief discussion of its interpretation follows.

From the printout provided in Figure 8.8, we can see that 24 students completed the 50-item test. At the top of the page, the minimum and maximum scores are provided, along with the mean and standard deviation. It is important to note that the KR-21 reliability for the test (near the upper-right corner) was equal to .81, well within the desirable range. (For further information regarding the calculations of the statistics mentioned here, please see Appendix C.)

The table in the middle of the page presents several pieces of information. For each item, the difficulty index (p) is presented in the second column. The correct response, as well as the distributions (i.e., the number of students who responded to each option) across all five options for each item, is presented next. First, notice that three of the items (Items 2, 3, and 8) were very easy items, as everyone answered them correctly. Several other items (e.g., Items 1, 5, 6, and 10) are borderline with respect to being too easy. None of these ten items appeared to be too difficult for the students.

The distribution of responses across the options provides information for distractor analysis. Specifically, the distractors for the three easy items identified earlier were completely ineffective since no one selected them. As a teacher, I might want to go back and re-examine the plausibility of the distractors for these items and possibly consider revising them in order to make them more effective. When examining the distractor distributions for other items, a couple of things should be noted. First, in Item 4 (which had the lowest difficulty level of the ten items), notice that more students missed the item than answered it correctly. Also notice that nine students selected option (C)—nearly as many as the number who answered the item correctly. I may want to take a look at that option to see if it is a well-written alternative, or if there is something vague or ambiguous about the way it is written, which could have resulted in confusion on the part of the students who selected it.

The discrimination indices are shown in the second table at the bottom of the page. Several of the discrimination values are quite low—although, fortunately, none are negative—which indicates that they require a closer look. Not surprisingly, Items 2, 3, and 8 had values equal to .00; since everyone taking the test answered correctly, obviously there was no difference between the upper and lower groups. Several others had values between .00 and .20, indicating again that I might want to scrutinize these items and their options a little closer prior to using them again. These low values indicate that there were few, if any, differences be-

tween the way high test scorers and low test scorers responded to those items.

As you saw demonstrated by the sample item analysis, it is crucial to note that several of the various indices support one another. Decisions about revising or even discarding an item should not be based solely on the examination of a single piece of information provided in the analysis, nor on the results of the statistical analyses alone. All pertinent information (i.e., difficulty, discrimination, and distractors) should be factored into those decisions.

Another reason for teachers to conduct item analyses is to develop and maintain an *item bank*. Each time an item is used and its statistical characteristics checked, the information could be recorded—either electronically or on 3" x 5" index cards. There is a substantial amount of time initially involved in this activity since new items must be written, administered, and analyzed. However, after awhile, teachers can simply go to their item banks and select suitable items for a given test, knowing that they have functioned effectively in the past.

Finally, item analysis information like that shown in Figure 8.8 can be obtained through specific statistical analysis software programs, such as ITEMAN (*www.assess.com/Software/iteman.htm*) and the Statistical Package for the Social Sciences, or SPSS (*www.spss.com*). Some of these software programs are quite expensive (near $1,000), while others are more affordable at around $300.

Figure 8.8 Sample printout from an item analysis

ANALYSIS OF TEST ITEMS

Number of students = 24
Number of items scored = 50
Maximum score = 46
Minimum score = 27

Mean score = 39.21
Standard deviation = 5.35
Reliability (KR-21) = .81

RESPONSE DISTRIBUTION

ITEM	DIFF (p)	CORR RESP	(A)	(B)	(C)	(D)	(E)
1	.83	A	20	1	2	1	•
2	1.00	C	•	•	24	•	•
3	1.00	A	24	•	•	•	•
4	.46	D	•	4	9	11	•
5	.88	C	•	•	21	3	•
6	.83	C	1	•	20	3	•
7	.71	A	17	7	•	•	•
8	1.00	C	•	•	24	•	•
9	.67	C	3	4	16	1	•
10	.92	C	1	•	22	•	1

Discrimination Indices (Difference of Upper and Lower 20%)

ITEM	PROP UPPER	PROP LOWER	D (DIFFER)
1	1.00	.80	.20
2	1.00	1.00	.00
3	1.00	1.00	.00
4	.40	.40	.00
5	1.00	.80	.20
6	1.00	.60	.40
7	.80	.40	.40
8	1.00	1.00	.00
9	1.00	.40	.60
10	1.00	.80	.20

It should be noted that if you perform item analyses by hand, you may not want to perform one for every test you give (Chase, 1999). Even periodic item analyses provide very useful information to the classroom teacher. Information and procedures for conducting item analyses by hand are provided through several Web sites appearing in the "Related Web Sites" section for this chapter (see page 193).

VALIDITY AND RELIABILITY OF OBJECTIVE TEST ITEMS

It is imperative that teachers determine the quality of the data resulting from students' test scores. Test scores can certainly provide valid and reliable information upon which to base—at least, in part—academic decisions about students. With respect to validity, we are ultimately trying to answer the following two questions: "Are we measuring what we intend to measure?" and "To what degree do we have confidence in the decisions we make based on those measures?" Of primary concern to classroom teachers is content evidence of validity for their tests. This is most appropriately achieved by means of a validation or content review of the items appearing on a test. An excellent practice is to have one or more experienced colleagues—familiar with the subject matter and level of student in the course or grade level—look over the test items prior to their administration to students (Tanner, 2001). This allows someone who is not familiar with the particular items to offer constructive feedback on their potential.

The issue of establishing the reliability of data resulting from objective tests is a little more straightforward. Reliability is best established through the use of statistical analyses and, specifically, the calculation of a reliability coefficient. For most classroom test situations, this would consist of the computation of a KR-21 (or other measure of internal consistency) reliability coefficient, as you saw demonstrated in the previous section on item analysis.

SUMMARY

Objective test items are those items with a single correct response. When scored, the judgment of the scorer does not influence an individual student's score in any way. These items typically assess lower levels of student cognitive skills, such as knowledge and comprehension. Objective items can be developed to measure higher-level skills, but they are much more difficult and time consuming to write for this purpose.

Objective items have several advantages. These include the relative ease with which they can be administered, scored, and analyzed; more content can be sampled efficiently; and the scores tend to be relatively reliable. Limitations include the time required to develop high-quality items, subjectivity in the decisions of content to be addressed by individual items, and that poor readers may be penalized, since these items rely on the comprehension of the prompt, problem, or statement presented in the item. A complete set of guidelines, presented in Figure 8.1, will aid teachers in the development of objective tests.

Another concept that can assist in the development of quality objective tests is that of a table of specifications. This table helps teachers specify the relation between specific content to be addressed on a test and the various cognitive levels of Bloom's taxonomy. It is highly advantageous to specify such a table prior to beginning the development of the actual test items.

The three main types of objective items are multiple-choice, matching, and alternate-choice items. All have particular advantages and limitations with which teachers should be familiar prior to administering such items to their students. Guidelines for developing these three main types of items have been summarized in Figures 8.4, 8.6, and 8.7, respectively. Several variations on the basic format of multiple-choice and alternate-choice items were also discussed.

A useful method of evaluating the quality of objective test items can be accomplished through statistical analysis of the actual student response, a process known as item analysis. Four main statistical indices are reported from an item analysis: item difficulty (proportion answering an item correctly), item discrimination (the difference between the proportion of correct answers for the highest-scoring students and the proportion of correct answers for the lowest-scoring students), distractor analysis (effectiveness of incorrect options), and reliability. These indices can be calculated by hand (for shorter tests) or by means of item-analysis software.

The validity of objective test items—primarily content evidence of validity—is most appropriately assessed by means of a content review. Experienced colleagues who are familiar with the content look over the test items prior to their implementation. Reliability of these test items is appropriately calculated and reported as a KR-21 reliability coefficient (see Appendix C).

⌐ **Chapter 8 *Related Web Sites*** 💻

❖ **Improving Your Test Questions** (*www.oir.uiuc.edu/dme/exams/ITQ.html*)
This site, maintained by the Division of Measurement and Evaluation at the University of Illinois at Urbana-Champaign, provides many good suggestions for writing high quality test items, including multiple-choice, true-false, matching, as well as completion, essay, and others. Included is some thought-provoking information about deciding between objective and subjective test items.

❖ **Checklist for Writing Test Items** (*www.tgsa.edu/online/cybrary/checklst.html*)
This Web site provides a series of checklists for writing various types of test items, both objective and subjective. Included are several additional references.

❖ **Creating Effective Classroom Tests: Writing Test Items**
(*www.taesig.8m.com/createv.html*)
Christine Coombe and Nancy Hubley have authored this electronic "textbook" with several chapters available online. Chapter V presents guidelines and suggestions for writing high-quality objective test items.

❖ **Creating Effective Classroom Tests: Statistics** (*www.taesig.8m.com/createviii.html*)
Chapter VIII of this resource by Coombe and Hubley provides some basic information about the types of statistics that can be computed when analyzing test data. These statistics include the mean, the pass/fail rate, and histograms.

❖ **Creating Effective Classroom Tests: Statistics Worksheet**
(*www.taesig.8m.com/createix.html*)
Coombe and Hubley have provided a worksheet template for assisting teachers in analyzing their own test data. Use this template or adapt it to fit your classroom needs.

❖ **Eight Simple Steps to Item Analysis**
(*www.edu.uleth.ca/courses/ed3604/iteman/eight/eight.html*)
Dr. Robert Runté, University of Lethbridge (Alberta, Canada), has put together this very useful Web page that "walks" you through the process of performing item analyses by hand. He presents a fairly straightforward process, and includes a sample form for compiling the results ("ITEM ANALYSIS FORM—TEACHER CONSTRUCTED TESTS"). He even offers some "short cuts," if you are pressed for time. Finally, Dr. Runté stresses that "You will note the complete lack of complicated statistics…no tricky formulas required for this." This site is highly recommended.

QUESTIONS FOR REVIEW

1. Discuss the relative advantages and disadvantages of objective test items as compared to performance assessments.

2. Using the guidelines provided in this chapter, identify the problem with the following multiple-choice item and rewrite it appropriately:

   ```
   Which of the following is an example of a crustacean?

   A) a shark
   B) a crab
   C) a starfish
   D) a rusty car
   ```

3. Using the guidelines provided, identify the problem with the following multiple-choice item and rewrite it appropriately:

   ```
   Validity is

   A) an important characteristic of a test.
   B) similar to reliability.
   C) the degree to which evidence and theory support the interpretations
      of test scores entailed by proposed uses of tests.
   D) the opposite of reliability.
   ```

4. Using the guidelines provided, identify the problem with the following multiple-choice item and rewrite it appropriately:

   ```
   Which of the following instruments uses a reed to make sound?

   A) an oboe
   B) a French horn
   C) a conductor
   D) a piano
   E) none of the above
   ```

5. Using the guidelines provided, identify the problem with the following multiple-choice item and rewrite it appropriately:

   ```
   Which is not a disadvantage of a multiple-choice item?

   A) scored objectively
   B) susceptible to guessing
   C) can be time consuming to construct
   ```

6. Using the guidelines provided, identify the problem with the following matching item and rewrite it appropriately:

_____	George Washington	A. site of Boston Tea Party
_____	Thomas Jefferson	B. wrote Declaration of Independence
_____	Lexington	C. announced arrival of British
_____	Paul Revere	D. first president
_____	Boston Harbor	E. site of important battle with British

7. Using the guidelines provided, identify the problem with the following true-false item and rewrite it appropriately:

    A golf ball hit with a driver will always go
    farther than one hit with a 9-iron.   T   F

8. Using the guidelines provided, identify the problem with the following true-false item and rewrite it appropriately:

    Most of the time, you should not use 9-1-1
    to call a television repairman.   T   F

9. Using the guidelines provided, identify the problem with the following true-false item and rewrite it appropriately:

    According to your textbook, there are four
    advantages of alternate-choice items.   T   F

10. A teacher notices the following values for D for four items. What is the appropriate interpretation of each?
    a.   +.60
    b.   +.20
    c.   .00
    d.   –.30

ENRICHMENT ACTIVITIES

1. Identify content for a lesson or unit that you will likely teach and assess. Develop a table of specifications covering five to six main areas of content from the unit for a 20-item objective test. Share your tables with your class.

2. For the table of specifications you developed above, develop a written test containing multiple-choice, matching, and true-false items. Prepare and format your test so that it would essentially be ready to copy and distribute to your students. Share your written tests with your class.

3. Develop a short (e.g., five-item) written "test" containing only multiple-choice items on any topic (perhaps current events). Administer your test to a minimum of 10 people (they might be friends, classmates, or family members). Once they have completed the test, conduct an item analysis by hand. Calculate and show the item difficulty indices, item discrimination indices, and the option response distribution. Which items worked well? Which are in need of revision? Should any be discarded entirely? Interpret the results and share them in small groups.

Chapter 9

Subjective Test Items

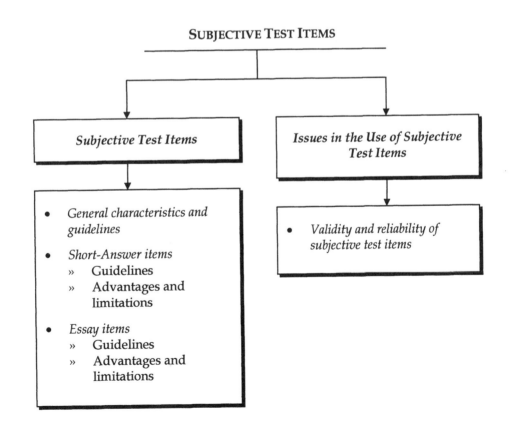

SUBJECTIVE TEST ITEMS

Subjective Test Items

- *General characteristics and guidelines*
- *Short-Answer items*
  » Guidelines
  » Advantages and limitations
- *Essay items*
  » Guidelines
  » Advantages and limitations

Issues in the Use of Subjective Test Items

- *Validity and reliability of subjective test items*

INTRODUCTION

Presented in this chapter is the other group of written, pencil-and-paper test items, namely *subjective test items*. Similar to objective test items, these types of items have been utilized in classrooms for many years. Teachers have found subjective items to be very versatile tools for assessing student learning.

It is worth reiterating that there is a commonly held belief among educators that the development of written test items is a relatively simple procedure. Although unique in their own right, subjective items share one important characteristic with objective items: Developing high-quality items requires a good deal of knowledge, skill, and practice. In this chapter, we will examine the characteristics, guidelines for development, and advantages and limitations of two main types of subjective test items.

GENERAL CHARACTERISTICS OF SUBJECTIVE TEST ITEMS

Among the various types of items used on pencil-and-paper classroom tests, subjective test items have the longest history (Nitko, 2001). Similar to objective test items, subjective items are so named because of the way in which they are scored. **Subjective test items** typically do not have a single correct response. Ordinarily, these items have several possible correct responses, or may have only one correct response but several possible ways to arrive at or express that answer. Furthermore, the subjective judgment of the

scorer can have an influence on a student's score. These types of items are also referred to as *free-response, constructed-response,* and *supply-type* items since students are presented with a prompt of some sort and then required to create their own answer (Gallagher, 1998). No possible answers are provided to them as they are with objective, or selected-response, items.

The use of subjective test items is appropriate for assessing lower-level cognitive skills as well as those at higher levels. Even though subjective items may address knowledge as the target skill, they usually involve a different kind of thinking on the part of the student (Tanner, 2001). These items require students to *produce* what they know, instead of merely *recognizing* the best response from a set of options.

Generally speaking, subjective test items have several advantages over their objective counterparts. Subjective items allow students to search for ideas and concepts that are not restricted to a preestablished set of options presented by the teacher (Gredler, 1999). They enable the teacher to follow a student's line of logic, argument, or justification (Tanner, 2001). Furthermore, subjective items tend to be relatively easy to construct (Tanner, 2001).

Although subjective items take little time to construct, they require more time for students to respond to them (Tanner, 2001). Related to this limitation is the fact that since more time is required to respond, less content can be adequately sampled in a given testing period. Some subjective items allow a great deal in depth of response, but a test consisting of them sacrifices quite a bit in terms of breadth of content coverage.

An additional limitation of subjective items is that some formats can be very time-consuming to score (Tanner, 2001). They are also difficult to score in a manner that eliminates the effects of the teacher's subjectivity, therefore creating problems with respect to the reliability of resulting scores.

It should be noted that many of the *general* guidelines discussed in Chapter 8 regarding the development of objective test items also apply to the development of subjective test items. Several of those specifically appropriate for subjective items are reiterated in Figure 9.1. In the following sections, the two main types of subjective items—short-answer and essay—will be discussed. Guidelines for the specific development of each will be summarized, as will the advantages and limitations of each.

Figure 9.1 General guidelines for developing subjective tests

Developing Subjective Tests:

General Guidelines

1. Subjective test items should cover important content and skills.
2. The reading level and vocabulary of each item should be as simple as possible.
3. Each subjective item should be stated in an unambiguous manner; confusing sentence structure and wording should be avoided.
4. Subjective items should not consist of verbatim statements or phrases lifted from the text.
5. Clues to the correct answer should not be provided.
6. Vary the types of items that appear on classroom tests.
7. Group items similar in format together, so that each type appears in a separate section.
8. Each section should be preceded by clear directions.
9. Within each section, order the items from easiest to most difficult.
10. Although all item types will not appear on every test, they should be arranged in the following order: true-false, matching, short answer, multiple-choice, and subjective items.
11. Provide adequate space for students to respond to each item.
12. Avoid splitting an item between two pages.

Short-Answer Items

Often, students are required to respond to an item with a word, short phrase, number, or other type of brief response. These types of items are known as **short-answer items** (Gallagher, 1998; Nitko, 2001). Short-answer items are most commonly formatted as either questions or incomplete sentences. The version consisting of an incomplete sentence is commonly referred to as a **completion** or **fill-in-the-blank item**. Generally speaking, if an item is phrased as a question, it is designated a *short-answer item*; if it contains a blank to be filled in by the student, it is labeled a *completion item*. In this section, these two variations will be discussed as the same general format. This is largely because virtually any completion item can be rewritten as a short-answer item and vice versa (Oosterhof, 1999 & 2001). The difference involves merely taking a statement and revising it to read as a question (or vice versa). For example, the following two items are essentially equivalent, with the first formatted as a short-answer item and the second as a completion item:

1) Who is the author of *Innocents Abroad*?

2) The author of *Innocents Abroad* is _____.

Notice that both of the above items look like multiple-choice items without the options (Gallagher, 1998). This is the primary difference between the short-answer and multiple-choice items. Very similar content and skills are being assessed, but students must create (or recall) their answers from memory, as opposed to selecting them from a list of provided options.

Short-answer items are most efficient at assessing lower-level thinking skills (Airasian, 2000 & 2001), but can also be used to assess higher-order thinking skills (Gredler, 1999; Nitko, 2001). They can be used to assess skills such as, but certainly not limited to, the ability to make relatively simple interpretations (e.g., counting the number of syllables in a word, or demonstrating an understanding of the concept of numerical place value) or the ability to solve numerical problems in mathematics and science (e.g., manipulating mathematical symbols in order to balance a chemical equation).

Short-answer and completion items are quite popular at all levels of education basically due to the ease with which they can be constructed (Tanner, 2001), as you will soon see. Short-answer items are also relatively easy to score (Trice, 2000), although not as easy as objective items (Gallagher, 1998). Since the responses must be handwritten by the student, they cannot be read by an optical computer scanner (Gallagher, 1998). It is important for teachers to remember that the specific nature of the response should be determined in advance by the teacher. This concept is somewhat similar to performance assessments in that it is necessary to specify the performance criteria that will be used to judge student work. This is probably most important when using short-answer items, as opposed to completion items, since short-answer items may consist of phrases or even up to two complete sentences (Gredler, 1999). This process is essentially equivalent to drafting correct or model responses prior to scoring the students' responses (Gallagher, 1998).

Two important issues in the scoring of these items are spelling and sentence structure (Gredler, 1999). If spelling and sentence structure are to be assessed as part of students' responses, they should be assessed separately from the content of the responses (Gredler, 1999). In other words, they should receive two independent scores: one for content, and one for spelling and structure. Furthermore, students should be informed *at the beginning of the instruction* that these two components will be assessed on tests.

With respect to scoring, it is important to note two final concerns. First, students may provide an answer that is correct but not what the teacher had intended. In these situations, teachers should award credit for these types of answers and do so uniformly for all students (Airasian, 2000 & 2001; Gallagher, 1998). Second, teachers must determine if these "unexpectedly correct" answers are the result of a poorly written item or a lack of student learning. If an item was poorly written and did not make clear the task for the students, the teacher should avoid penalizing students and award them credit. On the other hand, if the nature of the "incorrect-correct" response demonstrates a lack

of student comprehension or understanding, credit should not be awarded (Airasian, 2000 & 2001). Teacher decisions of this nature are subjective and are not necessarily easy ones to make. The ability to do so will come with experience.

It is also beneficial to consider a commonly used variation of the completion item. Many novice teachers and item-writers like to provide their students with a list of possible responses to a series of completion items. When this type of list is provided, the entire nature of the items has changed. These items are no longer subjective (i.e., constructed-response) items. Since a list of answers has been furnished to students and appear on the test, these items are, in reality, objective (i.e., matching) items. Therefore, different types of skills (recognition versus recall) are actually being assessed. For this reason, short-answer and completion items tend to be more difficult than selection items covering the same content (Chase, 1999).

Guidelines for Developing Short-Answer Items

In this section, guidelines and suggestions for writing short-answer items are presented (Chase, 1999; Gallagher, 1998; Gredler, 1999; Nitko, 2001; Oosterhof, 1999 & 2001; Tanner, 2001; Trice, 2000). They are as follows:

- *Short-answer items should be worded specifically and clearly.* Since short-answer items are usually brief, it is very important that the item clearly direct students to the desired answer. Items that are stated specifically tend to have fewer responses that are correct, but unintended, by the teacher. For example, consider the following item:

```
William Shakespeare wrote
_____.
```

A wide variety of responses to this item could be provided by students (e.g., "plays," "books," "with a pen," or "at night"), all of which could be correct, but would not be the answer desired by the teacher (e.g., *Romeo and Juliet*). An improved version of this item might be:

```
Romeo and Juliet was written by
_____.
```

However, similar undesirable responses could also be received here (e.g., "its author," "a man," or "a playwright"). The following version provides even more clarification:

```
Romeo and Juliet was written by
an English playwright whose
name was _____.
```

- *In completion items, place the blank near or at the end of the statement.* Items containing blanks near the beginning of the statement require students to mentally rearrange the wording in order to be able to respond to it, creating a degree of unnecessary confusion. Consider two versions of the same item, created by changing the position of the blank:

```
_____ is the name of
the capital city of New York.
```

```
The name of the capital city of
New York is _____.
```

The second version presents the prompt in a clearer fashion for students.

- *Avoid copying statements verbatim.* Using verbatim statements from a textbook, for example, only encourages students to memorize rather than comprehend information. These statements are also frequently taken out of context, which leads to ambiguous or vague items.

- *Omit important words only.* A completion item should require students to recall or otherwise identify important facts and concepts, not trivial types of information.

- *Use only one or two blanks.* Completion items with more than two blanks can become extremely unintelligible or ambiguous, creating what Trice (2000) calls a "Swiss-cheese item." Consider the following item:

```
The _____ produced by the
_____ is used by the
green _____ to change
_____ and _____
into _____. This process
is known as _____.
```

We could only imagine the creativity that could be demonstrated by students attempting to fill in those blanks. An improved version of this item, which also focuses on important information, appears next:

```
The process in which green
plants use the sun's energy to
turn water and carbon dioxide
into food is called
```

_____.

- *Standardize the length of blanks*. Varying the length of blanks in completion items can serve as unintended clues to students who are paying close attention to the format of the items rather than their content. For example, shorter blanks indicate that the desired response contains only a few letters, which may provide an important clue to students. To avoid these types of clues, keep all blanks the same length, but be sure to provide ample room for students to fill in their responses.

These guidelines for writing short-answer and completion items have been summarized in Figure 9.2.

Advantages and Limitations of Short-Answer Items

A primary advantage of short-answer items is that they are relatively easy to construct, provided teachers adhere to the guidelines presented in Figure 9.2 (Johnson & Johnson, 2002; Oosterhof, 1999 & 2001). Writing short-answer and completion items does take a little practice, but writing this item type is still easier than writing multiple-choice items, for example. With short-answer and completion items, only the stem needs to be written; no response options need to be written.

Another important advantage is that since no response options are provided from which students can choose, the probability of correctly guessing the response is substantially reduced (Airasian, 2000 & 2001; Gallagher, 1998; Gredler, 1999; Johnson & Johnson, 2002).

Figure 9.2 General guidelines for developing short-answer items

---

Developing Short-Answer Items:
General Guidelines

1. Short-answer items should be worded specifically and clearly.

2. In completion items, place the blank near or at the end of the statement.

3. Avoid copying statements verbatim.

4. Omit important words only.

5. Use only one or two blanks.

6. Standardize the length of blanks.

The opportunity for students to guess is always a possibility; however, with short-answer or completion items, they are "guessing" from memory, as opposed to simply guessing from a list provided to them. Finally, short-answer items tend to be quite reliable (Chase, 1999).

The main limitation of these items is that their primary use tends to be limited to lower-level thinking skills (Chase, 1999; Johnson & Johnson, 2002). As stated earlier, they can be written at higher levels of the cognitive domain, but writing quality higher-level items takes a good deal of practice and experience.

Scoring can be made difficult by the occurrence of spelling errors and poor sentence structure (Chase, 1999; Gallagher, 1998; Gredler, 1999; Oosterhof, 1999 & 2001). If these are important components of the students' responses, assess them separately. If these types of errors are not essential components, it is best to try to ignore them and assess only the content of the response.

Essay Items

In the previous chapter, we examined test items that required students to select brief responses from a set of options or determine the legitimacy of brief statements. In this chapter, thus far, we have discussed item types that require students to provide brief answers to questions or complete the missing information in statements. However, numerous situations arise where teachers are interested in assessing students' abilities to develop more

extensive responses. **Essay items** are questions or prompts that require students to write paragraphs or develop themes as responses (Johnson & Johnson, 2002). They might even consist of the development of a monthly budget for a family on a fixed income—anything that results in the creation of a somewhat lengthy response, either written or oral (Gallagher, 1998). They offer the greatest opportunity for students to construct their own responses (Airasian, 2000 & 2001). These items involve a wider variety of thinking skills, since students must recall, select, organize, and apply what they have learned and must do so in their own words.

Answers to essay items may be as short as a few sentences or as long as several pages (Chase, 1999). The shorter variety of essay item is typically referred to as a *restricted-response essay item*. Those requiring longer responses are known as *extended-response essay items*. The point at which a restricted-response essay becomes an extended-response essay is a "gray area," to say the least. It is better not to think of this classification as an "either-or" dichotomy, but rather as a continuum, with a potentially infinite number of essay response lengths possible.

Restricted response   *Extended response*

When using restricted-response essay items, teachers in some way restrict or limit the nature of the student response (Nitko, 2001). The item may be posed in such a manner as to elicit specific information; in other words, students are "directed" toward what the correct answer should include. Typically, both the content of the answer and the form of the written response are limited by the teacher. An example of a restricted-response essay item follows. Notice that students are instructed to provide only three reasons and are further instructed to "compare" only rating scales and checklists:

```
Discuss three reasons for the
preference of rating scales over
checklists for scoring perform-
ance assessments.
```

In contrast, extended-response essays permit students to freely express their own ideas, discuss various interrelationships among those ideas, and use their own organization in structuring their answers (Nitko, 2001). There is typically not one answer that is viewed by the teacher as being correct. A student's score is based on the ability to present views or opinions and support them with facts. Furthermore, scoring is contingent upon the content skill and knowledge possessed by the teacher. An example of an extended-response essay item, covering the same content as the restricted-response item shown above, is presented next. Notice how students' responses could be quite varied in terms of content and structure:

```
Discuss various ways in which
decisions about how to score as-
sessment activities can serve
different purposes when communi-
cating results to students and
parents.
```

Essay items are most appropriately used to assess complex thinking skills and learning outcomes (Chase, 1999). They can be used efficiently for analysis, synthesis, and evaluative skills. In that regard, essay items are sometimes used exclusively or are used as part of a larger performance assessment task (Gredler, 1999). It is not considered good practice to use essay items for the assessment of lower-level skills, such as knowledge and comprehension. Too much time and effort are required to use essays for that purpose (Gredler, 1999; Tanner, 2001). This can be accomplished much more efficiently through the use of objective items, which allow for more complete content coverage.

Scoring essay items represents the ultimate in scoring complexity and is notoriously unreliable (Airasian, 2000 & 2001; Johnson & Johnson, 2002). Different teachers may award different grades for identical answers, and the same teacher might award different grades for the same answer read at different times. There is also a tendency for teachers to award lower grades based on—or, at least, be influenced by—response characteristics (such as illegible writing or poor spelling and grammar), knowledge of student identities, or the location of papers in the stack of essays (Airasian, 2000 & 2001).

Scoring essays is time consuming and tiring (Airasian, 2000 & 2001). Because teachers read answers to the same essay item 15, 20, or even 60 times, boredom and fatigue can also influence scores awarded by teachers. It is best to take short breaks when scoring essays in order to avoid the fatigue factor.

Since the development of a response to an essay resembles the development of a response to a performance assessment task, it is recommended that essays be scored using similar techniques (Airasian, 2000 & 2001; Gallagher, 1998; Oosterhof, 1999 & 2001; Nitko, 2001). Specifically, this involves making decisions about scoring responses with an overall score or providing more specific feedback in the form of separate scores for each important component. If an overall score is to be awarded, a *holistic rubric* (as discussed in Chapter 6) should be developed and utilized. In contrast, if it is important to provide more specific feedback to students, an *analytic rubric* should be used.

Since scoring responses to essay items involves quite a bit of subjectivity, it is critical that the teacher take steps to improve the objectivity of the scoring process. Airasian (2000 & 2001) and Gallagher (1998) have offered several suggestions that can improve the objectivity of this process. These include:

- *Define ahead of time what constitutes a "correct" response.*
- *Use a carefully designed rubric or checklist for scoring.*

- *Decide, and inform students, how hand-writing, spelling, grammar, and organization will be scored.*
- *Whenever possible, score student responses anonymously.*
- *When tests involve several essay items, score all students' responses to the first item before moving on to the second.*

It is important to note that following these suggestions will reduce the subjectivity in scoring, but will not eliminate it entirely.

Guidelines for Developing Essay Items

In this section, guidelines for developing essay items are presented (Gallagher, 1998; Gredler, 1999; Nitko, 2001; Oosterhof, 1999 & 2001; Tanner, 2001; Trice, 2000). These guidelines include:

- *Essays should consist of the application of essential knowledge to new situations.* This is probably the epitome of assessing higher-order thinking skills. If knowledge is not being applied or evaluated with respect to *new* situations or scenarios, teachers are likely—and merely—assessing recall and comprehension skills, which can be accomplished more efficiently using previously discussed techniques.
- *Essays should present a clear and focused task to students.* Since they are open-ended and allow students to "flex their creative muscles," teachers should present a clear and unambiguous task to which students can respond. It is important to avoid such phrases as "Tell all you know..." or "Discuss everything you know

about…," which do nothing to focus a student's response. Consider the following item, which accompanied a passage from *Hamlet*, within which the teacher wanted students to discuss the characterization in this particular passage of the play:

```
Write an essay analyzing the
passage.
```

Undoubtedly, the teacher had something in mind for a response when this item was written. However, it is unlikely that the students are being guided toward that desirable response with this unfocused version of the item. An improved version might read:

```
Describe the characters' moti-
vation in this passage. Iden-
tify the factors that caused
each character to react as he
or she did.
```

It is much more likely that this second version will result in the type of response the teacher had hoped to see.

- *Specify for students the desired length, time limits, and evaluative criteria.* Teachers should inform students of these types of desirable qualities ahead of time. Usually, teachers have in mind a desired length of a response to an essay item. It is important to note that virtually any essay question can be answered in a paragraph—or in a book! Furthermore, if guidelines are not provided to students, some will respond with the former and some

with the latter. Informing them of the basis for scoring their responses also familiarizes them with the desirable qualities their responses should include. This may be accomplished by sharing with them the actual rubric that will be used to score their answer. Using the previous example, we might see something like this:

```
Describe the characters' moti-
vation in this passage. Iden-
tify 2-3 factors for each char-
acter that caused him or her to
react as he or she did. Limit
your response to two pages. (30
minutes/10 points)
```

- *Develop a model response.* As previously mentioned, teachers should anticipate the types of responses they will receive from their students. Developing a model response, containing all desirable qualities and content, helps teachers to envision specific components that students should and should not provide.

These guidelines for writing essay items have been summarized in Figure 9.3.

Advantages and Limitations of Essay Items

Essays can be used to elicit a wide variety of responses from students, spanning the continuum from knowledge to evaluation skills (Johnson & Johnson, 2002). Included in this advantage is that students are afforded the opportunity to create their own responses (Airasian, 2000 & 2001).

Figure 9.3 General guidelines for developing essay items

```
┌─────────────────────────────────────────────────────────────┐
│                                                               │
│                  Developing Essay Items:                      │
│                    General Guidelines                         │
│                                                               │
│   1.   Essays should consist of the application of essential  │
│        knowledge to new situations.                           │
│                                                               │
│   2.   Essays should present a clear and focused task to      │
│        students.                                              │
│                                                               │
│   3.   Specify for students the desired length, time limits,  │
│        and evaluative criteria.                               │
│                                                               │
│   4.   Develop a model response.                              │
│                                                               │
└─────────────────────────────────────────────────────────────┘
```

Another advantage of essays is that guessing is substantially reduced (Chase, 1999; Johnson & Johnson, 2002). Students must be able to recall and organize, in some fashion, larger amounts of information that they have learned. This, however, does create an opportunity for students to "bluff," which is a distinct disadvantage of essay items (Chase, 1999; Airasian, 2000 & 2001). *Bluffing* occurs when students actually know very little about the content and skills being addressed in the item, but write so creatively as to appear familiar with it. Their hope is to receive at least some partial credit.

Other limitations of essays include the fact that they are very time consuming to score (Airasian, 2000 & 2001; Chase, 1999). In fact, the vast majority of a teacher's work related to the use of essays is spent scoring student responses to them. Additionally, they may severely restrict the coverage of content from an instructional unit (Nitko, 2001; Oosterhof, 1999 & 2001). This is due to essays not only being time consuming for teachers to score, but also time consuming for students to answer. Finally, unless specific guidelines for the scoring of essays are strictly adhered to, the scoring will very likely be unreliable (Gredler, 1999; Nitko, 2001; Oosterhof, 1999 & 2001).

VALIDITY AND RELIABILITY OF SUBJECTIVE TEST ITEMS

With respect to establishing the validity of subjective test items, we are once again concerned with determining if we are actually measuring what we intend to measure, and if we can be confident in decisions that result from scores received on subjective items. As with objective items, the main concern to classroom teachers is content evidence of validity for their subjective items. A content review of any subjective items appearing on a test allows someone other than yourself, who is not familiar with the particular items, to offer constructive feedback on their potential.

The issue of the reliability of subjective items is somewhat different from that of objective items. Since there are not nearly as many subjective items as objective items that could appear on a test—and, since the scoring differs from a simple "correct" or "incorrect" alternative—subjective item scores cannot be subjected to an item analysis or calculation of a reliability coefficient as objective item scores can. Even with the use of thoroughly developed scoring rubrics, subjective judgments will be made by teachers when scoring responses to essay items; this subjectivity cannot be entirely eliminated. Following the guidelines for developing scoring rubrics (presented in Chapter 6), along with the suggestions for scoring essays presented in this chapter, will improve the reliability of scoring short-answer and, particularly, essay items.

SUMMARY

Subjective test items are those that do not typically have only one correct response. They may have several possible correct answers, or may have only one, but several ways in which students can arrive at it. Short-answer and essay items are appropriate for assessing student learning along the entire continuum of Bloom's taxonomy (see Chapter 2).

Generally speaking, subjective items have several distinct advantages over other forms of written test items. They allow students to construct their own responses, as opposed to simply selecting the correct answer from a set of teacher-developed options. Because of this fact, the potential for guessing is substantially reduced, although bluffing becomes a potential hindrance. Subjective items do not take a great deal of time for teachers to construct, but are limited by the fact that they are time consuming for students to answer and for teachers to score. General guidelines for preparing subjective tests are presented in Figure 9.1.

The two main types of subjective items are short-answer, including completion, and essay items. Teachers should be familiar with their respective advantages and limitations prior to developing and using them on classroom tests. Guidelines for developing these types of subjective items have been summarized in Figures 9.2 and 9.3.

Content evidence of the validity of subjective test items is assessed by means of a content review, usually by an experienced colleague familiar with the content. Reliability of these test items tends to be low but can be enhanced by following suggestions provided in this chapter.

~🖱 **Chapter 9** *Related Web Sites* 💻

❖ **Improving Your Test Questions** (*www.oir.uiuc.edu/dme/exams/ITQ.html*)
This site, maintained by the Division of Measurement and Evaluation at the University of Illinois at Urbana-Champaign, provides many good suggestions for writing high-quality test items, including multiple-choice, true-false, matching, as well as completion, essay, and others. Included is some thought-provoking information about deciding between objective and subjective test items.

❖ **Checklist for Writing Test Items** (*www.tgsa.edu/online/cybrary/checklst.html*)
This Web site provides a series of checklists for writing various types of test items, both objective and subjective. Included are several additional references.

❖ **Creating Effective Classroom Tests: Writing Subjective Test Items**
(*www.taesig.8m.com/createvi.html*)
Christine Coombe and Nancy Hubley have authored this electronic "textbook" with several chapters available online. Chapter VI presents guidelines and suggestions for writing high-quality subjective test items.

QUESTIONS FOR REVIEW

1. Discuss the relative advantages and disadvantages of subjective test items as compared to performance assessments.

2. Using the guidelines provided in this chapter, identify the problem(s) with the following short-answer item and rewrite it appropriately:

   ```
   A rotating storm that forms in the _____ Ocean and moves
   in a _____ direction is called a _____.
   ```

3. Using the guidelines provided, identify the problem(s) with the following short-answer item and rewrite it appropriately:

   ```
   _____ and _____ are the names of the two rivers that
   meet in Pittsburgh.
   ```

4. Rewrite the following multiple-choice item as a short-answer item.

   ```
   Which of the following instruments uses reeds to make sound?

   A) an oboe
   B) a French horn
   C) a conductor
   D) a piano
   E) none of the above
   ```

5. Rewrite the multiple-choice item in Question 4 above as a completion item.

6. Using the guidelines provided, identify the problem with the following short-answer item and rewrite it appropriately:

   ```
   Where is the Pacific Ocean? _____.
   ```

7. Using the guidelines provided in this chapter, identify the problem(s) with the following restricted-response essay item and rewrite it appropriately:

   ```
   State the three examples of moral dilemmas that we discussed in class.
   ```

8. Using the guidelines provided, identify the problem with the following extended-response essay item and rewrite it appropriately:

   ```
   After reading the chapter on the Vietnam War, discuss everything you
   know about Vietnam. [45 minutes/20 points]
   ```

9. For the restricted-response essay item listed below, discuss the things a teacher might do to be objective while scoring responses:

   ```
   Compare and contrast the circulatory systems of fish and mammals.
   Limit your discussion to three characteristics. [10 minutes/5 points]
   ```

10. Discuss the similarities and differences between essay items and performance assessment tasks.

ENRICHMENT ACTIVITIES

1. Identify content for a lesson or unit that you will likely teach and assess. Develop a table of specifications covering five to six main areas of content from the unit for a 20-item subjective test. Share your tables with your class.

2. For the table of specifications you developed above, develop a written test containing short-answer and essay items. Prepare and format your test so that it would essentially be ready to copy and distribute to your students. Share your written tests with your class.

3. Develop an essay item in your own teaching area. Anticipate desirable student responses and compose a scoring key or rubric for their actual responses. Your key should list the critical aspects that represent a good answer and the number of points each aspect will be worth. Share your essay item with your classmates.

PART IV:

ADDITIONAL ASSESSMENT ISSUES

Chapter 10
Grading Systems

Chapter 11
Interpreting Standardized Tests

Chapter 12
Assessing Group Work

Chapter 13
Assessing Affective Characteristics

Notes

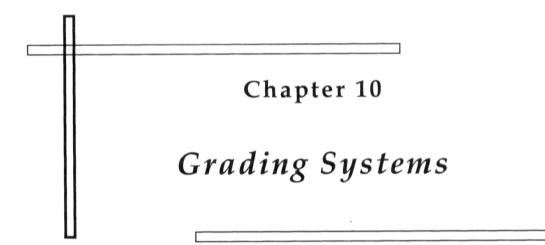

Chapter 10

Grading Systems

Overview of Chapter 10

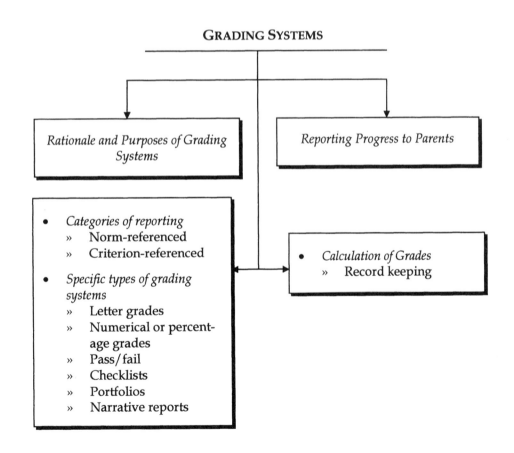

GRADING SYSTEMS

Rationale and Purposes of Grading Systems

Reporting Progress to Parents

- *Categories of reporting*
  - » Norm-referenced
  - » Criterion-referenced
- *Specific types of grading systems*
  - » Letter grades
  - » Numerical or percentage grades
  - » Pass/fail
  - » Checklists
  - » Portfolios
  - » Narrative reports

- *Calculation of Grades*
  - » Record keeping

INTRODUCTION

This chapter presents discussions of grades and grading systems. Grading is the primary means by which the results of assessments are summarized and communicated to interested parties. It is typically seen as the culminating activity following a series of preceding steps (Tanner, 2001). Recall that Figure 1.2 (you may want to revisit this diagram from Chapter 1) shows the detailed relationships between tests, measurements, assessments, evaluations, and assessment systems. Tests and other procedures yield measurements, which, when combined together, form assessments. These assessments serve as the basis for evaluations, or educational decisions. However, a crucial step in this process is that the assessments must be graded as the initial phase of the evaluative decision-making process.

Assigning grades to student work is the summative function of assessment (Nitko, 2001). We will learn more about the specific purposes of grading below, but first it is important to realize that summative grading serves as the basis for communicating the status of students' achievement to students, parents, administrators, and others.

Grading is often seen as one of the most difficult and troublesome aspects of teaching (Nitko, 2001). This difficulty is sometimes counterbalanced if teachers realize that grading and evaluation are simply the final steps in the instructional process:

planning → instruction → assessment → grading and evaluation

Teachers should not treat grading as an "afterthought." It should be considered as an integral part of the instructional process.

RATIONALE AND PURPOSES OF GRADING SYSTEMS

Grading is defined as the process of using a formal system for purposes of summarizing and reporting student achievement and progress. Assigning grades to students and their academic work is an important professional responsibility of teachers (Airasian, 2000 & 2001). It is important not only because teachers carry out this responsibility numerous times during a school year, but also because of the important consequences that grading can have for students.

Grades can be assigned to individual measurements (e.g., a test or a paper) or to assessments (i.e., groups of measurements) (Airasian, 2000 & 2001). The latter is commonly done at the end of grading periods or at the end of a school year.

Grading essentially involves the comparison of a student's performance to some standards or criteria (Airasian, 2000 & 2001). Imagine that Rosie, a fifth-grader, tells you that she received a score of 93 on a mathematics test. What might your reaction to her score be? Do you think her performance was good, average, or poor? At this point, that question cannot be answered. Something that serves as the basis for comparison is needed. Her score of 93 simply describes her performance; it does not "grade" her performance. For example, it would be helpful to know how many possible points there were on the math test. If 100 points were possible, we might conclude that Rosie performed well on the test. However, if there were 200 possible points, we would arrive at a substantially different conclusion. Similarly, we might want to know how Rosie did when compared to her classmates. Knowing that she earned a score of 93 does not tell us this.

The primary reason that teachers grade is that nearly all school districts require summative judgments, in some form, about their students (Airasian, 2000 & 2001; Johnson & Johnson, 2002). Grading is the necessary activity that leads to those summative judgments. Regardless of the type of grading system or reporting format used, student grades are always based on teachers' judgments. In fact, many experts believe that the single most important characteristic of the process of grading is its reliance on teachers' judgments (Airasian, 2000 & 2001; Chase, 1999). These judgments are not guesses, nor are they certainties; they should be based on the accumulation of valid and reliable evidence.

The main purpose of grades is to communicate information about a student's academic achievement and progress (Airasian, 2000 & 2001; Chase, 1999; Gallagher, 1998; Gredler, 1999; Tanner, 2001). This information might be used for administrative purposes (e.g., to deter-mine a student's class standing and appropriateness for promotion to the next grade), to communicate information about specific academic performance to students and parents, and for educational and career planning. A final purpose of grading, which will be described in detail below, is that grades can serve as a source of motivation for students (Airasian, 2000 & 2001; Gredler, 1999).

It is important to examine some important, and necessary, criteria for grading systems. First and foremost, grades must be fair (Gredler, 1999; Johnson & Johnson, 2002). Grades must also be accurate (Gredler, 1999). Students' grades are the primary determinant of the specific educational and career opportunities available to them. They can serve as the basis for determining academic recognition and honors, as well as placement into advanced courses. Grades are very powerful, and for this reason, assigning grades may be the most serious responsibility that classroom teachers have (Johnson & Johnson, 2002). The extent to which student grades are fair and accurate determines their defensibility (Gredler, 1999).

Grades should be based on a sufficient amount of data collected systematically throughout the course (Gallagher, 1998; Gredler, 1999). Furthermore, this systematically collected data must be valid. When teachers ensure that the data are both sufficient and valid, they also ensure that the grades they assign are accurate (Gredler, 1999). Just as one student is unlikely to accurately represent an entire population of students, so too is one measurement unlikely to represent the overall academic ability of a given student. The larger the number of valid components used to calculate a grade, the more likely the grade will be representative of the student's academic performance (Gallagher, 1998).

At the same time, however, it is not good practice to grade "everything in sight." For *summative* grading, it is not necessary—nor is it practical—to grade every homework problem, all seatwork, problems worked at the chalkboard, and responses to oral questions. Gallagher (1998) stresses that there must be a balance between the time given to assessment relative to the time given to instruction. There is nothing wrong with "grading" (or correcting) these types of activities in order to provide corrective comments in the form of *formative* feedback (Gredler, 1999). It is an altogether different situation to grade everything and figure all those scores into a summative grade. In fact, many educators believe that informing students that everything will be graded is equivalent to making a threat (Gallagher, 1998). Typically, a major part of instruction consists of learning through practice, which logically implies that students may answer problems or questions incorrectly until they have had ample opportunity to fully understand and master the material. For example, when first teaching students how to multiply and divide three-digit numbers, most of us would likely expect students to incor-

rectly answer some problems until they have had more practice (Frisbie & Waltman, 1992). Grading those first attempts does not only appear to be unfair, but might likely also result in a final grade that is at least somewhat misleading. Since not all student work is graded, it is important that students know in advance which measures will actually "count" toward their final grade (Gallagher, 1998).

Obviously, establishing a grading system where some assignments are corrected with only formative comments can also have detrimental effects. Some students will realize that since the assignments are not being graded, there is no real need to complete them (Gallagher, 1998; Gredler, 1999). A logical question might be, "Shouldn't these students be penalized for not completing the work?" These students might legitimately need less practice than others; they should not be punished for this (Gallagher, 1998). If they do need practice, but choose not to do the work, they will see that need reflected by the low grades they receive on more formal assessments. This should help them to see the link between practice and assessment without the teacher having to resort to a sort of "grades as punishment" mentality.

What specific types of student work should be included in a summative grade? Most teachers would agree that the results of formal assessments (e.g., written tests and large-scale projects) should be included in a final grade. Quizzes, homework, and seatwork may be included, depending on how they are viewed by the teacher (Airasian, 2000 & 2001). If these types of work are seen as practice for students that is closely tied to the instruction, teachers may decide not to include them in students' grades. On the other hand, some teachers view these assignments as indicators of how well students have learned their daily lessons and therefore include them as part of the grade (Airasian, 2000 & 2001). As with most grading issues, the final decisions about the specific components of students' grades rest with the individual classroom teacher.

A related issue about dimensions of student grades includes other factors such as attendance, effort, attitude, conduct, and class participation (Gallagher, 1998). Unless these items are specifically related to the instructional objectives, they should be excluded from grades (Oosterhof, 1999 & 2001). Many school districts use a multi-symbol grading system, which allows teachers to indicate a student's status or progress in nonacademic areas separately from academic performance, and to do so on the same report card. If you wish to report on these types of student behaviors—which are usually assessed through informal assessments—but your district's grading system does not permit you to do so independently, it is best to find another mechanism (such as a letter or a parent-teacher conference) of reporting them (Chase, 1999). If, based on academic work, a student earns a high mark in a course, but has that mark lowered due to poor conduct or a lack of participation, that

lowered mark inaccurately reports the student's academic performance.

An alternative situation in which to use factors such as effort and participation is in cases when students' composite marks place them on the boundary between two adjacent grades (Airasian, 2000 & 2001; Nitko, 2001). The results of informal assessments, such as observations of effort or participation, may be used as the justification for raising a grade that falls just below the borderline (Airasian, 2000 & 2001). However, it is best to remember that decisions about raising or lowering a borderline *academic* grade are best made using additional achievement information (Nitko, 2001).

As mentioned earlier, grades often serve as a source of motivation for students. There are educators who believe that grades introduce a false sort of incentive for achievement into the learning process (Chase, 1999). They believe that the intrinsic value of learning should serve as the sole motivator and that grades should be abolished (Oosterhof, 1999 & 2001). However, the existence of this "intrinsic motivation" is rarely the case. When comparing liberal to more stringent grading systems, we observe a decline in motivation with those that are more liberal (Chase, 1999).

The fact remains that grades serve as a substantial source of academic motivation for many students, albeit predominantly for already high-achieving students (Nitko, 2001). From a student perspective, high grades are associated with desirable qualities; low grades, with less desirable qualities (Oosterhof, 1999 & 2001). However, teachers should not use grades as a means of disciplining students (Oosterhof, 1999 & 2001). There is a tendency for teachers to reduce the credit (possibly even awarding zero points) that a student receives on an assignment that is submitted late or when caught cheating. When the student's grade is calculated at a later time, it may be reduced, perhaps quite substantially so, due to the effect of this "zero." However, this is poor practice. The lowered grade will then be interpreted as an indication of the student's academic performance, which in this case might be quite inaccurate. The fact that the student receives a score of zero is not synonymous with the student's having zero achievement, as represented by the score (Oosterhof, 1999 & 2001). Situations such as these are best described as disciplinary issues, not academic ones, and should be treated as such.

CATEGORIES OF REPORTING PROGRESS AND ACHIEVEMENT

As mentioned earlier, grading involves the comparison of a student's performance or progress to some standards or criteria. This is the basic mechanism for judging the quality of a student's performance. There exist several categories that can serve as the basis for comparisons of student performance. The categories most commonly used in classrooms involve comparisons of a student's performance with

- the performance of other students;
- predefined standards of performance;
- the student's own ability level; or
- the student's prior performance—an indication of improvement (Airasian, 2000 & 2001; Chase, 1999).

We will focus our discussion on the first two types of comparisons since they tend to be used across entire classes, schools, and districts. The third and fourth categories are not typically used by the regular classroom teacher, as they rely more heavily on teacher perceptions and subjectivity (Airasian, 2000 & 2001), which can call into question their validity and reliability. These two systems may be more appropriately used to assign grades to the performances and work habits of students who are receiving special educational services.

Norm-Referenced Comparisons

When teachers assign grades to students based on their performance compared with that of other students, they are using a **norm-referenced grading system**. Norm-referenced grading is also sometimes referred to as *relative grading, curving the class*, and *grading on the curve* (Airasian, 2000 & 2001; Chase, 1999; Gredler, 1999). The basis for comparison in a norm-referenced system of grading is the performance of all other students in the class. For example, if Maria receives a high grade in social studies, it means that she performed better than many of her classmates. Obviously, a low grade has the opposite meaning.

In a norm-referenced system of grading, not all students can receive the top grade, regardless of how well each performs (Airasian, 2000 & 2001). This system is designed to ensure that grades that span all possible grading categories will be received. Suppose we were going to report grades using a traditional letter grading system (i.e., A–B–C–D–F). Regardless of the actual number of points earned, some students would receive "A"s, some would receive "B"s, and some would receive "F"s. In other words, the grade awarded in a norm-referenced system is not based solely on the extent to which the student mastered the material that was taught (Airasian, 2000 & 2001). For example, it is possible to correctly answer 35 questions out of a possible 100 and receive an "A"—indicating that a score of 35 was better than that of most of the other students in the class. On the other hand, a student might earn 93 out of 100 points and receive a "D" due to the fact that most of the other students scored 95 and above.

Norm-referenced reporting assumes that student performance will always span across all possible grades and that the distribution across those grades can be specified in advance (Gredler, 1999). When teachers employ a norm-referenced system of grading, they must determine in advance their desired proportional distribution across the grading scale (Airasian, 2000 & 2001; Chase, 1999). This can vary from school to school or even from teacher to teacher, but a sample distribution might look like this:

Top 15% .... *"A" grade*
Next 30% .... *"B" grade*
Next 35% .... *"C" grade*
Next 10% .... *"D" grade*
Lowest 10% .... *"F" grade*

Following the administration of a written test, for example, a teacher would score the tests and arrange the students in order of their scores from highest to lowest. The top 15% of students would each receive a grade of "A," the next 30% would each receive a "B," and so on. Therefore, in a class comprising 33 students, the top 5 scorers would receive "A"s, the next 10 would receive "B"s, the next 12 would receive "C"s, the next 3 would receive "D"s, and the 3 lowest scores would receive "F"s. This same logic—and distribution—would apply to cumulative grades being calculated at the end of a term.

There is no absolute system of "curving" grades; teachers construct their own distributions by considering the individual students, subject areas, and their own beliefs about grades (Airasian, 2000 & 2001). Some teachers believe in awarding mostly "A"s and "B"s, while others give mostly "C"s. Often, each class performs differently and therefore should be treated differently; percentages may be adjusted from year to year (Gredler, 1999). Regardless of the proportions used, teachers must keep in mind that it is important for their system to appear fair.

A disadvantage of norm-referenced systems of comparison is that they tend to create very competitive classrooms. Students' success depends not only on their ability, but possibly more so on the performance of others (Airasian, 2000 & 2001). All students do not have a fair and equal opportunity to achieve their desired grade. It does not matter how well Jason performs; if others do better than he does, his grade is essentially lowered. This fact also has a tendency to reduce student co-operation and willingness to work together (Airasian, 2000 & 2001). Another disadvantage of norm-referenced grades is that the meaning of the letter grade is not always clear. Even the seemingly "objective" cutoff points for the specification of letter grades are arbitrary (i.e., predetermined by the teacher).

Criterion-Referenced Comparisons

Many teachers do not grade their students using a system that simply compares students to one another. These teachers might opt for the most commonly used grading system in public schools, known as criterion-referenced grading (Airasian, 2000 & 2001). In **criterion-referenced grading**, student performance is compared to a preestablished set of performance standards. This system of grading is seen as being much more fair as compared to norm-referenced grading since students are not competing for grades; the basis for grades is an individual student's performance (Airasian, 2000 & 2001; Gallagher, 1998; Gredler, 1999).

In a criterion-referenced approach to grading, all students can earn "A"s, just as it is possible for no student to earn an "A." The grades simply depend on the extent to which the performance criteria have been achieved and demonstrated by the student (Chase, 1999).

There are two types of performance standards that can be used in a criterion-referenced system of grading. The first type is known as *performance-based criteria* and involves the detailed specification of particular behaviors that students must perform in order to receive a certain grade (Airasian, 2000 & 2001). This approach is quite similar to rubric scoring, as was discussed in Chapter 6. For example, imagine that a teacher is preparing to teach a unit on estimation and is establishing the performance criteria. The teacher devises the following scoring rubric for assigning grades for the unit:

"A"   *Makes accurate estimations. Uses appropriate mathematical operations with no mistakes. Draws logical conclusions supported by graph. Sound explanations of thinking.*

"B"   *Makes good estimations. Uses appropriate mathematical operations with few mistakes. Draws logical conclusions supported by graph. Good explanations of thinking.*

"C"   *Attempts estimations, although many inaccurate. Uses inappropriate mathematical operations, but with no mistakes. Draws conclusions not supported by graph. Offers little explanation.*

"D"   *Makes inaccurate estimations. Uses inappropriate mathematical operations. Draws no conclusions related to graph. Offers no explanations of thinking.*

The teacher implements the criteria by observing each student during a culminating estimation activity and assigns grades according to the rubric. Notice that the students' grades will depend solely on how each performed in comparison to the criteria.

The second—and much more common—type of performance standard is known as *percentage-based criteria* (Airasian, 2000 & 2001). This type uses cutoff scores based on the percentage of items answered correctly or points earned on a measurement or other assignment. The following is an example of probably the most widely used standard of this type (Airasian, 2000 & 2001):

> 90%–100% .... "A" grade
> 80%–89% .... "B" grade
> 70%–79% .... "C" grade
> 60%–69% .... "D" grade
> Less than 60% .... "F" grade

Obviously, in this system there is no limit to the number of students who can receive a particular grade and there is no pre-established distribution of grades, as in a norm-referenced system. Similar to the norm-referenced system, this system requires teachers to determine the appropriate cut scores in light of the subject matter and their personal beliefs about grading (Airasian, 2000 & 2001). One teacher may use 93% as the cutoff score for an "A," while another may use 85%. Some schools have specific policies regarding the percentage-based cutoff scores, and all teachers must use that sys-

tem. However, many school districts permit teachers to make their own professional decisions regarding specific percentage-based criteria.

SPECIFIC TYPES OF GRADING SYSTEMS

Grading systems vary immensely from school district to school district, sometimes even within the *same* school district. Furthermore, elementary schools typically use systems that differ from those used in secondary schools. There are several systems in use today, some more predominantly than others. These systems include letter grades, numerical or percentage grades, pass/fail grading, checklists, portfolios, and narrative reports.

Letter Grades

Nearly everyone is familiar with the *letter grading system* (i.e., A–B–C–D–F), in which a grade of "A" represents the highest level of achievement and a grade of "F" denotes "failure" and indicates a notable lack of progress or achievement (Chase, 1999). This system is probably the oldest grading system still in use, largely because educators and parents believe they understand it (Chase, 1999; Gredler, 1999).

Letter grades are efficient because they summarize an entire term's work with a single grade. However, this advantage is also somewhat of a limitation. A single grade cannot adequately describe an individual student's strengths and weaknesses (Chase, 1999; Gredler, 1999; Johnson & Johnson, 2002). For example, if Carmen receives a grade of "B" in reading and writing skills, that grade provides no indication of the areas in which Carmen needs to improve. Furthermore, Carmen and Mary both may have received grades of "B," but for very different reasons. Often, letter grades are more beneficial when accompanied by some sort of descriptive information.

When letter grades are used in elementary settings, they may be adapted in order to avoid the finer distinctions of placing students into five possible grade categories (Chase, 1999). Elementary letter grade systems may use only three possible grades, such as "M" ("meritorious"), "S" ("satisfactory"), and "U" ("unsatisfactory"). Secondary schools do not typically have the luxury of making these adaptations, since a somewhat common system must exist for purposes of standardizing grade-point averages, which must be provided on college admissions applications.

In a letter grading system, there exists a potential for imprecision (Johnson & Johnson, 2002; Tanner, 2001). For example, suppose that the following grading scale for letter grades is being used in a seventh-grade mathematics class:

90–100 points...........“A” grade
80–89 points...........“B” grade
70–79 points...........“C” grade
60–69 points...........“D” grade
Less than 60 points...........“F” grade

At the end of the term, one student earns 99 of the possible 100 points, and another student earns 90 points. Obviously, both students receive "A"s, but there probably is a substantial difference in their levels of achievement, as represented by the difference of 9 points. A similar problem occurs when one student earns 60 points and another earns 59. The first student receives a grade of "D," and the second receives an "F." There is a meaningful discrepancy in the letter grades received, but that discrepancy is the result of a mere 1-point difference in performance. This problem can be remedied and letter grades made more precise when a plus/minus system is incorporated into a letter grading system (Tanner, 2001). For example, the previous grading scale might be revised as follows:

98–100 points...........“A+” grade
93–97 points...........“A” grade
90–92 points...........“A-” grade
87–89 points...........“B+” grade
83–86 points...........“B” grade
80–82 points...........“B-” grade
77–79 points...........“C+” grade
73–76 points...........“C” grade
70–72 points...........“C-” grade
67–69 points...........“D+” grade
63–66 points...........“D” grade
60–62 points...........“D-” grade
Less than 60 points...........“F” grade

This option allows for more precision in reported letter grades; however, seldom do teachers have control over the decision to include a plus/minus system. Those decisions are usually made at the district level.

Numerical or Percentage Grades

Another alternative to avoiding the imprecision of some letter grading systems is to simply report the actual number or percentage of points earned and, thus, escape the necessity of converting the value to a letter grade. These types of grades are known as *numerical* or *percentage grades*. However, there is still a tendency—especially for parents—to phone the teacher and ask, "I see that my daughter earned 82% of the points in your class, but is that a 'B' or a 'C'?" This problem may be avoided by reporting both the percentage and the corresponding letter grade in a system sometimes referred to as a *multigrade system*.

These types of grades are also limited by the fact that they do not provide specific feedback on areas of student weakness. They provide only an overall indication of student achievement (Oosterhof, 1999 & 2001).

Pass/Fail

An alternative to letter and numerical or percentage grades is the pass/fail designation. *Pass/fail systems of grading*, synonymous with *pass/no pass* or *credit/no credit* plans, are used most often in colleges for courses that students want to explore outside their chosen field of study (Gredler, 1999; Oosterhof, 1999 & 2001). This grading option permits students to investigate new topics that they might otherwise avoid because of anticipated low grades without the possible adverse effects on their grade-point average

(Chase, 1999; Oosterhof, 1999 & 2001). In elementary schools, pass/fail systems are often recommended for students with learning disabilities (Gredler, 1999).

The distinct advantage of this system is that it reduces the anxiety students often feel when striving for an 'A' or a 'B.' A pass/fail grading system basically collapses all letter grades into only two possible categories (Oosterhof, 1999 & 2001). The following is an example of a possible grading scale in a pass/fail system:

75–100 points..........."Pass" grade
Less than 75 points..........."Fail" grade

However, with only two possible categories in which students are graded, pass/fail systems provide much less information and feedback to students and teachers about the level of performance and achievement (Gredler, 1999). Furthermore, students tend to work harder when they realize they are working for a specific letter grade, and especially if they see their grades slipping a bit (Chase, 1999). Pass/fail systems have less of a motivational quality than do other systems of grading.

Checklists

A variation of the pass/fail system, which overcomes its primary limitation, is grading through the use of a *checklist*. Checklists still represent a type of dichotomous grading (i.e., only two options); however, very specific feedback can be provided to students and parents (Tanner, 2001). The primary goal of checklists is to provide a detailed analysis of student strengths and weaknesses (Johnson & Johnson, 2002). Checklists consist of specific performance criteria that students are expected to achieve. Specific feedback, as opposed to a single overall grade, is then provided to students.

One benefit of checklists is that in addition to academic skills, other factors of student behavior can be included, especially since checklists separate each factor or skill and allow teachers to evaluate them individually (Oosterhof, 1999 & 2001). It is not uncommon to see factors such as effort, classroom behavior, and other social and behavior skills appear alongside academic skills (Gredler, 1999). Since an overall grade is not being provided, there should be no fear of combining "apples and oranges" into one overall grade that supposedly represents students' academic achievement. Each remains a separate skill or behavior and can be graded as such. For these reasons, checklists are used quite frequently at the elementary level (Chase, 1999).

Portfolios

In Chapter 7, the use of portfolios was described in detail. *Portfolios* can be used to facilitate student growth, to document progress, and to showcase student work (Gredler, 1999). When portfolios are used as a means of providing summative grades, they are evaluated through the use of formal scoring rubrics. Portfolio use, in place of summative letter grades, is

typically done district-wide and the decision to do so is made at the district level, not by individual teachers in a particular school.

Narrative Reports

A final type of grading system is used primarily in the early years in lieu of letter grades in order to provide thorough description of student strengths and weaknesses (Gredler, 1999). *Narrative reports* tend to be thorough but brief. Typically, a paragraph is written for each academic skill and social/behavioral area. Each paragraph contains a summary for that particular area, including specific examples. Goals and plans for the future may also be included. It is important to remember that the report should be tactful but also accurate about the identification and nature of any deficiencies (Gredler, 1999; Oosterhof, 1999 & 2001).

Narrative reports may also be used quite effectively as a supplement to letter grades (Oosterhof, 1999 & 2001). They can include relevant information that serves to clarify the letter grade received. This can be very beneficial since teachers know best the various dimensions of the work of their students, as well as the progress they are making. This information is often not communicated through the limited use of letter grades (Nitko, 2001).

CALCULATION OF GRADES

The most common method of calculating grades is the *total point* approach. In this approach, each assessment is allotted a certain number of points, which makes it relatively easy for teachers to calculate final grades (Marzano, 2000). For each student, the teacher simply adds up the points for the various assignments and then divides the total number of points earned by the total number of possible points. If desired by the teacher, these proportions can then be converted into percentages by multiplying the value by 100. These could then be reported as numerical or percentage grades or converted to letter or pass/fail grades.

A variation of this method involves recording the calculated percentages (as described above) and then weighting them according to the relative importance of each assessment (Marzano, 2000). The determination of these weights can be based on a variety of factors, such as the relative importance of the individual assessments or the relative amount of instructional time spent on the topics covered on the assessments. The percentages are then multiplied by the relative weights. The resulting weighted percentages are then added up and the sum is divided by the total weights to obtain an average score, which is then typically converted to letter or pass/fail grades.

An important issue related to grading is that of measurement error. Recall from Chapter 3 that all measurements contain error. Errors in measurement can affect a student's observed score resulting from a given measurement. This concept is typically expressed as the following formula:

observed score = true score ± error score

The true score represents the student's actual understanding or skill and, therefore, achievement level. The error component represents any part of the observed score caused by factors other than the student's true understanding (e.g., fatigue, confusion, guessing) (Marzano, 2000). These errors in measurement cause the student's observed score to be higher or lower than it should be. In other words, error can work in favor of or against a student. This, therefore, results in inaccurate scores, at least to some degree.

Knowledge of this concept is especially important when it comes to calculating grades. Imagine the following scenario for a teacher who uses the total point method of calculating grades: This teacher's cutoff point for an "A" is 90%, and a student earns a total percentage of points equal to 89.5%. The teacher decides not to give the student the benefit of the doubt, adheres to the 90% cutoff, and assigns a grade of "B." In a situation such as this, it is important for teachers to reflect on how many additional points might have been required in order to achieve the additional .5%, thus "bumping" the grade from "B" to "A." Knowing that measurement error may have caused the student's true score to be lowered is important when making decisions about such borderline cases, and may result in the student receiving an "A" instead of a "B." Of course, teachers must still make subjective decisions about the proximity of a score to the cutoff in order to be considered borderline (Frisbie & Waltman, 1992). This, of course, calls into question the validity and reliability of grades, especially when being used for high-stakes decisions, such as college admissions.

Record Keeping

Individual scores, as well as overall grades, are typically maintained by the classroom teacher in a gradebook. A sample page from a gradebook is shown in Figure 10.1. Notice that the rows represent individual students and consist of scores and grades for each one, while the columns represent the various scored and graded activities that occur throughout the grading period.

REPORTING PROGRESS TO PARENTS

Whether they are recorded on individual measurements or on report cards, grades are the most common way that achievement and progress are communicated to students and parents (Airasian, 2000 & 2001). Grades are the most prominent feature of *report cards*. Most report cards also include definitions of the individual grade marks (Chase, 1999). However, these are usually not very helpful in understanding how a student has performed. Report cards also typically indicate the number of days absent and tardy. Some report cards, especially those at the elementary level, include space for the teacher to provide written comments, although the space is ordinarily too small to write anything other than a generalization about the student (Chase, 1999).

Figure 10.1 Sample page from a gradebook

Student Name	Assignments													
	M	T	W	T	F	M	T	W	T	F	M	T	W	T
1														
2														
3														
4														
5														
6														
7														
8														

A sample of an elementary school report card is shown in Figure 10.2. This particular example, at the fourth-grade level, is essentially a multigrade report card. Notice the "KEYS" in the upper-left portion. Both letter grades (A/B/C/D/F) and an alternative scale (*/+/-) are defined. Teachers in this particular school district assign letter grades only to overall performance (denoted "OVERALL GRADE" on the report card) in a subject area. Specific skills listed beneath each subject area are graded using the "*/+/-" scale. This report card typifies the extent to which teachers' judgments are a crucial component to assigning overall grades.

A sample of a secondary school report card is presented in Figure 10.3. Again, notice that the specific marks are defined at the bottom of the card. Although this card is standardized a bit more, teachers still have the opportunity to provide evaluative marks not only about academic performance (A/B/C/D/F), but also about citizenship (P/CR/NC/I/NM) and work habits (O/S/N/U/W). There is also a place for teachers to select predetermined, computer-printable comments.

We have already seen, however, that grades (and, therefore, report cards) convey very limited information regarding academic achievement. In order to fully understand their child's school performance, parents need additional information communicated through letters and conferences.

Letters to parents are not used as much as they have been in the past; teachers of- ten choose to communicate directly with parents over the telephone. However, the advantage of a written letter is that it provides a permanent record of the communication (Chase, 1999). Letters permit teachers to speak in greater detail than they can through report cards. Teachers can describe activities that parents can do at home to assist in the learning process.

Obviously, letters to parents cannot be used as the sole means of communication. Schools have administrative structures and requirements that necessitate the use of grades (Chase, 1999). Grades are necessary in order to certify that graduation requirements have been met. They are often necessary for admission to postsecondary institutions. However, letters can serve as an excellent supplement to report cards when a teacher believes that additional information could be helpful and should be provided to a student's parents.

Parent-teacher conferences are another mechanism for reporting progress to parents. The primary advantage of parent-teacher conferences is the opportunity for face-to-face dialogue; in other words, communication becomes a two-way process, as opposed to the unidirectional flow of communication that results from sending report cards or letters home to parents. Many parents believe that the most useful information about their children's progress is learned during regularly scheduled conferences (Gredler, 1999). Conferences also tend to increase parental involvement in the child's education, (Oosterhof, 1999 & 2001).

Figure 10.2 Sample of an elementary school report card

Bowling Green Schools

Fourth Grade

KEYS

Grade	
A = 93 - 100%	
B = 85 - 92%	Excellent = *
C = 70 - 84%	Satisfactory = +
D = 62 - 69%	Needs Improvement = -
F = 0 - 61%	

no mark indicates the outcome has either not been taught or assessed

Student's Name

Reading

	1	2	3	4
Completed Assignments				
Read at Grade Level				
Effort				

demonstrated an interest in reading
identified and interpreted vocabulary
located the main idea and supporting details
summarized the text
demonstrated understanding of the text by retelling
analyzed text by using appropriate strategies

English / Writing

	1	2	3	4
Completed Assignments				
Writing				
Effort				

demonstrated understanding of the writing process
wrote an organized and logical response
used a variety of words and sentence patterns
used the correct mechanics of writing
used correct spelling
used legible handwriting
demonstrated an awareness of word usage and grammar skills
demonstrated the ability to stay on topic with supporting details

Spelling

	1	2	3	4
Overall Grade				
Completed Assignments				
End of Year Average				
Effort				

Health

	1	2	3	4
Overall Grade				
Completed Assignments				
End of Year Average				
Effort				

Copyright 2000, Bowling Green City School District

Math

	1	2	3	4
Overall Grade				
Completed Assignments				
End of Year Average				
Effort				

The learner demonstrated an understanding of:
geometry
algebra
measurement
problem-solving strategies
numbers and number relations
patterns, relations, and functions
estimation and mental math
organizing data using analysis and probability
demonstrated mastery of:
addition facts
subtraction facts
multiplication facts
division facts

Science

	1	2	3	4
Overall Grade				
Completed Assignments				
End of Year Average				
Effort				

used the scientific method
correctly used measuring instruments
created and used a simple key
assessments

Social Studies

	1	2	3	4
Overall Grade				
Completed Assignments				
End of Year Average				
Effort				

The learner demonstrated an understanding of:
historical/cultural significance of the area
charts, maps, and graphs
economic process
the democratic process
assessment

revised 8/23/01

Permission to reprint granted by Superintendent, Bowling Green City Schools, Bowling Green, Ohio.

Figure 10.3 Sample of a secondary school report card

GRADE REPORT

sasI/SASIxp #213249

| STUDENT NAME | TEACHER | STUDENT NUMBER | CREDIT | GRADE LEVEL | REPORT PERIOD | FROM | TO |
| PRD | COURSE | MARK | CREDIT | CITZ | W/H | CLASS ABS. | TEACHER COMMENTS |

MARKS
A EXCELLENT
B ABOVE AVERAGE
C AVERAGE
D BELOW AVERAGE
F FAILING

CITIZENSHIP
P PASSING
CR CREDIT
NC NO CREDIT
I INCOMPLETE
NM NO MARK

WORK HABITS
O OUTSTANDING
S SATISFACTORY
N NEEDS IMPROVEMENT
U UNSATISFACTORY
W WITHDREW

Permission to reprint granted by Superintendent, Bowling Green City Schools, Bowling Green, Ohio.

Similar to letters, conferences are not a substitute for report cards; they work best when used to supplement the information that is provided on a report card (Chase, 1999). Additionally, they work most efficiently at the elementary level, where a teacher might need to meet with 25–30 sets of parents. At the secondary level, conferences with parents of all students would be almost impossible to carry out. One option at the secondary level is to conduct a parent-teacher conference when it is warranted by a specific situation.

Parent-teacher conferences should be friendly and nonconfrontational (Chase, 1999). Teachers should be well prepared for the meeting and evidence of general observations and comments should be available if requested by parents. This evidence might consist of portfolio entries, formal tests, projects, or other work samples. Negative comments should be balanced appropriately with positive ones. The ultimate goal of a parent-teacher conference is for the teacher and parents to work together for the scholastic well-being of the student (Gallagher, 1998).

SUMMARY

Grading is defined as the process of using a formal system for purposes of summarizing and reporting student achievement and progress. Grading is a vitally important professional role of the classroom teacher. This is due largely to the substantial consequences that grading can have for students. Grading is usually done because summative judgments of students are required by nearly every school district. Grades are mainly used to communicate information about students to parents, administrators, and the students themselves.

Grading systems must be fair. Important decisions are made about students and often those decisions are a direct result of their school performance, as represented by their grades. It is important that grades be based on sufficient and accurate data. However, teachers should not grade every piece of student work for purposes of determining summative grades. Individual teachers typically decide which works will be included in formulating student grades. If factors such as attendance and effort are to be summarized, they should be reported separately from academic work.

Grading involves the comparison of student performance to a preestablished standard. Comparisons in a norm-referenced system are based on the performance of other students in the class, while comparisons in a criterion-referenced system are based on performance criteria. Two types of performance standards are performance-based criteria and percentage-based criteria.

Grading systems vary immensely from district to district. There are several types of grading systems, with letter grading being the most commonly used. Other grading systems include numerical or percentage grades, pass/fail or credit/no credit systems, and checklists.

Portfolios and narrative reports are less commonly used alternatives.

Student information can be communicated to parents in a variety of ways. Report cards are the most popular method, although they provide only limited information. Letters and parent-teacher conferences provide teachers with the opportunity to offer greater detail to parents.

⌐ Chapter 10 *Related Web Sites* 💻

❖ **Grading Systems** (*www1.umn.edu/ohr/teachlearn/MinnCon/grading1.html*)
The Center for Teaching and Learning Services at the University of Minnesota developed this page, which offers good summaries of norm-referenced and criterion-referenced grading systems. Advantages and disadvantages, as well as possible modifications and questions to ask yourself before deciding on each type of system are included. Alternative systems such as contract grading and peer grading are also discussed.

❖ **Grading Systems** (*www.unc.edu/depts/ctl/fyc10.html*)
The Center for Teaching and Learning at the University of North Carolina at Chapel Hill has also developed a site that offers a comprehensive discussion about norm-referenced ("relative") and criterion-referenced ("absolute") grading systems.

❖ **Grading Systems by Country** (*www.reko.ac.at/grades.htm*)
This site provides brief summaries of the predominant grading systems in countries — and in some cases, provinces *within* countries — around the world. It is interesting to see how students are graded around the world — from A̲fghanistan to Z̲imbabwe.

❖ **Gradekeeper — Gradebook Software for Windows and Macintosh**
(*www.gradekeeper.com/*)
Gradekeeper is an easy-to-use — and extremely affordable — gradebook software program. You can maintain grades and attendance records for an entire school year. This site offers a quick tour of its features. The program can be downloaded free of charge for a 30-day trial (*www.gradekeeper.com/download.htm*). If you decide you like it, a single license or a school license can be purchased.

❖ **gradepoint** (*www.egradepoint.com/*)
Gradepoint is another gradebook software program. It offers more features than Gradekeeper but is less affordable. It also includes a free 30-day trial, available as a download or on CD-ROM.

QUESTIONS FOR REVIEW

1. Why is it highly desirable for grades to be based on some predetermined standards?

2. Explain why teachers' judgments are an integral part of assigning grades to students.

3. Describe the basic difference between norm-referenced and criterion-referenced grading systems.

4. Which grading system, norm-referenced or criterion-referenced, fails to meet the basic requirement of fairness in grading? Why?

5. Eileen earned points that total 270 out of 300 points (90%) for a grading period, but received a grade of "C" in science class. What system of comparison is likely being used to determine this grade? What problems can you identify with the grade she received?

6. Describe the basic assumption that guides the use of norm-referenced grading systems.

7. How is criterion-referenced grading, using performance-based criteria, similar to rubric scoring?

8. Letter grades are the predominant grading system used in the United States. Briefly discuss the main advantage and primary limitation to the use of letter grades.

9. What is the purpose of a *multigrade* system?

10. Even though they have distinct advantages, teachers cannot simply substitute letters to parents and parent-teacher conferences for report cards. Why?

ENRICHMENT ACTIVITIES

1. Think back to your days in school and specifically to your experiences with testing and assessment. List and discuss some of your memories regarding your experiences with various forms of assessment. For the most part, are those memories positive or negative? What caused them to be either positive or negative? Were those factors connected with the tests themselves, or were they a result of how the scores from the tests were used? Share your experiences in small groups.

2. Imagine that your principal approaches you and asks that you develop the "ideal" grading system and report card for your school. What would your report card look like? What components would it include? Be prepared to share your grading systems and report cards in small groups.

3. Not all types of student work (e.g., tests, homework, projects, research papers, presentations, performances, etc.) and work habits (e.g., effort, participation, etc.) are appropriate for every subject area in school; when they are appropriate, it may not be suitable to formally grade all types of student work. In other words, some work may be appro-

priate for *summative* grading, while it may be more fitting for other types to be used for *formative* feedback. For different grade levels and content areas, list the types of student work and habits that you believe should be incorporated into formal grades. Share your responses—and rationale for them—in small groups.

Notes

Chapter 11

Interpreting Standardized Tests

Overview of Chapter 11

INTERPRETING STANDARDIZED TESTS

- *Methods used for scoring*
  - » Norm-referenced
    - ~ Raw scores
    - ~ Percentile ranks
    - ~ Grade-equivalent scores
    - ~ Standardized scores
  - » Criterion-referenced
    - ~ Percent correct
    - ~ Speed of performance
    - ~ Quality of performance
    - ~ Precision of performance

- *Interpreting student performance*
  - » Standard error of measurement
  - » Confidence intervals

- *Uses of test results for teachers*
  - » Analyzing student performance
  - » Communicating to parents

INTRODUCTION

In Chapter 1, you received a brief introduction to standardized testing. Recall that a *standardized test* is defined as an assessment that is administered, scored, and interpreted in identical fashion for all examinees, regardless of when or where they were assessed. Regardless of whether students are being tested in Maine, Ohio, Oklahoma, or California, they are read the same instructions, respond to the same (or very similar) test questions, and have the same amount of time to complete the test. Furthermore, the scores have the same meaning in every school (Airasian, 2000 & 2001; Chase, 1999; Tanner, 2001). These uniform features of test administration and interpretation are what makes a test "standardized."

The reason behind the need for standardization of testing programs is that this process allows educators to have a sense of the average level of performance, as well as a range of scores, for a well-defined group of students (Chase, 1999). This well-defined group of students might consist of a national sample of fourth-graders or of ninth-graders. If a given student scores well above the national average and at the high end of the range, we might conclude that the student is proficient in that content or skill area. In contrast, if a student scores well below the average, it could be concluded that the student is deficient in that area. Without standardization procedures, this type of comparison would not be possible. The main purpose, then, of standardized test-

ing is to allow for the assessment of common characteristics among large numbers of students from varied and dissimilar backgrounds (Tanner, 2001). Classroom teachers have almost no control over this form of assessment; the tests are developed and scored externally (Airasian, 2000 & 2001). Nonetheless, it is important for teachers to understand the nature of standardized tests and, more important, to understand how to interpret and utilize the test results (Johnson & Johnson, 2002).

Standardized tests fall into two main categories: achievement and aptitude (Chase, 1999; Johnson & Johnson, 2002). *Achievement tests* measure academic skills across a wide variety of content areas, including reading comprehension, mathematics, spelling, social studies, and science. *Aptitude tests* are designed to measure potential or future academic achievement in specific areas. Examples of standardized tests include the *California Achievement Tests* (CAT), the *Comprehensive Tests of Basic Skills* (CTBS), the *Iowa Tests of Basic Skills* (ITBS), the *Metropolitan Achievement Tests* (MAT), and *PRAXIS I* and *II.* Many states also utilize standardized tests, which have been mandated by state legislatures or boards of education and which are developed internally (Airasian, 2000 & 2001). The results of these *state-mandated tests* typically inform decisions about high school graduation or promotion to the next grade.

Some standardized tests have no predetermined score that indicates passing or failing performance. These tests are known as **norm-referenced tests**. The results of this type of standardized test report student achievement or aptitude in relation to the performance of other students, usually a well-defined group. In contrast, **criterion-referenced tests** typically compare a student's performance to some preestablished criteria or objectives. The resulting scores basically translate into the degree of accuracy with which a student has mastered specific content. In examining the results of criterion-referenced tests, an individual student's performance is not dependent on the performance of others. These tests often include some sort of "cut" score for determining passage.

The focus of this chapter is on the types of scores that are presented on for-mal test reports for both norm-referenced and criterion-referenced tests. You will also read about how teachers can use test results to guide instruction and intervention.

METHODS OF REPORTING SCORES ON STANDARDIZED TESTS

Norm-referenced and criterion-referenced tests serve very different purposes in terms of reporting student performance. The types of scores reported for the tests reflect these fundamental differences. Figure 11.1 summarizes the various scores used for each type of test. The scores for each type of test will be discussed separately, beginning with criterion-referenced tests.

Figure 11.1 Summary of methods of reporting scores on standardized tests

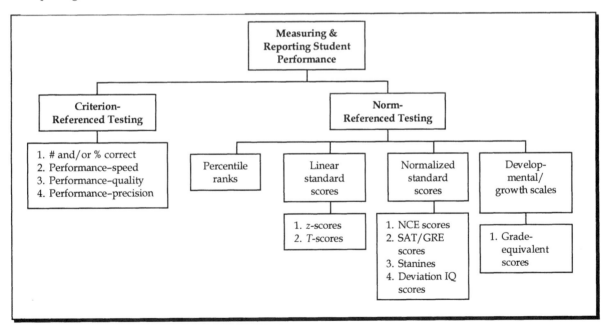

Criterion-Referenced Test Scores

The results from the administration of a criterion-referenced test enable teachers to draw inferences about the level of student performance relative to a large domain (Nitko, 2001). Individual student scores are not compared with—nor are they dependent on—the performance of others. Criterion-referenced tests provide evidence that essentially helps educators answer the following questions:

> *What does this student know? What can this student do? What content and skills has the student mastered?*

Scores resulting from criterion-referenced tests are relatively simple to interpret. They do not have well-derived, statistically based scoring systems as do norm-referenced tests (Nitko, 2001). The predominant way that the results of criterion-referenced tests are reported is in terms of *raw scores*, usually as a *number* or *percentage of items answered correctly*. Typically, a percentage of items answered correctly is provided for each subtest appearing on the entire test. This allows students, teachers, and parents to see the percentage of the sampled content domain the student has mastered.

Although less commonly used, Nitko (2001) points out several other methods of reporting the results for criterion-referenced tests. *Speed of performance* is simply the amount of time it takes for a student to complete a task or the number of tasks a student can complete in a fixed amount of time (e.g., the number of words typed in one minute, or the time it takes to run a mile). *Quality of performance* consists of a rating that indicates the level at which a student performs (e.g., "excellent," or "4 out of 5"). Finally, *precision of performance* involves measuring the degree of accuracy with which a student completes a task (e.g., accurately weighing a sample to the nearest gram). These last three types of scores are typically used for classroom assessments, but are rarely measured by standardized tests.

Norm-Referenced Test Scores

When norm-referenced standardized tests are administered to students, the results are reported in a way that permits comparisons with a well-defined group of other students who have taken the same assessment (Nitko, 2001). Individual student scores are dependent on the performance of other students. Norm-referenced tests provide evidence that assists educators in answering the following questions:

> *What is the relative standing of this student across this broad domain of content? How does the student compare to other similar students?*

The makeup of the group functioning as the comparison students forms the basis for interpreting scores resulting from norm-referenced tests. This well-defined group of students, known as a **norm group**, is given the same assessment under the same conditions (e.g., same time limits, same materials, same directions).

Comparisons to norm groups enable educators to describe achievement levels of students across different subject areas, to identify strengths and weaknesses across the curriculum, and to identify areas of deficiency—and subsequent intervention strategies—within each subject area (Nitko, 2001).

Descriptions of norm groups are typically provided in the test manuals that accompany the actual tests (Silverlake, 1999). The performance of the norm group on a particular assessment is intended to represent the current level of achievement for a specific group of students, usually a certain grade level (Nitko, 2001). It is important to realize that the average performance of the norm group does *not* represent a standard to be attained or exceeded by all students in every school across the country. Instead, comparisons to the norm group can assist educators in making decisions about the general range or level of performance to expect from their students.

There are several types of norms that can be reported in norm-referenced tests. These include local norm groups, special norm groups (e.g., composed of students who are blind or deaf), and school average norms. However, most norm-referenced tests rely on national norms (Airasian, 2000 & 2001; Nitko, 2001). *National norm groups* are supposed to be representative of the entire country. This representation is based on such characteristics as gender, race, ethnicity, culture, and socioeconomic status. The purpose of ob-

taining a *representative* norm group is to reduce any potential bias when comparing students from varied backgrounds around the country. Test publishers work very hard at ensuring representativeness, although "perfect" representation is never achieved (Nitko, 2001).

In addition to representativeness, norm groups must also be current. When scores from a norm group serve as the basis for comparison of student scores from around the country, the norm group scores must be recent (Gredler, 1999; Nitko, 2001). The national norms for the *Stanford Achievement Test*, for example, are revised every five years. The most current norms are based on between 500,000 and 600,000 student participants from kindergarten through grade 12 (Harcourt Educational Measurement, 2001). If the norm group scores are not recent, they will likely lead to misinterpretation of results and ultimately inappropriate educational decisions.

Publishers of norm-referenced tests have found it advantageous to sometimes transform scores so that they can be placed in some common distribution. This common distribution is called a *normal distribution*, also known as a *normal curve* or a *"bell-shaped curve."* Normal distributions have three main characteristics (Gredler, 1999). These are:

(1) The distribution is symmetrical (i.e., the left and right halves are mirror images of each other).

(2) The *mean* (or arithmetic average), *median* (the score that separates the up-

per 50% of scores from the lower 50% of scores), and the *mode* (the most frequently occurring score) are the same score and are located at the center of the distribution.

(3) The percentage of cases in each *standard deviation* (or the average distance of individual scores away from the mean) is known precisely.[1]

The normal distribution was derived over 250 years ago (Nitko, 2001). When first invented, it was based on the belief that nearly all physical characteristics in humans were, by nature, distributed randomly around an average value. Furthermore, the vast majority of cases were located in the middle of the distribution (indicating that most people are approximately average). A very small fraction of cases can be found at the extreme ends of the distribution. This serves as an indication that, with respect to most characteristics, the majority of people are relatively similar to one another (e.g., approximately "average" height), with a minority of people at the high (i.e., very tall) and low (i.e., very short) ends. This idea of randomly and normally distributed physical characteristics has since carried over into the realm of mental measurement.

As shown in Figure 11.2, each standard deviation in a normal distribution contains a fixed percentage of cases (Nitko, 2001). The mean ± one standard deviation contains approximately 68% of

the individuals making up the distribution; 95% of the cases are within two standard deviations of the mean; and over 99% of the cases are within three standard deviations. From the figure, it should be clear that 50% of the cases (or scores) are located above the mean (this should also make intuitive sense). Moreover, nearly 16% of the scores are greater than one standard deviation above the mean.

This information about the percentage of cases in the various segments of the distribution is key to the interpretation of scores resulting from norm-referenced standardized tests. A main purpose of a normal distribution is to help educators get a sense of how high or low a given score is in relation to an entire distribution of scores (Chase, 1999). This serves as the basis for many of the scores we will discuss next.

Raw Scores

In the section on criterion-referenced test scores, you read about the use of raw scores. Raw scores are the main method of reporting results of criterion-referenced tests. Norm-referenced test reports also typically provide the raw scores (i.e., the number of items answered correctly) obtained by students on various tests and subtests. However, this is not very useful when interpreting the results of a norm-referenced test (Airasian, 2000 & 2001). More important, teachers need to know how a particular student's raw score compares to the specific norm group. In order to make these types of comparisons,

---

[1] To learn more about the mean, median, mode, and standard deviation (including how to calculate each), see Appendix C.

raw scores must first be converted to some other score scale. These new scales are referred to as **transformed** or **derived scores**, and include such scores as percentile ranks, z-scores, T-scores, normal curve equivalent scores, deviation IQ scores, and stanines.

Percentile Ranks

A **percentile rank** is a single number that indicates the percentage of the norm group that scored below a given raw score (Chase, 1999). Possible values for percentile ranks range from 1 to 99. However, since percentile ranks indicate various percentages of individuals above and below scores that are normally distributed, they do not represent equal units (Chase, 1999). Percentile ranks are much more compactly arranged in the middle of the normal distribution, since that is where the majority of individuals fall. (You can clearly see that this is true if you examine the percentile equivalents in Figure 11.3.)

Figure 11.2 Characteristics of the normal distribution

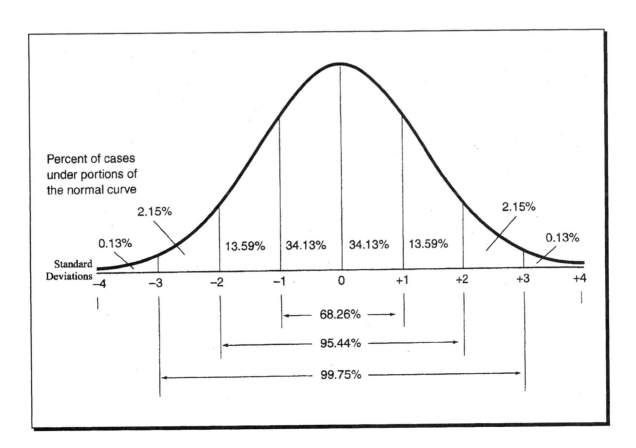

Let us consider a concrete example. Recall the fictitious SMART test we discussed earlier in this textbook. The publishers of the SMART would create a test report for all students who take the test in March, for example. Each student's report will include a percentile rank for all subtests appearing on the report. Let us assume that Mark correctly answers 34 out of a possible 45 items on the reading portion. When converted, this raw score of 36 converts to a percentile rank equal to 86. This means that, based on his raw score, Mark scored higher than 86% of the other students (in the norm group) who took the test. In other words, 86% of the other students answered fewer than 36 items correctly.

Percentile ranks are among the most frequently reported derived scores, yet are also among the most frequently misunderstood (Airasian, 2000 & 2001; Gredler, 1999). A common misinterpretation of these numbers is that they are equivalent to the percentages of items answered correctly. In our example above, Mark correctly answered 76% (i.e., 34 out of 45) of the items. It is important to realize that this implies a criterion-referenced (i.e., the score that he actually received) rather than a norm-referenced (i.e., his score in relation to others) interpretation.

Percentile ranks indicate relative standing, but have some limitations when compared to other types of derived scores we will discuss shortly. Percentile ranks are expressed in "ordinal" units, which means that the distance between units on a percentile scale are not equal (Chase, 1999; Glutting, n.d.; Gredler, 1999). The distance between the 49th and 50th percentiles is much smaller—due to the much larger number of individuals clustered at the center of the distribution—than the distance between the 1st and 2nd percentiles (Oosterhof, 1999 & 2001). In fact, the distance between the 1st and 3rd percentiles is exactly the same as the distance between the 16th and 50th percentiles (Glutting, n.d.). Since units are not equal, a difference in student performance for two students located at the extreme right end of the distribution (e.g., a one-unit difference) will appear less important on a percentile rank scale than the same difference for two students located in the middle of the distribution. For example, a one raw-score unit difference for students scoring near the mean (i.e., near the middle of the distribution) may differ by several percentile ranks, while two students located in the tail of the distribution with a one raw-score unit difference might both have the same percentile rank (Glutting, n.d.).

There is sometimes a dangerous temptation for teachers and parents to average percentile ranks in order to find a student's "typical" performance, or to subtract them in order to find the difference between two scores. Since percentiles do not represent equal units, they should not be mathematically manipulated in such a manner. In other words, they cannot be added, subtracted, multiplied, or divided as a means of further comparing students' relative standings or comparing student gains or losses (Glutting, n.d.; Oosterhof, 1999 & 2001).

Grade-Equivalent Scores

Another type of derived score that frequently appears on norm-referenced test reports is the grade-equivalent score. A **grade-equivalent score** indicates the grade in the norm group for which a certain raw score was the median performance (Oosterhof, 1999 & 2001; Silverlake, 1999), and is intended to estimate a student's developmental level (Airasian, 2000 & 2001). Grade-equivalent scores consist of two numerical components, separated by a period. The first number indicates the grade level, and the second indicates the month during that particular school year, which ranges from "0" (equivalent to September) to "9" (equivalent to June) (Chase, 1999; Gredler, 1999; Oosterhof, 1999 & 2001). For example, Patty receives a raw score of 67 on the mathematics portion of the third-grade SMART. This score is transformed to a grade-equivalent score of 4.2. This means that Patty's performance corresponds to the performance of a typical student taking the same test in November (i.e., the second month) of fourth-grade.

Grade-equivalent scores are often misinterpreted as standards that all students should be expected to achieve (Chase, 1999; Gredler, 1999; Oosterhof, 1999 & 2001). It is again important to remember that a criterion-referenced interpretation such as this is an inappropriate use of a grade-equivalent score, which is a norm-referenced score. Similarly, grade-equivalent scores are not intended to indicate appropriate grade-level placement. If Eric receives a score of 5.1 in mathematics on the third-grade SMART, we should not assume that he is ready for fifth-grade math, which is again a criterion-referenced interpretation and inappropriate use of the score (Gredler, 1999; Tanner, 2001). We could not know where Eric stands with respect to fourth-grade material since he was tested on third-grade content.

A final limitation of grade-equivalent scores is that although the scores represent months, they actually do not represent equal units (Chase, 1999; Gredler, 1999). For example, gains made in reading achievement from grade 1.0 to grade 1.5 very likely are greater than reading achievement gains made from grade 6.0 to grade 6.5.

With respect to grade-equivalent scores, it is important to remember that the scores represent what is considered "typical" or "average." If the scores for the norm group result in a normal distribution, half of the total group of students who take the test will score below the average for the group (Tanner, 2001).

Standardized Scores

You have seen that both percentile ranks and grade-equivalent scores exist on scales with unequal units. This characteristic seriously limits the interpretability and utility of each type of score. **Stan-**

dardized scores (also known as *standard scores*) are obtained when raw scores are transformed in order to "fit" a distribution whose characteristics are known and fixed (Tanner, 2001). Specifically, this distribution is the normal distribution and the scores are reported in standard deviation units, which are equal across the entire continuum. As a result of these transformations, scores can be interpreted in a way that is unaffected by the characteristics of a particular test. Regardless of the test, standardized scores efficiently indicate whether a particular score is typical, above average, or below average compared to others who took the test, as well as the magnitude of the variation away from the mean (Tanner, 2001).

Moreover, standardized scores allow for comparisons of test performance across two different measures (Chase, 1999). For example, suppose you want to compare students' performances on a standardized reading test and a standardized mathematics test. However, the reading test is composed of 65 items and the math test contains 34 items. The mean score on the reading test is 45 and on the math test is 24. Simply comparing raw scores would not tell you very much about a student's relative standing. If Catherine received a raw score of 40 (i.e., 40 out of 65) on the reading test and a raw score of 30 (i.e., 30 out of 45) on the math test, it would be incorrect to say that she performed better on the reading test, even though she answered more items correctly. (Remember, we are examining test

performance from a norm-referenced perspective.) One should notice that her score of 40 on the reading test is below the average, while her score of 30 on mathematics is above average. This type of norm-referenced comparison is possible only through the use of standardized scores.

Standardized scores simply report performance on various scales in terms of how many standard deviations the score is away from the mean. There are several types of standardized scores. The main types on which we will focus our discussion include *z*-scores, *T*-scores, stanines, normal curve equivalent (NCE) scores, and deviation IQ scores. As you will see later, these scores are essentially analogous to one another; they are simply being reported on different scales.

Z-scores are typically referred to as the most basic standard score (Gredler, 1999). They exist on a continuum, where more than 99% of the scores range from −3.00 to +3.00. The sign indicates whether the raw score is above or below the mean; the numerical value indicates how many standard deviations it is located away from the mean. A student's *z*-score is calculated in the following manner:

(1) Subtract the mean of the set of scores from the student's raw score.
(2) Divide the resulting value by the standard deviation for the set of scores.

Assume that the following information resulted from the administration of a standardized test: The mean is 75 and the standard deviation is 8. A student whose raw score is 75 would receive a z-score equal to 0 (i.e., zero standard deviation units away from the mean). Another student whose raw score is 91 receives a z-score of +2.00 (i.e., two standard deviation units *above* the mean). Finally, a student who earns a raw score of 63 would receive a z-score of –1.50 (i.e., 1¹/₂ standard deviation units *below* the mean).

One distinct disadvantage of z-scores is that by definition, half the students will receive scores below the mean. In other words, they will receive z-scores with negative values. It is very difficult to explain to students and to parents how a student could receive a –2.50 on a standardized test (Nitko, 2001). Understanding the proper interpretation requires knowledge of the mean, standard deviation, and norm-referencing, in general. Receiving negative scores on an academic achievement test can also have adverse effects on a student's level of motivation.

One way that this characteristic can be overcome is through the use of T-scores. A **T-score** provides the location of a raw score in a distribution that has a mean of 50 and a standard deviation of 10 (Chase, 1999; Gredler, 1999). Using the z-score scale as our guide, more than 99% of the T-scores on a standardized test will range from 20 (three standard deviations below the mean) to 80 (three standard deviations above the mean). A student's T-score is calculated in the following manner:

(1) Calculate a z-score and multiply that value by 10 (the "new" value for a standard deviation).

(2) Add 50 (the "new" value for the mean) to the resulting value.

Notice that the use of this scale eliminates any negative score values (Chase, 1999; Nitko, 2001).

If we examine the hypothetical example from our previous discussion about z-scores, the first student's z-score of +2.00 would equate to a T-score of 50; the second student would have a T-score of 70; and the third would have a T-score of 35. This comparison of z-scores and T-scores can be seen in Figure 11.3.

Although T-scores offer an improvement over z-scores, they too can be misinterpreted. Since they range from approximately 20 to 80 (i.e., the mean ± three standard deviations), they are often confused for percentages. A T-score of 60 (i.e., one standard deviation above the mean) can be *mis*interpreted as meaning that a student answered 60% of the items correctly. Once again, this is essentially a criterion-referenced interpretation; T-scores provide norm-referenced information.

The results of both the *Scholastic Assessment Test* (SAT) and *Graduate Record Examination* (GRE) are reported on a different type of scale, yet the scores convey the same basic information. The **SAT/GRE scores**[2] are reported on a scale

---

[2] These scores are also known as CEEB scores (for the College Entrance Examination Board, which originally developed them).

that has a mean of 500 and a standard deviation of 100. Once again, possible scores on the SAT and GRE range from a low of 200 (i.e., three standard deviations below the mean) to a high of 800 (i.e., three standard deviations above the mean) (see Figure 11.3). A student's SAT or GRE score is calculated in the following manner:

(1) Calculate a *z*-score and multiply that value by 100 (the "new" value for a standard deviation).
(2) Add 500 (the "new" value for the mean) to the resulting value.

Stanines are yet another scale on which to report norm-referenced performance, but do so by representing a band of scores (Chase, 1999). A **stanine** (short for "standard nine") provides the location of a raw score in a specific *segment* of the normal distribution (Nitko, 2001). Furthermore, stanines range in value from 1 (i.e., the extreme low end) to 9 (i.e., the extreme high end), where the mean is equal to 5 and the standard deviation is equal to 2 (see Figure 11.3). Each band actually spans one-half a standard deviation (Chase, 1999).

All individuals falling in a specific interval are assigned the stanine number of that interval (Nitko, 2001). For example, individuals with percentile ranks ranging from 40-59 fall into stanine 5; those with percentile ranks from 60-76 would be assigned to stanine 6; and so on. Stanines can typically be interpreted in the following manner: stanine scores of 1, 2, and 3 indicate below average performance;

scores of 4, 5, and 6 indicate average performance; and scores of 7, 8, and 9 indicate above average performance (Airasian, 2000 & 2001).

The main disadvantage of stanines is that they represent more coarse groupings of scores, especially when compared to percentile ranks (Nitko, 2001). However, a stanine is likely a more accurate estimate of the student's achievement because it represents a band or range within which the student truly belongs (Gredler, 1999). An individual's stanine is calculated in the following manner:

(1) Calculate a *z*-score and multiply that value by 2 (the "new" value for a standard deviation).
(2) Add 5 (the "new" value for the mean) to the resulting value.

Normal curve equivalent (also known as **NCE) scores** have a mean of 50 and a standard deviation of 21.06. Similar to percentile ranks, NCE scores range from 1 to 99. The "strange" value for the standard deviation has been established so that NCE scores will match percentile ranks at three specific points: 1, 50, and 99 (Chase, 1999; Oosterhof, 1999 & 2001). The basic advantage of NCE scores is that they represent equal units across the entire continuum (i.e., 1 to 99), unlike percentile ranks (Chase, 1999; Oosterhof, 1999 & 2001). NCE scores are calculated in similar fashion to the scores previously discussed:

(1) Calculate a *z*-score and multiply that value by 21.06 (the "new" value for a standard deviation).

(2) Add 50 (the "new" value for the mean) to the resulting value.

A final type of standardized score, used primarily with assessments of mental ability, is a deviation IQ score (Nitko, 2001). **Deviation IQ scores** provide the location of a raw score in a normal distribution having a mean of 100 and a standard deviation equal to 15 or 16 (depending on the specific test). For a test with a standard deviation set at 15, an individual's deviation IQ score is calculated in the following manner:

(1) Calculate a *z*-score and multiply that value by 15 (the "new" value for a standard deviation).
(2) Add 100 (the "new" value for the mean) to the resulting value.

As mentioned earlier in this section, all norm-referenced scores provide essentially identical information concerning the location of an individual raw score in a distribution, but simply do so on different scales. Figure 11.3 shows the relative correspondence between the normal distribution and the various standard score scales we have discussed. It is important to notice the unequal nature of percentile ranks, as well as the 1st and 9th stanines, which represent much larger bands than the other stanines.

INTERPRETING STUDENT PERFORMANCE

When interpreting student performance on norm-referenced measures, it is important to remember that no educational assessment is perfect. Error exists in all test scores (Airasian, 2000 & 2001). A test is given at a specific moment in time, and a variety of factors can affect—both positively and negatively—students' test scores. Some of these factors might be that a student was ill on the day of the test or recently experienced a traumatic event, such as a death in the family. These types of events would likely result in lowered student performance. In contrast, a student might be exceptionally good at guessing, which would result in performance above the true ability level of the student. Norm-referenced test scores, which factor in this measurement error, are also often included on test reports. The concepts of *standard error of measurement* and *confidence intervals* are important in understanding how to interpret these scores.

Standard Error of Measurement and Confidence Intervals

A **standard error of measurement (SEM)**, also known simply as a *standard error*, is the average amount of measurement error across students in the norm group. It is basically interpreted as the standard deviation of all errors in measurement. If the standard error is both added to and subtracted from the score a student receives on a standardized test, a range of student performance is defined. This range serves as an estimate within which the student's *true* performance probably lies. In other words,

Confidence Interval = Score ± Standard Error

Figure 11.3 Comparison of various types of standard scores and their relation to the normal distribution

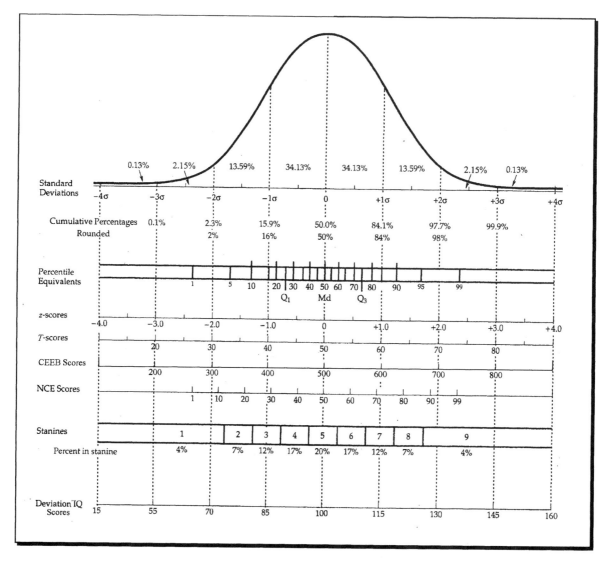

This range is known as a **confidence interval**, or *confidence band*.[3] The purpose of confidence intervals is to establish a band or range of scores that we are *reasonably* confident includes the student's true ability or achievement score (Gredler, 1999). Recall from Figure 11.2 that the mean ± one standard deviation contains approximately 68% of the individuals in a normal distribution of test scores. A somewhat related interpretation can be made for confidence intervals. For exam-

---

[3] To learn more about the calculation of the standard error of measurement, see Appendix C.

ple, assume that the standard error for a given standardized test is calculated to be equal to 3.5. A student receives a score of 64 on the test. The resulting confidence interval (based on the addition and subtraction of one standard error) for that student would be 60.5 to 67.5. This confidence interval is interpreted in the following manner: *If it were possible to test the student repeatedly under ideal conditions, 68% of the student's scores would fall within this interval* (Gredler, 1999). In other words, 68% of the student's possible scores would be located between 60.5 and 67.5. A student's obtained score plus and minus one standard error is sometimes referred to as the *68% confidence interval.* An alternative interpretation is to say that *we are 68% confident that the student's true ability score lies between 60.5 and 67.5.*

Since the interpretation of standard errors and the resulting confidence intervals are based on a normal distribution, we can generalize our example in order to provide various statements regarding the precision of the student's test scores. Again, using Figure 11.2 as a reference, we could conclude:

(1) We can be approximately 68% confident that the student's true scores lie in the range of 60.5 to 67.5 (i.e., within one standard error, or 64 ± 3.5).

(2) We can be approximately 96% confident that the student's true scores lie in the range of 57 to 71 [i.e., within two standard errors, or 64 ± (2)(3.5)].

(3) We can be approximately 99% confident that the student's true scores lie

in the range of 53.5 to 74.5 [i.e., within three standard errors, or 64 ± (3)(3.5)].

Although we would typically like to be as confident as possible when interpreting test results, confidence and precision have an inverse relationship. In other words, notice that as confidence increases (a good thing), precision decreases (a not-so-good thing). It is not very informative to say that we are 99% sure that a student's true achievement spans a more-than-20-unit range on the scale. The 68% confidence interval is typically seen as a meaningful compromise between confidence and precision.

On norm-referenced test reports, confidence intervals are typically presented around a student's obtained percentile rank scores. These are often referred to as *national percentile bands.* Figure 11.4 shows an example of three students' scores, including their respective confidence bands. For each student, notice that the obtained score is located in the middle of the band, although this will not always be the case since percentile ranks are not equal units. It is further important to note that Annette's performance is clearly better than that of Collette. However, Bob and Annette could actually be performing at nearly the same level, or Bob's performance could even be above that of Annette due to the fact that their bands overlap. In other words, when the bands overlap, there is no real difference between estimates of the true achievement levels for students.

Figure 11.4 Examples of percentile rank confidence bands (standard error = 4)

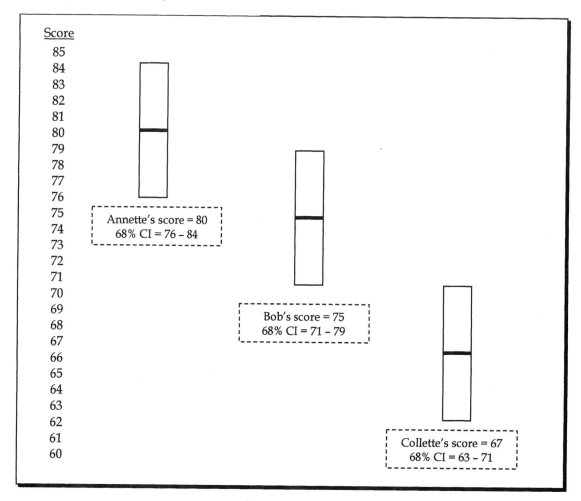

This interpretation can be extended to comparisons of the relative performances on various subtest scores for an individual student. For example, the current version of the *Metropolitan Achievement Test* (v. 8) provides norm-referenced scores on a total of fourteen tests and/or subtests. When examining the national percentile bands for an individual student, it is important to examine the overlap of subtest bands. If the bands for two subtests do not overlap, there is a significant difference in the performance in those areas.

USES OF TEST RESULTS FOR TEACHERS

There are two main ways that classroom teachers can make use of standardized test results. These results can be used to assist teachers in (1) revising instruction for entire classes or courses, and (2) developing specific intervention strategies for individual students (Mertler, 2001c).

The concept of teachers making decisions about their instructional practices and intervention strategies is nothing new. Teachers have been doing that forever; it is an integral part of being an educational professional. What occurs less frequently in schools and individual classrooms is the use of standardized test results as one additional source of information about students. This typically occurs as a result of the seemingly overwhelming amount of information provided on test reports. I have heard teachers comment that "There is so much information here! I don't know where to start!" This idea of *data-driven decision making* is not new, but it does take some practice on the part of the classroom

teacher. Focusing on a few key pieces of information on test reports and essentially ignoring other data is one method of avoiding this overwhelming feeling.

When examining test results for the purpose of revising instruction, the best practice is to interpret results provided for an entire class or course (Mertler, 2001c). This report is one of many that is typically provided to classroom teachers. It allows the classroom teacher to see how students are performing across the curriculum as a whole. Areas in which students are deficient may be identified following the process shown in Figure 11.5.

Figure 11.5 Steps in a generic process for identifying curricular areas in which students are deficient (focusing on group instruction)

```
                    ┌─────────────────────────────┐
                    │   Standardized Test Scores  │
                    └─────────────────────────────┘
                                  │
                                  ▼
```

1. Identify any content area or subtest where there are high percentages of students who performed below average.
2. Based on these percentages, rank order the 6–8 content areas or subtests with the poorest performance.
3. From this list, select 1–2 content areas to examine further by addressing the following:
   - *Where is this content addressed in our district's curriculum?*
   - *At what point in the school are these concepts/skills taught?*
   - *How are the students taught these concepts/skills?*
   - *How are students required to demonstrate that they have mastered the concepts/skills? In other words, how are they assessed in the classroom?*
4. Identify new/different methods of instruction, reinforcement, assessment, etc.

```
                                  │
                                  ▼
                    ┌─────────────────────────────┐
                    │      Revise Instruction     │
                    └─────────────────────────────┘
```

Any deficiencies, as identified by poor performance across a majority of students, should be targeted by the teacher for instructional revision. For example, teachers may want to consider any or all of the following questions for areas identified as deficient:

(1) Where is this content addressed in our district's curriculum?

(2) At what point in the school are these concepts/skills taught?

(3) How are the students taught these concepts/skills?

(4) How are students required to demonstrate that they have mastered the concepts/skills? In other words, how are they assessed in the classroom?

Answers to these questions, as well as others that are raised during the process, will often provide important information and will ultimately guide decisions regarding instructional revisions. Standardized test data may also be used very effectively in order to guide the development of individualized intervention strategies. First, however, it is important to remember that general achievement tests are intended to survey basic skills across a broad domain of content (Chase, 1999). On some subtests of most any standardized achievement test, a specific subtest may consist of as few as 5 or 6 items. Recall that the fewer number of items on a subtest, the less reliable the scores will be (Airasian, 2000 & 2001). Careless errors committed or lucky guesses by students may substantially alter the score on that subtest, especially if they are reported as percentages of items answered correctly or as percentile ranks. Therefore, it is important not only to examine the raw scores and percentile ranks, but also the total number of items possible on a given test prior to making any intervention decisions.

Most publishers of standardized achievement tests provide both criterion- and norm-referenced results on individual student reports. Many results are reported in terms of *average* performance (i.e., below average, average, above average). It is again important to remember that average simply means that half of the norm group scored above and half scored below that particular score (Gallagher, 1998). Teachers should take great care to avoid the *over*interpretation of test scores (Airasian, 2000 & 2001).

The process for examining test results in order to help guide the development of interventions is essentially the same as that summarized in Figure 11.5. The primary difference is to remember that you are essentially revising instruction for one individual student and that you make instructional decisions accordingly. A process for using standardized test data to guide intervention decisions is presented in Figure 11.6.

Figure 11.6 Steps in a generic process for identifying curricular areas in which students are deficient (focusing on individual intervention)

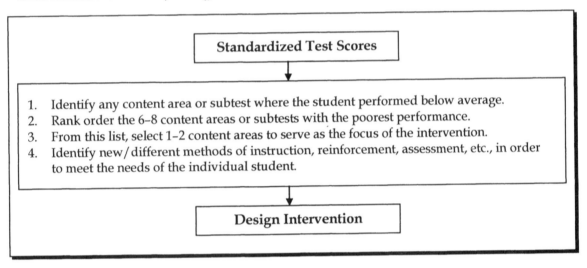

Standardized Test Scores

1. Identify any content area or subtest where the student performed below average.
2. Rank order the 6–8 content areas or subtests with the poorest performance.
3. From this list, select 1–2 content areas to serve as the focus of the intervention.
4. Identify new/different methods of instruction, reinforcement, assessment, etc., in order to meet the needs of the individual student.

Design Intervention

Analyzing Student Performance: An Example

Analyzing test reports resulting from the administration of standardized tests can be a daunting task for the classroom teacher. My advice is to focus on key pieces of information provided on the reports. As an example, let us examine a test report (shown in Figure 11.7) for a fictitious student, Elizabeth Tomlinson, who took the *Metropolitan Achievement Test* (v. 8).

The test report is separated into two sections. The top of the report contains a table (labeled **A** in Figure 11.7) of norm-referenced test results. There are a variety of scores reported here, but remember that most of them essentially provide analogous information. Each test and subtest is listed in the column titled **TESTS AND TOTAL**. The next two col-

umns provide the number of items on each subtest as well as the number of items this student answered correctly in each (i.e., her raw scores, labeled **1** in the figure). The next column (which is unlabeled in the figure) contains a scaled score similar to a GRE or SAT score, but that is calculated on a scale unique to this particular test.

The next column, titled **National PR-S** and labeled **2** in the figure, contains important norm-referenced information for teachers. The **PR** (i.e., the first number) represents the percentile rank and the **S** (i.e., the second number) represents the stanine score. Recall from Figure 11.3 that these two types of scores present very similar information. For example, a percentile rank near the middle of the distribution (e.g., 45 to 55) will be roughly

Figure 11.7 Sample student report on the *Metropolitan Achievement Test* (v. 8) for a fictitious student

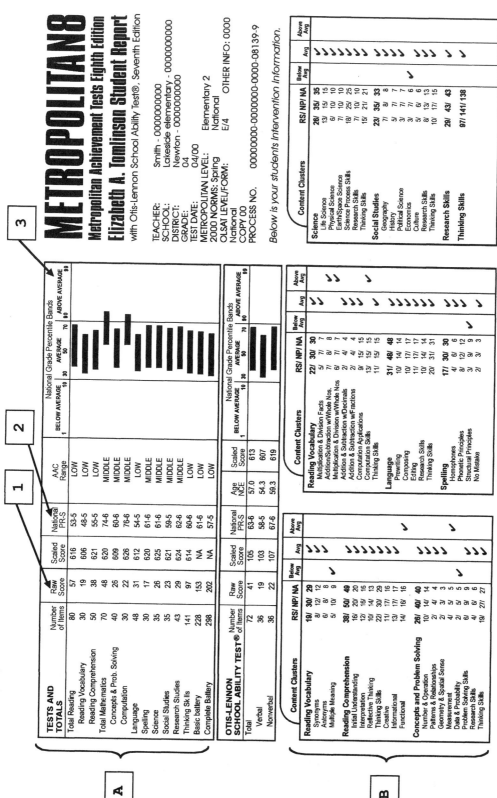

Source: Metropolitan Achievement Tests, 8th Edition. Copyright © 2000 by Harcourt, Inc. Reproduced with permission.

equivalent to a stanine score of 5. You can see this demonstrated in the Reading Vocabulary (48–5) and Reading Comprehension (55–5) scores for Elizabeth. In fact, most of Elizabeth's scores are fairly good, with percentile ranks ranging from 48 to 76 (stanine scores ranging from 5 to 6).

The last graphic on the right side of the table (labeled **3** in the figure) presents the national percentile bands for the 68% confidence level. Notice again how these parallel the results shown by the percentile ranks and stanine scores. All of the bands on the report overlap with one another, indicating that Elizabeth did not perform significantly better on one test than on any of the others.

The second section at the bottom of the page (labeled **B**) contains the criterion-referenced information for Elizabeth. For each content cluster, there are three numerical values provided: **RS** is the raw score, **NP** is the number of items possible, and **NA** is the number of items attempted. This information allows the teacher to see the relative importance of each content area addressed on the test. Notice that Elizabeth scored in the "average" and "above average" ranges in most content areas. The exceptions were "Multiple Meaning (Reading Vocabulary)," "Data and Probability (Concepts and Problem Solving)," "Structural Principles (Spelling)," and "Economics (Social Studies)." This information would be essential in designing an intervention plan for Elizabeth.

Communicating Test Performance to Parents

When it comes to explaining the results of standardized tests to parents, the responsibility rests almost solely with the classroom teacher (Nitko, 2001). Although there is typically a brief report that is sent home to parents, teachers must be prepared to explain and answer questions about what the scores actually mean regarding their child's performance. The best advice to follow is to present the results clearly and concisely, avoid technical assessment-related jargon, and respond to parent questions or comments in a nondefensive manner (Gredler, 1999).

Most parents will not understand what is meant by a stanine score or may misinterpret a percentile rank. Teachers should try to explain these scores in as simple a manner as possible. Be sure that parents understand the focus of the particular test (e.g., achievement or ability) and avoid references to "intelligence" due to the negative reactions that people sometimes have to it (Gredler, 1999). Additionally, it is usually beneficial to discuss a student's performance in terms of confidence bands (without calling them such!). Focusing on the fact that these scores represent an *estimate* of student achievement—as opposed to a precise level of achievement—will provide a more accurate interpretation of the results.

Finally, if intervention strategies are warranted as a result of a student's performance, communicate to parents the correspondence between test performance and intervention techniques or instructional strategies that may be implemented in the future.

SUMMARY

Standardized assessments are those that are administered, scored, and interpreted in identical fashion for all students who were assessed. Standardized testing programs were devised as a result of the need for educators to gain a sense of the "average" as well as the overall range of performance for students in specific grade levels. Although classroom teachers have little or no control over this form of assessment, it is vitally important for them to understand how to interpret and utilize the results.

Categories of standardized tests include achievement tests (i.e., those that measure academic skills) and ability tests (i.e., those that measure potential achievement). Tests with no predetermined passing score are known as norm-referenced tests and report performance in relation to that of other similar students. Those tests with preestablished cut scores are known as criterion-referenced tests.

There are several types of scores used to report performance in standardized tests. Scores resulting from criterion-referenced tests (which are intended to answer the question "What content and skills has this student mastered?") are reported as the number or percentage of items answered correctly. In contrast, scores resulting from norm-referenced tests (which are intended to answer the question "How does this student compare to other similar students?") are reported on a variety of score scales. These scores, which are based on comparisons to a well-defined norm group, basically report the same information, but do so on different scales. These scores include percentile ranks, grade-equivalent scores, z-scores, T-scores, SAT/GRE scores, normal curve equivalent scores, and deviation IQ scores.

Since standardized tests are intended to estimate students' levels of achievement, score interpretation is often enhanced through the use of confidence bands. These scores provide a range of possible scores within which we are relatively confident that a student's true achievement falls.

Data-driven decision making is an important use of standardized test results. Using student test data as an additional source of information can assist teachers in revising their instruction or in developing intervention strategies for specific students who may be experiencing difficulties in specific content areas. The generic processes outlined in Figures 11.5 and 11.6 provide a good starting point to support teachers in these efforts.

Another important role of the teacher is the communication of student performance to parents. Summarizing the results in a clear manner, avoiding technical jargon, and responding appropriately to parent questions are key factors to effective communication of test results.

⌐🖱 **Chapter 11 *Related Web Sites*** 🖥

❖ **Questions to Ask When Evaluating Tests** (*www.ericae.net/pare/getvn.asp?v=4&n=2*)
Larry Rudner's article, which appears in *Practical Assessment, Research, & Evaluation*, reviews some important questions that teachers should ask about standardized tests. Not only will the answers to these questions help teachers select appropriate tests, but they will also help in appropriately interpreting the results.

❖ **Talking to Your High School Students about Standardized Tests**
(*www.ericae.net/pare/getvn.asp?v=1&n=4*)
This article, authored by Carolyn Boccella Bagin, specifies some ways that teachers can help students prepare for standardized tests. Although the article was designed with secondary students in mind, many of the suggestions can be easily applied to elementary settings.

❖ **Proficiency Test Materials** (*www.ode.state.oh.us/proficiency/samples.asp*) and **Sample Test Questions** (*www.stmary.k12.la.us/leap.htm*)
These two sites provide sample standardized tests from several state-mandated standardized testing programs. The items, or complete tests in some cases, are available free of charge in a downloadable format. The complete tests come from the Ohio Proficiency Testing Program, with individual sample items from the states of Illinois, Kentucky, and Missouri.

❖ **Explaining Test Results to Parents** (*www.ericae.net/pare/getvn.asp?v=1&n=1*)
This brief article by Thomas Eissenberg and Larry Rudner provides very helpful suggestions for ways that teachers can communicate the purpose and results of standardized tests to parents. Specific suggestions are provided for ways to explain stanines, percentile ranks, and grade-equivalent scores.

❖ **Integrating Testing with Teaching** (*www.ericae.net/pare/getvn.asp?v=1&n=6*)
Herbert Rudman discusses various ways in which the results of testing can be linked to teaching, as well as how testing can be used to help teachers and administrators.

QUESTIONS FOR REVIEW

1. In your own words, describe the basic differences between norm-referenced and criterion-referenced standardized tests.

2. Paulette receives both norm-referenced and criterion-referenced scores for her performance on a standardized test in science. The norm-referenced scores indicate that she scores at the 85th percentile in "Earth and Space Science," but the criterion-referenced information indicates that she is deficient (i.e., failed to meet the performance criteria) in this area. Is this possible? Why or why not?

3. Juan, a sixth-grade student, receives a grade-equivalent score of 7.6 on a standardized vocabulary test. Write a statement offering an interpretation of this score.

4. What is the primary difference between percentile ranks and normal curve equivalent scores?

5. Using the information provided in Figure 11.3, approximate the values on the scales below that correspond to a *z*-score of +.50:

   a. percentile rank = ?
   b. *T*-score = ?
   c. stanine = ?
   d. NCE score = ?

6. What is the main reason for reporting confidence bands on standardized test reports?

For Questions 7–10, refer to the diagram below:

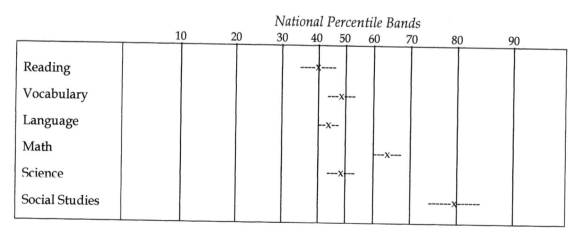

7. Which test has the largest standard error of measure? How do you know?

8. Which pair(s) of test scores are significantly different from each other?

9. The following interpretation of the percentile rank is incorrect; rewrite it so that it is accurate.

    The student correctly answered almost 80% of the social studies items.

10. The following interpretation is incorrect; rewrite it so that it is accurate.

    The student's true reading achievement is at the 40ᵗʰ percentile.

ENRICHMENT ACTIVITIES

1. Interview one or two teachers and/or parents about standardized tests. What kinds of information do they receive from standardized test reports? Which types of scores do they find most meaningful? Do they find the results to be consistent with those from other types of student performance, especially grades? Share the information you discover with others in your class.

2. Closely examine the test report shown in Figure 11.7. Assume that you are Elizabeth's teacher and your responsibility is to write a letter to her parents explaining her test performance. You may want to let the following suggestions guide your letter:
   - *Elizabeth's parents will receive a copy of this test report.*
   - *Elizabeth's parents are not testing experts and will basically want to know how their daughter performed.*
   - *You should start with some information about the test and its purpose.*
   - *Interpret the information about Elizabeth's performance, focusing on her strengths and weaknesses.*
   - *You do not have to convey every piece of information provided in the report. On the contrary, provide only the information that is most important and do so in a way that her parents can understand.*

   Be prepared to share your letters in small groups.

3. Again, closely examine the test report shown in Figure 11.7. In a paragraph or two, outline an appropriate intervention plan for Elizabeth, based on her test performance. Use Figure 11.6 as a guide. Share your intervention plans with other students in your class.

Notes

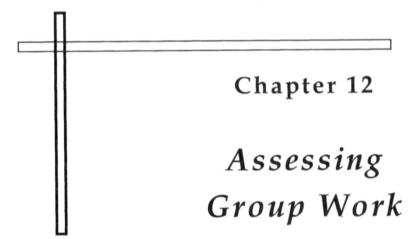

Chapter 12

Assessing Group Work

Overview of Chapter 12

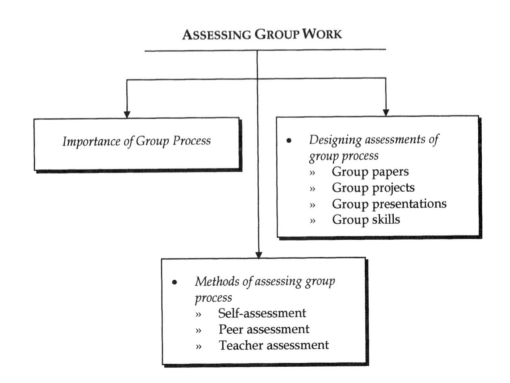

ASSESSING GROUP WORK

Importance of Group Process

- *Designing assessments of group process*
  - » Group papers
  - » Group projects
  - » Group presentations
  - » Group skills

- *Methods of assessing group process*
  - » Self-assessment
  - » Peer assessment
  - » Teacher assessment

INTRODUCTION

To this point, our focus in this textbook has been the assessment of *individual* student performance. In this chapter, however, we will examine assessment as it relates to the performances of *groups* of students. Assessing group work is not as straightforward as it may seem; it should not be viewed as a simple extension of individual student assessment resulting from the inclusion of more students. There are several issues that must be addressed and important questions answered prior to assigning, and ultimately assessing, group work.

THE IMPORTANCE OF GROUP PROCESS

More and more classrooms—at all levels of education—are increasingly emphasizing cooperative learning strategies, which allow teachers to obtain a more thorough picture of students' accomplishments (Airasian, 2000 & 2001; Tombari & Borich, 1999). These strategies involve small groups consisting of two to six students. The groups are presented with a task or problem they must solve by working together. Collaboration has long been seen as a mechanism for fostering student learning, as well as for other outcomes, such as self-esteem, social skills, and attitudes toward others (Webb, 1997). Not only is collaborative group work seen as an important *instructional* strategy, but the time has come for it to be valued as an important *assessment* strategy (Tombari & Borich, 1999; Webb, 1997). Doing so will ultimately create a stronger parallel between how students are taught and how they are assessed.

In classroom environments where cooperative learning is implemented, there are three basic purposes of student assessment (Airasian, 2000 & 2001; Webb, 1997):

(1) measuring each individual member's level of learning resulting from the group process, as well as the contribution of each member to the group's solution;
(2) measuring the quality of the group's solution to the problem; and
(3) measuring students' ability to collaborate with others as part of a team.

Assessment of these types of skills is quite different when compared to the historical purpose of student assessment: to measure individual achievement and competence. The impetus behind the inclusion of group work in classrooms is the idea that students often learn more by collaborating with others than when working in isolated environments (Webb, 1997). Assessments can still measure how well individual students perform, but only after allowing them the opportunity to learn from their peers in a collaborative climate. The primary focus of assessment remains on the individual student, but the group process allows students to learn more or to learn in a different manner (Tombari & Borich, 1999).

For example, imagine you are teaching a science unit on ecology; students' understanding of pH and how it is affected by various factors is important. The assessment for the unit might be divided into three separate assessment activities. First, students could be required to individually list solutions that can cause the pH of water to increase and to decrease. Second, in small groups, students could design, conduct, interpret, and summarize an experiment investigating the effects of various solutions on the pH level of water. Finally, in the third part of the assessment, students could individually critique the summary report of another group's experiment. Students' scores on the first part of the assessment reflect their own knowledge, while scores on the third part reflect their own knowledge plus what they learned through the group process (Webb, 1997).

The second purpose of assessment in cooperative learning environments is to measure the quality of the group's solution to the problem or task. Since the majority of tasks completed in the workplace is accomplished in teams or small groups, it has become increasingly important for teachers to determine what students can accomplish when working in collaborative groups (Webb, 1997).

The final purpose of assessment is to measure the extent to which students can successfully interact and work with others (Webb, 1997). Included in this assessment is the determination of how well students can function as part of a team. Cooperation, compromise, interpersonal communication, ability to help others, and a willingness to be helped by others are im-

portant workforce readiness skills valued by prospective employers. These types of skills can be assessed through teacher observations and through the use of peer or self-reports.

Several types of group processes can emerge when students are placed in a collaborative group situation (Webb, 1997). Depending on the nature and purpose of the assessment, as well as the specific decisions the teacher is trying to make as a result of those assessments, these various processes may work in favor of or against these three purposes of assessment of group learning. Webb (1997) has outlined six types of group processes with which teachers should be familiar. These are:

(1) *Working together.* Students work together in order to build on each other's ideas to construct new knowledge, skills, and understanding they did not previously possess.

(2) *Conflict and controversy.* Having disagreements and subsequently resolving them can be quite beneficial for learning. Students must listen to the opinions of others, as well as provide justification for their own. They may need to seek out new information in order to resolve the conflict. Suppression of disagreements—often an indication that one group member is dominating the work—can be a substantial barrier to learning.

(3) *Giving and receiving help.* Research has shown that students can learn by explaining material to other students

and by receiving explanation in return. This process can help students reorganize and clarify material. Failure of students to seek or to offer assistance can reinforce misunderstandings and, therefore, impede learning.

(4) *Equality of participation.* Most students tend to learn through active participation. However, students do not always have equal opportunities for involvement and participation, especially when the group includes outgoing, domineering, or energetic members. The social status of individual group members may also have an impact on the relative level of student participation.

(5) *Diffusion of responsibility.* Often, groups will include members who are content to sit back and let the other members do all the work. This may occur in situations where students believe that their contributions will not be valued or included. To compound the problem, the students who are doing all the work may realize that this is occurring and begin to "slack off" in order to avoid being taken advantage of. Obviously, this occurrence is detrimental to both individual and group learning.

(6) *Division of labor.* One way to avoid the problem associated with diffusion of responsibility is to divide the work and assign each group member a specific portion of the task to complete. The disadvantage of this procedure is

that students will then only learn their respective assigned portion of the task or material (known as the *expert model* of group process) and will not be exposed to all aspects of the problem (known as the *interchangeable model*) (Trice, 2000).

Although teachers should be aware of these various group processes, they should not try to address all of them within a single assessment. The effectiveness of desirable group processes, as well as the removal of undesirable ones, is dependent on the goal of the assessment. Prior to designing the specific assessment(s), teachers should closely examine their desired goals and educational decisions they wish to make about student learning through the use of group work (Tombari & Borich, 1999).

DESIGNING ASSESSMENTS OF GROUP PROCESS

The preceding list demonstrates that group processes can have both positive and negative effects on individual and group learning. It is important to consider what you will assess. Most likely, if you are incorporating group work into your instruction, you are interested in subject matter learning, as well as students' abilities to engage in appropriate group skills. Three types of group work that focus on the mastery of subject matter are group papers, group projects, and group presentations.

Group Papers

Although students have a great deal of exposure to writing individual papers, few students have experience writing group papers. Group papers involve a good deal of compromise based on constructive feedback. The general process, adapted from Trice (2000), is summarized below:

(1) Students conduct individual research on specific portions of the topic.
(2) Students write brief papers on their portions.
(3) The brief papers are shared among all members of the group.
(4) Students are provided with feedback on their individual papers, taking into consideration that they will later be merged into one.
(5) Students revise their papers based on feedback received.
(6) Students merge the papers and collectively develop an introduction and conclusion.

The papers are then evaluated using some sort of scoring instrument, where both individual and group work can be assessed. The relative weighting of the two portions should be carefully considered by the teacher.

Group Projects

Group projects are probably the most common type of group work assigned to students. The main purpose of group projects as an assessment technique is to determine whether students can work to-

gether in cooperative groups to plan and create a high-quality product (Nitko, 2001). Similar to group papers, group projects require students to examine their goals as a group and to assign various responsibilities. A general process that can be used to guide the development and completion of group projects is summarized below (Weber, 1999). This process includes the following steps:

(1) On chart paper, students brainstorm their goals for the project.
(2) Students further brainstorm the activities and/or products necessary to meet the goals.
(3) Specific tasks are delegated to various members of the group.
(4) Break the tasks into two or three time frames, which allow the group to reassemble for checks of progress and considerations of cohesiveness.
(5) Monitor progress through to completion of the project.

Group Presentations

Group presentations are quite similar in process to group papers. Students divide the labor based on subtopics and are responsible for their individual portions. However, in preparation for the actual presentation, students must get together to "rehearse" the presentation. Feedback is provided to the members of the group on their respective portions. Students should be encouraged by their teacher to ensure that the presentation does not appear to be merely a conglomeration of several individual presentations on related topics, but rather a cohesive and connected performance.

Group Skills

In addition to the learning of content, it is often desirable to assess students' collaborative work skills. Tombari & Borich (1999) have developed guidelines for specifically assessing collaborative skills related to group work. These steps are listed and discussed below and are also summarized in Figure 12.1.

Step 1: *Clarify your reasons for wanting to assess group skills*. To reiterate our previous discussion, making decisions about the reasons behind wanting to assess group work often fosters desirable group processes and reduces those less desirable. It is important for teachers to make these clarifications in their own minds.

Step 2: *Describe the assessment context*. Decide specifically what you will have students do as the assessment activity and on which associated group processes the activity will focus. These important decisions ultimately serve as the basis for assessing particular group skills.

Step 3: *Identify and describe each collaborative skill*. Determine the particular skills you want to assess. These might include such skills as interpersonal communication, ability to compromise, ability to get along with others, willingness to offer help to others, and willingness to receive help from others.

Step 4: *Design an appropriate scoring instrument*. As you undoubtedly know from previous chapters, several options are available to you. Group processes and skills can be assessed through the use of checklists, analytic rubrics, or holistic rubrics. An example of an analytic rubric for assessing group skills is presented in Figure 12.2.

Figure 12.1 Step-by-step procedure for assessing collaborative work skills

---

Assessing Collaborative Work Skills:

Step-by-Step Procedure

Step 1:   Clarify your reasons for wanting to assess group skills.

Step 2:   Describe the assessment context.

Step 3:   Identify and describe each collaborative skill.

Step 4:   Design an appropriate scoring instrument.

Figure 12.2 Sample analytic rubric for assessing group skills

CATEGORY	Excellent (4)	Good (3)	Satisfactory (2)	Needs Improvement (1)	Score
Contributions to the Group	Almost always provides useful ideas in the group and in classroom discussion. A definite leader who contributes a lot of effort.	Usually provides useful ideas in the group and in classroom discussion. A strong group member who tries hard.	Sometimes provides useful ideas in the group and in classroom discussion. A satisfactory group member who does what is required.	Rarely provides useful ideas in the group or in classroom discussion. May refuse to participate.	
Quality of Work	Provides work of the highest quality.	Provides high-quality work.	Provides work that sometimes needs to be checked by others to ensure quality.	Provides work that usually needs to be checked by others to ensure quality.	
Problem Solving	Actively looks for and suggests solutions to problems.	Refines solutions suggested by others.	Does not suggest or refine solutions, but is willing to try others' suggestions.	Does not try to solve problems or help others solve problems. Lets others do the work.	
Attitude	Almost never is publicly critical of the project or the work of others. Almost always has a positive attitude about the task(s).	Rarely is publicly critical of the project or the work of others. Often has a positive attitude about the task(s).	Occasionally is publicly critical of the project or the work of others. Sometimes has a positive attitude about the task(s).	Often is publicly critical of the project or the work of others. Often has a negative attitude about the task(s).	
Working with Others	Almost always listens to, shares with, and supports the efforts of others. Tries to keep people working well together.	Usually listens to, shares, with, and supports the efforts of others. Does not cause "waves" in the group.	Often listens to, shares with, and supports the efforts of others, but sometimes is not a good team member.	Rarely listens to, shares with, or supports the efforts of others. Often is not a good team player.	

Generated by the author from Rubistar (*http://rubistar.4teachers.org/*)

METHODS FOR ASSESSING GROUP PROCESS

The most common practice employed when assessing group work is to assign a single grade to the group's solution and to give that grade to each member of the group (Airasian, 2000 & 2001). Of course, this practice assumes that all members of the group have contributed equally to the solution, which is often not the case. Both the student who contributes and learns much and the student who contributes and learns little receive the same grade. However, if the teacher stresses that individual contributions are of greater importance than that of the group, many of the benefits of the group process will be lost (Airasian, 2000 & 2001). In these situations, a competitive climate is often established. Obviously, this does not lend itself to the fostering of cooperative learning among group members. Assessing and grading students in group situations creates dilemmas for the classroom teacher not typically encountered when assessing the individual student.

There is no single solution to these dilemmas; often, teachers must make subjective, yet professional, decisions about the purpose of the assessment and how best to address these problems associated with group work (Airasian, 2000 & 2001). Many teachers are content to award the same grade to all group members. Others rely on their observations of individual students during group work and subsequently adjust individual grades to reflect their observations of participation,

contribution, and understanding. This practice can allow for the incorporation—albeit unintentional—of bias into the grade-adjusting procedure. Still other teachers require students to assess themselves or peers as a means of determining individual contributions to the group. Three specific methods of assessing group processes are self-assessment, peer assessment, and teacher assessment.

Self-Assessment

One commonly used method of assessing group process is to have students assess their own participation (Trice, 2000). It is recommended that this technique be used for students in upper-elementary grades and secondary schools, since these students will likely have had greater exposure to group work. Self-assessments can be used to assess students' level of effort, amount of time put into a project, portions of the process with which students felt confident and those with which students experienced difficulties (Trice, 2000). Students can also indicate aspects of the process or project that they liked or disliked. An example of a student self-assessment rubric is presented in Figure 12.3.

There is the tendency for some students to assess themselves in a less-than-honest manner. Students may indicate that they are good at everything and that they contributed a great deal to the group process and product. Student self-assessments can be examined alongside other

Figure 12.3 Sample rubric for group
process student self-assessment

Name: _____ Group #: _____

Using the scale below, place the appropriate number in the blank next to each statement.
Be as honest as you can. This information will <u>not</u> be used as part of your grade.

    1 · · · **2** · · · **3** · · · **4** · · · **5**
   room for   **did well**
   improvement

1. I listened to everyone in the group. _____
2. I contributed to my group. _____
3. My group worked well together. _____
4. I said what I wanted to say. _____
5. My group worked well because _____
_____
6. I would work better in a group if I _____
_____
7. I like to work in a group because _____
_____
8. I do not like to a work in group because _____
_____

Adapted from *http://www.elm.maine.edu/assessments/Mayflower/swork2.stm*

other assessments—including peer and teacher assessments (see below). By sitting down individually with students after the completion of the group project and informally comparing their self-assessments to these other sources of information, teachers can help students learn more about themselves, as well as their skill and comfort levels, with respect to group process (Trice, 2000).

Peer Assessment

Another common approach to assessing group process is to have each team member assess the other members of the group individually (Trice, 2000). In theory, this is a very effective approach since the other group members have the best perspective for assessing the contributions and participation of individual students. Again, there may be problems associated with the use of peer assessments since some students may assess their friends higher than others in the group. Furthermore, there may be a tendency for students to rate others on more global characteristics (e.g., general likeability, appearance, etc.) as opposed to the specific contributions to their particular group.

Parents may have objections to the concept of peer assessment (Trice, 2000). Teachers should make sure that students understand the purpose behind peer assessment—namely to provide formative feedback to the teacher and the individual student. Peer assessments should not be factored into formal grades. An example of a peer assessment rubric is presented in Figure 12.4.

Teacher Assessment

One specific strategy that offers some advantages over the previous two methods places the entire responsibility for assessment on the classroom teacher. This technique involves the combination of both individual and group grades (Airasian, 2000 & 2001; Nitko, 2001). The teacher assigns a grade for the quality of the group-based product or solution to the problem. Each student in the group receives the same grade for the group's work. The teacher then requires individual students to complete follow-up activities related to the group's solution or product. These activities—which necessitate the use of separate rubrics (Nitko, 2001)—might consist of written tests, self-reflections, oral examinations, or individual reports. The purpose of these individualized activities is to determine the extent to which individual students understand the material and can apply the group's solution to other, similarly related types of problems. Each student then receives an individual grade for this portion of the assessment. In essence, each student receives two grades for the overall project, which may be weighted appropriately and differentially by the teacher. This approach allows for the assessment of group participation and contribution while maintaining the individual student's responsibility for subject matter learning (Airasian, 2000 & 2001; Johnson & Johnson, 2002).

Figure 12.4 Sample rubric for group process peer assessment

1 • • • 2 • • • 3 • • • 4 • • • 5

room for improvement ... **did well**

	Student Name		
	_____	_____	_____
1. Listened to everyone in the group.	____	____	____
2. Contributed to the group.	____	____	____
3. Worked well with others.	____	____	____
4. Voiced opinions.	____	____	____

SUMMARY

The importance of incorporating group process into classrooms is being realized by more and more educators. Collaboration in small groups can foster student learning, as well as other outcomes, such as attitudes, social skills, and self-esteem. With the increasing frequency of collaborative work groups in classrooms, teachers must become accustomed to assessing the various products and processes associated with their use.

Four basic purposes of student assessment in cooperative learning environments include measuring individual student learning, the contribution of the individual to the group, the quality of the group's product, and the ability of students to work collaboratively. When assessing students' abilities to work together in a group setting, several processes can emerge and serve as focal points for the assessment. These include the abilities to work together, resolve conflicts, give and receive assistance, participate equally, and appropriately divide the labor associated with the group task.

Three main types of group work allow the classroom teacher to assess both content learning and group skills. Group papers, group projects, and group presentations allow students to reinforce their content understanding while developing skills in brainstorming, compromise, and giving and receiving constructive feedback.

The assessment of group skills differs from the assessment of content learning and mastery in that the focus is on student skills and not on subject matter material. Since competency or proficiency on these skills can span a wide continuum, they are most appropriately assessed through the use of specially designed rubrics.

When assessing group process, self-assessments are an effective technique because they permit students to reflect on and assess their own participation and contribution to the group. They can indicate likes and dislikes, as well as strengths and weaknesses. Peer assessments are also beneficial since group members have the best perspective for assessing other members because they have been working closely with them. However, both of these techniques should be used in conjunction with teacher assessments. These three sources of assessment information allow the teacher to assess students with respect to both individual content mastery and group skills.

It is important to keep in mind that placing students in groups does not necessarily mean that they will function efficiently or productively (Webb, 1997). Group work is not a panacea for every student to learn efficiently (Weber, 1999). Students need practice at working together toward a collaborative goal. They may need assistance or reinforcement when faced with problems associated with the various group processes, which can emerge during the process.

⌒⊖ **Chapter 12** *Related Web Sites* 🖥

❖ **Assessing Group Work** (*learn.lincoln.ac.nz/groupwork/assessment/assessment.htm*)
This site, developed at Lincoln University in New Zealand, provides an overview of
the principles of assessing group work. Included is a link to more specific information about peer assessment.

❖ **Group Performance Rating Scale**
(*www.eed.state.ak.us/tls/frameworks/wrldlang/wlinstr3.html#GroupPerformance*)
The Alaska Department of Education and Early Development shows several types of
assessment instruments. This specific URL takes you to an example of a rating scale
used to assess the effectiveness of a collaborative group.

❖ **Group Project Rating Scale**
(*www.eed.state.ak.us/tls/frameworks/wrldlang/wlinstr3.html#GroupProject*)
A second sample instrument provided by the Alaska Department of Education &
Early Development is a specific peer assessment rubric, which focuses on group
members collectively, as opposed to each individual member.

❖ **Collaboration Rubric**
(*projects.edtech.sandi.net/morse/oceanhealth/rubrics/collrubric.html*)
This page contains a very informative example of an analytic rubric. The focus of the
rubric is eight collaborative work skills, assessed along a four-point continuum.

❖ **Student Self-Assessment Rubric**
(*www.spschools.org/rhem/WebQuest/studentrubric.html*)
This sample of a rubric allows students to assess themselves on eight criteria, focusing primarily on participation and cooperation.

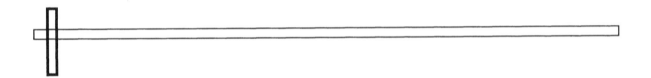

QUESTIONS FOR REVIEW

1. Name the three basic purposes of assessment in cooperative learning environments.

2. What might you tell a new teacher about the advantages of implementing cooperative learning strategies in his or her classroom?

3. An inherent part of group work is the existence of conflict and disagreement. How can this characteristic be beneficial to learning?

4. Briefly discuss the issues associated with group members who are content to sit back and let others do all the work of the group.

5. With respect to dividing the labor associated with a group task, distinguish between the *expert model* and the *interchangeable model*.

6. Why is it important to clarify your reasons for wanting to assess group skills?

7. Why is it important to assess group skills through the use of a rubric instead of a checklist?

8. What are the limitations associated with the use of self-assessments? How can they be overcome?

9. How might you respond to a parent who expresses dissatisfaction with your use of peer assessments for group work?

10. What are teachers responsible for, and for what should they observe when assigning group work?

ENRICHMENT ACTIVITIES

1. Select a topic for instruction at your grade level or within your subject area that would lend itself to a collaborative project. Identify both the content and collaborative work skills you would like your students to master. Will you use self-assessments, peer assessments, and/or teacher assessments? Draft two separate rubrics for the assessment—one for content learning and one for work skills. Share your projects and rubrics in small groups.

2. Make a list of advantages and disadvantages of assigning and assessing group work. Do you believe that the benefits outweigh the potential limitations? Will you integrate group work into your classroom? If so, in what ways? Share your responses in small groups.

3. Imagine that your instructor, in the middle of your term, decided to replace the final examination in the course with a group project. In small groups, brainstorm ideas about

what that project might look like. Next, decide whether you would rather have a final examination or a group project as the culminating assessment activity in the course. Why? Share your decisions and rationale in your small groups.

Chapter 13

Assessing
Affective Characteristics

Overview of Chapter 13

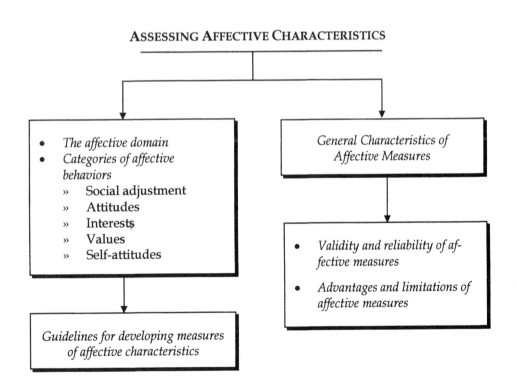

INTRODUCTION

Up to this point, our main focus has been on the assessment of subject matter learning (i.e., cognitive skills). The lone exception was the assessment of group skills (such as interpersonal communication and cooperation) in the previous chapter. In this chapter, we will focus our attention on characteristics such as attitudes, values, and emotions—in other words, characteristics that make up the *affective domain.*

THE AFFECTIVE DOMAIN AND CATEGORIES OF AFFECTIVE BEHAVIORS

In Chapter 2, you were briefly introduced to the affective domain of Bloom's taxonomy. Recall that the **affective domain** was defined as the domain of student behaviors that addresses attitudes, emotions, values, interests, feelings, etc. Affective characteristics are *constructs*; that is, they are unobservable internal characteristics that may be inferred only from students' actions in situations or their responses to carefully designed questions (Gredler, 1999). There are five hierarchical levels or categories that make up the affective domain of Bloom's taxonomy. The categories, along with their respective descriptions (Al-Belushi, n.d.; McMillan, 2001), are provided below:

- *Receiving*: defined as a student's willingness to attend to classroom activities; concerned with getting, holding, and directing the student's attention; illustrated by listening attentively,

showing awareness of the importance of learning, and controlling attention in a positive manner.

- *Responding*: defined as active participation by the student; the student not only attends to the situation, but also reacts to it in some way; illustrated by completing class work, voluntarily participating in class discussions and other tasks, asking relevant questions, and providing assistance to other students.

- *Valuing*: defined as the worth or value that a student attaches to a particular object, phenomenon, or behavior; the behavior of valuing or assigning worth is not forced upon the student; the focus is on the student's intrinsic value system; instructional behaviors or outcomes such as "attitudes" and "appreciation" are included here, which might be illustrated by showing concern for the welfare of others, helping others with problems, sharing materials with other students, encouraging others to do well, asking for permission before using others' materials, and commending others, when appropriate.

- *Organization*: defined as bringing together different values, resolving conflicts between them, and building an internally consistent value system; the emphasis is on comparing, relating, and synthesizing values; instructional behaviors or outcomes—such as "developing a philosophy of life (or credo)"—would be included here, which might be illustrated by accepting responsibility for actions, understanding and accepting his or her own strengths and limitations, and formulating a life plan consistent with abilities, interests, and beliefs.

- *Characterization*: defined as possessing a value system that has controlled the student's behavior long enough for the student to have developed a characteristic lifestyle; the behavior is consistent and predictable; instructional outcomes that emphasize typical or characteristic behavior would be included here, which might be illustrated by demonstrating self-reliance and independence, cooperation, and self-discipline.

The procedures for writing objectives for the affective domain are identical to those used for writing objectives for the cognitive domain (see Chapter 2, pages 39–40). Two examples of objectives written to assess affective characteristics follow:

- *The students will voluntarily participate in class discussions by asking relevant questions and responding appropriately to questions posed by the teacher.*
- *When working in teams with students of different races, the students will demonstrate an improvement in attitude toward nondiscrimination of race, as measured by a checklist.*

Although most classroom teachers believe that affective characteristics, such as attitudes toward learning, are important, few teachers give explicit attention to "shaping" and assessing them (Popham, 2002). In most cases, when teachers do try to assess affect, they tend to do so through the use of informal observation techniques, as opposed to a more formal, systematic collection of evidence. Even though teachers are aware that students who are confident about their ability to learn—who like the school subjects they study, who have a positive attitude toward learning, and who respect and show concern for others—are more likely to be motivated and involved in learning, systematic assessment of affect in students is fairly uncommon (McMillan, 2001; Popham, 2002).

There are several good reasons for teachers to assess affective behaviors and outcomes. First, they may encounter students who would not be classified as intellectually "gifted" but still experience a great deal of academic success. This may be due in part, or perhaps entirely, to the fact that they are motivated and hardworking individuals. Conversely, some students tend to give up on themselves and refuse to try if they believe that they are not worthy of a particular challenge. In these situations, affect may be equally as important as—if not more important than—cognitive ability (Popham, 2002). Having a sense of what attitudes and values students possess is valuable in terms of structuring subsequent instruction. This level of understanding attitudes and values can occur only through formal methods of assessment.

A second important reason for assessing affect is that formal affective assessments administered at the end of a unit will tend to guide the inclusion of affective instruction (Popham, 2002). As with cognitive measures, if teachers know that they will later be assessing specific affective traits, there will be a tendency for some degree of instruction to focus on those traits. If affective outcomes are important enough to be assessed, they are also important enough to be taught.

Third, affective assessments can also be used *during* instruction as a means of monitoring students' status with regard to affect (Popham, 2002). It might be extremely informative to learn how students' interest in or attitudes toward a given topic are changing. For example, imagine that a science teacher provided students with a beginning-of-the-year (e.g., September) self-report about their attitudes and interests in studying scientific concepts. The teacher discovered that 70% of the students were interested in science, so much so that several indicated that they were interested in taking more courses, perhaps even in college. The teacher administered the same instrument in early November and discovered that the percentage had dropped to 30% of the students expressing an interest in studying science further. Something happened during the course of those six or seven weeks that caused many of the students to lose interest in the subject matter. This kind of feedback could certainly provide some meaningful information regarding how one might revise or adjust the instruction in order to increase student motivation and interest.

Despite the desirability of assessing affective characteristics, teachers should be aware that there are several legitimate reasons why affective assessment can be rather difficult. First, the assessment of affective outcomes is filled with obstacles (McMillan, 2001). Since it is difficult to measure such internal, unobservable characteristics, there tend to be many sources of error that ultimately result in low reliability. A somewhat "new" source of error we have not previously considered is the fact that many students will not take assessments of affect seriously enough in order to provide accurate information. There might also be an inclination to please the teacher with *socially acceptable responses*. In other words, students sometimes respond to questions in the way they think their teacher wants them to respond. Finally, error can also be attributed to the many affective traits that are influenced by temporary moods or feelings. When students are experiencing an exceptionally good day or an extremely bad day, results of affective assessments will not be accurate.

Second, especially at the secondary school level, schools are organized and graded according to subject matter areas. The primary focus of this organizational scheme is the attainment of cognitive outcomes, separate from affective ones. Consequently, this means that affective assessment tends to be considered only after the assessment of cognitive skills has occurred, and there tends to be little time left in the school day or year for this type of assessment (McMillan, 2001).

Finally, in recent years, there has been increased pressure from political and religious groups opposed to the instruction of anything other than traditional academic outcomes in public school settings (McMillan, 2001; Popham, 2002). These groups contend that schools have no right to teach (or assess) attitudes, values, or beliefs that may be contrary to the belief systems of the groups. In many of these cases, teachers simply decide to avoid affect altogether, thus avoiding the potential controversies and arguments with special-interest groups.

Affective characteristics or behaviors may be categorized in many ways (Gredler, 1999; McMillan, 2001; Popham, 2002). There are, however, several common categories of affective characteristics with which classroom teachers should be familiar. They include social adjustments, attitudes, interests, values, and self-attitudes. Each of these categories is described below.

Social Adjustment

Social adjustment refers to adaptive behavior and social development as indicated by students' responses to school rules, responsibility, and good interpersonal relationships with teachers and peers (Gredler, 1999). Specific social behaviors include assertiveness, friendliness, cooperation, collaboration, empathy,

and conflict resolution (McMillan, 2001). The trend toward the inclusion of students with low intellectual functioning or poor academic skills into regular classrooms has heightened the importance of social adjustment. Students with learning disabilities, for example, may also have poor work habits or may have difficulties in reacting appropriately in social situations, especially with their peers.

Attitudes

Attitudes are described as relatively stable, consistent internal tendencies that influence what students are likely to do with respect to social situations, established institutions, and similar phenomena (Gredler, 1999; McMillan, 2001). This internal state constitutes some degree of reaction, ranging from positive–negative or favorable–unfavorable, toward an object, person, situation, or group of objects or persons (McMillan, 2001). It is important to realize that attitudes are not simply preferences; they involve ingrained beliefs about the particular situation, object, or person, and also include long-term perceptions and feelings (Gredler, 1999).

Attitudes have objects; in other words, we tend to think in terms of attitudes *toward* something (McMillan, 2001). Therefore, in school settings, we could talk about attitudes toward things such as school, homework, extracurricular activities, teachers, and specific subjects. However, it is important that "attitude toward a subject," for example, not be confused or used synonymously with "satisfaction with a course." Attitudes are typically deeply held beliefs, not mere expressions of approval or disapproval, likes or dislikes (Gredler, 1999).

Interests

Preferences for participating in particular activities characterize **interests**. They differ from attitudes because the target of interests are activities (as opposed to attitudes toward social situations, objects, or institutions) (Gredler, 1999). Teachers who possess knowledge of their students' interests can help themselves in two ways. First, teachers can select supplemental instructional materials or design examples or applications that are of interest to the majority of students in a class. Second, teachers can use this information to select or develop classroom activities that may be used to reinforce positive student behaviors (Gredler, 1999).

Values

Values are defined as standards that determine end states of existence, as well as modes of self-conduct and presentation of self to others (Gredler, 1999; McMillan, 2001). "End states of existence" are conditions and aspects of ourselves and our world that we want, such as world peace, freedom, happiness, social acceptance, and wisdom (McMillan, 2001). "Modes of conduct" are exemplified by what we think is appropriate and needed in everyday society and in our everyday existence, such as being honest, ambitious, loving, responsible, and helpful (McMillan, 2001;

Popham, 2002). Typically, these types of values can be placed into several categories consistent with different areas of our lives, such as moral, political, social, aesthetic, economic, technological, and religious (McMillan, 2001).

In school settings, teachers are usually restricted—both openly and covertly—to teaching and assessing those values that are closely tied to academics and those that are necessary for making effective contributions to society and to the workplace (McMillan, 2001). Many of these values relate directly to developing character and becoming a "good citizen." However, many values can be somewhat controversial, especially to particular groups, as previously mentioned. It is recommended that teachers focus their attention on less controversial—but sufficiently meaningful—values, such as honesty, integrity, justice, freedom, respect, courage, compassion, and tolerance (McMillan, 2001; Popham, 2002).

Self-Attitudes

Beliefs and feelings about oneself are essential to effective classroom learning (Gredler, 1999). **Self-attitudes** include such characteristics as *self-concept* (the general image one has about himself or herself), *self-esteem* (the degree of confidence and satisfaction in oneself), and *self-efficacy* (the perception of one's own capability to perform successfully). Self-attitudes are very important in classroom settings because they influence students' willingness to undertake academic tasks and take risks in academic and social settings (Gredler, 1999).

Since self-attitudes can be affected by many things (including appearance, race, and gender), it is often best for teachers to focus on *academic* self-concept, self-esteem, or self-efficacy (McMillan, 2001). The information that ensues from the assessment of these more focused self-attitudes will result in more accurate assessments of self as they relate specifically to academics. This, in turn, will create a more meaningful connection to the curriculum and, ultimately, to the academic achievement levels of students.

GUIDELINES FOR DEVELOPING MEASURES OF AFFECTIVE BEHAVIORS

The assessment of affective behaviors can be carried out at various levels of complexity (Popham, 2002). From a practical standpoint, classroom assessment of affect in students must be relatively easy, or teachers are not going to practice it. This is especially true when weighed against the relative importance of assessing cognitive outcomes. If time and effort are limiting factors, cognitive outcomes would—and, arguably, *should*—be assessed first. There are essentially two methods of assessing affective outcomes that can be feasibly utilized by the classroom teacher. These are teacher observations and student self-reports (McMillan, 2001). These two categories of affective assessment techniques will be discussed momentarily.

McMillan (2001) has identified three important considerations to keep in mind when assessing affect. First, realize that emotions and feelings (considered unstable) can change quickly, especially in young children and adolescents. In order to obtain an accurate portrait of a student's feelings, it is necessary to conduct several measurements of affect over a substantial period of time. This, then, would permit a teacher to have a general, overall sense of the student's prevalent affect. The predominant recommendation is to measure these types of affective traits repeatedly over several weeks.

Second, it is best to try to use as many different types of measures as possible. For example, as you will soon see, self-reports have several limitations. By incorporating them with teacher observations, it is possible to see if the self-reports are consistent. Again, this creates a more accurate picture of affect in a particular student.

Third, an initial decision should be made regarding interest in individual or group results concerning affect. This is ultimately related to the overall purpose of the teacher's decision to assess affect in the first place. For example, if the purpose of assessing affect is to report the results to parents, information is obviously needed at the individual student level. In contrast, if the purpose of affective assessment is to revise and improve classroom instruction, a teacher would want to gather information for the entire class or course. This approach is sometimes more advantageous since teachers can rely on anonymous self-reports.

Anonymity is considered to be an important component to affective assessment (McMillan, 2001; Popham, 2002). Therefore, it is discussed here as a final consideration for the implementation of affective assessment in the classroom. In order for teachers to draw accurate inferences from student self-reports of affect, students must respond honestly. Many students have a tendency to provide socially acceptable responses to affective measures. This is especially true when they believe that their responses could be traced back to them, and that they might receive some sort of punishment or chastisement for the way they feel.

In order to avoid these kinds of situations, Popham (2002) offers several guidelines for enhancing the anonymity of student self-reports. These include:

(1) *Directions.* The directions on a self-report instrument should stress the importance of honest answers. Furthermore, students should be explicitly instructed that they not put their names anywhere on the instrument.

(2) *Response restriction.* Self-reports should be formatted so that the only type of mark students need to make on the paper is a checkmark, circling of preferred response, etc. Any type of item that requests handwritten information from students will likely lead students to believe that the teacher will be able to identify them based on their style of handwriting. It

is best not to permit handwriting of any kind on affective instruments.

(3) *Collection.* Procedures should be developed for collecting completed instruments that again limit the potential for teachers—or other students—to identify specific students and their responses. Teachers may utilize special collection boxes and instruct students to fold their papers before placing them in the box. Of course, for this to be effective, students should be informed of the method of collection in advance.

It is important to make sure that students do not believe that their responses can be traced back to them, and that they feel comfortable in responding. This does not *guarantee* that students will respond honestly, but it will increase the odds of receiving honest responses.

Teacher Observations

Teacher observations were discussed extensively in Chapter 5. The acts of watching and listening to students in natural settings can provide valuable information regarding their attitudes, beliefs, and feelings, especially with respect to the ways in which they interact with their peers. Recall several important considerations and guidelines of which to be aware when using observations as a form of affective assessment:

(1) Many events in the classroom are observed either simultaneously or in very quick succession.

(2) Most events that go on in the class-room go unnoticed.

(3) Observations often require infer-ences, which may be erroneous.

(4) Know what you want to observe.

(5) Document observations that must be recalled at a later time.

Teacher observations may be un-structured or structured in nature. Un-structured observation is essentially what was discussed in Chapter 5. An *unstruc-tured observation* is open-ended; there is no checklist or rating scale on which to re-cord your observations. However, it is a bit more formal in that the teacher knows the specific affective trait on which atten-tion will be focused. At some point during or following the observation, the teacher will likely make brief anecdotal notes as a means of recording the observation.

In contrast to this technique, struc-tured observation requires a good deal more preparation (Gredler, 1999; McMil-lan, 2001). In using *structured observations*, a checklist or rating scale must be devel-oped prior to the observation. This in-strument is then used as the means for recording the observations. The format of a checklist is fairly straightforward. Be-haviors are listed and a space for indicat-ing frequency is provided for each. Fre-quency can be indicated on the form with marks such as "check–no check," "yes–no," "observed–not observed," or with the number of times a behavior oc-curred. An example of a checklist using a frequency approach is shown in Figure 13.1.

Alternatively, a rating scale can be used as the means of recording structured observations. Rating scales differ from checklists in that the response options are not limited to only two options or a mere indication of frequency. Typically, a rating scale provides the teacher with a range or continuum of options along which the ob-servation can be recorded. Examples of rating scale response options include "agree–disagree" scales (typically known as *Likert scales*), and scales that indicate degrees of frequency, quality, or profi-ciency (known as *Likert-type scales*). Rating scales often provide greater detail with respect to the specific affective traits being observed since responses are not limited to "yes–no," etc. An example of a rating scale, for the same behaviors as depicted in Figure 13.1, is shown in Figure 13.2.

Student Self-Reports

The only real difference between the rating scales previously discussed and *student self-report instruments* or *inventories* is that a teacher completes the observation rating scale, whereas the student com-pletes the self-report. Numerous pub-lished self-report inventories exist; how-ever, many of them were not designed for use by the classroom teacher (McMillan, 2001). They are intended more for re-search or for use by trained psychologists than for practical affective assessment in classroom settings.

Figure 13.1 Sample structured observation
instrument, using a frequency approach

Observation Form:
"Following Directions"

1. Follows directions first time given. `/ / /`
2. Follows directions after second verbal prompt. `/ /`
3. Follows directions after nonverbal prompt.
4. Follows directions with individualized teacher intervention. `/`

Figure 13.2 Sample rating scale, using Likert-type
response options

Rating Scale:
"Following Directions"

	Always	Often	Sometimes	Seldom	Never
1. Follows directions first time given.	☐	☐	☐	☐	☐
2. Follows directions after second verbal prompt.	☐	☐	☐	☐	☐
3. Follows directions after nonverbal prompt.	☐	☐	☐	☐	☐
4. Follows directions with individualized teacher intervention.	☐	☐	☐	☐	☐

One of the biggest challenges faced by teachers who want to use self-report inventories is that students might not take them seriously (McMillan, 2001). This fact requires that the teacher design an inventory with simple, understandable statements or questions. Furthermore, teachers should encourage students to take them seriously and respond as honestly as possible, since there is nothing to lose and something to be gained by being cooperative and providing meaningful feedback (McMillan, 2001).

The typical structure of a student self-report inventory is a selected-response format. Similar to a selected-response test item (see Chapter 8), students are provided with a series of statements or questions and are directed to circle (or otherwise indicate) their preferred response from those provided. Again, Likert scales are often utilized in student self-reports. An example of a Likert scale self-report instrument is shown in Figure 13.3.

Figure 13.3 Sample self-report inventory using Likert response options

Attitudes Toward School
Student Self-Report

		Strongly Disagree	Disagree	Neutral	Agree	Strongly Agree
1.	I like school.	☐	☐	☐	☐	☐
2.	I enjoy coming to school every day.	☐	☐	☐	☐	☐
3.	I like my teachers.	☐	☐	☐	☐	☐
4.	I like doing my homework.	☐	☐	☐	☐	☐
5.	I enjoy learning new things.	☐	☐	☐	☐	☐
6.	I have lots of friends at school.	☐	☐	☐	☐	☐
7.	I enjoy participating in extracurricular activities.	☐	☐	☐	☐	☐
8.	My teachers care about my academic growth.	☐	☐	☐	☐	☐
9.	My teachers care about my personal growth.	☐	☐	☐	☐	☐
10.	My teachers care about my social growth.	☐	☐	☐	☐	☐

One important characteristic of a self-report inventory is that statements or questions should be worded positively; if it is necessary to word a statement in the negative, teachers should somehow highlight terms like *not*, *no*, and *never* by underlining or italicizing them. Students may read the statements quickly, "glossing over" the negative term. This could result in a self-report that is in direct opposition to what the student actually feels.

Another consideration that should be made prior to the development of a self-report inventory is the appropriate reading and/or comprehension level of the students involved. Students in early grades may not understand how to respond to a Likert scale. A self-report instrument for young students should have a response scale that is comparable with their reading and skill levels. An example of this type of self-report instrument is shown in Figure 13.4.

Figure 13.4 Sample self-report inventory appropriate for younger students

Attitudes Toward School
Student Self-Report

		I like it a lot.	It's okay.	I don't like it.
1.	Reading books	☺	😐	☹
2.	Math work	☺	😐	☹
3.	Science experiments	☺	😐	☹
4.	Art projects	☺	😐	☹
5.	Physical education	☺	😐	☹
6.	Writing stories	☺	😐	☹
7.	Homework	☺	😐	☹
8.	School	☺	😐	☹

VALIDITY AND RELIABILITY OF AFFECTIVE MEASURES

The techniques and approaches described in this chapter can result in valid and reliable decisions regarding the affective characteristics of students, provided several potential hazards are avoided. Teachers must ensure that their decisions about student affect are based on objective observations, and are not the result of hearsay or other potentially erroneous sources of information. Also, prior identification and specification of the particular affective characteristics to be assessed provide beneficial guidance to the observation itself. This prevents teachers from feeling like they must assess all forms of affective outcomes simultaneously.

The validity of student self-reports may be questionable if students refrain from responding in a truthful manner. By following the guidelines presented earlier in the chapter for encouraging students to respond honestly and for protecting their anonymity, teachers will enhance the quality of the information they receive from affective measures.

For both teacher observations and student self-reports, the primary concern with respect to reliability is the lack of sufficient information provided by affective measures. This is especially true when inadequate samples of students' affective behaviors are gathered. Too many possible sources of error can adversely influence the consistency of the information gathered. Teachers should be sure that they base decisions regarding affective students' outcomes on multiple and diverse measures.

ADVANTAGES AND LIMITATIONS OF AFFECTIVE MEASURES

Teacher observations have several advantages as well as limitations. Unstructured observations have the advantage of occurring in a natural setting. Furthermore, teachers' observations are not restricted to only those items that appear on the checklist or rating scale; they are free to observe any and all behaviors displayed by students (McMillan, 2001). The main limitation of unstructured observations is that they require teachers to write formal notes about what was observed. This can be very time consuming, especially if a teacher wishes to do it for each student.

Structured observations have the limitation of requiring more preparation than unstructured ones. An additional limitation is that they substantially restrict what a teacher is able to observe—or at least, is able to record on the instrument. Advantages include the fact that they provide more structure or organization to the observation (hence, they tend to "guide" the observation). Additionally, structured observations tend to be more feasible and manageable for busy classroom teachers.

Student self-report instruments also require extensive preparation. Similar to structured observations, they restrict what students are able to respond to regarding the particular affective trait being assessed. The main advantage is that students can respond directly about their feelings and attitudes. However, as you read earlier, this can also serve as a potential limitation in situations where students do not feel comfortable being entirely honest or feel pressured to provide socially acceptable responses.

SUMMARY

Affective characteristics are defined as student behaviors that address attitudes, feelings, beliefs, interests, and values. They are unobservable internal characteristics (i.e., constructs) that can be inferred only from student actions or responses to questions or scenarios. The hierarchical levels of the affective domain of Bloom's taxonomy include receiving, responding, valuing, organization, and characterization. The main categories of affective behaviors include social adjustments, attitudes, interests, values, and self-attitudes.

Although most classroom teachers believe that affective behaviors and outcomes are important, few teachers formally and systematically assess them. Affect should be assessed because knowledge of attitudes and values can offer meaningful contributions to structuring future learning. Additionally, if teachers plan to assess affect, they are more likely to incorporate it into daily instruction. Finally, affective assessments can also provide a unique type of feedback regarding current instruction.

Teachers must also be aware that affective assessment can be difficult. The idea of social acceptability can create an additional type of measurement error. With the majority of the school day focused on the assessment of cognitive skills, it is also difficult to find time to incorporate affective assessment into daily instruction. Finally, many special-interest groups tend to apply pressure to schools with regard to the "appropriateness" of affective instruction and assessment.

There are four important considerations to bear in mind when developing measures of affective behaviors. First, teachers should be aware that behaviors such as emotions and feelings can change quickly, and may not result in an accurate portrait of a particular student. Second, it is important to use as many different types of measures of affect as possible. Third, the purpose behind the decision to assess affect—to provide individual-level information, or to revise group-level instruction—should be specified. Finally, affective measures should be designed to maintain the anonymity of the student.

Two specific methods of measuring affect are teacher observations and student self-reports. Teacher observations may be unstructured or structured. Unstructured observations permit teachers to assess students in a natural setting. The observation is open-ended and requires anecdotal notes to be written at a later time. Structured observations are more formal than their unstructured counterpart. No anecdotal notes are required since the observation is recorded on a checklist or rating scale. Checklists simply allow the teacher to indicate whether or not a specific behavior was present. In contrast, rating scales do not limit teachers to a dichotomous set of responses. Rating scale options exist on a continuum, such as level of agreement, frequency of occurrence, degree of quality, or degree of proficiency. Student self-reports are quite similar to structured teacher observations. The only real difference is that self-reports are completed by the student as opposed to the teacher.

Assessments of affect can result in valid and reliable decisions about students, provided several guidelines are followed. Decisions must be based on objective observations, honest student responses, and multiple and diverse measures.

Chapter 13 Related Web Sites 💻

❖ **Affective Domain** (*www.geocities.com/eltsqu/Affective.htm*)
This site was developed by Ali Hussain Al-Belushi, an instructor of English as a Foreign Language at a university in the country of Oman. Thorough descriptions of the five categories in the affective domain are provided, along with several very good examples.

❖ **Affective Domain** (*www.itc.utk.edu/~jklittle/edsmrt521/affective.html*)
An alternative set of descriptions of the five affective categories is provided on this page developed at the University of Tennessee. The page includes illustrations as well as sample instructional objectives.

❖ **Bloom's Taxonomy of Educational Objectives**
(*www.tedi.uq.edu.au/Assess/Assessment/bloomtax.html*)
This site includes information on all three domains in Bloom's taxonomy. Important to the topic in this chapter, specific action verbs to help in the writing of objectives in the affective domain are included.

❖ **Classroom Assessment Techniques Useful in Assessing Different Affective Domains** (*edtech.clas.pdx.edu/presentations/measure_outcomes/affect_assess.htm*)
Several specific types of affective behaviors (e.g., self-concept, interpersonal relations, and moral development) are listed, along with examples of appropriate affective assessment techniques.

❖ **Student Self-Assessment for Affective Thinking Behaviors**
(*www.tesd.k12.pa.us/stoga/Forms/student%20self%20assessment%20for%20afftective%20thinking%20behaviors1%E2%80%A6.pdf*)
This self-assessment survey of affective thinking behaviors was developed at Conestoga High School in Berwyn, Pennsylvania. It provides a very good example of a brief, self-assessment rating scale.

❖ **Assessment in the Affective Domain** (*www.sasked.gov.sk.ca/docs/physed/physed6-9/pg046.pdf*)
An example of a rubric for assessing affective behaviors is provided on this Web page from the Saskatchewan (Canada) Education Community, Government of Saskatchewan.

QUESTIONS FOR REVIEW

1. How is the affective domain of Bloom's taxonomy similar to the taxonomy of the cognitive domain? (You may want to revisit the discussion of Bloom's cognitive domain in Chapter 2.)

2. What are several reasons that classroom teachers do not systematically assess affect on a regular basis?

3. What is the difference between *attitudes* and *interests*?

4. In your own words, describe the difference between *self-concept* and *self-esteem*.

5. A teacher administers a self-report instrument about attitudes toward and feelings about a course to all students in a class. The students are directed to place their names at the top of the paper. What types of adverse affects can occur from this direction?

6. What are the relative advantages and disadvantages of unstructured observations as compared to structured observations?

7. Describe what is meant by a *socially acceptable response*.

8. Why is it important to avoid using negative wording in statements that appear on a self-report instrument?

9. Imagine that you and five of your friends are applying for the same full-time teaching position. As part of the screening process, the school district requires each of you to complete a self-report on personal work habits. At the risk of losing this position, what might you tell the district's representatives about the validity of the information resulting from the self-reports?

10. An affective self-report of academic self-efficacy asks students to indicate their extent of agreement with statements such as "I believe that I will be successful later in life." What problems might be associated with this type of statement?

ENRICHMENT ACTIVITIES

1. Identify some affective characteristics (within a common category, such as attitudes, values, or feeling) and construct a brief self-report instrument to assess those traits. Administer the instrument to a small group of students. After they have completed the self-report, ask them about their feelings toward the questions, and perhaps the wording of each. How difficult was it to develop the self-report instrument? Discuss your responses in small groups.

2. Think about the grade level and/or subjects you would like to teach someday. Imagine that you were limited to only two affective traits that you could assess. Identify these two "most crucial" characteristics. Why did you select them? How will you likely measure each? Share your ideas in small groups.

3. Spend some time with a classroom teacher talking about affective assessment. Try to discover information concerning their ideas about, opinions of, and attitudes toward affective assessment. Use the following questions to guide your interview:

   • Do you routinely assess affective behaviors in your classroom? If not, why not?
   • How important do you believe affective assessment is?
   • What types of approaches or techniques do you use to assess affect?
   • What do you see as the strengths and limitations of different techniques, such as unstructured observations, structured observations, and self-reports?
   • What do you find most difficult about assessing affective behaviors in your students?

Appendix A:

The Standards for Teacher Competence in the Educational Assessment of Students [1]

Developed by the
American Federation of Teachers
National Council on Measurement in Education
National Education Association

The professional education associations began working in 1987 to develop standards for teacher competence in student assessment out of concern that the potential educational benefits of student assessments be fully realized. The committee appointed to this project completed its work in 1990 following reviews of earlier drafts by members of the measurement, teaching, and teacher preparation and certification communities. Parallel committees of affected associations are encouraged to develop similar statements of qualifications for school administrators, counselors, testing directors, supervisors, and other educators in the near future. These statements are intended to guide the preservice and inservice preparation of educators, the accreditation of preparation programs, and the future certification of all educators.

A standard is defined here as a principle generally accepted by the professional associations responsible for this document. Assessment is defined as the process of obtaining information that is used to make educational decisions about students; to give feedback to the student about his or her progress, strengths, and weaknesses; to judge instructional effectiveness and curricular adequacy; and to inform policy. The various assessment techniques include, but are not limited to, formal and informal observation, qualitative analysis of pupil performance and products, paper-and-pencil tests, oral questioning, and analysis of student records. The assessment competencies included here are the knowledge and skills critical to a teacher's role as educator. It is understood that there are many competencies beyond assessment competencies that teachers must possess.

---

[1]   Obtained on March 12, 2002 from *http://www.unl.edu/buros/article3.html*
      This is not copyrighted material. Reproduction and dissemination are encouraged.

By establishing standards for teacher competence in student assessment, the associations subscribe to the view that student assessment is an essential part of teaching and that good teaching cannot exist without good student assessment. Training to develop the competencies covered in the standards should be an integral part of preservice preparation. Further, such assessment training should be widely available to practicing teachers through staff development programs at the district and building levels.

The standards are intended for use as:

- a guide for teacher educators as they design and approve programs for teacher preparation,
- a self-assessment guide for teachers in identifying their needs for professional development in student assessment,
- a guide for workshop instructors as they design professional development experiences for inservice teachers, and
- an impetus for educational measurement specialists and teacher trainers to conceptualize student assessment and teacher training in student assessment more broadly than has been the case in the past.

The standards should be incorporated into future teacher training and certification programs. Teachers who have not had the preparation these standards imply should have the opportunity and support to develop these competencies before the standards enter into the evaluation of these teachers.

The Approach Used to Develop the Standards

The members of the associations that supported this work are professional educators involved in teaching, teacher education, and student assessment. Members of these associations are concerned about the inadequacy with which teachers are prepared for assessing the educational progress of their students, and thus sought to address this concern effectively. A committee named by the associations first met in September 1987 and affirmed its commitment to defining standards for teacher preparation in student assessment. The committee then undertook a review of the research literature to identify needs in student assessment, current levels of teacher training in student assessment, areas of teacher activities requiring competence in using assessments, and current levels of teacher competence in student assessment.

The members of the committee used their collective experience and expertise to formulate and then revise statements of important assessment competencies. Drafts of these competencies went through several revisions by the committee before the standards were released for public review. Comments by reviewers from each of the associations were then used to prepare a final statement.

The Scope of a Teacher's Professional Role and Responsibilities for Student Assessment

There are seven standards in this document. In recognizing the critical need to revitalize classroom assessment, some standards focus on classroom-based competencies. Because of teachers' growing roles in education and policy decisions beyond the classroom, other standards address assessment competencies underlying teacher participation in decisions related to assessment at the school, district, state, and national levels.

The scope of a teacher's professional role and responsibilities for student assessment may be described in terms of the following activities. These activities imply that teachers need competence in student assessment and sufficient time and resources to complete them in a professional manner.

- **Activities Occurring Prior to Instruction**
  (a) Understanding students' cultural backgrounds, interests, skills, and abilities as they apply across a range of learning domains and/or subject areas;
  (b) understanding students' motivations and their interests in specific class content;
  (c) clarifying and articulating the performance outcomes expected of pupils; and
  (d) planning instruction for individuals or groups of students.
- **Activities Occurring During Instruction**
  (a) Monitoring pupil progress toward instructional goals;
  (b) identifying gains and difficulties pupils are experiencing in learning and performing;
  (c) adjusting instruction;
  (d) giving contingent, specific, and credible praise and feedback;
  (e) motivating students to learn; and
  (f) judging the extent of pupil attainment of instructional outcomes.
- **Activities Occurring After the Appropriate Instructional Segment (e.g., lesson, class, semester, grade)**
  (a) Describing the extent to which each pupil has attained both short- and long-term instructional goals;
  (b) communicating strengths and weaknesses based on assessment results to students, and parents or guardians;
  (c) recording and reporting assessment results for school-level analysis, evaluation, and decision making;
  (d) analyzing assessment information gathered before and during instruction to understand each student's progress to date and to inform future instructional planning;
  (e) evaluating the effectiveness of instruction; and
  (f) evaluating the effectiveness of the curriculum and materials in use.
- **Activities Associated with a Teacher's Involvement in School Building and School District Decision Making**
  (a) Serving on a school or district committee examining the school's and district's strengths and weaknesses in the development of its students;
  (b) working on the development or selection of assessment methods for school building or school district use;
  (c) evaluating school district curriculum; and
  (d) other related activities.

- **Activities Associated with a Teacher's Involvement in a Wider Community of Educators**
  (a) Serving on a state committee asked to develop learning goals and associated assessment methods;
  (b) participating in reviews of the appropriateness of district, state, or national student goals and associated assessment methods; and
  (c) interpreting the results of state and national student assessment programs.

Each standard that follows is an expectation for assessment knowledge or skill that a teacher should possess in order to perform well in the five areas just described. As a set, the standards call on teachers to demonstrate skill at selecting, developing, applying, using, communicating, and evaluating student assessment information and student assessment practices. A brief rationale and illustrative behaviors follow each standard.

The standards represent a conceptual framework or scaffolding from which specific skills can be derived. Work to make these standards operational will be needed even after they have been published. It is also expected that experience in the application of these standards should lead to their improvement and further development.

Standards for Teacher Competence in Educational Assessment of Students

1. Teachers should be skilled in choosing assessment methods appropriate for instructional decisions.

Skills in choosing appropriate, useful, administratively convenient, technically adequate, and fair assessment methods are prerequisite to good use of information to support instructional decisions. Teachers need to be well acquainted with the kinds of information provided by a broad range of assessment alternatives and their strengths and weaknesses. In particular, they should be familiar with criteria for evaluating and selecting assessment methods in light of instructional plans.

Teachers who meet this standard will have the conceptual and application skills that follow. They will be able to use the concepts of assessment error and validity when developing or selecting their approaches to classroom assessment of students. They will understand how valid assessment data can support instructional activities such as providing appropriate feedback to students, diagnosing group and individual learning needs, planning for individualized educational programs, motivating students, and evaluating instructional procedures. They will understand how invalid information can affect instructional decisions about students. They will also be able to use and evaluate assessment options available to them, considering, among other things, the cultural, social, economic, and language backgrounds of students. They will be aware that different assessment approaches can be incompatible with certain instructional goals and may impact quite differently on their teaching.

Teachers will know, for each assessment approach they use, its appropriateness for making decisions about their pupils. Moreover, teachers will know where to find information about and/or reviews of various assessment methods. Assessment options are diverse and include text- and curriculum-embedded questions and tests, standardized criterion-referenced and norm-referenced tests, oral questioning, spontaneous and structured performance assessments, portfolios, exhibitions, demonstrations, rating scales, writing samples, paper-and-pencil tests, seatwork and homework, peer- and self-assessments, student records, observations, questionnaires, interviews, projects, products, and others' opinions.

2. Teachers should be skilled in developing assessment methods appropriate for instructional decisions.

While teachers often use published or other external assessment tools, the bulk of the assessment information they use for decision-making comes from approaches they create and implement. Indeed, the assessment demands of the classroom go well beyond readily available instruments.

Teachers who meet this standard will have the conceptual and application skills that follow. Teachers will be skilled in planning the collection of information that facilitates the decisions they will make. They will know and follow appropriate principles for developing and using assessment methods in their teaching, avoiding common pitfalls in student assessment. Such techniques may include several of the options listed at the end of the first standard. The teacher will select the techniques that are appropriate to the intent of the teacher's instruction.

Teachers meeting this standard will also be skilled in using student data to analyze the quality of each assessment technique they use. Since most teachers do not have access to assessment specialists, they must be prepared to do these analyses themselves.

3. The teacher should be skilled in administering, scoring, and interpreting the results of both externally produced and teacher-produced assessment methods.

It is not enough that teachers are able to select and develop good assessment methods; they must also be able to apply them properly. Teachers should be skilled in administering, scoring, and interpreting results from diverse assessment methods.

Teachers who meet this standard will have the conceptual and application skills that follow. They will be skilled in interpreting informal and formal teacher-produced assessment results, including pupils' performances in class and on homework assignments. Teachers will be able to use guides for scoring essay questions and projects, stencils for scoring response-choice questions, and scales for rating performance assessments. They will be able to use these in ways that produce consistent results.

Teachers will be able to administer standardized achievement tests and be able to interpret the commonly reported scores: percentile ranks, percentile band scores, standard scores, and grade equivalents. They will have a conceptual understanding of the summary indexes commonly reported with assessment results: measures of central tendency, dispersion, relationships, reliability, and errors of measurement.

Teachers will be able to apply these concepts of score and summary indices in ways that enhance their use of the assessments that they develop. They will be able to analyze assessment results to identify pupils' strengths and weaknesses. If they get inconsistent results, they will seek other explanations for the discrepancy or other data to attempt to resolve the uncertainty before arriving at a decision. They will be able to use assessment methods in ways that encourage students' educational development and that do not inappropriately increase students' anxiety levels.

4. Teachers should be skilled in using assessment results when making decisions about individual students, planning teaching, developing curriculum, and school improvement.

Assessment results are used to make educational decisions at several levels: in the classroom about students, in the community about a school and a school district, and in society, generally, about the purposes and outcomes of the educational enterprise. Teachers play a vital role when participating in decision making at each of these levels and must be able to use assessment results effectively.

Teachers who meet this standard will have the conceptual and application skills that follow. They will be able to use accumulated assessment information to organize a sound instructional plan for facilitating students' educational development. When using assessment results to plan and/or evaluate instruction and curriculum, teachers will interpret the results correctly and avoid common misinterpretations, such as basing decisions on scores that lack curriculum validity. They will be informed about the results of local, regional, state, and national assessments and about their appropriate use for pupil, classroom, school, district, state, and national educational improvement.

5. Teachers should be skilled in developing valid pupil grading procedures that use pupil assessments.

Grading students is an important part of professional practice for teachers. Grading is defined as indicating both a student's level of performance and a teacher's valuing of that performance. The principles for using assessments to obtain valid grades are known and teachers should employ them.

Teachers who meet this standard will have the conceptual and application skills that follow. They will be able to devise, implement, and explain a procedure for developing grades composed of marks from various assignments, projects, in-class activities, quizzes, tests, and/or other assessments that they may use. Teachers will understand and be able to articulate why the grades they assign are rational, justified, and fair, acknowledging that such grades reflect their preferences and judgments. Teachers will be able to recognize and to avoid faulty grading procedures such as using grades as punishment. They will be able to evaluate and to modify their grading procedures in order to improve the validity of the interpretations made from them about students' attainments.

6. Teachers should be skilled in communicating assessment results to students, parents, other lay audiences, and other educators.

Teachers must routinely report assessment results to students and to parents or guardians. In addition, they are frequently asked to report or to discuss assessment results with other educators and with diverse lay audiences. If the results are not communicated effectively, they may be misused or not used. To communicate effectively with others on matters of student assessment, teachers must be able to use assessment terminology appropriately and must be able to articulate the meaning, limitations, and implications of assessment results. Furthermore, teachers will sometimes be in a position that will require them to defend their own assessment procedures and their interpretations of them. At other times, teachers may need to help the public to interpret assessment results appropriately.

Teachers who meet this standard will have the conceptual and application skills that follow. Teachers will understand and be able to give appropriate explanations of how the interpretation of student assessments must be moderated by the student's socioeconomic, cultural, language, and other background factors. Teachers will be able to explain that assessment results do not imply that such background factors limit a student's ultimate educational development. They will be able to communicate to students and to their parents or guardians how they may assess the student's educational progress. Teachers will understand and be able to explain the importance of taking measurement errors into account when using assessments to make decisions about individual students. Teachers will be able to explain the limitations of different informal and formal assessment methods. They will be able to explain printed reports of the results of pupil assessments at the classroom, school-district, state, and national levels.

7. Teachers should be skilled in recognizing unethical, illegal, and otherwise inappropriate assessment methods and uses of assessment information.

Fairness, the rights of all concerned, and professional ethical behavior must undergird all student assessment activities, from the initial planning for and gathering of information to the interpretation, use, and communication of the results. Teachers must be well versed in their own ethical and legal responsibilities in assessment. In addition, they should also attempt to have the inappropriate assessment practices of others discontinued whenever they are encountered. Teachers should also participate with the wider educational community in defining the limits of appropriate professional behavior in assessment.

Teachers who meet this standard will have the conceptual and application skills that follow. They will know those laws and case decisions that affect their classroom, school district, and state assessment practices. Teachers will be aware that various assessment procedures can be misused or overused resulting in harmful consequences such as embarrassing students, violating a student's right to confidentiality, and inappropriately using students' standardized achievement test scores to measure teaching effectiveness.

Notes

Appendix B:

The Code of Fair Testing Practices in Education [1]

Prepared by the Joint Committee on Testing Practices

The Code of Fair Testing Practices in Education states the major obligations to test takers of professionals who develop or use educational tests. The Code is meant to apply broadly to the use of tests in education (admissions, educational assessment, educational diagnosis, and student placement). The Code is not designed to cover employment testing, licensure or certification testing, or other types of testing. Although the Code has relevance to many types of educational tests, it is directed primarily at professionally developed tests such as those sold by commercial test publishers or used in formally administered testing programs. The Code is not intended to cover tests made by individual teachers for use in their own classrooms.

The Code addresses the roles of test developers and test users separately. Test users are people who select tests, commission test development services, or make decisions on the basis of test scores. Test developers are people who actually construct tests as well as those who set policies for particular testing programs. The roles may, of course, overlap as when a state education agency commissions test development services, sets policies that control the test development process, and makes decisions on the basis of the test scores.

The Code presents standards for educational test developers and users in four areas:

A. Developing/Selecting Tests
B. Interpreting Scores
C. Striving for Fairness
D. Informing Test Takers

Organizations, institutions, and individual professionals who endorse the Code commit themselves to safeguarding the rights of test takers by following the principles listed. The

---

[1] Obtained on March 12, 2002 from *http://www.apa.org/science/fairtestcode.html*
    This is not copyrighted material. Reproduction and dissemination are encouraged.

Code is intended to be consistent with the relevant parts of The Standards for Educational and Psychological Testing (AERA, NCME, 1985). However, the Code differs from the Standards in both audience and purpose. The Code is meant to be understood by the general public; it is limited to educational tests; and the primary focus is on those issues that affect the proper use of tests. The Code is not meant to add new principles over and above those in the Standards or to change the meaning of the Standards. The goal is rather to represent the spirit of a selected portion of the Standards in a way that is meaningful to test takers and/or their parents of guardians. It is the hope of the Joint Committee on Testing Practices that the Code will also be judged to be consistent with existing codes of conduct and standards of other professional groups who use educational tests.

A. Developing/Selecting Appropriate Tests

Many of the statements in the Code refer to the selection of existing tests. However, in customized testing programs, test developers are engaged to construct new tests. In those situations, the test development process should be designed to help ensure that the completed tests will be in compliance with the Code.

Test developers should provide the information that test users need to select appropriate tests.

Test Developers Should:

1. Define what each test measures and what the test should be used for. Describe the populations(s) for which the test is appropriate.
2. Accurately represent the characteristics, usefulness, and limitations of tests for their intended purposes.
3. Explain relevant measurement concepts as necessary for clarity at the level of detail that is appropriate for the intended audience(s).
4. Describe the process of test development. Explain how the context and skills to be tested were selected.
5. Provide evidence that the test meets its intended purpose(s).
6. Provide either representative samples or complete copies of test questions, directions, answer sheets, manuals, and score reports to qualified users.
7. Indicate the nature of the evidence obtained concerning the appropriateness of each test for groups of different racial, ethnic, or linguistic backgrounds who are likely to be tested.
8. Identify and publish any specialized skills needed to administer each test and to interpret scores correctly.

Test users should select tests that meet the purpose for which they are to be used and that are appropriate for the intended test-taking populations.

Test Users Should:

1. First define the purpose for testing and the population to be tested. Then, select a test for that purpose and that population based on a thorough review of the available information.
2. Investigate potentially useful sources of information, in addition to test scores, to corroborate the information provided by tests.
3. Read the materials provided by test developers and avoid using tests for which unclear or incomplete information is provided.
4. Become familiar with how and when the test was developed and tried out.
5. Read independent evaluations of a test and of possible alternative measures. Look for evidence required to support the claims of test developers.
6. Examine specimen sets, disclosed tests or samples of questions, directions, answer sheets, manuals, and score reports before selecting a test.
7. Ascertain whether the test content and norms group(s) or comparison group(s) are appropriate for the intended test takers.

Select and use only those tests for which the skills needed to administer the test and interpret scores correctly are available.

B. Interpreting Scores

Test developers should help users interpret scores correctly.

Test Developers Should:

1. Provide timely and easily understood score reports that describe test performance clearly and accurately. Also explain the meaning and limitations of reported scores.
2. Describe the population(s) represented by any norms or comparison group(s), the dates the data were gathered, and the process used to select the samples of test takers.
3. Warn users to avoid specific, reasonable anticipated misuses of test scores.
4. Provide information that will help users follow reasonable procedures for setting passing scores when it is appropriate to use such scores with the test.
5. Provide information that will help users gather evidence to show that the test is meeting its intended purpose(s).

Test users should interpret scores correctly.

Test Users Should:

1. Obtain information about the scale used for reporting scores, the characteristics of any norms or comparison group(s), and the limitations of the scores.
2. Interpret scores taking into account any major differences between the norms or comparison groups and the actual test takers. Also take into account any differences in test administration practices or familiarity with the specific questions in the test.
3. Avoid using tests for purposes not specifically recommended by the test developer unless evidence is obtained to support the intended use.

4. Explain how any passing scores were set and gather evidence to support the appropriateness of the scores.
5. Obtain evidence to help show that the test is meeting its intended purpose(s).

C. Striving for Fairness

Test developers should strive to make tests that are as fair as possible for test takers of different races, gender, ethnic backgrounds, or handicapping conditions.

Test Developers Should:

1. Review and revise test questions and related materials to avoid potentially insensitive content or language.
2. Investigate the performance of test takers of different races, gender, and ethnic backgrounds when samples of sufficient size are available. Enact procedures that help to ensure that differences in performance are related primarily to the skills under assessment rather than to irrelevant factors.
3. When feasible, make appropriately modified forms of tests or administration procedures available for test takers with handicapping conditions. Warn test users of potential problems in using standard norms with modified tests or administration procedures that result in noncomparable scores.

Test users should select tests that have been developed in ways that attempt to make them as fair as possible for test takers of different races, gender, ethnic backgrounds, or handicapping conditions.

Test Users Should:

1. Evaluate the procedures used by test developers to avoid potentially insensitive content or language.
2. Review the performance of test takers of different races, gender, and ethnic backgrounds when samples of sufficient size are available. Evaluate the extent to which performance differences may have been caused by inappropriate characteristics of the test.
3. When necessary and feasible, use appropriately modified forms of tests or administration procedures for test takers with handicapping conditions. Interpret standard norms with care in light of the modifications that were made.

D. Informing Test Takers

Under some circumstances, test developers have direct communication with test takers. Under other circumstances, test users communicate directly with test takers. Whichever group communicates directly with test takers should provide the information described below.

Test Developers or Test Users Should:

1. When a test is optional, provide test takers or their parents/guardians with information to help them judge whether the test should be taken, or if an available alternative to the test should be used.
2. Provide test takers with the information they need to be familiar with the coverage of the test, the types of question formats, the directions, and appropriate test-taking strategies. Strive to make such information equally available to all test takers.

Under some circumstances, test developers have direct control of tests and test scores. Under other circumstances, test users have such control. Whichever group has direct control of tests and test scores should take steps described below.

Test Developers or Test Users Should:

1. Provide test takers or their parents/guardians with information about rights test takers may have to obtain copies of tests and completed answer sheets, retake tests, have tests rescored, or cancel scores.
2. Tell test takers or their parents/guardians how long scores will be kept on file and indicate to whom and under what circumstances test scores will or will not be released.
3. Describe the procedures that test takers or their parents/guardians may use to register complaints and have problems resolved.

The Code has been developed by the Joint Committee of Testing Practices, a cooperative effort of several professional organizations, that has as its aim the advancement, in the public interest, of the quality of testing practices. The Joint Committee was initiated by the American Educational Research Association (AERA), the American Psychological Association (APA), and the National Council on Measurement in Education (NCME). In addition to these three groups, the American Association for Counseling and Development/Association for Measurement and Evaluation in Counseling and Development, and the American Speech-Language-Hearing Association also now sponsor the Joint Committee.

Notes

Appendix C:

A Guide to Descriptive Statistics

The purpose of descriptive statistics is to summarize, organize, and simplify a set of measurements, such as test scores. There are four basic categories of descriptive statistics: (1) measures of central tendency, (2) measures of variability, (3) measures of relative position, and (4) measures of correlation. Descriptive statistical procedures in each of these categories will be described, followed by a discussion of calculations of internal consistency reliability and the standard error of measurement. The sample data set shown below will be used as a working example throughout the discussions of calculations in this appendix.

Student	Exam 1	Exam 2
Joseph	30	19
Brian	24	23
Mathew	28	21
John	23	11
Brandon	28	30
Jason	23	25
Angie	35	27
Rebecca	33	25
Juan	29	31
Melissa	25	19
Jennifer	24	20
Andrew	30	19
Eric	30	23
Maureen	16	23
Chris	30	18
Amber	30	25
Gary	22	19
Jeff	31	21

MEASURES OF CENTRAL TENDENCY

A measure of central tendency is a single value that represents the average or typical value in a set of scores. There are three measures of central tendency: (1) the mean, (2) the median, and (3) the mode.

The Mean

The *mean* is the arithmetic average of a set of scores. It is symbolized by $\overline{X}$ or M, and is calculated by summing all scores and dividing the resulting value by the number of scores in the set. The formula for calculating the mean is

$$\overline{X} = M = \frac{\sum X}{n}$$

where $\sum X$ is the sum of scores (i.e., $\sum$ means "the sum of"), X is each individual score, and n is the number of scores in the set. For our sample set of scores, the mean for Exam 1 is

$$\overline{X} = M = \frac{\sum X}{n} = \frac{491}{18} = 27.27778 = 27.3$$

The mean for Exam 2 is approximately equal to 22.2.

The Median

The *median* is the point in a set of scores that divides the distribution into two equal halves; it is the midpoint of the scores. In order to identify the midpoint of the scores, the scores must first be arranged in order from highest to lowest. The median is then determined by counting up or down until the midpoint is reached. If there is an odd number of scores in the set, the median is simply the middlemost score. If there is an even number, the midpoint is defined as being halfway between the two middlemost scores (in other words, it is the mean of the middlemost scores). For Exam 1, the scores would be arranged as follows:

16 22 23 23 24 24 25 28 <u>28</u> <u>29</u> 30 30 30 30 30 31 33 35

Since there are eighteen scores, we find the two middlemost scores. They are 28 and 29. Therefore, the median is calculated as the mean of these two scores, or 28.5. The median for Exam 2 is 22 (see below).

11 18 19 19 19 19 20 21 <u>21</u> <u>23</u> 23 23 25 25 25 27 30 31

The Mode

The *mode* is defined as the most frequently occurring score in the set. It is quite easy to determine, since it involves no mathematical calculations. It involves arranging the scores as was done to determine the median, and determining which scores occur most often. The mode for Exam 1 is 30; the mode for Exam 2 is 19. It is possible for a set of scores to have more than one mode. For example, this would be the case in a situation where five students earned scores of 25 and five students earned scores of 28. This distribution is then described as bimodal. If more than two modes exist, the distribution is said to be multimodal.

MEASURES OF VARIABILITY

While measures of central tendency provide information about the typical score in a set, measures of variability summarize the amount of spread in the scores. The most commonly used measure of variability is the standard deviation.

The Standard Deviation

The *standard deviation* is defined as a type of average distance of the scores from the mean. The formula for computing the standard deviation is

$$SD = \sqrt{\frac{\sum (X - M)^2}{n - 1}}$$

where SD is the standard deviation, $\sum (X - M)^2$ is the sum of all of the squared differences between each score and the mean, and n is the number of scores in the set. The steps in the calculation of a standard deviation are as follows:

(1) Find the difference between each student's score and the mean.
(2) Square each of these differences.
(3) Sum the squared differences.
(4) Divide the sum by the number of scores minus 1.
(5) Find the square root of the resulting quotient.

This resulting value, the standard deviation, is a measure of the average distance of the scores away from the mean. The following table and subsequent calculations result in the computation of the standard deviation for Exam 1.

Student	Exam 1	$(X-M)$	$(X-M)^2$
Joseph	30	2.7	7.29
Brian	24	-3.3	10.89
Mathew	28	.7	.49
John	23	-4.3	18.49
Brandon	28	.7	.49
Jason	23	-4.3	18.49
Angie	35	7.7	59.29
Rebecca	33	5.7	32.49
Juan	29	1.7	2.89
Melissa	25	-2.3	5.29
Jennifer	24	-3.3	10.89
Andrew	30	2.7	7.29
Eric	30	2.7	7.29
Maureen	16	-11.3	127.69
Chris	30	2.7	7.29
Amber	30	2.7	7.29
Gary	22	-5.3	28.09
Jeff	31	3.7	13.69

$$\sum(X-M)^2 = 365.62$$

$$\frac{\sum(X-M)^2}{n-1} = \frac{365.62}{17} = 21.51$$

$$SD = \sqrt{\frac{\sum(X-M)^2}{n-1}} = \sqrt{\frac{365.62}{17}} = \sqrt{21.51} = 4.64$$

Therefore, the standard deviation for Exam 1 is equal to 4.64. The standard deviation for Exam 2 is equal to 4.72.

MEASURES OF RELATIVE POSITION

Measures of relative position are statistical measures that describe where an individual student lies in relation to all others within a set of scores. Recall that they are one type of standard score. Two of the most common measures of relative position are *z*-scores and *T*-scores.

z-score

A *z-score* specifies the precise location of each student's score within a distribution of a set of scores. The sign indicates whether the score is above or below the mean; the numerical value indicates the distance away from the mean in standard deviation units. The formula for calculating a z-score is

$$z = \frac{X - M}{SD}$$

where z is the value of the z-score, X is each individual raw score, M is the mean of the set of scores, and SD is the standard deviation for the scores. For example, suppose we wanted to determine the relative position of two students, Brian and Rebecca, on Exam 1. These calculations appear below.

Brian: $z = \dfrac{X - M}{SD} = \dfrac{24 - 27.3}{4.64} = \dfrac{-3.3}{4.64} = -.71$

Rebecca: $z = \dfrac{X - M}{SD} = \dfrac{33 - 27.3}{4.64} = \dfrac{5.7}{4.64} = +1.23$

Therefore, Brian's score is nearly three-fourths of a standard deviation below the mean, while Rebecca's score is almost one-and-a-quarter standard deviations above the mean.

T-score

A *T-score* is another type of standard score, simply reported on a different scale. A *T*-score reports the same information as does its corresponding z-score. The formula for calculating a *T*-score is

$$T = 50 + 10z$$

where T is the value of the T-score and z is the student's z-score. Converting the two z-scores above to T-scores would give us the following:

Brian: $T = 50 + 10z = 50 + 10(-.71) = 50 + (-7.1) = 42.9$

Rebecca: $T = 50 + 10z = 50 + 10(+1.23) = 50 + 12.3 = 62.3$

MEASURES OF CORRELATION

Correlation coefficients describe the extent to which two measures are related; they are very useful in assessment settings. They can be used to establish the degree of relationship between two measures, which can then be used as a basis for predicting future performance on one of those measures, provided the student has a score on the other measure. Correlation coefficients are also used in the calculation of specific measures of reliability, namely test-retest and alternate-forms reliabilities. There are several types of correlation coefficients that can be computed, but perhaps the most common method is the *Pearson product-moment correlation*. In order to calculate a correlation coefficient, each student must have scores on *each* of the two measures. The formula for calculating the Pearson correlation is

$$r = \frac{\sum(X - M_X)(Y - M_Y)}{\sqrt{\left[\sum(X - M_X)^2\right]\left[\sum(Y - M_Y)^2\right]}}$$

where r is the value of the Pearson correlation, $\sum(X - M_X)(Y - M_Y)$ is known as the "sum of products" (the product of the difference between a student's score on measure X and the mean of measure X and the difference between a student's score on measure Y and the mean of measure Y), $\sum(X - M_X)^2$ is the sum of the squared differences between each raw score and the mean for measure X, and $\sum(Y - M_Y)^2$ is the sum of the squared differences between each raw score and the mean for measure Y. The table and subsequent calculations that appear on the next page result in the computation of the Pearson correlation between Exam 1 and Exam 2.

Student	Exam 1 (X)	$(X-M_X)$	$(X-M_X)^2$	Exam 2 (Y)	$(Y-M_Y)$	$(Y-M_Y)^2$	$(X-M_X)(Y-M_Y)$
Joseph	30	2.7	7.29	19	-3.2	10.24	-8.64
Brian	24	-3.3	10.89	23	.8	.64	-2.64
Mathew	28	.7	.49	21	-1.2	1.44	-.84
John	23	-4.3	18.49	11	-11.2	125.44	48.16
Brandon	28	.7	.49	30	7.8	60.84	5.46
Jason	23	-4.3	18.49	25	2.8	7.84	-12.04
Angie	35	7.7	59.29	27	4.8	23.04	36.96
Rebecca	33	5.7	32.49	25	2.8	7.84	15.96
Juan	29	1.7	2.89	31	8.8	77.44	14.96
Melissa	25	-2.3	5.29	19	-3.2	10.24	7.36
Jennifer	24	-3.3	10.89	20	-2.2	4.84	7.26
Andrew	30	2.7	7.29	19	-3.2	10.24	-8.64
Eric	30	2.7	7.29	23	.8	.64	2.16
Maureen	16	-11.3	127.69	23	.8	.64	-9.04
Chris	30	2.7	7.29	18	-4.2	17.64	-11.34
Amber	30	2.7	7.29	25	2.8	7.84	7.56
Gary	22	-5.3	28.09	19	-3.2	10.24	16.96
Jeff	31	3.7	13.69	21	-1.2	1.44	-4.44

$$r = \frac{\Sigma(X-M_X)(Y-M_Y)}{\sqrt{[\Sigma(X-M_X)^2][\Sigma(Y-M_Y)^2]}} = \frac{105.18}{\sqrt{(365.62)(378.52)}} = \frac{105.18}{\sqrt{138394.48}} = \frac{105.18}{372.01} = .28$$

This correlation coefficient of .28 represents a fairly weak relationship between Exam 1 and Exam 2.

MEASURES OF INTERNAL CONSISTENCY

Internal consistency is a statistical estimate of the reliability of a test that is administered only once. For this reason, this type of reliability estimate is most useful for classroom teachers. One of the easiest internal consistency formulae to use is the *Kuder-Richardson formula 21* (also known as KR-21). The formula for calculating KR-21 internal consistency is

$$r_{total} = \frac{(K)(SD)^2 - M(K-M)}{(SD)^2(K-1)}$$

where r_{total} is the reliability index for the total test, K is the number of items on the test, M is the mean for the test, and SD is the standard deviation of the test. Imagine that Exam 1 consists of 40 items. The mean, calculated earlier, is equal to 27.3, and the standard deviation is 4.64. Therefore the internal consistency reliability index for the exam, using the KR-21 formula, is shown below.

$$r_{total} = \frac{(40)(4.64)^2 - (27.3)(40-27.3)}{(4.64)^2(40-1)} = \frac{(40)(21.53) - (27.3)(12.7)}{(21.53)(39)} = \frac{514.49}{839.67} = .61$$

As the number of items on a test increases, the reliability of the test tends to improve. Imagine that the teacher of Exam 1 wants to know by how much the reliability would increase if the test were doubled to 80 items. The Spearman-Brown prophecy formula was designed to estimate what the reliability coefficient will become after lengthening a particular test. The formula for calculating the Spearman-Brown reliability is

$$r_{est} = \frac{nr}{1 + (n-1)r}$$

where r_{est} is the estimated new reliability coefficient, r is the original reliability coefficient, and n is the number of times the test is lengthened. If the teacher were to double the number of items on the original Exam 1, the new reliability would be estimated as follows:

$$r_{est} = \frac{nr}{1 + (n-1)r} = \frac{(2)(.61)}{1 + (2-1)(.61)} = \frac{1.22}{1.61} = .76$$

Therefore, by increasing the number of test items on Exam 1 from 40 to 80, the reliability coefficient improves from .61 to .76.

STANDARD ERROR OF MEASUREMENT

The *standard error of measurement* is another way of expressing the reliability of a test. The standard error is an estimate of how often you can expect test errors of a given size. Although it is a function of other characteristics of a test, generally speaking, a small value (e.g., less than 3.0) for the standard error indicates high reliability; a large value for the standard error indicates low reliability. The formula for calculating the standard error of measurement is

$$SE_m = SD\sqrt{1-r}$$

where SE_m is the standard error of measurement, SD is the standard deviation, and r is the reliability coefficient (i.e., the KR-21 coefficient) for the test.

As you can see, the standard error of measurement is a function of a test's standard deviation and reliability. For Exam 1, the standard error of measurement is:

$$SE_m = SD\sqrt{1-r} = (4.64)\sqrt{1-.61} = (4.64)(.62) = 2.88$$

The standard error of measurement for Exam 2 is equal to 3.10. Notice that higher reliability and smaller standard deviations are associated with smaller standard errors. This is the more desirable situation for classroom tests.

EXERCISES TO ACCOMPANY THE CALCULATIONS IN APPENDIX C

Complete the specified calculations for the sets of scores provided in the table.

STUDENT	EXAM 1	EXAM 2
Alexander	27	29
Elaine	27	29
Robert	24	27
Melissa	31	28
Joshua	27	22
Lisa	33	25
Laura	20	21
Heather	33	29
Carolyn	22	24
Brian	25	25
Christa	29	25
Beth Ann	26	19
Molli	27	25
Matthew	27	28
Nicole	23	24
Brandon	28	23
Amy	31	21
Christie	33	28
Alani	24	29
Wendy	35	31

1. Determine the mean, median, and mode for Exam 1.

2. Calculate the standard deviation for Exam 1.

3. Determine the mean, median, and mode for Exam 2.

4. Calculate the standard deviation for Exam 2.

5. What is the *z*-score for Heather on Exam 1? For Brandon on Exam 2?

6. What is Heather's *T*-score on Exam 1? Brandon's *T*-score on Exam 2?

7. Calculate the Pearson product-moment correlation between the two tests.

8. Calculate the KR-21 internal consistency reliability for Exam 2 (containing 40 items).

9. Estimate the new reliability for Exam 2 if the test were doubled (i.e., 80 items).

10. Estimate the new reliability for Exam 2 if the test were tripled (i.e., 120 items).

Classroom Assessment Glossary

Action verbs (2)[1] verbs that specify the observable behaviors in instructional objectives.

Affective domain (2; 13) domain of student behaviors that addresses attitudes, emotions, values, interests, feelings, etc.

Alternate-choice item (4; 8) objective test item consisting of a statement followed by only two options.

Alternate-forms coefficient (3) reliability coefficient resulting from an alternate-forms estimate of reliability; serves as a measure of equivalence.

Alternate-forms method (3) method of estimating reliability where two forms of a test are administered to the same group of students at essentially the same time; results in an alternate-forms coefficient.

Alternative assessment (1; 4) any assessment not considered to be traditional (e.g., pencil-and-paper test); helps overcome the limitations of traditional assessments.

Analytic rubric (5; 6) a scoring guide where the separate, individual parts of a product or performance are scored first, then summed to obtain a total score; used in scoring performance assessments.

Anecdotal record (5) a short, written record of student behavior, including the context in which the behavior occurred.

Answer key (8) a list of the correct answers to a test; the primary method of scoring student responses to objective items.

Assessment method (1; 2; 3) a process involving a structured situation that includes samples of particular characteristics or behaviors that results in a numerical or narrative score.

---

1 The number(s) in parentheses refer to the chapter(s) in which the term is discussed.

Assessment system (1) all the systematic methods and procedures that are used to obtain information about behaviors and upon which educational decisions are based.

Attitudes (13) relatively stable, consistent internal tendencies that influence what students are likely to do with respect to social situations, established institutions, and similar phenomena.

Authentic assessments (1; 4; 6) assessment methods that involve the real application of a skill beyond its instructional context; facts and concepts are *applied* in an attempt to solve real-world problems.

Bloom's taxonomy (2) classification system for instructional objectives and subsequent student behaviors; includes the cognitive, affective, and psychomotor domains.

Checklist (5; 6) a list of behaviors or student outcomes, where the teacher simply indicates whether each behavior or outcome has been observed.

Coefficient of stability (3) reliability coefficient resulting from a test-retest estimate of reliability; serves as a measure of consistency over time.

Cognitive domain (2) domain of student behaviors that addresses intellectual capabilities.

Competency test (1) see *criterion-referenced assessment.*

Completion item (4; 9) subjective test item in which the student must supply the missing word or words.

Concurrent evidence (of validity) (3) a form of criterion-related evidence in which the criterion is measured at the same time or consists of some measure that is available at the same time.

Confidence interval (11) a band or range of scores that we are *reasonably* confident includes a student's true ability or achievement score; also known as a *confidence band.*

Construct evidence (of validity) (3) the degree to which an assessment measures an intended hypothetical construct (an underlying, unobservable trait).

Constructed-response item (1; 4; 9) see *subjective assessments.*

Content evidence (of validity) (3) the extent to which the *content* addressed by assessment items, tasks, or activities adequately samples (i.e., is representative of) the larger domain of performance; determines the degree to which an assessment measures the intended content area.

Continuous-feedback model (1) model of teaching and assessment based on the basic principle that, if provided with additional time to learn, the vast majority of students could master the content presented to them in schools.

Correction true-false item (8) variation of a true-false item that requires students to rewrite statements that they indicate as being false.

Correlation coefficient (3) a statistical value that indicates the extent to which the scores on one measure agree with the scores on another measure.

Criterion evidence (of validity) (3) the extent to which the scores resulting from an assessment are related to the scores on another, well-established assessment method.

Criterion-referenced assessment (1) assessment methods that compare a student's performance to some pre-established criteria or objectives.

Criterion-referenced grading (10) grades are assigned to students based on their performance compared to a preestablished set of performance standards.

Curriculum frameworks (2) see *curriculum guides*.

Curriculum guide (2) a set of guidelines that specify topics to be taught and the order in which they should be taught for specific grade levels and/or subject areas.

Derived scores (11) scores resulting from the conversion of raw scores on norm-referenced tests that permit comparisons with norm group; see also *transformed scores*.

Deviation IQ score (11) standardized score that gives the location of a raw score in a normal distribution having a mean of 100 and a standard deviation equal to 15 or 16.

Diagnostic assessment (1) assessment methods that are used to determine what students already know and can do; designed to identify the nature of specific student difficulties.

Distractor (8) an incorrect response option of a multiple-choice test item.

Distractor analysis (8) in an item analysis, provides information about the pattern of responses for incorrect options.

Documentation portfolio (7) the type of portfolio used to provide an ongoing record of student progress.

Educational objective (2) see *instructional objective*.

Embedded alternate-choice item (8) type of alternate-choice item consisting of a series of alternate-choice items embedded in a paragraph.

Equivalent-forms method (3) method of estimating reliability where two forms of a test that measure the same skills but with slightly different items are administered to the same group of students at about the same time.

Essay items (4; 9) subjective items where students must construct a response to some prompt (a question, situation, or problem).

Evaluation (1) the use of assessment information to make judgments about students, teachers, or educational programs.

Extended response essay items (4; 9) essay items that allow students to respond by freely expressing their own ideas and to use their own organization of their answers.

Face evidence (of validity) (3) an informal impression of the extent to which the users or takers of tests believe that the tests are valid.

Fill-in-the-blank item (4; 9) see *completion item*.

Formal assessments (1) assessments that are planned in advance of their administration; they lack spontaneity.

Formative evaluation (1) a process that leads to decisions that occur during instruction, for the purpose of determining what adjustments to instruction should be made; typically based on informal assessments.

Grade-equivalent score (11) score indicating the grade in the norm group for which a certain raw score was the average performance.

Grading (10) the process of using a formal system for purposes of summarizing and reporting student achievement and progress.

GRE/SAT score (11) standardized score on a scale that has a mean of 500 and a standard deviation of 100; also known as CEEB score.

Higher-level cognitive behaviors (2) thinking skills that go beyond simple memorization and understanding.

Holistic rubric (5; 6) a scoring guide where the overall process or product is scored as a whole, without judging the component parts separately; used in scoring performance assessments.

Informal assessments (1; 4) assessments that are not planned in advance and are very spontaneous.

Instructional objective (2; 3) statement that clearly describes what students are expected to learn or to be able to do following instruction.

Integrated assessment model (1) model of teaching and assessment that is based on the notion that instruction should focus on meaningful learning and thinking.

Interests (13) preferences held by students for participating in particular activities.

Internal consistency (3) method of estimating reliability requiring only one administration of a test.

Interrater consistency (3) method of establishing reliability of qualitative assessment; based on the calculation of the percent agreement between two or more raters of student performance or products.

Item analysis (8) the process of statistically analyzing the characteristics of objective test items for purposes of making decisions about the items.

Item difficulty (8) in an item analysis, the proportion of students who answer the item correctly; symbolized by p.

Item discrimination (8) in an item analysis, the difference between the proportion of correct answers for the highest-scoring students and the proportion of correct answers for the lowest-scoring students; symbolized by D.

Kuder-Richardson method (3) method of estimating reliability equal to the average of all possible split-half combinations; see *split-half method*.

Lesson plan (2) detailed plan for each individual lesson to be taught.

Lower-level cognitive behaviors (2) thinking skills that focus on basic thinking strategies, such as rote memorization, recall of information, and simple understanding of subject matter.

Mastery test (1) see *criterion-referenced assessment*.

Matching items (4; 8) an objective test item typically consisting of two lists of terms, the stimuli on the left and the responses on the right.

Measure (1) a process involving a structured situation that includes samples of particular characteristics or behaviors that results in a numerical or narrative score.

Multiple true-false items (8) a variation of an alternate-choice item consisting of several statements, each utilizing the same stem, and requiring a determination of truth or falsity.

Multiple-choice items (4; 8) objective test items consisting of a stem and a set of possible answers known as options.

Nonstandardized assessment (1) teacher-made assessment methods developed for use within a single classroom and with a single set of students.

Normal curve equivalent (NCE) scores (11) standardized score scale with a mean of 50 and a standard deviation of 21.06; range in value from 1 to 99.

Norm group (1; 11) the well-defined group of students that serves as the basis for comparing students' test performance in norm-referenced assessments.

Norm-referenced assessment (1) assessment methods that show where an individual student's performance lies in relation to other students.

Norm-referenced grading (10) grades that are assigned to students based on a comparison of a student's performance with the performance of other students.

Objective assessment (1) assessment methods that have only one correct answer; the judgment of the scorer has no influence on the student's score; answers are selected from a set of options.

Objectives-referenced test (1) see *criterion-referenced assessment*.

Objective test items (4; 8) see *objective assessment*.

Observations (4; 5) informal method of assessment that involves watching and/or listening to students as they carry out some activity.

Percentile rank (11) a number that indicates the percentage of the norm group that scored below a given raw score on a norm-referenced test.

Performance-based assessment (4; 6) an assessment activity that provides direct observation of student performance; usually an authentic assessment; also known as *performance assessment*.

Performance criteria (6) specific observable standards by which student performances or products are assessed.

Performance task (6) the actual prompt or activity supplied to students as part of a performance assessment.

Portfolio assessment (4; 7) purposeful, organized collection of student work that can be used to describe students' efforts, progress, and/or achievement in a subject area.

Portfolio, documentation (7) see *documentation portfolio*.

Portfolio, showcase (7) see *showcase portfolio*.

Predictive evidence (of validity) (3) a form of criterion-related evidence in which the criterion is measured sometime in the future.

Process assessment (6) a performance assessment that specifically targets procedures used by students to solve a problem or complete a task.

Product assessment (6) a performance assessment that results in a tangible outcome.

Psychomotor domain (2) domain of student behaviors that addresses physical and manipulative activities.

Qualitative assessment (1; 3) assessment methods that result in verbal descriptions of a student characteristic or behavior.

Quantitative assessment (1; 3) assessment methods that yield numerical scores that serve as estimates of a student characteristic or behavior.

Questioning (4; 5) informal assessment characterized by unplanned and spontaneous oral inquiries posed by the teacher to be answered by the students.

Rating scale (5; 6) a list of behaviors or student outcomes where teachers can indicate the frequency or degree to which a student exhibits a characteristic.

Reliability (3) the consistency of measurements when the testing procedure is repeated on a population of individuals or groups.

Reliability coefficient (3) a correlation coefficient used as a measure of reliability.

Restricted response essay items (4; 9) essay items that limit what the student is permitted to answer; also known as *short-answer items*.

Rubric (5; 6) a scoring guide, consisting of specific preestablished performance criteria used in evaluating student work on performance assessments.

Rubric, analytic (5; 6) see *analytic rubric*.

Rubric, holistic (5; 6) see *holistic rubric*.

SAT/GRE score (11) standardized score on a scale that has a mean of 500 and a standard deviation of 100; also known as CEEB score.

Scoring rubric (6) see *rubric*.

Selected-response items (1; 4; 8) see *objective assessment*.

Self-attitudes (13) beliefs and feelings about oneself.

Short-answer items (4; 9) type of subjective test items requiring students to respond with a word, short phrase, number, or other type of brief response.

Showcase portfolio (7) a specific type of portfolio used to highlight and display a student's best accomplishments.

Social adjustment (13) adaptive behavior and social development as indicated by students' responses to school rules, responsibility, and interpersonal relationships with teachers and peers.

Split-half method (3) method of estimating internal consistency involving the separation of one test into two comparable halves.

Standard error of measurement (SEM) (11) the average amount of measurement error across students in the norm group; also known as *standard error*.

Standardized assessments (1) assessments that are administered, scored, and interpreted in identical fashion for all examinees, regardless of when or where they were assessed.

Standardized scores (11) raw scores transformed to "fit" a distribution whose characteristics are known and fixed; also known as *standard scores*.

Stanine (11) standardized score that provides the location of a raw score in a specific *segment* of the normal distribution; range in value from 1 to 9, where the mean is equal to 5 and the standard deviation is equal to 2.

Stem (8) component of a multiple-choice test item that defines the problem or provides the prompt to which students must select the correct response.

Stimuli (8) one of the lists in a matching item which is typically composed of concepts or names that are to be matched with responses.

Structured-response items (1; 8) see *objective assessment*.

Student reflections (5) brief narratives or self-reports written by students concerning the subject matter being studied.

Subjective assessment (1) assessment methods that have several possible correct responses, or those which may have only a single correct response but several possible ways to arrive at that answer; the judgment of the scorer can have influence on the student's score.

Subjective test items (4; 8) see *subjective assessment*.

Summative evaluation (1) a process based on assessments that occur after instruction, for the purpose of determining achievement of instructional objectives; consists solely of formal assessments.

Supply items (1) see *subjective assessment*.

Table of specifications (8) a chart showing the relation between objectives, instructional content, and taxonomic levels of Bloom's cognitive domain.

Teacher observations (4; 5) see *observations*.

Teacher questions (4; 5) see *questioning*.

Teacher-supplied items (1) see *objective assessment*.

Test (1; 2) a formal set of questions or tasks, often administered to a group of students, that address particular cognitive capabilities learned in a specific course or subject area.

Test-retest method (3) method of estimating reliability where a test is administered to the same group of students at about the same time; results in a coefficient of stability.

Testwiseness (1) the ability to use assessment-taking strategies, clues from poorly written items; also, experience in taking tests to improve one's score beyond that which would be attained from mastery of the content.

Time-restricted model (1) model of teaching and assessment where assessment occurs only following the completion of instruction.

Traditional assessment (1; 4) pencil-and-paper methods of assessment, such as tests and quizzes; specific item types include multiple-choice, alternate-choice, matching, short-answer, and essay.

Transformed scores (11) scores resulting from the conversion of raw scores on norm-referenced tests that permit comparisons with norm group; see also *derived scores*.

True-false items (4; 8) alternate-choice items where the student indicates whether a statement is true or false.

***T*-score (11)** a standardized score scale that has a mean of 50 and a standard deviation of 10.

Unit plan (2) an outline or overview of a rather large section of content material to be covered during instruction.

Validity (3) the degree to which evidence and theory support the interpretations of test scores entailed by proposed uses of tests.

Validity coefficient (3) a correlation coefficient used as a measure of validity.

Values (13) standards that determine end states of existence, as well as modes of self-conduct and presentation of self to others, which are desirable.

Weekly plan (2) a brief overview of what will be covered each day of a given week for each subject, course, or class period.

Yes-no item (8) a variation of a traditional true-false item where the statement is changed to a question and the response options to "yes-no."

***z*-score (11)** standardized scores ranging from −3.00 to +3.00; the sign indicates whether the raw score is above or below the mean; the numerical value indicates how many standard deviations it is located away from the mean.

Notes

References

Airasian, P. W. (2000). *Assessment in the classroom: A concise approach* (2nd ed.). Boston: McGraw-Hill.

Airasian, P. W. (2001). *Classroom assessment: Concepts and applications* (4th ed.). Boston: McGraw-Hill.

Al-Belushi, A. H. (n.d.). *Affective domain*. Retrieved February 26, 2002, from http://www.geocities.com/eltsqu/Affective.htm

American Educational Research Association, American Psychological Association, & National Council on Measurement in Education. (1999). *Standards for educational and psychological testing*. Washington, D.C.: American Educational Research Association.

Arlington Central School District: Performance Assessment Tasks. (May 12, 1999). Retrieved November 16, 2001, from http://www.arlingtonschools.org/Curriculum/Assessment/math4dat.html

Charles, C. M., & Mertler, C. A. (2002). *Introduction to educational research* (4th ed.). Boston: Allyn & Bacon.

Chase, C. I. (1999). *Contemporary assessment for educators*. New York: Longman.

Children's Museum of Indianapolis. (1999). *Field guide to the universe: Modern astronomers*. Retrieved March 11, 2002, from http://www.childrensmuseum.org/cosmicquest/fieldguide/astro_modern.html

Code of Fair Testing Practices in Education. (1988) Washington, D.C.: Joint Committee on Testing Practices.

Danielson, C., & Abrutyn, L. (1997a). Introduction. In C. Danielson & L. Abrutyn, *An introduction to using portfolios in the classroom.* Alexandria, VA: Association for Supervision and Curriculum Development. Retrieved November 29, 2001, from http://www.ascd.org/readingroom/books/danielson97book.html#intro

Danielson, C., & Abrutyn, L. (1997b). The types of portfolios. In C. Danielson & L. Abrutyn, *An introduction to using portfolios in the classroom.* Alexandria, VA: Association for Supervision and Curriculum Development. Retrieved November 29, 2001, from http://www.ascd.org/readingroom/books/danielson97book.html#chap1

Forgette-Giroux, R., & Simon, M. (2000). Organizational issues related to portfolio assessment implementation in the classroom. *Practical Assessment, Research, & Evaluation,* 7(4). Available online: http://ericae.net/pare/getvn.asp?v=7&n=4

Fraenkel, J. R., & Wallen, N. E. (2000). *How to design and evaluate research in education* (4th ed.). Boston: McGraw-Hill.

Frary, R. B. (1995). More multiple-choice item writing do's and don'ts. *Practical Assessment, Research, & Evaluation,* 4(11). Available online: http://ericae.net/pare/getvn.asp?v=4&n=11

Frisbie, D. A., & Waltman, K. K. (1992). An NCME instructional module on developing a personal grading plan. *Educational Measurement: Issues and Practice,* 11(3), 35-42.

Gallagher, J. D. (1998). *Classroom assessment for teachers.* Upper Saddle River, NJ: Merrill.

Glutting, J. J. (n.d.). Overview of norm-referenced test score interpretation. In *Glutting's guide for norm-referenced test score interpretation, using a sample psychological report.* Retrieved February 11, 2002, from http://www.causeonline.org/Gluttings%20Guide.pdf

Gredler, M. E. (1999). *Classroom assessment and learning.* New York: Longman.

Gronlund, N. E. (2000). *How to write and use instructional objectives* (6th ed.). Upper Saddle River, NJ: Merrill.

Harcourt Educational Measurement. (2001). Technical Information. *Stanford Achievement Test Series.* San Antonio, TX. Retrieved February 6, 2002, from http://www.hemweb.com/trophy/achvtest/techinf.htm

Johnson, D. W., & Johnson, R. T. (2002). *Meaningful assessment: A manageable and cooperative process.* Boston: Allyn & Bacon.

Kehoe, J. (1995). Writing multiple-choice test items. *Practical Assessment, Research, & Evaluation, 4*(9). Available online: http://ericae.net/pare/getvn.asp?v=4&n=9

Magnan, B. (1991, January). Teaching idea: The one-minute paper. *Newsletter of the Teaching Resource Center for Faculty and Teaching Assistants,* The University of Virginia. Retrieved October 29, 2001, from http://trc.virginia.edu/tc/1991/OneMinute.htm

Marzano, R. J. (2000). *Transforming classroom grading.* Alexandria, VA: Association for Supervision and Curriculum Development.

McGovern, M. (2001a, August). *One-minute paper.* College of Nursing, Villanova University. Retrieved October 29, 2001, from http://www.nln.org/ce/mcgovern/tsld047.htm

McGovern, M. (2001b, August). *One-minute papers.* College of Nursing, Villanova University. Retrieved October 29, 2001, from http://www.nln.org/ce/mcgovern/tsld046.htm

McMillan, J. H. (2001). *Classroom assessment: Principles and practice for effective instruction* (2nd ed.). Boston: Allyn & Bacon.

Meisels, S. J., Harrington, H. L., McMahon, P., Dichtelmiller, M. L., & Jablon, J. R. (2002). *Thinking like a teacher: Using observational assessment to improve teaching and learning.* Boston: Allyn & Bacon.

Mertler, C. A. (2000). Teacher-centered fallacies of classroom assessment validity and reliability. *Mid-Western Educational Researcher, 13*(4), 29-35.

Mertler, C. A. (2001a). Designing scoring rubrics for your classroom. *Practical Assessment, Research, & Evaluation, 7*(25). Available online: http://ericae.net/pare/getvn.asp?v=7&n=25

Mertler, C. A. (2001b). *Using performance assessment in your classroom.* Unpublished manuscript (inservice training materials), Bowling Green State University.

Mertler, C. A. (2001c). *Interpreting proficiency test data: Guiding instruction and intervention.* Unpublished manuscript (inservice training materials), Bowling Green State University.

Montgomery, K. (2001). *Authentic assessment: A guide for elementary teachers.* New York: Longman.

Moskal, B. M. (2000). Scoring rubrics: what, when, and how? *Practical Assessment, Research, & Evaluation, 7*(3). Available online: http://ericae.net/pare/getvn.asp?v=7&n=3

Nitko, A. J. (2001). *Educational assessment of students* (3rd ed.). Upper Saddle River, NJ: Merrill.

Oosterhof, A. (1999). *Developing and using classroom assessments* (2nd ed.). Upper Saddle River, NJ: Merrill.

Oosterhof, A. (2001). *Classroom applications of educational measurement* (3rd ed.). Upper Saddle River, NJ: Merrill.

Pattonville (MO) School District: Show-Me Classroom Performance Assessment Project, Performance Assessments Index (High School). (1997). Retrieved November 16, 2001, from http://www.pattonville.k12.mo.us/services/showme_assessment/pdfdocs/HScannam.pdf

Popham, W. J. (2002). *Classroom assessment: What teachers need to know* (3rd ed.). Boston: Allyn & Bacon.

Quina, J. (1989). *Effective secondary teaching: Going beyond the bell curve.* New York: Harper & Row.

Rolheiser, C., Bower, B., & Stevahn, L. (2000). Determining the basics of student portfolios. In C. Rolheiser, B. Bower, & L. Stevahn, *The portfolio organizer: Succeeding with portfolios in your classroom.* Alexandria, VA: Association for Supervision and Curriculum Development. Retrieved November 29, 2001, from http://www.ascd.org/reading room/books/rolheiser00book.html#chapter1

Scriven, M. (1967). The methodology of evaluation. In R. W. Tyler (ed.), *Perspectives of curriculum evaluation* (pp. 39-83). Chicago: Rand McNally.

Shepard, L. A. (2000). The role of assessment in a learning culture. *Educational Researcher, 29*(7), 4-14.

Silverlake, A. C. (1999). *Comprehending test manuals: A guide and workbook.* Los Angeles, CA: Pyrczak.

Stix, A. (1996, November). *Creating rubrics through negotiable contracting and assessment.* Paper presented at the National Middle School Conference, Baltimore, MD. (ERIC Document Reproduction Service ED411273)

Tanner, D. E. (2001). *Assessing academic achievement.* Boston: Allyn & Bacon.

The Standards for Teacher Competence in the Educational Assessment of Students. (1990). Washington, D.C.: National Council on Measurement in Education.

Tombari, M., & Borich, G. (1999). *Authentic assessment in the classroom: Applications and practice.* Upper Saddle River, NJ: Merrill.

Trice, A. D. (2000). *A handbook of classroom assessment.* New York: Longman.

Webb, N. M. (1997). Assessing students in small collaborative groups. *Theory Into Practice, 36*(4), 205-213.

Weber, E. (1999). *Student assessment that works: A practical approach.* Boston: Allyn & Bacon.

Notes

Subject Index

Terms appearing in boldface type are defined in the Classroom Assessment Glossary.

A

achievement tests, 147, 254, 258, 299
action verbs, 40-41, 45, 292
   definition, 319
affective characteristics, 279-281, 289, 293
affective domain, 37, 278-280
   definition, 319
   levels of, 278
AFT, NCME, & NEA Standards, 16
alternate-choice item, 77, 81, 180-184
   advantages and limitations, 182-183
   definition, 319
   guidelines, 180-182
   variations, 183-184
alternate-forms coefficient, 62, 319
   definition, 319
alternate-forms method, 61-62
   definition, 319
alternative assessment, 10, 70
   definition, 319
American Federation of Teachers, 16, 295
American Psychological Association, 16, 50, 307, 327
anecdotal record, 8, 93-95
   definition, 319
answer key, 169, 174, 180
   definition, 319

aptitude tests, 54
assessing instruction, 22, 29, 41, 44
assessment method, 6-11
   definition, 319
assessment of affect, 294
   anonymity in the, 284, 289, 290
   reasons for, 279
   techniques
      student self-reports, 285
assessment system, 4-5
   definition, 320
attitudes, 279-283
   definition, 320
authentic assessments, 10, 70
   definition, 320

B

Bloom's taxonomy, 37-38
   definition, 320
   levels, 38

C

California Achievement Tests, 9, 238
CEEB scores, 247
checklist, 93, 95
   definition, 320
classroom tests, 164-168

Code of Fair Testing Practices in Education, 16, 18, 66, 303, 328
coefficient of stability, 61, 325
  definition, 320
cognitive domain, 37-38
  definition, 320
competency test, 10, 120, 273
  definition, 320
completion item, 78-79, 200-201
  definition, 320
Comprehensive Tests of Basic Skills, 238
concurrent evidence (of validity), 55-56
  definition, 320
confidence interval, 249-251
  definition, 320
constructed-response item, 11, 78, 82, 198, 201
  definition, 320
construct evidence (of validity), 55, 57, 66
  definition, 320
constructs, 278, 290
content evidence (of validity), 52-54
  definition, 320
continuous-feedback model, 24-26
  definition, 320
correction true-false item, 183
  definition, 320
correlation coefficient, 58-59, 61, 314-316
  definition, 320
courses of study, 36
criterion evidence of validity, 55-58
  definition, 320
criterion-referenced assessment, 10, 18, 320, 322-323
  definition, 320
criterion-referenced grading, 222, 233-234
  definition, 321
criterion-referenced tests, 185, 239-240, 242, 258
Cronbach's coefficient alpha (α) method, 63, 66, 68
curriculum framework, 36
  definition, 321
curriculum guide, 36, 46
  definition, 321

D

data-driven decisionmaking, 253
delivering instruction, 22, 29, 44
derived scores

definition, 321
descriptive statistics, 309
deviation IQ score, 243, 246, 258
  definition, 321
diagnostic assessment, 12
  definition, 321
distractor analysis, 185, 188, 192
  definition, 321
distractor, 76, 77, 169, 171
  definition, 321

E

educational objective, 37
  definition, 321
embedded alternate-choice item, 183
  definition, 321
equivalent-forms method, 61
  definition, 321
essay items, 77-78, 204-209
  advantages and limitations, 207-208
  definition, 321
  extended response, 78, 204
    definition, 321
  guidelines for developing, 206-207
  restricted response, 78, 204
    definition, 323
evaluation, 5
  definition, 321

F

face evidence (of validity), 56-57, 136
  definition, 321
Family and Education Rights and Privacy Act of 1974, The, 17
fill-in-the-blank item, 78, 200
  definition, 321
formal assessments, 6
  definition, 321
formative decision making, 24, 43
formative evaluation, 8-9
  definition, 321

G

gradebook, 228, 233
grade-equivalent score, 245, 258-260
  definition, 321
grading, 213, 215-218, 223, 232-233
  definition, 321

grading systems, 216-228
   categories of reporting
      criterion-referenced grading, 233-234
      norm-referenced grading, 220, 234
   non-academic areas, 219
   types of
      letter grades, 223-224
      numerical or percentage grades, 224-225
      pass/fail, 225
Graduate Record Examination, 9, 55, 247, 255
GRE/SAT score, 247-248
   definition, 321
group process, 265-271, 273
   designing assessments of, 266-269
      group papers, 266-267
      group presentations, 266-267
      group projects, 266-268
      group skills, 266, 268
   types of, 265-266
group skills, 266, 268
   assessment of
      peer assessment, 271-272, 275
      self-assessment, 270-271
      teacher assessment, 272
   rubric for assessing, 269

H

higher-level cognitive behaviors, 38
   definition, 322

I

inferences, 90
informal assessment methods, 6
informal assessments
   definition, 322
   teacher observations, 88-93
      definition, 324
   teacher questions, 97-100
      definition, 324
instruction
   assessing, 42-44
   delivering, 42
   planning, 30-41
instructional objective, 36-40
   writing, 39-40
   definition, 322
instructional process, 29
integrated assessment model, 26-28

definition, 322
interests, 282
   definition, 322
internal consistency, 62-63
   definition, 322
interrater consistency, 63
   definition, 322
Iowa Tests of Basic Skills, 9, 10, 238
ITEMAN, 189
item analysis, 184-191
   distractor analysis, 185, 188, 192
   item difficulty, 185-186
   item discrimination, 185-188
item difficulty, 185-186
   definition, 322
item discrimination, 185188
   definition, 322

K

KR-21 formula, 63, 188, 315-316
Kuder-Richardson method, 63
   definition, 322

L

lesson plan, 31-36
   definition, 322
   guidelines, 31-33
   sample form, 34
letter grades, 223-224
letters to parents, 229
Likert scales, 285, 287
Likert-type scales, 285
lower-level cognitive behaviors, 38
   definition, 322

M

mastery test, 10
   definition, 322
matching items, 77, 176-180
   advantages and limitations, 179-180
   definition, 322
   guidelines, 177-179
mean, 241, 246, 310
measure, 6
   definition, 322
measurement, 5
measures of central tendency, 310
measures of correlation, 314

measures of relative position, 312-313
measures of variability, 311-312
median, 310
Metropolitan Achievement Tests, 238, 256
mode, 310
motivating students, 97, 297-298
multiple true-false items, 184
  definition, 322
multiple-choice items, 169-176
  advantages and limitations, 173-175
  definition, 322
  guidelines, 170-173
  variations, 175-176

N

National Council on Measurement in
  Education, 16, 50, 295, 307, 327
National Education Association, 16, 295
national percentile bands, 251, 252, 257
natural setting, 88, 284, 289-290
nonstandardized assessment, 9
  definition, 322
normal curve equivalent (NCE) scores, 248
  definition, 322
normal distribution, 241, 242, 243, 245, 246,
  248, 249, 250, 251, 258, 260, 321, 324
norm group, 10, 240-241
  definition, 322
norm-referenced assessment, 10
  definition, 323
norm-referenced grading, 220-222
  definition, 323
norm-referenced tests, 239, 240-241, 258, 299
numerical grades, 224-225

O

objective assessment, 11
  definition, 323
objectives-referenced test, 10
  definition, 323
objective test items, 76-77
  characteristics and examples, 76-77
  definition, 323
  strengths and limitations, 77
objective tests, 76, 164-169
  guidelines for developing, 165-167
one-minute paper, 102
open-ended items, 78

P

parent-teacher conferences, 229
pass/fail grades, 225
Pearson product-moment correlation, 314
percentage grades, 224-225
percentile rank, 243-244
  definition, 323
performance-based assessment, 72-74
  basic requirements, 113-115
  characteristics, 110-113
  definition, 323
  developing rubrics, 132-133
  developing tasks, 116-120
  process assessment, 115
  product assessment, 115
performance criteria, 118
  definition, 323
performance task, 110, 116-120
  definition, 323
placing students, 12, 18
planning instruction, 30-41
plans
  lesson, 31-36
  unit, 30
  weekly, 31
portfolio assessment, 74-76
  characteristics, 144-148
  class, 150
  creating, 150
  definition, 323
  documentation, 149
    definition, 323
  evaluation, 150
  guiding steps, 153-154
  showcase, 149-150
    definition, 323
  student reflections in, 146
  uses of, 148
PRAXIS I and II, 9, 10, 238
precision of performance, 240
predictive evidence (of validity), 55-56, 58
  definition, 323
process assessment, 115
  definition, 323
product assessment, 115
  definition, 323
professionally developed tests, 16, 303
psychomotor domain, 37
  definition, 323

Q

qualitative assessment, 8
  definition, 323
quantitative assessment, 8
  definition, 323

R

rating scale, 73, 96
  definition, 323
raw scores, 242
relationship between validity and reliability,
  63-64
relevance, 52
reliability, 60
  definition, 323
  of qualitative assessments, 63
  of quantitative assessments, 61-63
  relationship with validity, 63-64
reliability coefficient, 61
  definition, 323
report cards, 228-229
  samples, 230-231
representativeness, 53
response options, 76
rubric, 73, 127-133
  analytic, 127-129
    definition, 319
    template, 130
  converting to grades, 131
  holistic, 127-128
    definition, 322
    template, 129

S

SAT/GRE score, 247-248
  definition, 324
Scholastic Assessment Test, 9-10, 55, 61, 247,
  255, 258
Science, Mathematics, and Reading Test
  (SMART), 50-51, 55, 64, 244-245
selected-response item, 76
  definition, 324
self-attitudes, 282-283
  definition, 324
self-concept, 282-283
self-efficacy, 282-283
self-esteem, 282-283
short-answer items, 78, 200-204

advantages and limitations, 203-204
  definition, 324
  guidelines, 201-203
social adjustment, 281
  definition, 324
split-half method, 62-63
  definition, 324
SPSS, 189
standard deviation, 63, 242311-312
standard error of measurement, 249-252, 316-
  317
  definition, 324
standardized assessments, 9
  definition, 324
standardized scores, 245-246
  definition, 324
standardized tests, 238-239
  criterion-referenced, 239-240
  interpreting student performance, 249-252
  methods of reporting scores on, 239
  norm-referenced, 240-242
Standards for Teacher Competence in the
  Educational Assessment of Students, The,
  16, 18-19, 66, 331
stanine, 248
  definition, 324
state-mandated tests, 238
stem, 76, 169
  definition, 324
stimuli, 77, 176, 178
  definition, 324
structured observations, 285
structured-response items, 11, 164
  definition, 324
student reflections, 146
  definition, 324
subjective assessment, 11
  definition, 324
subjective test items, 77-79
  definition, 324
summative decision making, 12, 24
summative evaluation, 9, 13
  definition, 324
supply items, 11, 78
  definition, 324

T

table of specifications, 166-168
  definition, 324

teacher-developed tests, 76
teacher observations, 88-93
   definition, 324
teacher questions, 97-100
   definition, 324
teacher-supplied items, 11
   definition, 324
teaching-assessment models, 22-28
  continuous-feedback model, 24-26
    definition, 320
  integrated assessment model, 26-28
    definition, 322
  time-restricted model, 22-24
    definition, 325
test, 6-7
   definition, 325
test administration, 238, 305
test publishers, 16, 303
test-retest method, 61
   definition, 325
testwiseness, 14
   definition, 325
time-restricted model, 22-24
   definition, 325
traditional assessment, 10, 76-79
   definition, 325
true-false items, 77, 180-183
   advantages and limitations, 182-183
   definition, 325
   guidelines, 180-182
   variations, 183-184
T-score, 247, 313
   definition, 325

U

unit plan, 30
   definition, 325
unstructured observations, 285

V

validity, 50-60
   definition, 325
   of qualitative assessments, 59
   of quantitative assessments, 56-59
   relationship with reliability, 63-64
   sources of evidence, 52
    concurrent, 55
    content, 52-54
    criterion, 55-58
    face, 56-57
    predictive, 55-56
validity coefficient, 58
   definition, 325
values, 282
   definition, 325

W

weekly plan, 31
   definition, 325

Z

z-**score**, 246-247, 313
   definition, 325